Praise for *Fundamentals of Data Engineering*

The world of data has been evolving for a while now. First there were designers. Then database administrators. Then CIOs. Then data architects. This book signals the next step in the evolution and maturity of the industry. It is a must read for anyone who takes their profession and career honestly.

—*Bill Inmon, creator of the data warehouse*

Fundamentals of Data Engineering is a great introduction to the business of moving, processing, and handling data. It explains the taxonomy of data concepts, without focusing too heavily on individual tools or vendors, so the techniques and ideas should outlast any individual trend or product. I'd highly recommend it for anyone wanting to get up to speed in data engineering or analytics, or for existing practitioners who want to fill in any gaps in their understanding.

—*Jordan Tigani, founder and CEO, MotherDuck, and founding engineer and cocreator of BigQuery*

If you want to lead in your industry, you must build the capabilities required to provide exceptional customer and employee experiences. This is not just a technology problem. It's a people opportunity. And it will transform your business. Data engineers are at the center of this transformation. But today the discipline is misunderstood. This book will demystify data engineering and become your ultimate guide to succeeding with data.

—*Bruno Aziza, Head of Data Analytics, Google Cloud*

What a book! Joe and Matt are giving you the answer to the question, "What must I understand to do data engineering?" Whether you are getting started as a data engineer or strengthening your skills, you are not looking for yet another technology handbook. You are seeking to learn more about the underlying principles and the core concepts of the role, its responsibilities, its technical and organizational environment, its mission—that's exactly what Joe and Matt offer in this book.

—Andy Petrella, founder of Kensu

This is the missing book in data engineering. A wonderfully thorough account of what it takes to be a good practicing data engineer, including thoughtful real-life considerations. I'd recommend all future education of data professionals include Joe and Matt's work.

—Sarah Krasnik, data engineering leader

It is incredible to realize the breadth of knowledge a data engineer must have. But don't let it scare you. This book provides a great foundational overview of various architectures, approaches, methodologies, and patterns that anyone working with data needs to be aware of. But what is even more valuable is that this book is full of golden nuggets of wisdom, best-practice advice, and things to consider when making decisions related to data engineering. It is a must read for both experienced and new data engineers.

—Veronika Durgin, data and analytics leader

I was honored and humbled to be asked by Joe and Matt to help technical review their masterpiece of data knowledge, *Fundamentals of Data Engineering*. Their ability to break down the key components that are critical to anyone wanting to move into a data engineering role is second to none. Their writing style makes the information easy to absorb, and they leave no stone unturned. It was an absolute pleasure to work with some of the best thought leaders in the data space. I can't wait to see what they do next.

—Chris Tabb, cofounder of LEIT DATA

Fundamentals of Data Engineering is the first book to take an in-depth and holistic look into the requirements of today's data engineer. As you'll see, the book dives into the critical areas of data engineering including skill sets, tools, and architectures used to manage, move, and curate data in today's complex technical environments.

More importantly, Joe and Matt convey their master of understanding data engineering and take the time to further dive into the more nuanced areas of data engineering and make it relatable to the reader. Whether you're a manager, experienced data engineer, or someone wanting to get into the space, this book provides practical insight into today's data engineering landscape.

—Jon King, Principal Data Architect

Two things will remain relevant to data engineers in 2042: SQL and this book. Joe and Matt cut through the hype around tools to extract the slowly changing dimensions of our discipline. Whether you're starting your journey with data or adding stripes to your black belt, *Fundamentals of Data Engineering* lays the foundation for mastery.

—*Kevin Hu, CEO of Metaplane*

In a field that is rapidly changing, with new technology solutions popping up constantly, Joe and Matt provide clear, timeless guidance, focusing on the core concepts and foundational knowledge required to excel as a data engineer. This book is jam packed with information that will empower you to ask the right questions, understand trade-offs, and make the best decisions when designing your data architecture and implementing solutions across the data engineering lifecycle. Whether you're just considering becoming a data engineer or have been in the field for years, I guarantee you'll learn something from this book!

—*Julie Price, Senior Product Manager, SingleStore*

Fundamentals of Data Engineering isn't just an instruction manual—it teaches you how to think like a data engineer. Part history lesson, part theory, and part acquired knowledge from Joe and Matt's decades of experience, the book has definitely earned its place on every data professional's bookshelf.

—*Scott Breitenother, founder and CEO, Brooklyn Data Co.*

There is no other book that so comprehensively covers what it means to be a data engineer. Joe and Matt dive deep into responsibilities, impacts, architectural choices, and so much more. Despite talking about such complex topics, the book is easy to read and digest. A very powerful combination.

—*Danny Leybzon, MLOps Architect*

I wish this book was around years ago when I started working with data engineers. The wide coverage of the field makes the involved roles clear and builds empathy with the many roles it takes to build a competent data discipline.

—*Tod Hansmann, VP Engineering*

A must read and instant classic for anyone in the data engineering field. This book fills a gap in the current knowledge base, discussing fundamental topics not found in other books. You will gain understanding of foundational concepts and insight into historical context about data engineering that will set up anyone to succeed.

—*Matthew Sharp, Data and ML Engineer*

Data engineering is the foundation of every analysis, machine learning model, and data product, so it is critical that it is done well. There are countless manuals, books, and references for each of the technologies used by data engineers, but very few (if any) resources that provide a holistic view of what it means to work as a data engineer. This book fills a critical need in the industry and does it well, laying the foundation for new and working data engineers to be successful and effective in their roles. This is the book that I'll be recommending to anyone who wants to work with data at any level.

—*Tobias Macey, host of* The Data Engineering Podcast

Fundamentals of Data Engineering

Plan and Build Robust Data Systems

Joe Reis and Matt Housley

Beijing · Boston · Farnham · Sebastopol · Tokyo

Fundamentals of Data Engineering

by Joe Reis and Matt Housley

Copyright © 2022 Joseph Reis and Matthew Housley. All rights reserved.

Published by O'Reilly Media, Inc., 1005 Gravenstein Highway North, Sebastopol, CA 95472.

O'Reilly books may be purchased for educational, business, or sales promotional use. Online editions are also available for most titles (*http://oreilly.com*). For more information, contact our corporate/institutional sales department: 800-998-9938 or *corporate@oreilly.com*.

Acquisitions Editor: Jessica Haberman	**Proofreader:** Amnet Systems, LLC
Development Editors: Nicole Taché and Michele Cronin	**Indexer:** Judith McConville
	Interior Designer: David Futato
Production Editor: Gregory Hyman	**Cover Designer:** Karen Montgomery
Copyeditor: Sharon Wilkey	**Illustrator:** Kate Dullea

July 2022:   First Edition

Revision History for the First Edition
2022-06-22:   First Release
2023-07-28:   Second Release

See *http://oreilly.com/catalog/errata.csp?isbn=9781098108304* for release details.

The O'Reilly logo is a registered trademark of O'Reilly Media, Inc. *Fundamentals of Data Engineering*, the cover image, and related trade dress are trademarks of O'Reilly Media, Inc.

The views expressed in this work are those of the authors, and do not represent the publisher's views. While the publisher and the authors have used good faith efforts to ensure that the information and instructions contained in this work are accurate, the publisher and the authors disclaim all responsibility for errors or omissions, including without limitation responsibility for damages resulting from the use of or reliance on this work. Use of the information and instructions contained in this work is at your own risk. If any code samples or other technology this work contains or describes is subject to open source licenses or the intellectual property rights of others, it is your responsibility to ensure that your use thereof complies with such licenses and/or rights.

978-1-098-10830-4

[LSI]

Table of Contents

Part I.   Foundation and Building Blocks

Part II. The Data Engineering Lifecycle in Depth

Part III. Security, Privacy, and the Future of Data Engineering

Preface

How did this book come about? The origin is deeply rooted in our journey from data science into data engineering. We often jokingly refer to ourselves as *recovering data scientists*. We both had the experience of being assigned to data science projects, then struggling to execute these projects due to a lack of proper foundations. Our journey into data engineering began when we undertook data engineering tasks to build foundations and infrastructure.

With the rise of data science, companies splashed out lavishly on data science talent, hoping to reap rich rewards. Very often, data scientists struggled with basic problems that their background and training did not address—data collection, data cleansing, data access, data transformation, and data infrastructure. These are problems that data engineering aims to solve.

What This Book Isn't

Before we cover what this book is about and what you'll get out of it, let's quickly cover what this book *isn't*. This book isn't about data engineering using a particular tool, technology, or platform. While many excellent books approach data engineering technologies from this perspective, these books have a short shelf life. Instead, we focus on the fundamental concepts behind data engineering.

What This Book Is About

This book aims to fill a gap in current data engineering content and materials. While there's no shortage of technical resources that address specific data engineering tools and technologies, people struggle to understand how to assemble these components into a coherent whole that applies in the real world. This book connects the dots of the end-to-end data lifecycle. It shows you how to stitch together various technologies to serve the needs of downstream data consumers such as analysts, data scientists, and machine learning engineers. This book works as a complement to O'Reilly books that cover the details of particular technologies, platforms, and programming languages.

The big idea of this book is the *data engineering lifecycle*: data generation, storage, ingestion, transformation, and serving. Since the dawn of data, we've seen the rise and fall of innumerable specific technologies and vendor products, but the data engineering lifecycle stages have remained essentially unchanged. With this framework, the reader will come away with a sound understanding for applying technologies to real-world business problems.

Our goal here is to map out principles that reach across two axes. First, we wish to distill data engineering into principles that can encompass *any relevant technology*. Second, we wish to present principles that will stand the test of *time*. We hope that these ideas reflect lessons learned across the data technology upheaval of the last twenty years and that our mental framework will remain useful for a decade or more into the future.

One thing to note: we unapologetically take a cloud-first approach. We view the cloud as a fundamentally transformative development that will endure for decades; most on-premises data systems and workloads will eventually move to cloud hosting. We assume that infrastructure and systems are *ephemeral* and *scalable*, and that data engineers will lean toward deploying managed services in the cloud. That said, most concepts in this book will translate to non-cloud environments.

Who Should Read This Book

Our primary intended audience for this book consists of technical practitioners, mid- to senior-level software engineers, data scientists, or analysts interested in moving into data engineering; or data engineers working in the guts of specific technologies, but wanting to develop a more comprehensive perspective. Our secondary target audience consists of data stakeholders who work adjacent to technical practitioners—e.g., a data team lead with a technical background overseeing a team of data engineers, or a director of data warehousing wanting to migrate from on-premises technology to a cloud-based solution.

Ideally, you're curious and want to learn—why else would you be reading this book? You stay current with data technologies and trends by reading books and articles on data warehousing/data lakes, batch and streaming systems, orchestration, modeling, management, analysis, developments in cloud technologies, etc. This book will help you weave what you've read into a complete picture of data engineering across technologies and paradigms.

Prerequisites

We assume a good deal of familiarity with the types of data systems found in a corporate setting. In addition, we assume that readers have some familiarity with SQL and Python (or some other programming language), and experience with cloud services.

Numerous resources are available for aspiring data engineers to practice Python and SQL. Free online resources abound (blog posts, tutorial sites, YouTube videos), and many new Python books are published every year.

The cloud provides unprecedented opportunities to get hands-on experience with data tools. We suggest that aspiring data engineers set up accounts with cloud services such as AWS, Azure, Google Cloud Platform, Snowflake, Databricks, etc. Note that many of these platforms have *free tier* options, but readers should keep a close eye on costs and work with small quantities of data and single node clusters as they study.

Developing familiarity with corporate data systems outside of a corporate environment remains difficult, and this creates certain barriers for aspiring data engineers who have yet to land their first data job. This book can help. We suggest that data novices read for high-level ideas and then look at materials in the Additional Resources section at the end of each chapter. On a second read through, note any unfamiliar terms and technologies. You can utilize Google, Wikipedia, blog posts, YouTube videos, and vendor sites to become familiar with new terms and fill gaps in your understanding.

What You'll Learn and How It Will Improve Your Abilities

This book aims to help you build a solid foundation for solving real-world data engineering problems.

By the end of this book you will understand:

- How data engineering impacts your current role (data scientist, software engineer, or data team lead)
- How to cut through the marketing hype and choose the right technologies, data architecture, and processes
- How to use the data engineering lifecycle to design and build a robust architecture
- Best practices for each stage of the data lifecycle

And you will be able to:

- Incorporate data engineering principles in your current role (data scientist, analyst, software engineer, data team lead, etc.)
- Stitch together a variety of cloud technologies to serve the needs of downstream data consumers
- Assess data engineering problems with an end-to-end framework of best practices
- Incorporate data governance and security across the data engineering lifecycle

Navigating This Book

This book is composed of four parts:

- Part I, "Foundation and Building Blocks"
- Part II, "The Data Engineering Lifecycle in Depth"
- Part III, "Security, Privacy, and the Future of Data Engineering"
- Appendices A and B: covering serialization and compression, and cloud networking, respectively

In Part I, we begin by defining data engineering in Chapter 1, then map out the data engineering lifecycle in Chapter 2. In Chapter 3, we discuss *good architecture*. In Chapter 4, we introduce a framework for choosing the right technology—while we frequently see technology and architecture conflated, these are in fact very different topics.

Part II builds on Chapter 2 to cover the data engineering lifecycle in depth; each lifecycle stage—data generation, storage, ingestion, transformation and serving—is covered in its own chapter. Part II is arguably the heart of the book, and the other chapters exist to support the core ideas covered here.

Part III covers additional topics. In Chapter 10, we discuss *security and privacy*. While security has always been an important part of the data engineering profession, it has only become more critical with the rise of for profit hacking and state sponsored cyber attacks. And what can we say of privacy? The era of corporate privacy nihilism is over—no company wants to see its name appear in the headline of an article on sloppy privacy practices. Reckless handling of personal data can also have significant legal ramifications with the advent of GDPR, CCPA, and other regulations. In short, security and privacy must be top priorities in any data engineering work.

In the course of working in data engineering, doing research for this book and interviewing numerous experts, we thought a good deal about where the field is going in the near and long term. Chapter 11 outlines our highly speculative ideas on the future of data engineering. By its nature, the future is a slippery thing. Time will tell if some of our ideas are correct. We would love to hear from our readers on how their visions of the future agree with or differ from our own.

In the appendices, we cover a handful of technical topics that are extremely relevant to the day-to-day practice of data engineering but didn't fit into the main body of the text. Specifically, engineers need to understand serialization and compression (see Appendix A) both to work directly with data files and to assess performance considerations in data systems, and cloud networking (see Appendix B) is a critical topic as data engineering shifts into the cloud.

Conventions Used in This Book

The following typographical conventions are used in this book:

Italic
    Indicates new terms, URLs, email addresses, filenames, and file extensions

`Constant width`
    Used for program listings, as well as within paragraphs to refer to program elements such as variable or function names, databases, data types, environment variables, statements, and keywords

This element signifies a tip or suggestion.

This element signifies a general note.

This element indicates a warning or caution.

How to Contact Us

Please address comments and questions concerning this book to the publisher:

O'Reilly Media, Inc.
1005 Gravenstein Highway North
Sebastopol, CA 95472
800-998-9938 (in the United States or Canada)
707-829-0515 (international or local)
707-829-0104 (fax)

We have a web page for this book, where we list errata, examples, and any additional information. You can access this page at *https://oreil.ly/fundamentals-of-data*.

Email *bookquestions@oreilly.com* to comment or ask technical questions about this book.

For news and information about our books and courses, visit *https://oreilly.com*.

Find us on LinkedIn: *https://linkedin.com/company/oreilly-media*

Follow us on Twitter: *https://twitter.com/oreillymedia*

Watch us on YouTube: *https://www.youtube.com/oreillymedia*

Acknowledgments

When we started writing this book, we were warned by many people that we faced a hard task. A book like this has a lot of moving parts, and due to its comprehensive view of the field of data engineering, it required a ton of research, interviews, discussions, and deep thinking. We won't claim to have captured every nuance of data engineering, but we hope that the results resonate with you. Numerous individuals contributed to our efforts, and we're grateful for the support we received from many experts.

First, thanks to our amazing crew of technical reviewers. They slogged through many readings and gave invaluable (and often ruthlessly blunt) feedback. This book would be a fraction of itself without their efforts. In no particular order, we give endless thanks to Bill Inmon, Andy Petrella, Matt Sharp, Tod Hansmann, Chris Tabb, Danny Lebzyon, Martin Kleppman, Scott Lorimor, Nick Schrock, Lisa Steckman, Veronika Durgin, and Alex Woolford.

Second, we've had a unique opportunity to talk with the leading experts in the field of data on our live shows, podcasts, meetups, and endless private calls. Their ideas helped shape our book. There are too many people to name individually, but we'd like to give shoutouts to Jordan Tigani, Zhamak Dehghani, Ananth Packkildurai,

Shruti Bhat, Eric Tschetter, Benn Stancil, Kevin Hu, Michael Rogove, Ryan Wright, Adi Polak, Shinji Kim, Andreas Kretz, Egor Gryaznov, Chad Sanderson, Julie Price, Matt Turck, Monica Rogati, Mars Lan, Pardhu Gunnam, Brian Suk, Barr Moses, Lior Gavish, Bruno Aziza, Gian Merlino, DeVaris Brown, Todd Beauchene, Tudor Girba, Scott Taylor, Ori Rafael, Lee Edwards, Bryan Offutt, Ollie Hughes, Gilbert Eijkelenboom, Chris Bergh, Fabiana Clemente, Andreas Kretz, Ori Reshef, Nick Singh, Mark Balkenende, Kenten Danas, Brian Olsen, Rhaghu Murthy, Greg Coquillo, David Aponte, Demetrios Brinkmann, Sarah Catanzaro, Michel Tricot, Levi Davis, Ted Walker, Carlos Kemeny, Josh Benamram, Chanin Nantasenamat, George Firican, Jordan Goldmeir, Minhaaj Rehman, Luigi Patruno, Vin Vashista, Danny Ma, Jesse Anderson, Alessya Visnjic, Vishal Singh, Dave Langer, Roy Hasson, Todd Odess, Che Sharma, Scott Breitenother, Ben Taylor, Thom Ives, John Thompson, Brent Dykes, Josh Tobin, Mark Kosiba, Tyler Pugliese, Douwe Maan, Martin Traverso, Curtis Kowalski, Bob Davis, Koo Ping Shung, Ed Chenard, Matt Sciorma, Tyler Folkman, Jeff Baird, Tejas Manohar, Paul Singman, Kevin Stumpf, Willem Pineaar, and Michael Del Balso from Tecton, Emma Dahl, Harpreet Sahota, Ken Jee, Scott Taylor, Kate Strachnyi, Kristen Kehrer, Taylor Miller, Abe Gong, Ben Castleton, Ben Rogojan, David Mertz, Emmanuel Raj, Andrew Jones, Avery Smith, Brock Cooper, Jeff Larson, Jon King, Holden Ackerman, Miriah Peterson, Felipe Hoffa, David Gonzalez, Richard Wellman, Susan Walsh, Ravit Jain, Lauren Balik, Mikiko Bazeley, Mark Freeman, Mike Wimmer, Alexey Shchedrin, Mary Clair Thompson, Julie Burroughs, Jason Pedley, Freddy Drennan, Jason Pedley, Kelly and Matt Phillipps, Brian Campbell, Faris Chebib, Dylan Gregerson, Ken Myers, Jake Carter, Seth Paul, Ethan Aaron, and many others.

If you're not mentioned specifically, don't take it personally. You know who you are. Let us know and we'll get you on the next edition.

We'd also like to thank the Ternary Data team (Colleen McAuley, Maike Wells, Patrick Dahl, Aaron Hunsaker, and others), our students, and the countless people around the world who've supported us. It's a great reminder the world is a very small place.

Working with the O'Reilly crew was amazing! Special thanks to Jess Haberman for having confidence in us during the book proposal process, our amazing and extremely patient development editors Nicole Taché and Michele Cronin for invaluable editing, feedback, and support. Thank you also to the superb production team at O'Reilly (Greg and crew).

Joe would like to thank his family—Cassie, Milo, and Ethan—for letting him write a book. They had to endure a ton, and Joe promises to never write a book again. ;)

Matt would like to thank his friends and family for their enduring patience and support. He's still hopeful that Seneca will deign to give a five-star review after a good deal of toil and missed family time around the holidays.

PART I

Foundation and Building Blocks

Data Engineering Described

If you work in data or software, you may have noticed data engineering emerging from the shadows and now sharing the stage with data science. Data engineering is one of the hottest fields in data and technology, and for a good reason. It builds the foundation for data science and analytics in production. This chapter explores what data engineering is, how the field was born and its evolution, the skills of data engineers, and with whom they work.

What Is Data Engineering?

Despite the current popularity of data engineering, there's a lot of confusion about what data engineering means and what data engineers do. Data engineering has existed in some form since companies started doing things with data—such as predictive analysis, descriptive analytics, and reports—and came into sharp focus alongside the rise of data science in the 2010s. For the purpose of this book, it's critical to define what *data engineering* and *data engineer* mean.

First, let's look at the landscape of how data engineering is described and develop some terminology we can use throughout this book. Endless definitions of *data engineering* exist. In early 2022, a Google exact-match search for "what is data engineering?" returns over 91,000 unique results. Before we give our definition, here are a few examples of how some experts in the field define data engineering:

> Data engineering is a set of operations aimed at creating interfaces and mechanisms for the flow and access of information. It takes dedicated specialists—data engineers—to maintain data so that it remains available and usable by others. In short, data engineers set up and operate the organization's data infrastructure, preparing it for further analysis by data analysts and scientists.

—From "Data Engineering and Its Main Concepts" by AlexSoft[1]

The first type of data engineering is SQL-focused. The work and primary storage of the data is in relational databases. All of the data processing is done with SQL or a SQL-based language. Sometimes, this data processing is done with an ETL tool.[2] The second type of data engineering is Big Data–focused. The work and primary storage of the data is in Big Data technologies like Hadoop, Cassandra, and HBase. All of the data processing is done in Big Data frameworks like MapReduce, Spark, and Flink. While SQL is used, the primary processing is done with programming languages like Java, Scala, and Python.

—Jesse Anderson[3]

In relation to previously existing roles, the data engineering field could be thought of as a superset of business intelligence and data warehousing that brings more elements from software engineering. This discipline also integrates specialization around the operation of so-called "big data" distributed systems, along with concepts around the extended Hadoop ecosystem, stream processing, and in computation at scale.

—Maxime Beauchemin[4]

Data engineering is all about the movement, manipulation, and management of data.

—Lewis Gavin[5]

Wow! It's entirely understandable if you've been confused about data engineering. That's only a handful of definitions, and they contain an enormous range of opinions about the meaning of *data engineering*.

Data Engineering Defined

When we unpack the common threads of how various people define data engineering, an obvious pattern emerges: a data engineer gets data, stores it, and prepares it for consumption by data scientists, analysts, and others. We define *data engineering* and *data engineer* as follows:

> *Data engineering* is the development, implementation, and maintenance of systems and processes that take in raw data and produce high-quality, consistent information that supports downstream use cases, such as analysis and machine learning. Data engineering is the intersection of security, data management, DataOps, data architecture, orchestration, and software engineering. A *data engineer* manages the data engineering lifecycle, beginning with getting data from source systems and ending with serving data for use cases, such as analysis or machine learning.

---

1 "Data Engineering and Its Main Concepts," AlexSoft, last updated August 26, 2021, *https://oreil.ly/e94py*.

2 *ETL* stands for *extract, transform, load*, a common pattern we cover in the book.

3 Jesse Anderson, "The Two Types of Data Engineering," June 27, 2018, *https://oreil.ly/dxDt6*.

4 Maxime Beauchemin, "The Rise of the Data Engineer," January 20, 2017, *https://oreil.ly/kNDmd*.

5 Lewis Gavin, *What Is Data Engineering?* (Sebastapol, CA: O'Reilly, 2020), *https://oreil.ly/ELxLi*.

The Data Engineering Lifecycle

It is all too easy to fixate on technology and miss the bigger picture myopically. This book centers around a big idea called the *data engineering lifecycle* (Figure 1-1), which we believe gives data engineers the holistic context to view their role.

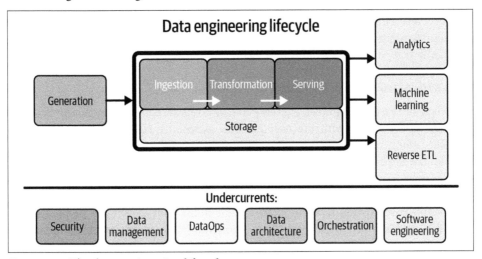

Figure 1-1. The data engineering lifecycle

The data engineering lifecycle shifts the conversation away from technology and toward the data itself and the end goals that it must serve. The stages of the data engineering lifecycle are as follows:

- Generation
- Storage
- Ingestion
- Transformation
- Serving

The data engineering lifecycle also has a notion of *undercurrents*—critical ideas across the entire lifecycle. These include security, data management, DataOps, data architecture, orchestration, and software engineering. We cover the data engineering lifecycle and its undercurrents more extensively in Chapter 2. Still, we introduce it here because it is essential to our definition of data engineering and the discussion that follows in this chapter.

Now that you have a working definition of data engineering and an introduction to its lifecycle, let's take a step back and look at a bit of history.

Evolution of the Data Engineer

> History doesn't repeat itself, but it rhymes.
>
> —A famous adage often attributed to Mark Twain

Understanding data engineering today and tomorrow requires a context of how the field evolved. This section is not a history lesson, but looking at the past is invaluable in understanding where we are today and where things are going. A common theme constantly reappears: what's old is new again.

The early days: 1980 to 2000, from data warehousing to the web

The birth of the data engineer arguably has its roots in data warehousing, dating as far back as the 1970s, with the *business data warehouse* taking shape in the 1980s and Bill Inmon officially coining the term *data warehouse* in 1989. After engineers at IBM developed the relational database and Structured Query Language (SQL), Oracle popularized the technology. As nascent data systems grew, businesses needed dedicated tools and data pipelines for reporting and business intelligence (BI). To help people correctly model their business logic in the data warehouse, Ralph Kimball and Inmon developed their respective eponymous data-modeling techniques and approaches, which are still widely used today.

Data warehousing ushered in the first age of scalable analytics, with new massively parallel processing (MPP) databases that use multiple processors to crunch large amounts of data coming on the market and supporting unprecedented volumes of data. Roles such as BI engineer, ETL developer, and data warehouse engineer addressed the various needs of the data warehouse. Data warehouse and BI engineering were a precursor to today's data engineering and still play a central role in the discipline.

The internet went mainstream around the mid-1990s, creating a whole new generation of web-first companies such as AOL, Yahoo, and Amazon. The dot-com boom spawned a ton of activity in web applications and the backend systems to support them—servers, databases, and storage. Much of the infrastructure was expensive, monolithic, and heavily licensed. The vendors selling these backend systems likely didn't foresee the sheer scale of the data that web applications would produce.

The early 2000s: The birth of contemporary data engineering

Fast-forward to the early 2000s, when the dot-com boom of the late '90s went bust, leaving behind a tiny cluster of survivors. Some of these companies, such as Yahoo, Google, and Amazon, would grow into powerhouse tech companies. Initially, these companies continued to rely on the traditional monolithic, relational databases and data warehouses of the 1990s, pushing these systems to the limit. As these systems buckled, updated approaches were needed to handle data growth. The new generation of the systems must be cost-effective, scalable, available, and reliable.

Coinciding with the explosion of data, commodity hardware—such as servers, RAM, disks, and flash drives—also became cheap and ubiquitous. Several innovations allowed distributed computation and storage on massive computing clusters at a vast scale. These innovations started decentralizing and breaking apart traditionally monolithic services. The "big data" era had begun.

The *Oxford English Dictionary* defines big data (*https://oreil.ly/8IaGH*) as "extremely large data sets that may be analyzed computationally to reveal patterns, trends, and associations, especially relating to human behavior and interactions." Another famous and succinct description of big data is the three *V*s of data: velocity, variety, and volume.

In 2003, Google published a paper on the Google File System, and shortly after that, in 2004, a paper on MapReduce, an ultra-scalable data-processing paradigm. In truth, big data has earlier antecedents in MPP data warehouses and data management for experimental physics projects, but Google's publications constituted a "big bang" for data technologies and the cultural roots of data engineering as we know it today. You'll learn more about MPP systems and MapReduce in Chapters 3 and 8, respectively.

The Google papers inspired engineers at Yahoo to develop and later open source Apache Hadoop in 2006.[6] It's hard to overstate the impact of Hadoop. Software engineers interested in large-scale data problems were drawn to the possibilities of this new open source technology ecosystem. As companies of all sizes and types saw their data grow into many terabytes and even petabytes, the era of the big data engineer was born.

Around the same time, Amazon had to keep up with its own exploding data needs and created elastic computing environments (Amazon Elastic Compute Cloud, or EC2), infinitely scalable storage systems (Amazon Simple Storage Service, or S3), highly scalable NoSQL databases (Amazon DynamoDB), and many other core data building blocks.[7] Amazon elected to offer these services for internal and external consumption through *Amazon Web Services* (AWS), becoming the first popular public cloud. AWS created an ultra-flexible pay-as-you-go resource marketplace by virtualizing and reselling vast pools of commodity hardware. Instead of purchasing hardware for a data center, developers could simply rent compute and storage from AWS.

---

6 Cade Metz, "How Yahoo Spawned Hadoop, the Future of Big Data," *Wired*, October 18, 2011, *https://oreil.ly/iaD9G*.

7 Ron Miller, "How AWS Came to Be," *TechCrunch*, July 2, 2016, *https://oreil.ly/VJehv*.

As AWS became a highly profitable growth engine for Amazon, other public clouds would soon follow, such as Google Cloud, Microsoft Azure, and DigitalOcean. The public cloud is arguably one of the most significant innovations of the 21st century and spawned a revolution in the way software and data applications are developed and deployed.

The early big data tools and public cloud laid the foundation for today's data ecosystem. The modern data landscape—and data engineering as we know it now—would not exist without these innovations.

The 2000s and 2010s: Big data engineering

Open source big data tools in the Hadoop ecosystem rapidly matured and spread from Silicon Valley to tech-savvy companies worldwide. For the first time, any business had access to the same bleeding-edge data tools used by the top tech companies. Another revolution occurred with the transition from batch computing to event streaming, ushering in a new era of big "real-time" data. You'll learn about batch and event streaming throughout this book.

Engineers could choose the latest and greatest—Hadoop, Apache Pig, Apache Hive, Dremel, Apache HBase, Apache Storm, Apache Cassandra, Apache Spark, Presto, and numerous other new technologies that came on the scene. Traditional enterprise-oriented and GUI-based data tools suddenly felt outmoded, and code-first engineering was in vogue with the ascendance of MapReduce. We (the authors) were around during this time, and it felt like old dogmas died a sudden death upon the altar of big data.

The explosion of data tools in the late 2000s and 2010s ushered in the *big data engineer*. To effectively use these tools and techniques—namely, the Hadoop ecosystem including Hadoop, YARN, Hadoop Distributed File System (HDFS), and MapReduce—big data engineers had to be proficient in software development and low-level infrastructure hacking, but with a shifted emphasis. Big data engineers typically maintained massive clusters of commodity hardware to deliver data at scale. While they might occasionally submit pull requests to Hadoop core code, they shifted their focus from core technology development to data delivery.

Big data quickly became a victim of its own success. As a buzzword, *big data* gained popularity during the early 2000s through the mid-2010s. Big data captured the imagination of companies trying to make sense of the ever-growing volumes of data and the endless barrage of shameless marketing from companies selling big data tools and services. Because of the immense hype, it was common to see companies using big data tools for small data problems, sometimes standing up a Hadoop cluster to process just a few gigabytes. It seemed like everyone wanted in on the big data action. Dan Ariely tweeted (*https://oreil.ly/cpL26*), "Big data is like teenage sex: everyone talks about it, nobody really knows how to do it, everyone thinks everyone else is doing it, so everyone claims they are doing it."

Figure 1-2 shows a snapshot of Google Trends for the search term "big data" to get an idea of the rise and fall of big data.

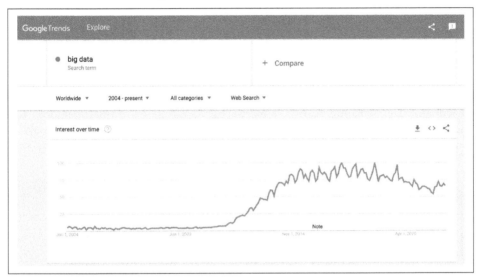

Figure 1-2. Google Trends for "big data" (March 2022)

Despite the term's popularity, big data has lost steam. What happened? One word: simplification. Despite the power and sophistication of open source big data tools, managing them was a lot of work and required constant attention. Often, companies employed entire teams of big data engineers, costing millions of dollars a year, to babysit these platforms. Big data engineers often spent excessive time maintaining complicated tooling and arguably not as much time delivering the business's insights and value.

Open source developers, clouds, and third parties started looking for ways to abstract, simplify, and make big data available without the high administrative overhead and cost of managing their clusters, and installing, configuring, and upgrading their open source code. The term *big data* is essentially a relic to describe a particular time and approach to handling large amounts of data.

Today, data is moving faster than ever and growing ever larger, but big data processing has become so accessible that it no longer merits a separate term; every company aims to solve its data problems, regardless of actual data size. Big data engineers are now simply *data engineers*.

The 2020s: Engineering for the data lifecycle

At the time of this writing, the data engineering role is evolving rapidly. We expect this evolution to continue at a rapid clip for the foreseeable future. Whereas data engineers historically tended to the low-level details of monolithic frameworks such as Hadoop, Spark, or Informatica, the trend is moving toward decentralized, modularized, managed, and highly abstracted tools.

Indeed, data tools have proliferated at an astonishing rate (see Figure 1-3). Popular trends in the early 2020s include the *modern data stack*, representing a collection of off-the-shelf open source and third-party products assembled to make analysts' lives easier. At the same time, data sources and data formats are growing both in variety and size. Data engineering is increasingly a discipline of interoperation, and connecting various technologies like LEGO bricks, to serve ultimate business goals.

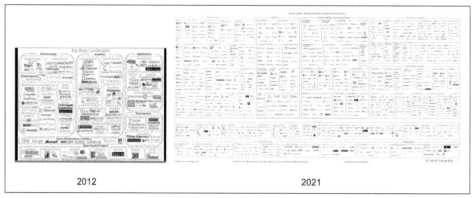

Figure 1-3. Matt Turck's Data Landscape (https://oreil.ly/TWTfM) in 2012 versus 2021

The data engineer we discuss in this book can be described more precisely as a *data lifecycle engineer*. With greater abstraction and simplification, a data lifecycle engineer is no longer encumbered by the gory details of yesterday's big data frameworks. While data engineers maintain skills in low-level data programming and use these as required, they increasingly find their role focused on things higher in the value chain: security, data management, DataOps, data architecture, orchestration, and general data lifecycle management.[8]

As tools and workflows simplify, we've seen a noticeable shift in the attitudes of data engineers. Instead of focusing on who has the "biggest data," open source projects and services are increasingly concerned with managing and governing data, making it easier to use and discover, and improving its quality. Data engineers are

---

8 *DataOps* is an abbreviation for *data operations*. We cover this topic in Chapter 2. For more information, read the DataOps Manifesto (*https://oreil.ly/jGoHM*).

now conversant in acronyms such as *CCPA* and *GDPR*;[9] as they engineer pipelines, they concern themselves with privacy, anonymization, data garbage collection, and compliance with regulations.

What's old is new again. While "enterprisey" stuff like data management (including data quality and governance) was common for large enterprises in the pre-big-data era, it wasn't widely adopted in smaller companies. Now that many of the challenging problems of yesterday's data systems are solved, neatly productized, and packaged, technologists and entrepreneurs have shifted focus back to the "enterprisey" stuff, but with an emphasis on decentralization and agility, which contrasts with the traditional enterprise command-and-control approach.

We view the present as a golden age of data lifecycle management. Data engineers managing the data engineering lifecycle have better tools and techniques than ever before. We discuss the data engineering lifecycle and its undercurrents in greater detail in the next chapter.

Data Engineering and Data Science

Where does data engineering fit in with data science? There's some debate, with some arguing data engineering is a subdiscipline of data science. We believe data engineering is *separate* from data science and analytics. They complement each other, but they are distinctly different. Data engineering sits upstream from data science (Figure 1-4), meaning data engineers provide the inputs used by data scientists (downstream from data engineering), who convert these inputs into something useful.

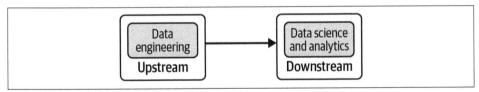

Figure 1-4. Data engineering sits upstream from data science

Consider the Data Science Hierarchy of Needs (Figure 1-5). In 2017, Monica Rogati published this hierarchy in an article (*https://oreil.ly/pGg9U*) that showed where AI and machine learning (ML) sat in proximity to more "mundane" areas such as data movement/storage, collection, and infrastructure.

---

9 These acronyms stand for *California Consumer Privacy Act* and *General Data Protection Regulation*, respectively.

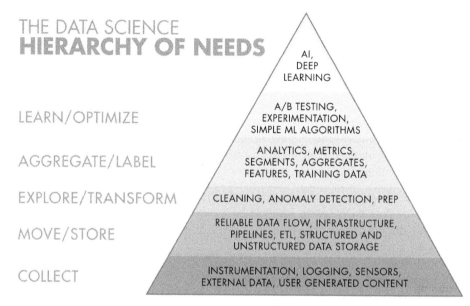

THE DATA SCIENCE
HIERARCHY OF NEEDS

AI, DEEP LEARNING

LEARN/OPTIMIZE — A/B TESTING, EXPERIMENTATION, SIMPLE ML ALGORITHMS

AGGREGATE/LABEL — ANALYTICS, METRICS, SEGMENTS, AGGREGATES, FEATURES, TRAINING DATA

EXPLORE/TRANSFORM — CLEANING, ANOMALY DETECTION, PREP

MOVE/STORE — RELIABLE DATA FLOW, INFRASTRUCTURE, PIPELINES, ETL, STRUCTURED AND UNSTRUCTURED DATA STORAGE

COLLECT — INSTRUMENTATION, LOGGING, SENSORS, EXTERNAL DATA, USER GENERATED CONTENT

Figure 1-5. The Data Science Hierarchy of Needs (https://oreil.ly/pGg9U)

Although many data scientists are eager to build and tune ML models, the reality is an estimated 70% to 80% of their time is spent toiling in the bottom three parts of the hierarchy—gathering data, cleaning data, processing data—and only a tiny slice of their time on analysis and ML. Rogati argues that companies need to build a solid data foundation (the bottom three levels of the hierarchy) before tackling areas such as AI and ML.

Data scientists aren't typically trained to engineer production-grade data systems, and they end up doing this work haphazardly because they lack the support and resources of a data engineer. In an ideal world, data scientists should spend more than 90% of their time focused on the top layers of the pyramid: analytics, experimentation, and ML. When data engineers focus on these bottom parts of the hierarchy, they build a solid foundation for data scientists to succeed.

With data science driving advanced analytics and ML, data engineering straddles the divide between getting data and getting value from data (see Figure 1-6). We believe data engineering is of equal importance and visibility to data science, with data engineers playing a vital role in making data science successful in production.

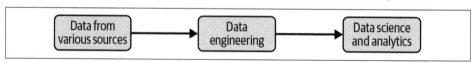

Data from various sources → Data engineering → Data science and analytics

Figure 1-6. A data engineer gets data and provides value from the data

Data Engineering Skills and Activities

The skill set of a data engineer encompasses the "undercurrents" of data engineering: security, data management, DataOps, data architecture, and software engineering. This skill set requires an understanding of how to evaluate data tools and how they fit together across the data engineering lifecycle. It's also critical to know how data is produced in source systems and how analysts and data scientists will consume and create value after processing and curating data. Finally, a data engineer juggles a lot of complex moving parts and must constantly optimize along the axes of cost, agility, scalability, simplicity, reuse, and interoperability (Figure 1-7). We cover these topics in more detail in upcoming chapters.

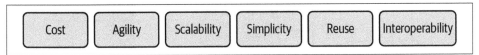

Figure 1-7. The balancing act of data engineering

As we discussed, in the recent past, a data engineer was expected to know and understand how to use a small handful of powerful and monolithic technologies (Hadoop, Spark, Teradata, Hive, and many others) to create a data solution. Utilizing these technologies often requires a sophisticated understanding of software engineering, networking, distributed computing, storage, or other low-level details. Their work would be devoted to cluster administration and maintenance, managing overhead, and writing pipeline and transformation jobs, among other tasks.

Nowadays, the data-tooling landscape is dramatically less complicated to manage and deploy. Modern data tools considerably abstract and simplify workflows. As a result, data engineers are now focused on balancing the simplest and most cost-effective, best-of-breed services that deliver value to the business. The data engineer is also expected to create agile data architectures that evolve as new trends emerge.

What are some things a data engineer does *not* do? A data engineer typically does not directly build ML models, create reports or dashboards, perform data analysis, build key performance indicators (KPIs), or develop software applications. A data engineer should have a good functioning understanding of these areas to serve stakeholders best.

Data Maturity and the Data Engineer

The level of data engineering complexity within a company depends a great deal on the company's data maturity. This significantly impacts a data engineer's day-to-day job responsibilities and career progression. What is data maturity, exactly?

Data maturity is the progression toward higher data utilization, capabilities, and integration across the organization, but data maturity does not simply depend on the age or revenue of a company. An early-stage startup can have greater data maturity than a 100-year-old company with annual revenues in the billions. What matters is the way data is leveraged as a competitive advantage.

Data maturity models have many versions, such as Data Management Maturity (DMM) (*https://oreil.ly/HmX62*) and others, and it's hard to pick one that is both simple and useful for data engineering. So, we'll create our own simplified data maturity model. Our data maturity model (Figure 1-8) has three stages: starting with data, scaling with data, and leading with data. Let's look at each of these stages and at what a data engineer typically does at each stage.

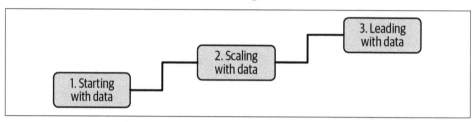

Figure 1-8. Our simplified data maturity model for a company

Stage 1: Starting with data

A company getting started with data is, by definition, in the very early stages of its data maturity. The company may have fuzzy, loosely defined goals or no goals. Data architecture and infrastructure are in the very early stages of planning and development. Adoption and utilization are likely low or nonexistent. The data team is small, often with a headcount in the single digits. At this stage, a data engineer is usually a generalist and will typically play several other roles, such as data scientist or software engineer. A data engineer's goal is to move fast, get traction, and add value.

The practicalities of getting value from data are typically poorly understood, but the desire exists. Reports or analyses lack formal structure, and most requests for data are ad hoc. While it's tempting to jump headfirst into ML at this stage, we don't recommend it. We've seen countless data teams get stuck and fall short when they try to jump to ML without building a solid data foundation.

That's not to say you can't get wins from ML at this stage—it is rare but possible. Without a solid data foundation, you likely won't have the data to train reliable ML models nor the means to deploy these models to production in a scalable and repeatable way. We half-jokingly call ourselves "recovering data scientists" (*https:// oreil.ly/2wXbD*), mainly from personal experience with being involved in premature data science projects without adequate data maturity or data engineering support.

A data engineer should focus on the following in organizations getting started with data:

- Get buy-in from key stakeholders, including executive management. Ideally, the data engineer should have a sponsor for critical initiatives to design and build a data architecture to support the company's goals.

- Define the right data architecture (usually solo, since a data architect likely isn't available). This means determining business goals and the competitive advantage you're aiming to achieve with your data initiative. Work toward a data architecture that supports these goals. See Chapter 3 for our advice on "good" data architecture.

- Identify and audit data that will support key initiatives and operate within the data architecture you designed.

- Build a solid data foundation for future data analysts and data scientists to generate reports and models that provide competitive value. In the meantime, you may also have to generate these reports and models until this team is hired.

This is a delicate stage with lots of pitfalls. Here are some tips for this stage:

- Organizational willpower may wane if a lot of visible successes don't occur with data. Getting quick wins will establish the importance of data within the organization. Just keep in mind that quick wins will likely create technical debt. Have a plan to reduce this debt, as it will otherwise add friction for future delivery.

- Get out and talk to people, and avoid working in silos. We often see the data team working in a bubble, not communicating with people outside their departments and getting perspectives and feedback from business stakeholders. The danger is you'll spend a lot of time working on things of little use to people.

- Avoid undifferentiated heavy lifting. Don't box yourself in with unnecessary technical complexity. Use off-the-shelf, turnkey solutions wherever possible.

- Build custom solutions and code only where this creates a competitive advantage.

Stage 2: Scaling with data

At this point, a company has moved away from ad hoc data requests and has formal data practices. Now the challenge is creating scalable data architectures and planning for a future where the company is genuinely data-driven. Data engineering roles move from generalists to specialists, with people focusing on particular aspects of the data engineering lifecycle.

In organizations that are in stage 2 of data maturity, a data engineer's goals are to do the following:

- Establish formal data practices
- Create scalable and robust data architectures

- Adopt DevOps and DataOps practices
- Build systems that support ML
- Continue to avoid undifferentiated heavy lifting and customize only when a competitive advantage results

We return to each of these goals later in the book.

Issues to watch out for include the following:

- As we grow more sophisticated with data, there's a temptation to adopt bleeding-edge technologies based on social proof from Silicon Valley companies. This is rarely a good use of your time and energy. Any technology decisions should be driven by the value they'll deliver to your customers.
- The main bottleneck for scaling is not cluster nodes, storage, or technology but the data engineering team. Focus on solutions that are simple to deploy and manage to expand your team's throughput.
- You'll be tempted to frame yourself as a technologist, a data genius who can deliver magical products. Shift your focus instead to pragmatic leadership and begin transitioning to the next maturity stage; communicate with other teams about the practical utility of data. Teach the organization how to consume and leverage data.

Stage 3: Leading with data

At this stage, the company is data-driven. The automated pipelines and systems created by data engineers allow people within the company to do self-service analytics and ML. Introducing new data sources is seamless, and tangible value is derived. Data engineers implement proper controls and practices to ensure that data is always available to the people and systems. Data engineering roles continue to specialize more deeply than in stage 2.

In organizations in stage 3 of data maturity, a data engineer will continue building on prior stages, plus they will do the following:

- Create automation for the seamless introduction and usage of new data
- Focus on building custom tools and systems that leverage data as a competitive advantage
- Focus on the "enterprisey" aspects of data, such as data management (including data governance and quality) and DataOps
- Deploy tools that expose and disseminate data throughout the organization, including data catalogs, data lineage tools, and metadata management systems

- Collaborate efficiently with software engineers, ML engineers, analysts, and others
- Create a community and environment where people can collaborate and speak openly, no matter their role or position

Issues to watch out for include the following:

- At this stage, complacency is a significant danger. Once organizations reach stage 3, they must constantly focus on maintenance and improvement or risk falling back to a lower stage.
- Technology distractions are a more significant danger here than in the other stages. There's a temptation to pursue expensive hobby projects that don't deliver value to the business. Utilize custom-built technology only where it provides a competitive advantage.

The Background and Skills of a Data Engineer

Data engineering is a fast-growing field, and a lot of questions remain about how to become a data engineer. Because data engineering is a relatively new discipline, little formal training is available to enter the field. Universities don't have a standard data engineering path. Although a handful of data engineering boot camps and online tutorials cover random topics, a common curriculum for the subject doesn't yet exist.

People entering data engineering arrive with varying backgrounds in education, career, and skill set. Everyone entering the field should expect to invest a significant amount of time in self-study. Reading this book is a good starting point; one of the primary goals of this book is to give you a foundation for the knowledge and skills we think are necessary to succeed as a data engineer.

If you're pivoting your career into data engineering, we've found that the transition is easiest when moving from an adjacent field, such as software engineering, ETL development, database administration, data science, or data analysis. These disciplines tend to be "data aware" and provide good context for data roles in an organization. They also equip folks with the relevant technical skills and context to solve data engineering problems.

Despite the lack of a formalized path, a requisite body of knowledge exists that we believe a data engineer should know to be successful. By definition, a data engineer must understand both data and technology. With respect to data, this entails knowing about various best practices around data management. On the technology end, a data engineer must be aware of various options for tools, their interplay, and their trade-offs. This requires a good understanding of software engineering, DataOps, and data architecture.

Zooming out, a data engineer must also understand the requirements of data consumers (data analysts and data scientists) and the broader implications of data across the organization. Data engineering is a holistic practice; the best data engineers view their responsibilities through business and technical lenses.

Business Responsibilities

The macro responsibilities we list in this section aren't exclusive to data engineers but are crucial for anyone working in a data or technology field. Because a simple Google search will yield tons of resources to learn about these areas, we will simply list them for brevity:

Know how to communicate with nontechnical and technical people.
> Communication is key, and you need to be able to establish rapport and trust with people across the organization. We suggest paying close attention to organizational hierarchies, who reports to whom, how people interact, and which silos exist. These observations will be invaluable to your success.

Understand how to scope and gather business and product requirements.
> You need to know what to build and ensure that your stakeholders agree with your assessment. In addition, develop a sense of how data and technology decisions impact the business.

Understand the cultural foundations of Agile, DevOps, and DataOps.
> Many technologists mistakenly believe these practices are solved through technology. We feel this is dangerously wrong. Agile, DevOps, and DataOps are fundamentally cultural, requiring buy-in across the organization.

Control costs.
> You'll be successful when you can keep costs low while providing outsized value. Know how to optimize for time to value, the total cost of ownership, and opportunity cost. Learn to monitor costs to avoid surprises.

Learn continuously.
> The data field feels like it's changing at light speed. People who succeed in it are great at picking up new things while sharpening their fundamental knowledge. They're also good at filtering, determining which new developments are most relevant to their work, which are still immature, and which are just fads. Stay abreast of the field and learn how to learn.

A successful data engineer always zooms out to understand the big picture and how to achieve outsized value for the business. Communication is vital, both for technical and nontechnical people. We often see data teams succeed based on their communication with other stakeholders; success or failure is rarely a technology issue. Knowing how to navigate an organization, scope and gather requirements, control costs, and continuously learn will set you apart from the data engineers who rely solely on their technical abilities to carry their career.

Technical Responsibilities

You must understand how to build architectures that optimize performance and cost at a high level, using prepackaged or homegrown components. Ultimately, architectures and constituent technologies are building blocks to serve the data engineering lifecycle. Recall the stages of the data engineering lifecycle:

- Generation
- Storage
- Ingestion
- Transformation
- Serving

The undercurrents of the data engineering lifecycle are the following:

- Security
- Data management
- DataOps
- Data architecture
- Orchestration
- Software engineering

Zooming in a bit, we discuss some of the tactical data and technology skills you'll need as a data engineer in this section; we discuss these in more detail in subsequent chapters.

People often ask, should a data engineer know how to code? Short answer: yes. A data engineer should have production-grade software engineering chops. We note that the nature of software development projects undertaken by data engineers has changed fundamentally in the last few years. Fully managed services now replace a great deal of low-level programming effort previously expected of engineers, who now use managed open source, and simple plug-and-play software-as-a-service (SaaS) offerings. For example, data engineers now focus on high-level abstractions or writing pipelines as code within an orchestration framework.

Even in a more abstract world, software engineering best practices provide a competitive advantage, and data engineers who can dive into the deep architectural details of a codebase give their companies an edge when specific technical needs arise. In short, a data engineer who can't write production-grade code will be severely hindered, and we don't see this changing anytime soon. Data engineers remain software engineers, in addition to their many other roles.

What languages should a data engineer know? We divide data engineering programming languages into primary and secondary categories. At the time of this writing, the primary languages of data engineering are SQL, Python, a Java Virtual Machine (JVM) language (usually Java or Scala), and bash:

SQL
> The most common interface for databases and data lakes. After briefly being sidelined by the need to write custom MapReduce code for big data processing, SQL (in various forms) has reemerged as the lingua franca of data.

Python
> The bridge language between data engineering and data science. A growing number of data engineering tools are written in Python or have Python APIs. It's known as "the second-best language at everything." Python underlies popular data tools such as pandas, NumPy, Airflow, sci-kit learn, TensorFlow, PyTorch, and PySpark. Python is the glue between underlying components and is frequently a first-class API language for interfacing with a framework.

JVM languages such as Java and Scala
> Prevalent for Apache open source projects such as Spark, Hive, and Druid. The JVM is generally more performant than Python and may provide access to lower-level features than a Python API (for example, this is the case for Apache Spark and Beam). Understanding Java or Scala will be beneficial if you're using a popular open source data framework.

bash
> The command-line interface for Linux operating systems. Knowing bash commands and being comfortable using CLIs will significantly improve your productivity and workflow when you need to script or perform OS operations. Even today, data engineers frequently use command-line tools like awk or sed to process files in a data pipeline or call bash commands from orchestration frameworks. If you're using Windows, feel free to substitute PowerShell for bash.

The Unreasonable Effectiveness of SQL

The advent of MapReduce and the big data era relegated SQL to passé status. Since then, various developments have dramatically enhanced the utility of SQL in the data engineering lifecycle. Spark SQL, Google BigQuery, Snowflake, Hive, and many other data tools can process massive amounts of data by using declarative, set-theoretic SQL semantics. SQL is also supported by many streaming frameworks, such as Apache Flink, Beam, and Kafka. We believe that competent data engineers should be highly proficient in SQL.

Are we saying that SQL is a be-all and end-all language? Not at all. SQL is a powerful tool that can quickly solve complex analytics and data transformation problems. Given that time is a primary constraint for data engineering team throughput, engineers should embrace tools that combine simplicity and high productivity. Data engineers also do well to develop expertise in composing SQL with other operations, either within frameworks such as Spark and Flink or by using orchestration to combine multiple tools. Data engineers should also learn modern SQL semantics for dealing with JavaScript Object Notation (JSON) parsing and nested data and consider leveraging a SQL management framework such as dbt (Data Build Tool) (*https://www.getdbt.com*).

A proficient data engineer also recognizes when SQL is not the right tool for the job and can choose and code in a suitable alternative. A SQL expert could likely write a query to stem and tokenize raw text in a natural language processing (NLP) pipeline but would also recognize that coding in native Spark is a far superior alternative to this masochistic exercise.

Data engineers may also need to develop proficiency in secondary programming languages, including R, JavaScript, Go, Rust, C/C++, C#, and Julia. Developing in these languages is often necessary when popular across the company or used with domain-specific data tools. For instance, JavaScript has proven popular as a language for user-defined functions in cloud data warehouses. At the same time, C# and PowerShell are essential in companies that leverage Azure and the Microsoft ecosystem.

Keeping Pace in a Fast-Moving Field

> Once a new technology rolls over you, if you're not part of the steamroller, you're part of the road.
>
> —Stewart Brand

How do you keep your skills sharp in a rapidly changing field like data engineering? Should you focus on the latest tools or deep dive into fundamentals? Here's our advice: focus on the fundamentals to understand what's not going to change; pay attention to ongoing developments to know where the field is going. New paradigms and practices are introduced all the time, and it's incumbent on you to stay current. Strive to understand how new technologies will be helpful in the lifecycle.

The Continuum of Data Engineering Roles, from A to B

Although job descriptions paint a data engineer as a "unicorn" who must possess every data skill imaginable, data engineers don't all do the same type of work or have the same skill set. Data maturity is a helpful guide to understanding the types of data challenges a company will face as it grows its data capability. It's beneficial to look at some critical distinctions in the kinds of work data engineers do. Though these distinctions are simplistic, they clarify what data scientists and data engineers do and avoid lumping either role into the unicorn bucket.

In data science, there's the notion of type A and type B data scientists.[10] *Type A data scientists*—where *A* stands for *analysis*—focus on understanding and deriving insight from data. *Type B data scientists*—where *B* stands for *building*—share similar backgrounds as type A data scientists and possess strong programming skills. The type B data scientist builds systems that make data science work in production. Borrowing from this data scientist continuum, we'll create a similar distinction for two types of data engineers:

Type A data engineers
> *A* stands for *abstraction*. In this case, the data engineer avoids undifferentiated heavy lifting, keeping data architecture as abstract and straightforward as possible and not reinventing the wheel. Type A data engineers manage the data engineering lifecycle mainly by using entirely off-the-shelf products, managed services, and tools. Type A data engineers work at companies across industries and at all levels of data maturity.

Type B data engineers
> *B* stands for *build*. Type B data engineers build data tools and systems that scale and leverage a company's core competency and competitive advantage. In the data maturity range, a type B data engineer is more commonly found at companies in stage 2 and 3 (scaling and leading with data), or when an initial data use case is so unique and mission-critical that custom data tools are required to get started.

Type A and type B data engineers may work in the same company and may even be the same person! More commonly, a type A data engineer is first hired to set the foundation, with type B data engineer skill sets either learned or hired as the need arises within a company.

Data Engineers Inside an Organization

Data engineers don't work in a vacuum. Depending on what they're working on, they will interact with technical and nontechnical people and face different directions (internal and external). Let's explore what data engineers do inside an organization and with whom they interact.

---

10 Robert Chang, "Doing Data Science at Twitter," *Medium*, June 20, 2015, *https://oreil.ly/xqjAx*.

Internal-Facing Versus External-Facing Data Engineers

A data engineer serves several end users and faces many internal and external directions (Figure 1-9). Since not all data engineering workloads and responsibilities are the same, it's essential to understand whom the data engineer serves. Depending on the end-use cases, a data engineer's primary responsibilities are external facing, internal facing, or a blend of the two.

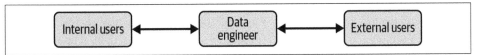

Figure 1-9. The directions a data engineer faces

An *external-facing* data engineer typically aligns with the users of external-facing applications, such as social media apps, Internet of Things (IoT) devices, and ecommerce platforms. This data engineer architects, builds, and manages the systems that collect, store, and process transactional and event data from these applications. The systems built by these data engineers have a feedback loop from the application to the data pipeline, and then back to the application (Figure 1-10).

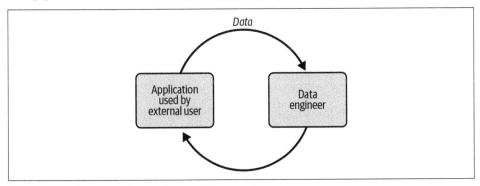

Figure 1-10. External-facing data engineer systems

External-facing data engineering comes with a unique set of problems. External-facing query engines often handle much larger concurrency loads than internal-facing systems. Engineers also need to consider putting tight limits on queries that users can run to limit the infrastructure impact of any single user. In addition, security is a much more complex and sensitive problem for external queries, especially if the data being queried is multitenant (data from many customers and housed in a single table).

An *internal-facing data engineer* typically focuses on activities crucial to the needs of the business and internal stakeholders (Figure 1-11). Examples include creating and maintaining data pipelines and data warehouses for BI dashboards, reports, business processes, data science, and ML models.

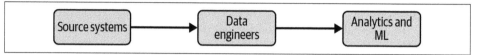

Figure 1-11. Internal-facing data engineer

External-facing and internal-facing responsibilities are often blended. In practice, internal-facing data is usually a prerequisite to external-facing data. The data engineer has two sets of users with very different requirements for query concurrency, security, and more.

Data Engineers and Other Technical Roles

In practice, the data engineering lifecycle cuts across many domains of responsibility. Data engineers sit at the nexus of various roles, directly or through managers, interacting with many organizational units.

Let's look at whom a data engineer may impact. In this section, we'll discuss technical roles connected to data engineering (Figure 1-12).

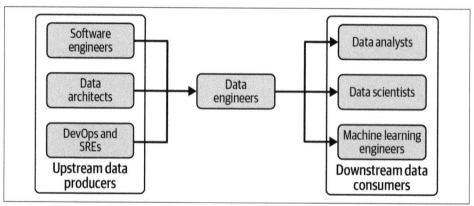

Figure 1-12. Key technical stakeholders of data engineering

The data engineer is a hub between *data producers*, such as software engineers, data architects, and DevOps or site-reliability engineers (SREs), and *data consumers*, such as data analysts, data scientists, and ML engineers. In addition, data engineers will interact with those in operational roles, such as DevOps engineers.

Given the pace at which new data roles come into vogue (analytics and ML engineers come to mind), this is by no means an exhaustive list.

Upstream stakeholders

To be successful as a data engineer, you need to understand the data architecture you're using or designing and the source systems producing the data you'll need. Next, we discuss a few familiar upstream stakeholders: data architects, software engineers, and DevOps engineers.

Data architects. Data architects function at a level of abstraction one step removed from data engineers. Data architects design the blueprint for organizational data management, mapping out processes and overall data architecture and systems.[11] They also serve as a bridge between an organization's technical and nontechnical sides. Successful data architects generally have "battle scars" from extensive engineering experience, allowing them to guide and assist engineers while successfully communicating engineering challenges to nontechnical business stakeholders.

Data architects implement policies for managing data across silos and business units, steer global strategies such as data management and data governance, and guide significant initiatives. Data architects often play a central role in cloud migrations and greenfield cloud design.

The advent of the cloud has shifted the boundary between data architecture and data engineering. Cloud data architectures are much more fluid than on-premises systems, so architecture decisions that traditionally involved extensive study, long lead times, purchase contracts, and hardware installation are now often made during the implementation process, just one step in a larger strategy. Nevertheless, data architects will remain influential visionaries in enterprises, working hand in hand with data engineers to determine the big picture of architecture practices and data strategies.

Depending on the company's data maturity and size, a data engineer may overlap with or assume the responsibilities of a data architect. Therefore, a data engineer should have a good understanding of architecture best practices and approaches.

Note that we have placed data architects in the *upstream stakeholders* section. Data architects often help design application data layers that are source systems for data engineers. Architects may also interact with data engineers at various other stages of the data engineering lifecycle. We cover "good" data architecture in Chapter 3.

Software engineers. Software engineers build the software and systems that run a business; they are largely responsible for generating the *internal data* that data engineers will consume and process. The systems built by software engineers typically generate application event data and logs, which are significant assets in their own

---

11 Paramita (Guha) Ghosh, "Data Architect vs. Data Engineer," Dataversity, November 12, 2021, *https://oreil.ly/TlyZY.*

right. This internal data contrasts with *external data* pulled from SaaS platforms or partner businesses. In well-run technical organizations, software engineers and data engineers coordinate from the inception of a new project to design application data for consumption by analytics and ML applications.

A data engineer should work together with software engineers to understand the applications that generate data, the volume, frequency, and format of the generated data, and anything else that will impact the data engineering lifecycle, such as data security and regulatory compliance. For example, this might mean setting upstream expectations on what the data software engineers need to do their jobs. Data engineers must work closely with the software engineers.

DevOps engineers and site-reliability engineers.   DevOps and SREs often produce data through operational monitoring. We classify them as upstream of data engineers, but they may also be downstream, consuming data through dashboards or interacting with data engineers directly in coordinating operations of data systems.

Downstream stakeholders

Data engineering exists to serve downstream data consumers and use cases. This section discusses how data engineers interact with various downstream roles. We'll also introduce a few service models, including centralized data engineering teams and cross-functional teams.

Data scientists.   Data scientists build forward-looking models to make predictions and recommendations. These models are then evaluated on live data to provide value in various ways. For example, model scoring might determine automated actions in response to real-time conditions, recommend products to customers based on the browsing history in their current session, or make live economic predictions used by traders.

According to common industry folklore, data scientists spend 70% to 80% of their time collecting, cleaning, and preparing data.[12] In our experience, these numbers often reflect immature data science and data engineering practices. In particular, many popular data science frameworks can become bottlenecks if they are not scaled up appropriately. Data scientists who work exclusively on a single workstation force themselves to downsample data, making data preparation significantly more complicated and potentially compromising the quality of the models they

---

12 A variety of references exist for this notion. Although this cliche is widely known, a healthy debate has arisen around its validity in different practical settings. For more details, see Leigh Dodds, "Do Data Scientists Spend 80% of Their Time Cleaning Data? Turns Out, No?" Lost Boy blog, January 31, 2020, *https://oreil.ly/szFww*; and Alex Woodie, "Data Prep Still Dominates Data Scientists' Time, Survey Finds," *Datanami*, July 6, 2020, *https://oreil.ly/jDVWF*.

produce. Furthermore, locally developed code and environments are often difficult to deploy in production, and a lack of automation significantly hampers data science workflows. If data engineers do their job and collaborate successfully, data scientists shouldn't spend their time collecting, cleaning, and preparing data after initial exploratory work. Data engineers should automate this work as much as possible.

The need for production-ready data science is a significant driver behind the emergence of the data engineering profession. Data engineers should help data scientists to enable a path to production. In fact, we (the authors) moved from data science to data engineering after recognizing this fundamental need. Data engineers work to provide the data automation and scale that make data science more efficient.

Data analysts. Data analysts (or business analysts) seek to understand business performance and trends. Whereas data scientists are forward-looking, a data analyst typically focuses on the past or present. Data analysts usually run SQL queries in a data warehouse or a data lake. They may also utilize spreadsheets for computation and analysis and various BI tools such as Microsoft Power BI, Looker, or Tableau. Data analysts are domain experts in the data they work with frequently and become intimately familiar with data definitions, characteristics, and quality problems. A data analyst's typical downstream customers are business users, management, and executives.

Data engineers work with data analysts to build pipelines for new data sources required by the business. Data analysts' subject-matter expertise is invaluable in improving data quality, and they frequently collaborate with data engineers in this capacity.

Machine learning engineers and AI researchers. Machine learning engineers (ML engineers) overlap with data engineers and data scientists. ML engineers develop advanced ML techniques, train models, and design and maintain the infrastructure running ML processes in a scaled production environment. ML engineers often have advanced working knowledge of ML and deep learning techniques and frameworks such as PyTorch or TensorFlow.

ML engineers also understand the hardware, services, and systems required to run these frameworks, both for model training and model deployment at a production scale. It's common for ML flows to run in a cloud environment where ML engineers can spin up and scale infrastructure resources on demand or rely on managed services.

As we've mentioned, the boundaries between ML engineering, data engineering, and data science are blurry. Data engineers may have some operational responsibilities over ML systems, and data scientists may work closely with ML engineering in designing advanced ML processes.

The world of ML engineering is snowballing and parallels a lot of the same developments occurring in data engineering. Whereas several years ago, the attention of ML was focused on how to build models, ML engineering now increasingly emphasizes incorporating best practices of machine learning operations (MLOps) and other mature practices previously adopted in software engineering and DevOps.

AI researchers work on new, advanced ML techniques. AI researchers may work inside large technology companies, specialized intellectual property startups (OpenAI, DeepMind), or academic institutions. Some practitioners are dedicated to part-time research in conjunction with ML engineering responsibilities inside a company. Those working inside specialized ML labs are often 100% dedicated to research. Research problems may target immediate practical applications or more abstract demonstrations of AI. DALL-E, Gato AI, AlphaGo, and GPT-3/GPT-4 are great examples of ML research projects. Given the pace of advancements in ML, these examples will very likely be quaint in a few years' time. We've provided some references in "Additional Resources" on page 32.

AI researchers in well-funded organizations are highly specialized and operate with supporting teams of engineers to facilitate their work. ML engineers in academia usually have fewer resources but rely on teams of graduate students, postdocs, and university staff to provide engineering support. ML engineers who are partially dedicated to research often rely on the same support teams for research and production.

Data Engineers and Business Leadership

We've discussed technical roles with which a data engineer interacts. But data engineers also operate more broadly as organizational connectors, often in a nontechnical capacity. Businesses have come to rely increasingly on data as a core part of many products or a product in itself. Data engineers now participate in strategic planning and lead key initiatives that extend beyond the boundaries of IT. Data engineers often support data architects by acting as the glue between the business and data science/analytics.

Data in the C-suite

C-level executives are increasingly involved in data and analytics, as these are recognized as significant assets for modern businesses. For example, CEOs now concern themselves with initiatives that were once the exclusive province of IT, such as cloud migrations or deployment of a new customer data platform.

Chief executive officer. Chief executive officers (CEOs) at nontech companies generally don't concern themselves with the nitty-gritty of data frameworks and software. Instead, they define a vision in collaboration with technical C-suite roles and company data leadership. Data engineers provide a window into what's possible with data. Data engineers and their managers maintain a map of what data is available to the organization—both internally and from third parties—in what time frame. They are also tasked to study primary data architectural changes in collaboration with other engineering roles. For example, data engineers are often heavily involved in cloud migrations, migrations to new data systems, or deployment of streaming technologies.

Chief information officer.   A chief information officer (CIO) is the senior C-suite executive responsible for information technology within an organization; it is an internal-facing role. A CIO must possess deep knowledge of information technology and business processes—either alone is insufficient. CIOs direct the information technology organization, setting ongoing policies while also defining and executing significant initiatives under the direction of the CEO.

CIOs often collaborate with data engineering leadership in organizations with a well-developed data culture. If an organization is not very high in its data maturity, a CIO will typically help shape its data culture. CIOs will work with engineers and architects to map out major initiatives and make strategic decisions on adopting major architectural elements, such as enterprise resource planning (ERP) and customer relationship management (CRM) systems, cloud migrations, data systems, and internal-facing IT.

Chief technology officer.   A chief technology officer (CTO) is similar to a CIO but faces outward. A CTO owns the key technological strategy and architectures for external-facing applications, such as mobile, web apps, and IoT—all critical data sources for data engineers. The CTO is likely a skilled technologist and has a good sense of software engineering fundamentals and system architecture. In some organizations without a CIO, the CTO or sometimes the chief operating officer (COO) plays the role of CIO. Data engineers often report directly or indirectly through a CTO.

Chief data officer.   The chief data officer (CDO) was created in 2002 at Capital One to recognize the growing importance of data as a business asset. The CDO is responsible for a company's data assets and strategy. CDOs are focused on data's business utility but should have a strong technical grounding. CDOs oversee data products, strategy, initiatives, and core functions such as master data management and privacy. Occasionally, CDOs manage business analytics and data engineering.

Chief analytics officer.   The chief analytics officer (CAO) is a variant of the CDO role. Where both roles exist, the CDO focuses on the technology and organization required to deliver data. The CAO is responsible for analytics, strategy, and decision making for the business. A CAO may oversee data science and ML, though this largely depends on whether the company has a CDO or CTO role.

Chief algorithms officer. A chief algorithms officer (CAO-2) is a recent innovation in the C-suite, a highly technical role focused specifically on data science and ML. CAO-2s typically have experience as individual contributors and team leads in data science or ML projects. Frequently, they have a background in ML research and a related advanced degree.

CAO-2s are expected to be conversant in current ML research and have deep technical knowledge of their company's ML initiatives. In addition to creating business initiatives, they provide technical leadership, set research and development agendas, and build research teams.

Data engineers and project managers

Data engineers often work on significant initiatives, potentially spanning many years. As we write this book, many data engineers are working on cloud migrations, migrating pipelines and warehouses to the next generation of data tools. Other data engineers are starting greenfield projects, assembling new data architectures from scratch by selecting from an astonishing number of best-of-breed architecture and tooling options.

These large initiatives often benefit from *project management* (in contrast to product management, discussed next). Whereas data engineers function in an infrastructure and service delivery capacity, project managers direct traffic and serve as gatekeepers. Most project managers operate according to some variation of Agile and Scrum, with Waterfall still appearing occasionally. Business never sleeps, and business stakeholders often have a significant backlog of things they want to address and new initiatives they want to launch. Project managers must filter a long list of requests and prioritize critical deliverables to keep projects on track and better serve the company.

Data engineers interact with project managers, often planning sprints for projects and ensuing standups related to the sprint. Feedback goes both ways, with data engineers informing project managers and other stakeholders about progress and blockers, and project managers balancing the cadence of technology teams against the ever-changing needs of the business.

Data engineers and product managers

Product managers oversee product development, often owning product lines. In the context of data engineers, these products are called *data products*. Data products are either built from the ground up or are incremental improvements upon existing products. Data engineers interact more frequently with *product managers* as the corporate world has adopted a data-centric focus. Like project managers, product managers balance the activity of technology teams against the needs of the customer and business.

Data engineers and other management roles

Data engineers interact with various managers beyond project and product managers. However, these interactions usually follow either the services or cross-functional models. Data engineers either serve a variety of incoming requests as a centralized team or work as a resource assigned to a particular manager, project, or product.

For more information on data teams and how to structure them, we recommend John Thompson's *Building Analytics Teams* (Packt) and Jesse Anderson's *Data Teams* (Apress). Both books provide strong frameworks and perspectives on the roles of executives with data, who to hire, and how to construct the most effective data team for your company.

 Companies don't hire engineers simply to hack on code in isolation. To be worthy of their title, engineers should develop a deep understanding of the problems they're tasked with solving, the technology tools at their disposal, and the people they work with and serve.

Conclusion

This chapter provided you with a brief overview of the data engineering landscape, including the following:

- Defining data engineering and describing what data engineers do
- Describing the types of data maturity in a company
- Type A and type B data engineers
- Whom data engineers work with

We hope that this first chapter has whetted your appetite, whether you are a software development practitioner, data scientist, ML engineer, business stakeholder, entrepreneur, or venture capitalist. Of course, a great deal still remains to elucidate in subsequent chapters. Chapter 2 covers the data engineering lifecycle, followed by architecture in Chapter 3. The following chapters get into the nitty-gritty of technology decisions for each part of the lifecycle. The entire data field is in flux, and as much as possible, each chapter focuses on the *immutables*—perspectives that will be valid for many years amid relentless change.

Additional Resources

- "The AI Hierarchy of Needs" (*https://oreil.ly/1RJOR*) by Monica Rogati
- The AlphaGo research web page (*https://oreil.ly/mNB6b*)
- "Big Data Will Be Dead in Five Years" (*https://oreil.ly/R2Rus*) by Lewis Gavin
- *Building Analytics Teams* by John K. Thompson (Packt)
- Chapter 1 of *What Is Data Engineering?* by Lewis Gavin (O'Reilly)
- "Data as a Product vs. Data as a Service" (*https://oreil.ly/iOUug*) by Justin Gage
- "Data Engineering: A Quick and Simple Definition" (*https://oreil.ly/eNAnS*) by James Furbush (O'Reilly)
- *Data Teams* by Jesse Anderson (Apress)
- "Doing Data Science at Twitter" (*https://oreil.ly/8rcYh*) by Robert Chang
- "The Downfall of the Data Engineer" (*https://oreil.ly/qxg6y*) by Maxime Beauchemin
- "The Future of Data Engineering Is the Convergence of Disciplines" (*https://oreil.ly/rDiqj*) by Liam Hausmann
- "How CEOs Can Lead a Data-Driven Culture" (*https://oreil.ly/7Kp6R*) by Thomas H. Davenport and Nitin Mittal
- "How Creating a Data-Driven Culture Can Drive Success" (*https://oreil.ly/UgzIZ*) by Frederik Bussler
- The Information Management Body of Knowledge website (*https://www.imbok.info*)
- "Information Management Body of Knowledge" Wikipedia page (*https://oreil.ly/Jk0KW*)
- "Information Management" Wikipedia page (*https://oreil.ly/SWj8k*)
- "On Complexity in Big Data" (*https://oreil.ly/r0jkK*) by Jesse Anderson (O'Reilly)
- "OpenAI's New Language Generator GPT-3 Is Shockingly Good—and Completely Mindless" (*https://oreil.ly/hKYeB*) by Will Douglas Heaven
- "The Rise of the Data Engineer" (*https://oreil.ly/R0QwP*) by Maxime Beauchemin
- "A Short History of Big Data" (*https://oreil.ly/BgzWe*) by Mark van Rijmenam
- "Skills of the Data Architect" (*https://oreil.ly/gImx2*) by Bob Lambert
- "The Three Levels of Data Analysis: A Framework for Assessing Data Organization Maturity" (*https://oreil.ly/bTTd0*) by Emilie Schario
- "What Is a Data Architect? IT's Data Framework Visionary" (*https://oreil.ly/2QBcv*) by Thor Olavsrud

- "Which Profession Is More Complex to Become, a Data Engineer or a Data Scientist?" thread on Quora (*https://oreil.ly/1MAR8*)
- "Why CEOs Must Lead Big Data Initiatives" (*https://oreil.ly/Zh4A0*) by John Weathington

CHAPTER 2

The Data Engineering Lifecycle

The major goal of this book is to encourage you to move beyond viewing data engineering as a specific collection of data technologies. The data landscape is undergoing an explosion of new data technologies and practices, with ever-increasing levels of abstraction and ease of use. Because of increased technical abstraction, data engineers will increasingly become *data lifecycle engineers*, thinking and operating in terms of the *principles* of data lifecycle management.

In this chapter, you'll learn about the *data engineering lifecycle*, which is the central theme of this book. The data engineering lifecycle is our framework describing "cradle to grave" data engineering. You will also learn about the undercurrents of the data engineering lifecycle, which are key foundations that support all data engineering efforts.

What Is the Data Engineering Lifecycle?

The data engineering lifecycle comprises stages that turn raw data ingredients into a useful end product, ready for consumption by analysts, data scientists, ML engineers, and others. This chapter introduces the major stages of the data engineering lifecycle, focusing on each stage's core concepts and saving details for later chapters.

We divide the data engineering lifecycle into five stages (Figure 2-1, top):

- Generation
- Storage
- Ingestion
- Transformation
- Serving data

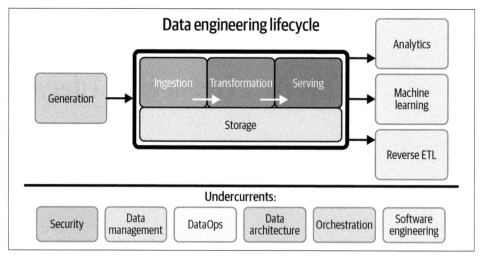

Figure 2-1. Components and undercurrents of the data engineering lifecycle

We begin the data engineering lifecycle by getting data from source systems and storing it. Next, we transform the data and then proceed to our central goal, serving data to analysts, data scientists, ML engineers, and others. In reality, storage occurs throughout the lifecycle as data flows from beginning to end—hence, the diagram shows the storage "stage" as a foundation that underpins other stages.

In general, the middle stages—storage, ingestion, transformation—can get a bit jumbled. And that's OK. Although we split out the distinct parts of the data engineering lifecycle, it's not always a neat, continuous flow. Various stages of the lifecycle may repeat themselves, occur out of order, overlap, or weave together in interesting and unexpected ways.

Acting as a bedrock are *undercurrents* (Figure 2-1, bottom) that cut across multiple stages of the data engineering lifecycle: security, data management, DataOps, data architecture, orchestration, and software engineering. No part of the data engineering lifecycle can adequately function without these undercurrents.

The Data Lifecycle Versus the Data Engineering Lifecycle

You may be wondering about the difference between the overall data lifecycle and the data engineering lifecycle. There's a subtle distinction between the two. The data engineering lifecycle is a subset of the whole data lifecycle (Figure 2-2). Whereas the full data lifecycle encompasses data across its entire lifespan, the data engineering lifecycle focuses on the stages a data engineer controls.

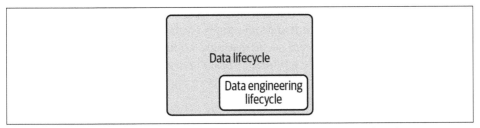

Figure 2-2. The data engineering lifecycle is a subset of the full data lifecycle

Generation: Source Systems

A *source system* is the origin of the data used in the data engineering lifecycle. For example, a source system could be an IoT device, an application message queue, or a transactional database. A data engineer consumes data from a source system but doesn't typically own or control the source system itself. The data engineer needs to have a working understanding of the way source systems work, the way they generate data, the frequency and velocity of the data, and the variety of data they generate.

Engineers also need to keep an open line of communication with source system owners on changes that could break pipelines and analytics. Application code might change the structure of data in a field, or the application team might even choose to migrate the backend to an entirely new database technology.

A major challenge in data engineering is the dizzying array of data source systems engineers must work with and understand. As an illustration, let's look at two common source systems, one very traditional (an application database) and the other a more recent example (IoT swarms).

Figure 2-3 illustrates a traditional source system with several application servers supported by a database. This source system pattern became popular in the 1980s with the explosive success of relational database management systems (RDBMSs). The application + database pattern remains popular today with various modern evolutions of software development practices. For example, applications often consist of many small service/database pairs with microservices rather than a single monolith.

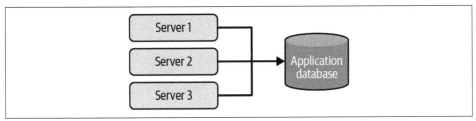

Figure 2-3. Source system example: an application database

Let's look at another example of a source system. Figure 2-4 illustrates an IoT swarm: a fleet of devices (circles) sends data messages (rectangles) to a central collection system. This IoT source system is increasingly common as IoT devices such as sensors, smart devices, and much more increase in the wild.

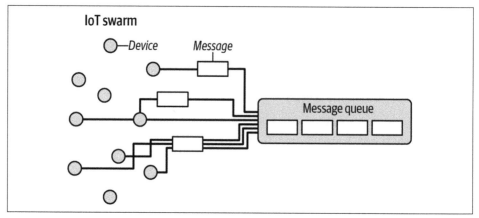

Figure 2-4. Source system example: an IoT swarm and message queue

Evaluating source systems: Key engineering considerations

There are many things to consider when assessing source systems, including how the system handles ingestion, state, and data generation. The following is a starting set of evaluation questions of source systems that data engineers must consider:

- What are the essential characteristics of the data source? Is it an application? A swarm of IoT devices?

- How is data persisted in the source system? Is data persisted long term, or is it temporary and quickly deleted?

- At what rate is data generated? How many events per second? How many gigabytes per hour?

- What level of consistency can data engineers expect from the output data? If you're running data-quality checks against the output data, how often do data inconsistencies occur—nulls where they aren't expected, lousy formatting, etc.?

- How often do errors occur?

- Will the data contain duplicates?

- Will some data values arrive late, possibly much later than other messages produced simultaneously?

- What is the schema of the ingested data? Will data engineers need to join across several tables or even several systems to get a complete picture of the data?

- If schema changes (say, a new column is added), how is this dealt with and communicated to downstream stakeholders?
- How frequently should data be pulled from the source system?
- For stateful systems (e.g., a database tracking customer account information), is data provided as periodic snapshots or update events from change data capture (CDC)? What's the logic for how changes are performed, and how are these tracked in the source database?
- Who/what is the data provider that will transmit the data for downstream consumption?
- Will reading from a data source impact its performance?
- Does the source system have upstream data dependencies? What are the characteristics of these upstream systems?
- Are data-quality checks in place to check for late or missing data?

Sources produce data consumed by downstream systems, including human-generated spreadsheets, IoT sensors, and web and mobile applications. Each source has its unique volume and cadence of data generation. A data engineer should know how the source generates data, including relevant quirks or nuances. Data engineers also need to understand the limits of the source systems they interact with. For example, will analytical queries against a source application database cause resource contention and performance issues?

One of the most challenging nuances of source data is the schema. The *schema* defines the hierarchical organization of data. Logically, we can think of data at the level of a whole source system, drilling down into individual tables, all the way to the structure of respective fields. The schema of data shipped from source systems is handled in various ways. Two popular options are schemaless and fixed schema.

Schemaless doesn't mean the absence of schema. Rather, it means that the application defines the schema as data is written, whether to a message queue, a flat file, a blob, or a document database such as MongoDB. A more traditional model built on relational database storage uses a *fixed schema* enforced in the database, to which application writes must conform.

Either of these models presents challenges for data engineers. Schemas change over time; in fact, schema evolution is encouraged in the Agile approach to software development. A key part of the data engineer's job is taking raw data input in the source system schema and transforming this into valuable output for analytics. This job becomes more challenging as the source schema evolves.

We dive into source systems in greater detail in Chapter 5; we also cover schemas and data modeling in Chapters 6 and 8, respectively.

Storage

You need a place to store data. Choosing a storage solution is key to success in the rest of the data lifecycle, and it's also one of the most complicated stages of the data lifecycle for a variety of reasons. First, data architectures in the cloud often leverage *several* storage solutions. Second, few data storage solutions function purely as storage, with many supporting complex transformation queries; even object storage solutions may support powerful query capabilities—e.g., Amazon S3 Select (*https://oreil.ly/XzcKh*). Third, while storage is a stage of the data engineering lifecycle, it frequently touches on other stages, such as ingestion, transformation, and serving.

Storage runs across the entire data engineering lifecycle, often occurring in multiple places in a data pipeline, with storage systems crossing over with source systems, ingestion, transformation, and serving. In many ways, the way data is stored impacts how it is used in all of the stages of the data engineering lifecycle. For example, cloud data warehouses can store data, process data in pipelines, and serve it to analysts. Streaming frameworks such as Apache Kafka and Pulsar can function simultaneously as ingestion, storage, and query systems for messages, with object storage being a standard layer for data transmission.

Evaluating storage systems: Key engineering considerations

Here are a few key engineering questions to ask when choosing a storage system for a data warehouse, data lakehouse, database, or object storage:

- Is this storage solution compatible with the architecture's required write and read speeds?
- Will storage create a bottleneck for downstream processes?
- Do you understand how this storage technology works? Are you utilizing the storage system optimally or committing unnatural acts? For instance, are you applying a high rate of random access updates in an object storage system? (This is an antipattern with significant performance overhead.)
- Will this storage system handle anticipated future scale? You should consider all capacity limits on the storage system: total available storage, read operation rate, write volume, etc.
- Will downstream users and processes be able to retrieve data in the required service-level agreement (SLA)?
- Are you capturing metadata about schema evolution, data flows, data lineage, and so forth? Metadata has a significant impact on the utility of data. Metadata represents an investment in the future, dramatically enhancing discoverability and institutional knowledge to streamline future projects and architecture changes.

- Is this a pure storage solution (object storage), or does it support complex query patterns (i.e., a cloud data warehouse)?

- Is the storage system schema-agnostic (object storage)? Flexible schema (Cassandra)? Enforced schema (a cloud data warehouse)?

- How are you tracking master data, golden records data quality, and data lineage for data governance? (We have more to say on these in "Data Management" on page 52.)

- How are you handling regulatory compliance and data sovereignty? For example, can you store your data in certain geographical locations but not others?

Understanding data access frequency

Not all data is accessed in the same way. Retrieval patterns will greatly vary based on the data being stored and queried. This brings up the notion of the "temperatures" of data. Data access frequency will determine the temperature of your data.

Data that is most frequently accessed is called *hot data*. Hot data is commonly retrieved many times per day, perhaps even several times per second—for example, in systems that serve user requests. This data should be stored for fast retrieval, where "fast" is relative to the use case. *Lukewarm data* might be accessed every so often—say, every week or month.

Cold data is seldom queried and is appropriate for storing in an archival system. Cold data is often retained for compliance purposes or in case of a catastrophic failure in another system. In the "old days," cold data would be stored on tapes and shipped to remote archival facilities. In cloud environments, vendors offer specialized storage tiers with very cheap monthly storage costs but high prices for data retrieval.

Selecting a storage system

What type of storage solution should you use? This depends on your use cases, data volumes, frequency of ingestion, format, and size of the data being ingested—essentially, the key considerations listed in the preceding bulleted questions. There is no one-size-fits-all universal storage recommendation. Every storage technology has its trade-offs. Countless varieties of storage technologies exist, and it's easy to be overwhelmed when deciding the best option for your data architecture.

Chapter 6 covers storage best practices and approaches in greater detail, as well as the crossover between storage and other lifecycle stages.

Ingestion

After you understand the data source, the characteristics of the source system you're using, and how data is stored, you need to gather the data. The next stage of the data engineering lifecycle is data ingestion from source systems.

In our experience, source systems and ingestion represent the most significant bottlenecks of the data engineering lifecycle. The source systems are normally outside your direct control and might randomly become unresponsive or provide data of poor quality. Or, your data ingestion service might mysteriously stop working for many reasons. As a result, data flow stops or delivers insufficient data for storage, processing, and serving.

Unreliable source and ingestion systems have a ripple effect across the data engineering lifecycle. But you're in good shape, assuming you've answered the big questions about source systems.

Key engineering considerations for the ingestion phase

When preparing to architect or build a system, here are some primary questions about the ingestion stage:

- What are the use cases for the data I'm ingesting? Can I reuse this data rather than create multiple versions of the same dataset?
- Are the systems generating and ingesting this data reliably, and is the data available when I need it?
- What is the data destination after ingestion?
- How frequently will I need to access the data?
- In what volume will the data typically arrive?
- What format is the data in? Can my downstream storage and transformation systems handle this format?
- Is the source data in good shape for immediate downstream use? If so, for how long, and what may cause it to be unusable?
- If the data is from a streaming source, does it need to be transformed before reaching its destination? Would an in-flight transformation be appropriate, where the data is transformed within the stream itself?

These are just a sample of the factors you'll need to think about with ingestion, and we cover those questions and more in Chapter 7. Before we leave, let's briefly turn our attention to two major data ingestion concepts: batch versus streaming and push versus pull.

Batch versus streaming

Virtually all data we deal with is inherently *streaming*. Data is nearly always produced and updated continually at its source. *Batch ingestion* is simply a specialized and convenient way of processing this stream in large chunks—for example, handling a full day's worth of data in a single batch.

Streaming ingestion allows us to provide data to downstream systems—whether other applications, databases, or analytics systems—in a continuous, real-time fashion. Here, *real-time* (or *near real-time*) means that the data is available to a downstream system a short time after it is produced (e.g., less than one second later). The latency required to qualify as real-time varies by domain and requirements.

Batch data is ingested either on a predetermined time interval or as data reaches a preset size threshold. Batch ingestion is a one-way door: once data is broken into batches, the latency for downstream consumers is inherently constrained. Because of limitations of legacy systems, batch was for a long time the default way to ingest data. Batch processing remains an extremely popular way to ingest data for downstream consumption, particularly in analytics and ML.

However, the separation of storage and compute in many systems and the ubiquity of event-streaming and processing platforms make the continuous processing of data streams much more accessible and increasingly popular. The choice largely depends on the use case and expectations for data timeliness.

Key considerations for batch versus stream ingestion

Should you go streaming-first? Despite the attractiveness of a streaming-first approach, there are many trade-offs to understand and think about. The following are some questions to ask yourself when determining whether streaming ingestion is an appropriate choice over batch ingestion:

- If I ingest the data in real time, can downstream storage systems handle the rate of data flow?
- Do I need millisecond real-time data ingestion? Or would a micro-batch approach work, accumulating and ingesting data, say, every minute?
- What are my use cases for streaming ingestion? What specific benefits do I realize by implementing streaming? If I get data in real time, what actions can I take on that data that would be an improvement upon batch?
- Will my streaming-first approach cost more in terms of time, money, maintenance, downtime, and opportunity cost than simply doing batch?
- Are my streaming pipeline and system reliable and redundant if infrastructure fails?
- What tools are most appropriate for the use case? Should I use a managed service (Amazon Kinesis, Google Cloud Pub/Sub, Google Cloud Dataflow) or stand up my own instances of Kafka, Flink, Spark, Pulsar, etc.? If I do the latter, who will manage it? What are the costs and trade-offs?
- If I'm deploying an ML model, what benefits do I have with online predictions and possibly continuous training?

- Am I getting data from a live production instance? If so, what's the impact of my ingestion process on this source system?

As you can see, streaming-first might seem like a good idea, but it's not always straightforward; extra costs and complexities inherently occur. Many great ingestion frameworks do handle both batch and micro-batch ingestion styles. We think batch is an excellent approach for many common use cases, such as model training and weekly reporting. Adopt true real-time streaming only after identifying a business use case that justifies the trade-offs against using batch.

Push versus pull

In the *push* model of data ingestion, a source system writes data out to a target, whether a database, object store, or filesystem. In the *pull* model, data is retrieved from the source system. The line between the push and pull paradigms can be quite blurry; data is often pushed and pulled as it works its way through the various stages of a data pipeline.

Consider, for example, the extract, transform, load (ETL) process, commonly used in batch-oriented ingestion workflows. ETL's *extract* (*E*) part clarifies that we're dealing with a pull ingestion model. In traditional ETL, the ingestion system queries a current source table snapshot on a fixed schedule. You'll learn more about ETL and extract, load, transform (ELT) throughout this book.

In another example, consider continuous CDC, which is achieved in a few ways. One common method triggers a message every time a row is changed in the source database. This message is *pushed* to a queue, where the ingestion system picks it up. Another common CDC method uses binary logs, which record every commit to the database. The database *pushes* to its logs. The ingestion system reads the logs but doesn't directly interact with the database otherwise. This adds little to no additional load to the source database. Some versions of batch CDC use the *pull* pattern. For example, in timestamp-based CDC, an ingestion system queries the source database and pulls the rows that have changed since the previous update.

With streaming ingestion, data bypasses a backend database and is pushed directly to an endpoint, typically with data buffered by an event-streaming platform. This pattern is useful with fleets of IoT sensors emitting sensor data. Rather than relying on a database to maintain the current state, we simply think of each recorded reading as an event. This pattern is also growing in popularity in software applications as it simplifies real-time processing, allows app developers to tailor their messages for downstream analytics, and greatly simplifies the lives of data engineers.

We discuss ingestion best practices and techniques in depth in Chapter 7. Next, let's turn to the transformation stage of the data engineering lifecycle.

Transformation

After you've ingested and stored data, you need to do something with it. The next stage of the data engineering lifecycle is *transformation*, meaning data needs to be changed from its original form into something useful for downstream use cases. Without proper transformations, data will sit inert, and not be in a useful form for reports, analysis, or ML. Typically, the transformation stage is where data begins to create value for downstream user consumption.

Immediately after ingestion, basic transformations map data into correct types (changing ingested string data into numeric and date types, for example), putting records into standard formats, and removing bad ones. Later stages of transformation may transform the data schema and apply normalization. Downstream, we can apply large-scale aggregation for reporting or featurize data for ML processes.

Key considerations for the transformation phase

When considering data transformations within the data engineering lifecycle, it helps to consider the following:

- What's the cost and return on investment (ROI) of the transformation? What is the associated business value?
- Is the transformation as simple and self-isolated as possible?
- What business rules do the transformations support?

You can transform data in batch or while streaming in flight. As mentioned in "Ingestion" on page 41, virtually all data starts life as a continuous stream; batch is just a specialized way of processing a data stream. Batch transformations are overwhelmingly popular, but given the growing popularity of stream-processing solutions and the general increase in the amount of streaming data, we expect the popularity of streaming transformations to continue growing, perhaps entirely replacing batch processing in certain domains soon.

Logically, we treat transformation as a standalone area of the data engineering lifecycle, but the realities of the lifecycle can be much more complicated in practice. Transformation is often entangled in other phases of the lifecycle. Typically, data is transformed in source systems or in flight during ingestion. For example, a source system may add an event timestamp to a record before forwarding it to an ingestion process. Or a record within a streaming pipeline may be "enriched" with additional fields and calculations before it's sent to a data warehouse. Transformations are ubiquitous in various parts of the lifecycle. Data preparation, data wrangling, and cleaning—these transformative tasks add value for end consumers of data.

Business logic is a major driver of data transformation, often in data modeling. Data translates business logic into reusable elements (e.g., a sale means "somebody bought

12 picture frames from me for $30 each, or $360 in total"). In this case, somebody bought 12 picture frames for $30 each. Data modeling is critical for obtaining a clear and current picture of business processes. A simple view of raw retail transactions might not be useful without adding the logic of accounting rules so that the CFO has a clear picture of financial health. Ensure a standard approach for implementing business logic across your transformations.

Data featurization for ML is another data transformation process. Featurization intends to extract and enhance data features useful for training ML models. Featurization can be a dark art, combining domain expertise (to identify which features might be important for prediction) with extensive experience in data science. For this book, the main point is that once data scientists determine how to featurize data, featurization processes can be automated by data engineers in the transformation stage of a data pipeline.

Transformation is a profound subject, and we cannot do it justice in this brief introduction. Chapter 8 delves into queries, data modeling, and various transformation practices and nuances.

Serving Data

You've reached the last stage of the data engineering lifecycle. Now that the data has been ingested, stored, and transformed into coherent and useful structures, it's time to get value from your data. "Getting value" from data means different things to different users.

Data has *value* when it's used for practical purposes. Data that is not consumed or queried is simply inert. Data vanity projects are a major risk for companies. Many companies pursued vanity projects in the big data era, gathering massive datasets in data lakes that were never consumed in any useful way. The cloud era is triggering a new wave of vanity projects built on the latest data warehouses, object storage systems, and streaming technologies. Data projects must be intentional across the lifecycle. What is the ultimate business purpose of the data so carefully collected, cleaned, and stored?

Data serving is perhaps the most exciting part of the data engineering lifecycle. This is where the magic happens. This is where ML engineers can apply the most advanced techniques. Let's look at some of the popular uses of data: analytics, ML, and reverse ETL.

Analytics

Analytics is the core of most data endeavors. Once your data is stored and transformed, you're ready to generate reports or dashboards and do ad hoc analysis on the data. Whereas the bulk of analytics used to encompass BI, it now includes other facets such as operational analytics and embedded analytics (Figure 2-5). Let's briefly touch on these variations of analytics.

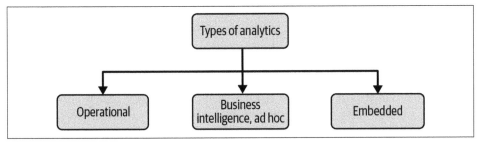

Figure 2-5. Types of analytics

Business intelligence.   BI marshals collected data to describe a business's past and current state. BI requires using business logic to process raw data. Note that data serving for analytics is yet another area where the stages of the data engineering lifecycle can get tangled. As we mentioned earlier, business logic is often applied to data in the transformation stage of the data engineering lifecycle, but a logic-on-read approach has become increasingly popular. Data is stored in a clean but fairly raw form, with minimal postprocessing business logic. A BI system maintains a repository of business logic and definitions. This business logic is used to query the data warehouse so that reports and dashboards align with business definitions.

As a company grows its data maturity, it will move from ad hoc data analysis to self-service analytics, allowing democratized data access to business users without needing IT to intervene. The capability to do self-service analytics assumes that data is good enough that people across the organization can simply access it themselves, slice and dice it however they choose, and get immediate insights. Although self-service analytics is simple in theory, it's tough to pull off in practice. The main reason is that poor data quality, organizational silos, and a lack of adequate data skills often get in the way of allowing widespread use of analytics.

Operational analytics.   Operational analytics focuses on the fine-grained details of operations, promoting actions that a user of the reports can act upon immediately. Operational analytics could be a live view of inventory or real-time dashboarding of website or application health. In this case, data is consumed in real time, either directly from a source system or from a streaming data pipeline. The types of insights in operational analytics differ from traditional BI since operational analytics is focused on the present and doesn't necessarily concern historical trends.

Embedded analytics.   You may wonder why we've broken out embedded analytics (customer-facing analytics) separately from BI. In practice, analytics provided to customers on a SaaS platform come with a separate set of requirements and complications. Internal BI faces a limited audience and generally presents a limited number of unified views. Access controls are critical but not particularly complicated. Access is managed using a handful of roles and access tiers.

With embedded analytics, the request rate for reports, and the corresponding burden on analytics systems, goes up dramatically; access control is significantly more complicated and critical. Businesses may be serving separate analytics and data to thousands or more customers. Each customer must see their data and only their data. An internal data-access error at a company would likely lead to a procedural review. A data leak between customers would be considered a massive breach of trust, leading to media attention and a significant loss of customers. Minimize your blast radius related to data leaks and security vulnerabilities. Apply tenant- or data-level security within your storage and anywhere there's a possibility of data leakage.

Multitenancy

Many current storage and analytics systems support multitenancy in various ways. Data engineers may choose to house data for many customers in common tables to allow a unified view for internal analytics and ML. This data is presented externally to individual customers through logical views with appropriately defined controls and filters. It is incumbent on data engineers to understand the minutiae of multitenancy in the systems they deploy to ensure absolute data security and isolation.

Machine learning

The emergence and success of ML is one of the most exciting technology revolutions. Once organizations reach a high level of data maturity, they can begin to identify problems amenable to ML and start organizing a practice around it.

The responsibilities of data engineers overlap significantly in analytics and ML, and the boundaries between data engineering, ML engineering, and analytics engineering can be fuzzy. For example, a data engineer may need to support Spark clusters that facilitate analytics pipelines and ML model training. They may also need to provide a system that orchestrates tasks across teams and support metadata and cataloging systems that track data history and lineage. Setting these domains of responsibility and the relevant reporting structures is a critical organizational decision.

The feature store is a recently developed tool that combines data engineering and ML engineering. Feature stores are designed to reduce the operational burden for ML engineers by maintaining feature history and versions, supporting feature sharing among teams, and providing basic operational and orchestration capabilities, such as backfilling. In practice, data engineers are part of the core support team for feature stores to support ML engineering.

Should a data engineer be familiar with ML? It certainly helps. Regardless of the operational boundary between data engineering, ML engineering, business analytics, and so forth, data engineers should maintain operational knowledge about their teams. A good data engineer is conversant in the fundamental ML techniques and related data-processing requirements, the use cases for models within their company, and the responsibilities of the organization's various analytics teams. This helps maintain efficient communication and facilitate collaboration. Ideally, data engineers will build tools in partnership with other teams that neither team can make independently.

This book cannot possibly cover ML in depth. A growing ecosystem of books, videos, articles, and communities is available if you're interested in learning more; we include a few suggestions in "Additional Resources" on page 71.

The following are some considerations for the serving data phase specific to ML:

- Is the data of sufficient quality to perform reliable feature engineering? Quality requirements and assessments are developed in close collaboration with teams consuming the data.
- Is the data discoverable? Can data scientists and ML engineers easily find valuable data?
- Where are the technical and organizational boundaries between data engineering and ML engineering? This organizational question has significant architectural implications.
- Does the dataset properly represent ground truth? Is it unfairly biased?

While ML is exciting, our experience is that companies often prematurely dive into it. Before investing a ton of resources into ML, take the time to build a solid data foundation. This means setting up the best systems and architecture across the data engineering and ML lifecycle. It's generally best to develop competence in analytics before moving to ML. Many companies have dashed their ML dreams because they undertook initiatives without appropriate foundations.

Reverse ETL

Reverse ETL has long been a practical reality in data, viewed as an antipattern that we didn't like to talk about or dignify with a name. *Reverse ETL* takes processed data from the output side of the data engineering lifecycle and feeds it back into source systems, as shown in Figure 2-6. In reality, this flow is beneficial and often necessary; reverse ETL allows us to take analytics, scored models, etc., and feed these back into production systems or SaaS platforms.

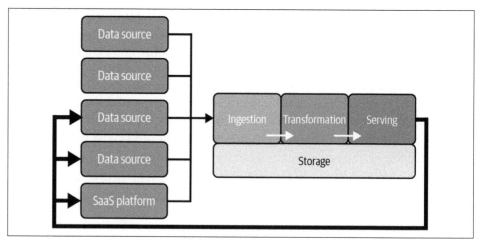

Figure 2-6. Reverse ETL

Marketing analysts might calculate bids in Microsoft Excel by using the data in their data warehouse, and then upload these bids to Google Ads. This process was often entirely manual and primitive.

As we've written this book, several vendors have embraced the concept of reverse ETL and built products around it, such as Hightouch and Census. Reverse ETL remains nascent as a practice, but we suspect that it is here to stay.

Reverse ETL has become especially important as businesses rely increasingly on SaaS and external platforms. For example, companies may want to push specific metrics from their data warehouse to a customer data platform or CRM system. Advertising platforms are another everyday use case, as in the Google Ads example. Expect to see more activity in reverse ETL, with an overlap in both data engineering and ML engineering.

The jury is out on whether the term *reverse ETL* will stick. And the practice may evolve. Some engineers claim that we can eliminate reverse ETL by handling data transformations in an event stream and sending those events back to source systems as needed. Realizing widespread adoption of this pattern across businesses is another matter. The gist is that transformed data will need to be returned to source systems in some manner, ideally with the correct lineage and business process associated with the source system.

Major Undercurrents Across the Data Engineering Lifecycle

Data engineering is rapidly maturing. Whereas prior cycles of data engineering simply focused on the technology layer, the continued abstraction and simplification of tools and practices have shifted this focus. Data engineering now encompasses far more than tools and technology. The field is now moving up the value chain, incorporating traditional enterprise practices such as data management and cost optimization and newer practices like DataOps.

We've termed these practices *undercurrents*—security, data management, DataOps, data architecture, orchestration, and software engineering—that support every aspect of the data engineering lifecycle (Figure 2-7). In this section, we give a brief overview of these undercurrents and their major components, which you'll see in more detail throughout the book.

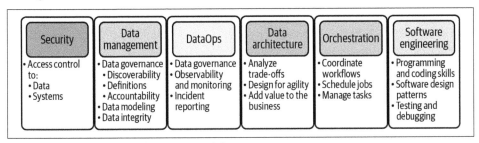

Figure 2-7. The major undercurrents of data engineering

Security

Security must be top of mind for data engineers, and those who ignore it do so at their peril. That's why security is the first undercurrent. Data engineers must understand both data and access security, exercising the principle of least privilege. The principle of least privilege (*https://oreil.ly/6RGAq*) means giving a user or system access to only the essential data and resources to perform an intended function. A common antipattern we see with data engineers with little security experience is to give admin access to all users. This is a catastrophe waiting to happen!

Give users only the access they need to do their jobs today, nothing more. Don't operate from a root shell when you're just looking for visible files with standard user access. When querying tables with a lesser role, don't use the superuser role in a database. Imposing the principle of least privilege on ourselves can prevent accidental damage and keep you in a security-first mindset.

People and organizational structure are always the biggest security vulnerabilities in any company. When we hear about major security breaches in the media, it often turns out that someone in the company ignored basic precautions, fell victim to a phishing attack, or otherwise acted irresponsibly. The first line of defense for data security is to create a culture of security that permeates the organization. All individuals who have access to data must understand their responsibility in protecting the company's sensitive data and its customers.

Data security is also about timing—providing data access to exactly the people and systems that need to access it and *only for the duration necessary to perform their work*. Data should be protected from unwanted visibility, both in flight and at rest, by using encryption, tokenization, data masking, obfuscation, and simple, robust access controls.

Data engineers must be competent security administrators, as security falls in their domain. A data engineer should understand security best practices for the cloud and on prem. Knowledge of user and identity access management (IAM) roles, policies, groups, network security, password policies, and encryption are good places to start.

Throughout the book, we highlight areas where security should be top of mind in the data engineering lifecycle. You can also gain more detailed insights into security in Chapter 10.

Data Management

You probably think that data management sounds very...corporate. "Old school" data management practices make their way into data and ML engineering. What's old is new again. Data management has been around for decades but didn't get a lot of traction in data engineering until recently. Data tools are becoming simpler, and there is less complexity for data engineers to manage. As a result, the data engineer moves up the value chain toward the next rung of best practices. Data best practices once reserved for huge companies—data governance, master data management, data-quality management, metadata management—are now filtering down to companies of all sizes and maturity levels. As we like to say, data engineering is becoming "enterprisey." This is ultimately a great thing!

The Data Management Association International (DAMA) *Data Management Body of Knowledge* (*DMBOK*), which we consider to be the definitive book for enterprise data management, offers this definition:

> Data management is the development, execution, and supervision of plans, policies, programs, and practices that deliver, control, protect, and enhance the value of data and information assets throughout their lifecycle.

That's a bit lengthy, so let's look at how it ties to data engineering. Data engineers manage the data lifecycle, and data management encompasses the set of best practices that data engineers will use to accomplish this task, both technically and strategically. Without a framework for managing data, data engineers are simply technicians operating in a vacuum. Data engineers need a broader perspective of data's utility across the organization, from the source systems to the C-suite, and everywhere in between.

Why is data management important? Data management demonstrates that data is vital to daily operations, just as businesses view financial resources, finished goods, or real estate as assets. Data management practices form a cohesive framework that everyone can adopt to ensure that the organization gets value from data and handles it appropriately.

Data management has quite a few facets, including the following:

- Data governance, including discoverability and accountability
- Data modeling and design
- Data lineage
- Storage and operations
- Data integration and interoperability
- Data lifecycle management
- Data systems for advanced analytics and ML
- Ethics and privacy

While this book is in no way an exhaustive resource on data management, let's briefly cover some salient points from each area as they relate to data engineering.

Data governance

According to *Data Governance: The Definitive Guide,* "Data governance is, first and foremost, a data management function to ensure the quality, integrity, security, and usability of the data collected by an organization."[1]

We can expand on that definition and say that data governance engages people, processes, and technologies to maximize data value across an organization while protecting data with appropriate security controls. Effective data governance is developed with intention and supported by the organization. When data governance is accidental and haphazard, the side effects can range from untrusted data to security breaches and everything in between. Being intentional about data governance will maximize the organization's data capabilities and the value generated from data. It will also (hopefully) keep a company out of the headlines for questionable or downright reckless data practices.

Think of the typical example of data governance being done poorly. A business analyst gets a request for a report but doesn't know what data to use to answer the question. They may spend hours digging through dozens of tables in a transactional database, wildly guessing at which fields might be useful. The analyst compiles a "directionally correct" report but isn't entirely sure that the report's underlying data is

---

1 Evren Eryurek et al., *Data Governance: The Definitive Guide* (Sebastopol, CA: O'Reilly, 2021), 1, *https://oreil.ly/LFT4d.*

accurate or sound. The recipient of the report also questions the validity of the data. The integrity of the analyst—and of all data in the company's systems—is called into question. The company is confused about its performance, making business planning impossible.

Data governance is a foundation for data-driven business practices and a mission-critical part of the data engineering lifecycle. When data governance is practiced well, people, processes, and technologies align to treat data as a key business driver; if data issues occur, they are promptly handled.

The core categories of data governance are discoverability, security, and accountability.[2] Within these core categories are subcategories, such as data quality, metadata, and privacy. Let's look at each core category in turn.

Discoverability. In a data-driven company, data must be available and discoverable. End users should have quick and reliable access to the data they need to do their jobs. They should know where the data comes from, how it relates to other data, and what the data means.

Some key areas of data discoverability include metadata management and master data management. Let's briefly describe these areas.

Metadata. *Metadata* is "data about data," and it underpins every section of the data engineering lifecycle. Metadata is exactly the data needed to make data discoverable and governable.

We divide metadata into two major categories: autogenerated and human generated. Modern data engineering revolves around automation, but metadata collection is often manual and error prone.

Technology can assist with this process, removing much of the error-prone work of manual metadata collection. We're seeing a proliferation of data catalogs, data-lineage tracking systems, and metadata management tools. Tools can crawl databases to look for relationships and monitor data pipelines to track where data comes from and where it goes. A low-fidelity manual approach uses an internally led effort where various stakeholders crowdsource metadata collection within the organization. These data management tools are covered in depth throughout the book, as they undercut much of the data engineering lifecycle.

Metadata becomes a byproduct of data and data processes. However, key challenges remain. In particular, interoperability and standards are still lacking. Metadata tools are only as good as their connectors to data systems and their ability to share

---

2 Eryurek, *Data Governance*, 5.

metadata. In addition, automated metadata tools should not entirely take humans out of the loop.

Data has a social element; each organization accumulates social capital and knowledge around processes, datasets, and pipelines. Human-oriented metadata systems focus on the social aspect of metadata. This is something that Airbnb has emphasized in its various blog posts on data tools, particularly its original Dataportal concept.[3] Such tools should provide a place to disclose data owners, data consumers, and domain experts. Documentation and internal wiki tools provide a key foundation for metadata management, but these tools should also integrate with automated data cataloging. For example, data-scanning tools can generate wiki pages with links to relevant data objects.

Once metadata systems and processes exist, data engineers can consume metadata in useful ways. Metadata becomes a foundation for designing pipelines and managing data throughout the lifecycle.

DMBOK identifies four main categories of metadata that are useful to data engineers:

- Business metadata
- Technical metadata
- Operational metadata
- Reference metadata

Let's briefly describe each category of metadata.

Business metadata relates to the way data is used in the business, including business and data definitions, data rules and logic, how and where data is used, and the data owner(s).

A data engineer uses business metadata to answer nontechnical questions about who, what, where, and how. For example, a data engineer may be tasked with creating a data pipeline for customer sales analysis. But what is a customer? Is it someone who's purchased in the last 90 days? Or someone who's purchased at any time the business has been open? A data engineer would use the correct data to refer to business metadata (data dictionary or data catalog) to look up how a "customer" is defined. Business metadata provides a data engineer with the right context and definitions to properly use data.

Technical metadata describes the data created and used by systems across the data engineering lifecycle. It includes the data model and schema, data lineage, field

---

3 Chris Williams et al., "Democratizing Data at Airbnb," *The Airbnb Tech Blog*, May 12, 2017, *https://oreil.ly/dM332*.

mappings, and pipeline workflows. A data engineer uses technical metadata to create, connect, and monitor various systems across the data engineering lifecycle.

Here are some common types of technical metadata that a data engineer will use:

- Pipeline metadata (often produced in orchestration systems)
- Data lineage
- Schema

Orchestration is a central hub that coordinates workflow across various systems. *Pipeline metadata* captured in orchestration systems provides details of the workflow schedule, system and data dependencies, configurations, connection details, and much more.

Data-lineage metadata tracks the origin and changes to data, and its dependencies, over time. As data flows through the data engineering lifecycle, it evolves through transformations and combinations with other data. Data lineage provides an audit trail of data's evolution as it moves through various systems and workflows.

Schema metadata describes the structure of data stored in a system such as a database, a data warehouse, a data lake, or a filesystem; it is one of the key differentiators across different storage systems. Object stores, for example, don't manage schema metadata; instead, this must be managed in a *metastore*. On the other hand, cloud data warehouses manage schema metadata internally.

These are just a few examples of technical metadata that a data engineer should know about. This is not a complete list, and we cover additional aspects of technical metadata throughout the book.

Operational metadata describes the operational results of various systems and includes statistics about processes, job IDs, application runtime logs, data used in a process, and error logs. A data engineer uses operational metadata to determine whether a process succeeded or failed and the data involved in the process.

Orchestration systems can provide a limited picture of operational metadata, but the latter still tends to be scattered across many systems. A need for better-quality operational metadata, and better metadata management, is a major motivation for next-generation orchestration and metadata management systems.

Reference metadata is data used to classify other data. This is also referred to as *lookup data*. Standard examples of reference data are internal codes, geographic codes, units of measurement, and internal calendar standards. Note that much of reference data is fully managed internally, but items such as geographic codes might come from standard external references. Reference data is essentially a standard for interpreting other data, so if it changes, this change happens slowly over time.

Data accountability. *Data accountability* means assigning an individual to govern a portion of data. The responsible person then coordinates the governance activities of other stakeholders. Managing data quality is tough if no one is accountable for the data in question.

Note that people accountable for data need not be data engineers. The accountable person might be a software engineer or product manager, or serve in another role. In addition, the responsible person generally doesn't have all the resources necessary to maintain data quality. Instead, they coordinate with all people who touch the data, including data engineers.

Data accountability can happen at various levels; accountability can happen at the level of a table or a log stream but could be as fine-grained as a single field entity that occurs across many tables. An individual may be accountable for managing a customer ID across many systems. For enterprise data management, a data domain is the set of all possible values that can occur for a given field type, such as in this ID example. This may seem excessively bureaucratic and meticulous, but it can significantly affect data quality.

Data quality.

> Can I trust this data?
>> —Everyone in the business

Data quality is the optimization of data toward the desired state and orbits the question, "What do you get compared with what you expect?" Data should conform to the expectations in the business metadata. Does the data match the definition agreed upon by the business?

A data engineer ensures data quality across the entire data engineering lifecycle. This involves performing data-quality tests, and ensuring data conformance to schema expectations, data completeness, and precision.

According to *Data Governance: The Definitive Guide*, data quality is defined by three main characteristics:[4]

Accuracy
Is the collected data factually correct? Are there duplicate values? Are the numeric values accurate?

Completeness
Are the records complete? Do all required fields contain valid values?

---

4 Eryurek, *Data Governance*, 113.

Timeliness
Are records available in a timely fashion?

Each of these characteristics is quite nuanced. For example, how do we think about bots and web scrapers when dealing with web event data? If we intend to analyze the customer journey, we must have a process that lets us separate humans from machine-generated traffic. Any bot-generated events misclassified as *human* present data accuracy issues, and vice versa.

A variety of interesting problems arise concerning completeness and timeliness. In the Google paper introducing the Dataflow model, the authors give the example of an offline video platform that displays ads.[5] The platform downloads video and ads while a connection is present, allows the user to watch these while offline, and then uploads ad view data once a connection is present again. This data may arrive late, well after the ads are watched. How does the platform handle billing for the ads?

Fundamentally, this problem can't be solved by purely technical means. Rather, engineers will need to determine their standards for late-arriving data and enforce these uniformly, possibly with the help of various technology tools.

Master Data Management

Master data is data about business entities such as employees, customers, products, and locations. As organizations grow larger and more complex through organic growth and acquisitions, and collaborate with other businesses, maintaining a consistent picture of entities and identities becomes more and more challenging.

Master data management (MDM) is the practice of building consistent entity definitions known as *golden records*. Golden records harmonize entity data across an organization and with its partners. MDM is a business operations process facilitated by building and deploying technology tools. For example, an MDM team might determine a standard format for addresses, and then work with data engineers to build an API to return consistent addresses and a system that uses address data to match customer records across company divisions.

MDM reaches across the full data cycle into operational databases. It may fall directly under the purview of data engineering but is often the assigned responsibility of a dedicated team that works across the organization. Even if they don't own MDM, data engineers must always be aware of it, as they might collaborate on MDM initiatives.

---

5 Tyler Akidau et al., "The Dataflow Model: A Practical Approach to Balancing Correctness, Latency, and Cost in Massive-Scale, Unbounded, Out-of-Order Data Processing," *Proceedings of the VLDB Endowment* 8 (2015): 1792–1803, *https://oreil.ly/Z6XYy*.

Data quality sits across the boundary of human and technology problems. Data engineers need robust processes to collect actionable human feedback on data quality and use technology tools to detect quality issues preemptively before downstream users ever see them. We cover these collection processes in the appropriate chapters throughout this book.

Data modeling and design

To derive business insights from data, through business analytics and data science, the data must be in a usable form. The process for converting data into a usable form is known as *data modeling and design*. Whereas we traditionally think of data modeling as a problem for database administrators (DBAs) and ETL developers, data modeling can happen almost anywhere in an organization. Firmware engineers develop the data format of a record for an IoT device, or web application developers design the JSON response to an API call or a MySQL table schema—these are all instances of data modeling and design.

Data modeling has become more challenging because of the variety of new data sources and use cases. For instance, strict normalization doesn't work well with event data. Fortunately, a new generation of data tools increases the flexibility of data models, while retaining logical separations of measures, dimensions, attributes, and hierarchies. Cloud data warehouses support the ingestion of enormous quantities of denormalized and semistructured data, while still supporting common data modeling patterns, such as Kimball, Inmon, and Data Vault. Data processing frameworks such as Spark can ingest a whole spectrum of data, from flat structured relational records to raw unstructured text. We discuss these data modeling and transformation patterns in greater detail in Chapter 8.

With the wide variety of data that engineers must cope with, there is a temptation to throw up our hands and give up on data modeling. This is a terrible idea with harrowing consequences, made evident when people murmur of the write once, read never (WORN) access pattern or refer to a *data swamp*. Data engineers need to understand modeling best practices as well as develop the flexibility to apply the appropriate level and type of modeling to the data source and use case.

Data lineage

As data moves through its lifecycle, how do you know what system affected the data or what the data is composed of as it gets passed around and transformed? *Data lineage* describes the recording of an audit trail of data through its lifecycle, tracking both the systems that process the data and the upstream data it depends on.

Data lineage helps with error tracking, accountability, and debugging of data and the systems that process it. It has the obvious benefit of giving an audit trail for the data lifecycle and helps with compliance. For example, if a user would like their data deleted from your systems, having lineage for that data lets you know where that data is stored and its dependencies.

Data lineage has been around for a long time in larger companies with strict compliance standards. However, it's now being more widely adopted in smaller companies as data management becomes mainstream. We also note that Andy Petrella's concept of Data Observability Driven Development (DODD) (*https://oreil.ly/3f4WS*) is closely related to data lineage. DODD observes data all along its lineage. This process is applied during development, testing, and finally production to deliver quality and conformity to expectations.

Data integration and interoperability

Data integration and interoperability is the process of integrating data across tools and processes. As we move away from a single-stack approach to analytics and toward a heterogeneous cloud environment in which various tools process data on demand, integration and interoperability occupy an ever-widening swath of the data engineer's job.

Increasingly, integration happens through general-purpose APIs rather than custom database connections. For example, a data pipeline might pull data from the Salesforce API, store it to Amazon S3, call the Snowflake API to load it into a table, call the API again to run a query, and then export the results to S3 where Spark can consume them.

All of this activity can be managed with relatively simple Python code that talks to data systems rather than handling data directly. While the complexity of interacting with data systems has decreased, the number of systems and the complexity of pipelines has dramatically increased. Engineers starting from scratch quickly outgrow the capabilities of bespoke scripting and stumble into the need for *orchestration*. Orchestration is one of our undercurrents, and we discuss it in detail in "Orchestration" on page 66.

Data lifecycle management

The advent of data lakes encouraged organizations to ignore data archival and destruction. Why discard data when you can simply add more storage ad infinitum? Two changes have encouraged engineers to pay more attention to what happens at the end of the data engineering lifecycle.

First, data is increasingly stored in the cloud. This means we have pay-as-you-go storage costs instead of large up-front capital expenditures for an on-premises data lake. When every byte shows up on a monthly AWS statement, CFOs see opportunities for savings. Cloud environments make data archival a relatively straightforward process. Major cloud vendors offer archival-specific object storage classes that allow long-term data retention at an extremely low cost, assuming very infrequent access (it should be noted that data retrieval isn't so cheap, but that's for another conversation). These storage classes also support extra policy controls to prevent accidental or deliberate deletion of critical archives.

Second, privacy and data retention laws such as the GDPR and the CCPA require data engineers to actively manage data destruction to respect users' "right to be forgotten." Data engineers must know what consumer data they retain and must have procedures to destroy data in response to requests and compliance requirements.

Data destruction is straightforward in a cloud data warehouse. SQL semantics allow deletion of rows conforming to a `where` clause. Data destruction was more challenging in data lakes, where write-once, read-many was the default storage pattern. Tools such as Hive ACID and Delta Lake allow easy management of deletion transactions at scale. New generations of metadata management, data lineage, and cataloging tools will also streamline the end of the data engineering lifecycle.

Ethics and privacy

The last several years of data breaches, misinformation, and mishandling of data make one thing clear: data impacts people. Data used to live in the Wild West, freely collected and traded like baseball cards. Those days are long gone. Whereas data's ethical and privacy implications were once considered nice to have, like security, they're now central to the general data lifecycle. Data engineers need to do the right thing when no one else is watching, because everyone will be watching someday.[6] We hope that more organizations will encourage a culture of good data ethics and privacy.

How do ethics and privacy impact the data engineering lifecycle? Data engineers need to ensure that datasets mask personally identifiable information (PII) and other sensitive information; bias can be identified and tracked in datasets as they are transformed. Regulatory requirements and compliance penalties are only growing. Ensure that your data assets are compliant with a growing number of data regulations, such as GDPR and CCPA. Please take this seriously. We offer tips throughout the book to ensure that you're baking ethics and privacy into the data engineering lifecycle.

DataOps

DataOps maps the best practices of Agile methodology, DevOps, and statistical process control (SPC) to data. Whereas DevOps aims to improve the release and quality of software products, DataOps does the same thing for data products.

---

6 We espouse the notion that ethical behavior is doing the right thing when no one is watching, an idea that occurs in the writings of C. S. Lewis, Charles Marshall, and many other authors.

Data products differ from software products because of the way data is used. A software product provides specific functionality and technical features for end users. By contrast, a data product is built around sound business logic and metrics, whose users make decisions or build models that perform automated actions. A data engineer must understand both the technical aspects of building software products and the business logic, quality, and metrics that will create excellent data products.

Like DevOps, DataOps borrows much from lean manufacturing and supply chain management, mixing people, processes, and technology to reduce time to value. As Data Kitchen (experts in DataOps) describes it:[7]

> DataOps is a collection of technical practices, workflows, cultural norms, and architectural patterns that enable:
>
> - Rapid innovation and experimentation delivering new insights to customers with increasing velocity
> - Extremely high data quality and very low error rates
> - Collaboration across complex arrays of people, technology, and environments
> - Clear measurement, monitoring, and transparency of results

Lean practices (such as lead time reduction and minimizing defects) and the resulting improvements to quality and productivity are things we are glad to see gaining momentum both in software and data operations.

First and foremost, DataOps is a set of cultural habits; the data engineering team needs to adopt a cycle of communicating and collaborating with the business, breaking down silos, continuously learning from successes and mistakes, and rapid iteration. Only when these cultural habits are set in place can the team get the best results from technology and tools.

Depending on a company's data maturity, a data engineer has some options to build DataOps into the fabric of the overall data engineering lifecycle. If the company has no preexisting data infrastructure or practices, DataOps is very much a greenfield opportunity that can be baked in from day one. With an existing project or infrastructure that lacks DataOps, a data engineer can begin adding DataOps into workflows. We suggest first starting with observability and monitoring to get a window into the performance of a system, then adding in automation and incident response. A data engineer may work alongside an existing DataOps team to improve the data engineering lifecycle in a data-mature company. In all cases, a data engineer must be aware of the philosophy and technical aspects of DataOps.

---

7 "What Is DataOps," DataKitchen FAQ page, accessed May 5, 2022, *https://oreil.ly/Ns06w*.

DataOps has three core technical elements: automation, monitoring and observability, and incident response (Figure 2-8). Let's look at each of these pieces and how they relate to the data engineering lifecycle.

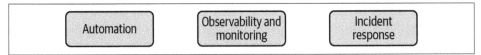

Figure 2-8. The three pillars of DataOps

Automation

Automation enables reliability and consistency in the DataOps process and allows data engineers to quickly deploy new product features and improvements to existing workflows. DataOps automation has a similar framework and workflow to DevOps, consisting of change management (environment, code, and data version control), continuous integration/continuous deployment (CI/CD), and configuration as code. Like DevOps, DataOps practices monitor and maintain the reliability of technology and systems (data pipelines, orchestration, etc.), with the added dimension of checking for data quality, data/model drift, metadata integrity, and more.

Let's briefly discuss the evolution of DataOps automation within a hypothetical organization. An organization with a low level of DataOps maturity often attempts to schedule multiple stages of data transformation processes using cron jobs. This works well for a while. As data pipelines become more complicated, several things are likely to happen. If the cron jobs are hosted on a cloud instance, the instance may have an operational problem, causing the jobs to stop running unexpectedly. As the spacing between jobs becomes tighter, a job will eventually run long, causing a subsequent job to fail or produce stale data. Engineers may not be aware of job failures until they hear from analysts that their reports are out-of-date.

As the organization's data maturity grows, data engineers will typically adopt an orchestration framework, perhaps Airflow or Dagster. Data engineers are aware that Airflow presents an operational burden, but the benefits of orchestration eventually outweigh the complexity. Engineers will gradually migrate their cron jobs to Airflow jobs. Now, dependencies are checked before jobs run. More transformation jobs can be packed into a given time because each job can start as soon as upstream data is ready rather than at a fixed, predetermined time.

The data engineering team still has room for operational improvements. A data scientist eventually deploys a broken DAG, bringing down the Airflow web server and leaving the data team operationally blind. After enough such headaches, the data engineering team members realize that they need to stop allowing manual DAG deployments. In their next phase of operational maturity, they adopt automated DAG deployment. DAGs are tested before deployment, and monitoring processes ensure that the new DAGs start running properly. In addition, data engineers block the deployment of new Python dependencies until installation is validated. After automation is adopted, the data team is much happier and experiences far fewer headaches.

One of the tenets of the DataOps Manifesto (*https://oreil.ly/2LGwL*) is "Embrace change." This does not mean change for the sake of change but rather goal-oriented change. At each stage of our automation journey, opportunities exist for operational improvement. Even at the high level of maturity that we've described here, further room for improvement remains. Engineers might embrace a next-generation orchestration framework that builds in better metadata capabilities. Or they might try to develop a framework that builds DAGs automatically based on data-lineage specifications. The main point is that engineers constantly seek to implement improvements in automation that will reduce their workload and increase the value that they deliver to the business.

Observability and monitoring

As we tell our clients, "Data is a silent killer." We've seen countless examples of bad data lingering in reports for months or years. Executives may make key decisions from this bad data, discovering the error only much later. The outcomes are usually bad and sometimes catastrophic for the business. Initiatives are undermined and destroyed, years of work wasted. In some of the worst cases, bad data may lead companies to financial ruin.

Another horror story occurs when the systems that create the data for reports randomly stop working, resulting in reports being delayed by several days. The data team doesn't know until they're asked by stakeholders why reports are late or producing stale information. Eventually, various stakeholders lose trust in the capabilities of the core data team and start their own splinter teams. The result is many different unstable systems, inconsistent reports, and silos.

If you're not observing and monitoring your data and the systems that produce the data, you're inevitably going to experience your own data horror story. Observability, monitoring, logging, alerting, and tracing are all critical to getting ahead of any problems along the data engineering lifecycle. We recommend you incorporate SPC to understand whether events being monitored are out of line and which incidents are worth responding to.

Petrella's DODD method mentioned previously in this chapter provides an excellent framework for thinking about data observability. DODD is much like test-driven development (TDD) in software engineering:[8]

---

8 Andy Petrella, "Data Observability Driven Development: The Perfect Analogy for Beginners," Kensu, accessed May 5, 2022, *https://oreil.ly/MxvSX*.

The purpose of DODD is to give everyone involved in the data chain visibility into the data and data applications so that everyone involved in the data value chain has the ability to identify changes to the data or data applications at every step—from ingestion to transformation to analysis—to help troubleshoot or prevent data issues. DODD focuses on making data observability a first-class consideration in the data engineering lifecycle.

We cover many aspects of monitoring and observability throughout the data engineering lifecycle in later chapters.

Incident response

A high-functioning data team using DataOps will be able to ship new data products quickly. But mistakes will inevitably happen. A system may have downtime, a new data model may break downstream reports, an ML model may become stale and provide bad predictions—countless problems can interrupt the data engineering lifecycle. *Incident response* is about using the automation and observability capabilities mentioned previously to rapidly identify root causes of an incident and resolve it as reliably and quickly as possible.

Incident response isn't just about technology and tools, though these are beneficial; it's also about open and blameless communication, both on the data engineering team and across the organization. As Werner Vogels, CTO of Amazon Web Services, is famous for saying, "Everything breaks all the time." Data engineers must be prepared for a disaster and ready to respond as swiftly and efficiently as possible.

Data engineers should proactively find issues before the business reports them. Failure happens, and when the stakeholders or end users see problems, they will present them. They will be unhappy to do so. The feeling is different when they go to raise those issues to a team and see that they are actively being worked on to resolve already. Which team's state would you trust more as an end user? Trust takes a long time to build and can be lost in minutes. Incident response is as much about retroactively responding to incidents as proactively addressing them before they happen.

DataOps summary

At this point, DataOps is still a work in progress. Practitioners have done a good job of adapting DevOps principles to the data domain and mapping out an initial vision through the DataOps Manifesto and other resources. Data engineers would do well to make DataOps practices a high priority in all of their work. The up-front effort will see a significant long-term payoff through faster delivery of products, better reliability and accuracy of data, and greater overall value for the business.

The state of operations in data engineering is still quite immature compared with software engineering. Many data engineering tools, especially legacy monoliths, are not automation-first. A recent movement has arisen to adopt automation best practices across the data engineering lifecycle. Tools like Airflow have paved the way for a new generation of automation and data management tools. The general practices we describe for DataOps are aspirational, and we suggest companies try to adopt them to the fullest extent possible, given the tools and knowledge available today.

Data Architecture

A data architecture reflects the current and future state of data systems that support an organization's long-term data needs and strategy. Because an organization's data requirements will likely change rapidly, and new tools and practices seem to arrive on a near-daily basis, data engineers must understand good data architecture. Chapter 3 covers data architecture in depth, but we want to highlight here that data architecture is an undercurrent of the data engineering lifecycle.

A data engineer should first understand the needs of the business and gather requirements for new use cases. Next, a data engineer needs to translate those requirements to design new ways to capture and serve data, balanced for cost and operational simplicity. This means knowing the trade-offs with design patterns, technologies, and tools in source systems, ingestion, storage, transformation, and serving data.

This doesn't imply that a data engineer is a data architect, as these are typically two separate roles. If a data engineer works alongside a data architect, the data engineer should be able to deliver on the data architect's designs and provide architectural feedback.

Orchestration

> We think that orchestration matters because we view it as really the center of gravity of both the data platform as well as the data lifecycle, the software development lifecycle as it comes to data.
>
> —Nick Schrock, founder of Elementl[9]

Orchestration is not only a central DataOps process, but also a critical part of the engineering and deployment flow for data jobs. So, what is orchestration?

Orchestration is the process of coordinating many jobs to run as quickly and efficiently as possible on a scheduled cadence. For instance, people often refer to orchestration tools like Apache Airflow as *schedulers*. This isn't quite accurate. A pure scheduler, such as cron, is aware only of time; an orchestration engine builds in metadata on job dependencies, generally in the form of a directed acyclic graph

---

9 Ternary Data, "An Introduction to Dagster: The Orchestrator for the Full Data Lifecycle - UDEM June 2021," YouTube video, 1:09:40, *https://oreil.ly/HyGMh*.

(DAG). The DAG can be run once or scheduled to run at a fixed interval of daily, weekly, every hour, every five minutes, etc.

As we discuss orchestration throughout this book, we assume that an orchestration system stays online with high availability. This allows the orchestration system to sense and monitor constantly without human intervention and run new jobs anytime they are deployed. An orchestration system monitors jobs that it manages and kicks off new tasks as internal DAG dependencies are completed. It can also monitor external systems and tools to watch for data to arrive and criteria to be met. When certain conditions go out of bounds, the system also sets error conditions and sends alerts through email or other channels. You might set an expected completion time of 10 a.m. for overnight daily data pipelines. If jobs are not done by this time, alerts go out to data engineers and consumers.

Orchestration systems also build job history capabilities, visualization, and alerting. Advanced orchestration engines can backfill new DAGs or individual tasks as they are added to a DAG. They also support dependencies over a time range. For example, a monthly reporting job might check that an ETL job has been completed for the full month before starting.

Orchestration has long been a key capability for data processing but was not often top of mind nor accessible to anyone except the largest companies. Enterprises used various tools to manage job flows, but these were expensive, out of reach of small startups, and generally not extensible. Apache Oozie was extremely popular in the 2010s, but it was designed to work within a Hadoop cluster and was difficult to use in a more heterogeneous environment. Facebook developed Dataswarm for internal use in the late 2000s; this inspired popular tools such as Airflow, introduced by Airbnb in 2014.

Airflow was open source from its inception and was widely adopted. It was written in Python, making it highly extensible to almost any use case imaginable. While many other interesting open source orchestration projects exist, such as Luigi and Conductor, Airflow is arguably the mindshare leader for the time being. Airflow arrived just as data processing was becoming more abstract and accessible, and engineers were increasingly interested in coordinating complex flows across multiple processors and storage systems, especially in cloud environments.

At this writing, several nascent open source projects aim to mimic the best elements of Airflow's core design while improving on it in key areas. Some of the most interesting examples are Prefect and Dagster, which aim to improve the portability and testability of DAGs to allow engineers to move from local development to production more easily. Argo is an orchestration engine built around Kubernetes primitives; Metaflow is an open source project out of Netflix that aims to improve data science orchestration.

We must point out that orchestration is strictly a batch concept. The streaming alternative to orchestrated task DAGs is the streaming DAG. Streaming DAGs remain challenging to build and maintain, but next-generation streaming platforms such as Pulsar aim to dramatically reduce the engineering and operational burden. We talk more about these developments in Chapter 8.

Software Engineering

Software engineering has always been a central skill for data engineers. In the early days of contemporary data engineering (2000–2010), data engineers worked on low-level frameworks and wrote MapReduce jobs in C, C++, and Java. At the peak of the big data era (the mid-2010s), engineers started using frameworks that abstracted away these low-level details.

This abstraction continues today. Cloud data warehouses support powerful transformations using SQL semantics; tools like Spark have become more user-friendly, transitioning away from low-level coding details and toward easy-to-use dataframes. Despite this abstraction, software engineering is still critical to data engineering. We want to briefly discuss a few common areas of software engineering that apply to the data engineering lifecycle.

Core data processing code

Though it has become more abstract and easier to manage, core data processing code still needs to be written, and it appears throughout the data engineering lifecycle. Whether in ingestion, transformation, or data serving, data engineers need to be highly proficient and productive in frameworks and languages such as Spark, SQL, or Beam; we reject the notion that SQL is not code.

It's also imperative that a data engineer understand proper code-testing methodologies, such as unit, regression, integration, end-to-end, and smoke.

Development of open source frameworks

Many data engineers are heavily involved in developing open source frameworks. They adopt these frameworks to solve specific problems in the data engineering lifecycle, and then continue developing the framework code to improve the tools for their use cases and contribute back to the community.

In the big data era, we saw a Cambrian explosion of data-processing frameworks inside the Hadoop ecosystem. These tools primarily focused on transforming and serving parts of the data engineering lifecycle. Data engineering tool speciation has not ceased or slowed down, but the emphasis has shifted up the ladder of abstraction, away from direct data processing. This new generation of open source tools assists engineers in managing, enhancing, connecting, optimizing, and monitoring data.

For example, Airflow dominated the orchestration space from 2015 until the early 2020s. Now, a new batch of open source competitors (including Prefect, Dagster, and Metaflow) has sprung up to fix perceived limitations of Airflow, providing better metadata handling, portability, and dependency management. Where the future of orchestration goes is anyone's guess.

Before data engineers begin engineering new internal tools, they would do well to survey the landscape of publicly available tools. Keep an eye on the total cost of ownership (TCO) and opportunity cost associated with implementing a tool. There is a good chance that an open source project already exists to address the problem they're looking to solve, and they would do well to collaborate rather than reinventing the wheel.

Streaming

Streaming data processing is inherently more complicated than batch, and the tools and paradigms are arguably less mature. As streaming data becomes more pervasive in every stage of the data engineering lifecycle, data engineers face interesting software engineering problems.

For instance, data processing tasks such as joins that we take for granted in the batch processing world often become more complicated in real time, requiring more complex software engineering. Engineers must also write code to apply a variety of *windowing* methods. Windowing allows real-time systems to calculate valuable metrics such as trailing statistics. Engineers have many frameworks to choose from, including various function platforms (OpenFaaS, AWS Lambda, Google Cloud Functions) for handling individual events or dedicated stream processors (Spark, Beam, Flink, or Pulsar) for analyzing streams to support reporting and real-time actions.

Infrastructure as code

Infrastructure as code (IaC) applies software engineering practices to the configuration and management of infrastructure. The infrastructure management burden of the big data era has decreased as companies have migrated to managed big data systems—such as Databricks and Amazon Elastic MapReduce (EMR)—and cloud data warehouses. When data engineers have to manage their infrastructure in a cloud environment, they increasingly do this through IaC frameworks rather than manually spinning up instances and installing software. Several general-purpose and cloud-platform-specific frameworks allow automated infrastructure deployment based on a set of specifications. Many of these frameworks can manage cloud services as well as infrastructure. There is also a notion of IaC with containers and Kubernetes, using tools like Helm.

These practices are a vital part of DevOps, allowing version control and repeatability of deployments. Naturally, these capabilities are vital throughout the data engineering lifecycle, especially as we adopt DataOps practices.

Pipelines as code

Pipelines as code is the core concept of present-day orchestration systems, which touch every stage of the data engineering lifecycle. Data engineers use code (typically Python) to declare data tasks and dependencies among them. The orchestration engine interprets these instructions to run steps using available resources.

General-purpose problem solving

In practice, regardless of which high-level tools they adopt, data engineers will run into corner cases throughout the data engineering lifecycle that require them to solve problems outside the boundaries of their chosen tools and to write custom code. When using frameworks like Fivetran, Airbyte, or Matillion, data engineers will encounter data sources without existing connectors and need to write something custom. They should be proficient in software engineering to understand APIs, pull and transform data, handle exceptions, and so forth.

Conclusion

Most discussions we've seen in the past about data engineering involve technologies but miss the bigger picture of data lifecycle management. As technologies become more abstract and do more heavy lifting, a data engineer has the opportunity to think and act on a higher level. The data engineering lifecycle, supported by its undercurrents, is an extremely useful mental model for organizing the work of data engineering.

We break the data engineering lifecycle into the following stages:

- Generation
- Storage
- Ingestion
- Transformation
- Serving data

Several themes cut across the data engineering lifecycle as well. These are the undercurrents of the data engineering lifecycle. At a high level, the undercurrents are as follows:

- Security

- Data management

- DataOps

- Data architecture

- Orchestration

- Software engineering

A data engineer has several top-level goals across the data lifecycle: produce optimum ROI and reduce costs (financial and opportunity), reduce risk (security, data quality), and maximize data value and utility.

The next two chapters discuss how these elements impact good architecture design, along with choosing the right technologies. If you feel comfortable with these two topics, feel free to skip ahead to Part II, where we cover each of the stages of the data engineering lifecycle.

Additional Resources

- "A Comparison of Data Processing Frameworks" (*https://oreil.ly/tq61F*) by Ludovic Santos

- DAMA International website (*https://oreil.ly/mu7oI*)

- "The Dataflow Model: A Practical Approach to Balancing Correctness, Latency, and Cost in Massive-Scale, Unbounded, Out-of-Order Data Processing" (*https://oreil.ly/nmPVs*) by Tyler Akidau et al.

- "Data Processing" Wikipedia page (*https://oreil.ly/4mllo*)

- "Data Transformation" Wikipedia page (*https://oreil.ly/tyF6K*)

- "Democratizing Data at Airbnb" (*https://oreil.ly/E9CrX*) by Chris Williams et al.

- "Five Steps to Begin Collecting the Value of Your Data" Lean-Data web page (*https://oreil.ly/F4mOh*)

- "Getting Started with DevOps Automation" (*https://oreil.ly/euVJJ*) by Jared Murrell

- "Incident Management in the Age of DevOps" Atlassian web page (*https://oreil.ly/O8zMT*)

- "An Introduction to Dagster: The Orchestrator for the Full Data Lifecycle" video (*https://oreil.ly/PQNwK*) by Nick Schrock

- "Is DevOps Related to DataOps?" (*https://oreil.ly/J8ZnN*) by Carol Jang and Jove Kuang

- "The Seven Stages of Effective Incident Response" Atlassian web page (*https://oreil.ly/Lv5XP*)
- "Staying Ahead of Debt" (*https://oreil.ly/uVz7h*) by Etai Mizrahi
- "What Is Metadata" (*https://oreil.ly/65cTA*) by Michelle Knight

CHAPTER 3

Designing Good Data Architecture

Good data architecture provides seamless capabilities across every step of the data lifecycle and undercurrent. We'll begin by defining *data architecture* and then discuss components and considerations. We'll then touch on specific batch patterns (data warehouses, data lakes), streaming patterns, and patterns that unify batch and streaming. Throughout, we'll emphasize leveraging the capabilities of the cloud to deliver scalability, availability, and reliability.

What Is Data Architecture?

Successful data engineering is built upon rock-solid data architecture. This chapter aims to review a few popular architecture approaches and frameworks, and then craft our opinionated definition of what makes "good" data architecture. Indeed, we won't make everyone happy. Still, we will lay out a pragmatic, domain-specific, working definition for *data architecture* that we think will work for companies of vastly different scales, business processes, and needs.

What is data architecture? When you stop to unpack it, the topic becomes a bit murky; researching data architecture yields many inconsistent and often outdated definitions. It's a lot like when we defined *data engineering* in Chapter 1—there's no consensus. In a field that is constantly changing, this is to be expected. So what do we mean by *data architecture* for the purposes of this book? Before defining the term, it's essential to understand the context in which it sits. Let's briefly cover enterprise architecture, which will frame our definition of data architecture.

Enterprise Architecture Defined

Enterprise architecture has many subsets, including business, technical, application, and data (Figure 3-1). As such, many frameworks and resources are devoted to enterprise architecture. In truth, architecture is a surprisingly controversial topic.

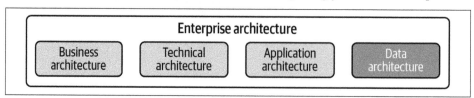

Figure 3-1. Data architecture is a subset of enterprise architecture

The term *enterprise* gets mixed reactions. It brings to mind sterile corporate offices, command-and-control/waterfall planning, stagnant business cultures, and empty catchphrases. Even so, we can learn some things here.

Before we define and describe *enterprise architecture*, let's unpack this term. Let's look at how enterprise architecture is defined by some significant thought leaders: TOGAF, Gartner, and EABOK.

TOGAF's definition

TOGAF is *The Open Group Architecture Framework*, a standard of The Open Group. It's touted as the most widely used architecture framework today. Here's the TOGAF definition:[1]

> The term "enterprise" in the context of "enterprise architecture" can denote an entire enterprise—encompassing all of its information and technology services, processes, and infrastructure—or a specific domain within the enterprise. In both cases, the architecture crosses multiple systems, and multiple functional groups within the enterprise.

Gartner's definition

Gartner is a global research and advisory company that produces research articles and reports on trends related to enterprises. Among other things, it is responsible for the (in)famous Gartner Hype Cycle. Gartner's definition is as follows:[2]

> Enterprise architecture (EA) is a discipline for proactively and holistically leading enterprise responses to disruptive forces by identifying and analyzing the execution of change toward desired business vision and outcomes. EA delivers value by presenting

---

1 The Open Group, *TOGAF Version 9.1*, *https://oreil.ly/A1H67*.

2 Gartner Glossary, s.v. "Enterprise Architecture (EA)," *https://oreil.ly/SWwQF*.

---

business and IT leaders with signature-ready recommendations for adjusting policies and projects to achieve targeted business outcomes that capitalize on relevant business disruptions.

EABOK's definition

EABOK is the *Enterprise Architecture Book of Knowledge,* an enterprise architecture reference produced by the MITRE Corporation. EABOK was released as an incomplete draft in 2004 and has not been updated since. Though seemingly obsolete, EABOK is frequently referenced in descriptions of enterprise architecture; we found many of its ideas helpful while writing this book. Here's the EABOK definition:[3]

> Enterprise Architecture (EA) is an organizational model; an abstract representation of an Enterprise that aligns strategy, operations, and technology to create a roadmap for success.

Our definition

We extract a few common threads in these definitions of enterprise architecture: change, alignment, organization, opportunities, problem-solving, and migration. Here is our definition of *enterprise architecture,* one that we feel is more relevant to today's fast-moving data landscape:

> Enterprise architecture is the design of systems to support *change in the enterprise,* achieved by *flexible and reversible decisions* reached through careful *evaluation of trade-offs.*

Here, we touch on some key areas we'll return to throughout the book: flexible and reversible decisions, change management, and evaluation of trade-offs. We discuss each theme at length in this section and then make the definition more concrete in the latter part of the chapter by giving various examples of data architecture.

Flexible and reversible decisions are essential for two reasons. First, the world is constantly changing, and predicting the future is impossible. Reversible decisions allow you to adjust course as the world changes and you gather new information. Second, there is a natural tendency toward enterprise ossification as organizations grow. Adopting a culture of reversible decisions helps overcome this tendency by reducing the risk attached to a decision.

Jeff Bezos is credited with the idea of one-way and two-way doors.[4] A *one-way door* is a decision that is almost impossible to reverse. For example, Amazon could have

---

3 EABOK Consortium website, *https://eabok.org.*

4 Jeff Haden, "Amazon Founder Jeff Bezos: This Is How Successful People Make Such Smart Decisions," *Inc.,* December 3, 2018, *https://oreil.ly/QwIm0.*

decided to sell AWS or shut it down. It would be nearly impossible for Amazon to rebuild a public cloud with the same market position after such an action.

On the other hand, a *two-way door* is an easily reversible decision: you walk through and proceed if you like what you see in the room or step back through the door if you don't. Amazon might decide to require the use of DynamoDB for a new microservices database. If this policy doesn't work, Amazon has the option of reversing it and refactoring some services to use other databases. Since the stakes attached to each reversible decision (two-way door) are low, organizations can make more decisions, iterating, improving, and collecting data rapidly.

Change management is closely related to reversible decisions and is a central theme of enterprise architecture frameworks. Even with an emphasis on reversible decisions, enterprises often need to undertake large initiatives. These are ideally broken into smaller changes, each one a reversible decision in itself. Returning to Amazon, we note a five-year gap (2007 to 2012) from the publication of a paper on the DynamoDB concept to Werner Vogels's announcement of the DynamoDB service on AWS. Behind the scenes, teams took numerous small actions to make DynamoDB a concrete reality for AWS customers. Managing such small actions is at the heart of change management.

Architects are not simply mapping out IT processes and vaguely looking toward a distant, utopian future; they actively solve business problems and create new opportunities. Technical solutions exist not for their own sake but in support of business goals. Architects identify problems in the current state (poor data quality, scalability limits, money-losing lines of business), define desired future states (agile data-quality improvement, scalable cloud data solutions, improved business processes), and realize initiatives through execution of small, concrete steps. It bears repeating:

> Technical solutions exist not for their own sake but in support of business goals.

We found significant inspiration in *Fundamentals of Software Architecture* by Mark Richards and Neal Ford (O'Reilly). They emphasize that trade-offs are inevitable and ubiquitous in the engineering space. Sometimes the relatively fluid nature of software and data leads us to believe that we are freed from the constraints that engineers face in the hard, cold physical world. Indeed, this is partially true; patching a software bug is much easier than redesigning and replacing an airplane wing. However, digital systems are ultimately constrained by physical limits such as latency, reliability, density, and energy consumption. Engineers also confront various nonphysical limits, such as characteristics of programming languages and frameworks, and practical constraints in managing complexity, budgets, etc. Magical thinking culminates in poor engineering. Data engineers must account for trade-offs at every step to design an optimal system while minimizing high-interest technical debt.

Let's reiterate one central point in our enterprise architecture definition: enterprise architecture balances flexibility and trade-offs. This isn't always an easy balance, and architects must constantly assess and reevaluate with the recognition that the world is dynamic. Given the pace of change that enterprises are faced with, organizations— and their architecture—cannot afford to stand still.

Data Architecture Defined

Now that you understand enterprise architecture, let's dive into data architecture by establishing a working definition that will set the stage for the rest of the book. *Data architecture* is a subset of enterprise architecture, inheriting its properties: processes, strategy, change management, and evaluating trade-offs. Here are a couple of definitions of data architecture that influence our definition.

TOGAF's definition

TOGAF defines data architecture as follows:[5]

> A description of the structure and interaction of the enterprise's major types and sources of data, logical data assets, physical data assets, and data management resources.

DAMA's definition

The DAMA *DMBOK* defines data architecture as follows:[6]

> Identifying the data needs of the enterprise (regardless of structure) and designing and maintaining the master blueprints to meet those needs. Using master blueprints to guide data integration, control data assets, and align data investments with business strategy.

Our definition

Considering the preceding two definitions and our experience, we have crafted our definition of *data architecture*:

> Data architecture is the design of systems to support the evolving data needs of an enterprise, achieved by flexible and reversible decisions reached through a careful evaluation of trade-offs.

How does data architecture fit into data engineering? Just as the data engineering lifecycle is a subset of the data lifecycle, data engineering architecture is a subset of general data architecture. *Data engineering architecture* is the systems and frameworks

---

5 The Open Group, *TOGAF Version 9.1*, https://oreil.ly/A1H67.

6 *DAMA - DMBOK: Data Management Body of Knowledge*, 2nd ed. (Technics Publications, 2017).

that make up the key sections of the data engineering lifecycle. We'll use *data architec-ture* interchangeably with *data engineering architecture* throughout this book.

Other aspects of data architecture that you should be aware of are operational and technical (Figure 3-2). *Operational architecture* encompasses the functional require-ments of what needs to happen related to people, processes, and technology. For example, what business processes does the data serve? How does the organization manage data quality? What is the latency requirement from when the data is pro-duced to when it becomes available to query? *Technical architecture* outlines how data is ingested, stored, transformed, and served along the data engineering lifecycle. For instance, how will you move 10 TB of data every hour from a source database to your data lake? In short, operational architecture describes *what* needs to be done, and technical architecture details *how* it will happen.

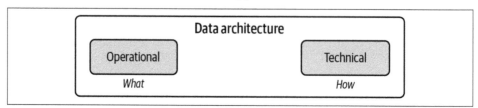

Figure 3-2. Operational and technical data architecture

Now that we have a working definition of data architecture, let's cover the elements of "good" data architecture.

"Good" Data Architecture

> Never shoot for the best architecture, but rather the least worst architecture.
> —Mark Richards and Neal Ford[7]

According to Grady Booch (*https://oreil.ly/SynOe*), "Architecture represents the sig-nificant design decisions that shape a system, where *significant* is measured by cost of change." Data architects aim to make significant decisions that will lead to good architecture at a basic level.

What do we mean by "good" data architecture? To paraphrase an old cliche, you know good when you see it. *Good data architecture* serves business requirements with a common, widely reusable set of building blocks while maintaining flexibility and making appropriate trade-offs. Bad architecture is authoritarian and tries to cram a bunch of one-size-fits-all decisions into a big ball of mud (*https://oreil.ly/YWfb1*).

---

7 Mark Richards and Neal Ford, *Fundamentals of Software Architecture* (Sebastopol, CA: O'Reilly, 2020), *https://oreil.ly/hpCp0*.

Agility is the foundation for good data architecture; it acknowledges that the world is fluid. *Good data architecture is flexible and easily maintainable.* It evolves in response to changes within the business and new technologies and practices that may unlock even more value in the future. Businesses and their use cases for data are always evolving. The world is dynamic, and the pace of change in the data space is accelerating. Last year's data architecture that served you well might not be sufficient for today, let alone next year.

Bad data architecture is tightly coupled, rigid, overly centralized, or uses the wrong tools for the job, hampering development and change management. Ideally, by designing architecture with reversibility in mind, changes will be less costly.

The undercurrents of the data engineering lifecycle form the foundation of good data architecture for companies at any stage of data maturity. Again, these undercurrents are security, data management, DataOps, data architecture, orchestration, and software engineering.

Good data architecture is a living, breathing thing. It's never finished. In fact, per our definition, change and evolution are central to the meaning and purpose of data architecture. Let's now look at the principles of good data architecture.

Principles of Good Data Architecture

This section takes a 10,000-foot view of good architecture by focusing on principles—key ideas useful in evaluating major architectural decisions and practices. We borrow inspiration for our architecture principles from several sources, especially the AWS Well-Architected Framework and Google Cloud's Five Principles for Cloud-Native Architecture.

The AWS Well-Architected Framework (*https://oreil.ly/4D0yq*) consists of six pillars:

- Operational excellence
- Security
- Reliability
- Performance efficiency
- Cost optimization
- Sustainability

Google Cloud's Five Principles for Cloud-Native Architecture (*https://oreil.ly/t63DH*) are as follows:

- Design for automation.
- Be smart with state.

- Favor managed services.
- Practice defense in depth.
- Always be architecting.

We advise you to carefully study both frameworks, identify valuable ideas, and determine points of disagreement. We'd like to expand or elaborate on these pillars with these principles of data engineering architecture:

1. Choose common components wisely.
2. Plan for failure.
3. Architect for scalability.
4. Architecture is leadership.
5. Always be architecting.
6. Build loosely coupled systems.
7. Make reversible decisions.
8. Prioritize security.
9. Embrace FinOps.

Principle 1: Choose Common Components Wisely

One of the primary jobs of a data engineer is to choose common components and practices that can be used widely across an organization. When architects choose well and lead effectively, common components become a fabric facilitating team collaboration and breaking down silos. Common components enable agility within and across teams in conjunction with shared knowledge and skills.

Common components can be anything that has broad applicability within an organization. Common components include object storage, version-control systems, observability, monitoring and orchestration systems, and processing engines. Common components should be accessible to everyone with an appropriate use case, and teams are encouraged to rely on common components already in use rather than reinventing the wheel. Common components must support robust permissions and security to enable sharing of assets among teams while preventing unauthorized access.

Cloud platforms are an ideal place to adopt common components. For example, compute and storage separation in cloud data systems allows users to access a shared storage layer (most commonly object storage) using specialized tools to access and query the data needed for specific use cases.

Choosing common components is a balancing act. On the one hand, you need to focus on needs across the data engineering lifecycle and teams, utilize common components that will be useful for individual projects, and simultaneously facilitate interoperation and collaboration. On the other hand, architects should avoid decisions that will hamper the productivity of engineers working on domain-specific problems by forcing them into one-size-fits-all technology solutions. Chapter 4 provides additional details.

Principle 2: Plan for Failure

> Everything fails, all the time.
>
> —Werner Vogels, CTO of Amazon Web Services[8]

Modern hardware is highly robust and durable. Even so, any hardware component will fail, given enough time. To build highly robust data systems, you must consider failures in your designs. Here are a few key terms for evaluating failure scenarios; we describe these in greater detail in this chapter and throughout the book:

Availability
The percentage of time an IT service or component is in an operable state.

Reliability
The system's probability of meeting defined standards in performing its intended function during a specified interval.

Recovery time objective
The maximum acceptable time for a service or system outage. The recovery time objective (RTO) is generally set by determining the business impact of an outage. An RTO of one day might be fine for an internal reporting system. A website outage of just five minutes could have a significant adverse business impact on an online retailer.

Recovery point objective
The acceptable state after recovery. In data systems, data is often lost during an outage. In this setting, the recovery point objective (RPO) refers to the maximum acceptable data loss.

Engineers need to consider acceptable reliability, availability, RTO, and RPO in designing for failure. These will guide their architecture decisions as they assess possible failure scenarios.

---

8 UberPulse, "Amazon.com CTO: Everything Fails," YouTube video, 3:03, *https://oreil.ly/vDVlX*.

Principle 3: Architect for Scalability

Scalability in data systems encompasses two main capabilities. First, scalable systems can *scale up* to handle significant quantities of data. We might need to spin up a large cluster to train a model on a petabyte of customer data or scale out a streaming ingestion system to handle a transient load spike. Our ability to scale up allows us to handle extreme loads temporarily. Second, scalable systems can *scale down*. Once the load spike ebbs, we should automatically remove capacity to cut costs. (This is related to principle 9.) An *elastic system* can scale dynamically in response to load, ideally in an automated fashion.

Some scalable systems can also *scale to zero*: they shut down completely when not in use. Once the large model-training job completes, we can delete the cluster. Many serverless systems (e.g., serverless functions and serverless online analytical processing, or OLAP, databases) can automatically scale to zero.

Note that deploying inappropriate scaling strategies can result in overcomplicated systems and high costs. A straightforward relational database with one failover node may be appropriate for an application instead of a complex cluster arrangement. Measure your current load, approximate load spikes, and estimate load over the next several years to determine if your database architecture is appropriate. If your startup grows much faster than anticipated, this growth should also lead to more available resources to rearchitect for scalability.

Principle 4: Architecture Is Leadership

Data architects are responsible for technology decisions and architecture descriptions and disseminating these choices through effective leadership and training. Data architects should be highly technically competent but delegate most individual contributor work to others. Strong leadership skills combined with high technical competence are rare and extremely valuable. The best data architects take this duality seriously.

Note that leadership does not imply a command-and-control approach to technology. It was not uncommon in the past for architects to choose one proprietary database technology and force every team to house their data there. We oppose this approach because it can significantly hinder current data projects. Cloud environments allow architects to balance common component choices with flexibility that enables innovation within projects.

Returning to the notion of technical leadership, Martin Fowler describes a specific archetype of an ideal software architect, well embodied in his colleague Dave Rice:[9]

> In many ways, the most important activity of *Architectus Oryzus* is to mentor the development team, to raise their level so they can take on more complex issues. Improving the development team's ability gives an architect much greater leverage than being the sole decision-maker and thus running the risk of being an architectural bottleneck.

An ideal data architect manifests similar characteristics. They possess the technical skills of a data engineer but no longer practice data engineering day to day; they mentor current data engineers, make careful technology choices in consultation with their organization, and disseminate expertise through training and leadership. They train engineers in best practices and bring the company's engineering resources together to pursue common goals in both technology and business.

As a data engineer, you should practice architecture leadership and seek mentorship from architects. Eventually, you may well occupy the architect role yourself.

Principle 5: Always Be Architecting

We borrow this principle directly from Google Cloud's Five Principles for Cloud-Native Architecture. Data architects don't serve in their role simply to maintain the existing state; instead, they constantly design new and exciting things in response to changes in business and technology. Per the EABOK (*https://oreil.ly/i58Az*), an architect's job is to develop deep knowledge of the *baseline architecture* (current state), develop a *target architecture*, and map out a *sequencing plan* to determine priorities and the order of architecture changes.

We add that modern architecture should not be command-and-control or waterfall but collaborative and agile. The data architect maintains a target architecture and sequencing plans that change over time. The target architecture becomes a moving target, adjusted in response to business and technology changes internally and worldwide. The sequencing plan determines immediate priorities for delivery.

Principle 6: Build Loosely Coupled Systems

> When the architecture of the system is designed to enable teams to test, deploy, and change systems without dependencies on other teams, teams require little communication to get work done. In other words, both the architecture and the teams are loosely coupled.
>
> —Google DevOps tech architecture guide[10]

---

9 Martin Fowler, "Who Needs an Architect?" *IEEE Software*, July/August 2003, *https://oreil.ly/wAMmZ*.

10 Google Cloud, "DevOps Tech: Architecture," Cloud Architecture Center, *https://oreil.ly/j4MT1*.

In 2002, Bezos wrote an email to Amazon employees that became known as the Bezos API Mandate:[11]

1. All teams will henceforth expose their data and functionality through service interfaces.

2. Teams must communicate with each other through these interfaces.

3. There will be no other form of interprocess communication allowed: no direct linking, no direct reads of another team's data store, no shared-memory model, no back-doors whatsoever. The only communication allowed is via service interface calls over the network.

4. It doesn't matter what technology they use. HTTP, Corba, Pubsub, custom protocols—doesn't matter.

5. All service interfaces, without exception, must be designed from the ground up to be externalizable. That is to say, the team must plan and design to be able to expose the interface to developers in the outside world. No exceptions.

The advent of Bezos's API Mandate is widely viewed as a watershed moment for Amazon. Putting data and services behind APIs enabled the loose coupling and eventually resulted in AWS as we know it now. Google's pursuit of loose coupling allowed it to grow its systems to an extraordinary scale.

For software architecture, a loosely coupled system has the following properties:

1. Systems are broken into many small components.

2. These systems interface with other services through abstraction layers, such as a messaging bus or an API. These abstraction layers hide and protect internal details of the service, such as a database backend or internal classes and method calls.

3. As a consequence of property 2, internal changes to a system component don't require changes in other parts. Details of code updates are hidden behind stable APIs. Each piece can evolve and improve separately.

4. As a consequence of property 3, there is no waterfall, global release cycle for the whole system. Instead, each component is updated separately as changes and improvements are made.

Notice that we are talking about *technical systems*. We need to think bigger. Let's translate these technical characteristics into organizational characteristics:

---

11 "The Bezos API Mandate: Amazon's Manifesto for Externalization," Nordic APIs, January 19, 2021, *https://oreil.ly/vIs8m*.

1. Many small teams engineer a large, complex system. Each team is tasked with engineering, maintaining, and improving some system components.

2. These teams publish the abstract details of their components to other teams via API definitions, message schemas, etc. Teams need not concern themselves with other teams' components; they simply use the published API or message specifications to call these components. They iterate their part to improve their performance and capabilities over time. They might also publish new capabilities as they are added or request new stuff from other teams. Again, the latter happens without teams needing to worry about the internal technical details of the requested features. Teams work together through *loosely coupled communication*.

3. As a consequence of characteristic 2, each team can rapidly evolve and improve its component independently of the work of other teams.

4. Specifically, characteristic 3 implies that teams can release updates to their components with minimal downtime. Teams release continuously during regular working hours to make code changes and test them.

Loose coupling of both technology and human systems will allow your data engineering teams to more efficiently collaborate with one another and with other parts of the company. This principle also directly facilitates principle 7.

Principle 7: Make Reversible Decisions

The data landscape is changing rapidly. Today's hot technology or stack is tomorrow's afterthought. Popular opinion shifts quickly. You should aim for reversible decisions, as these tend to simplify your architecture and keep it agile.

As Fowler wrote, "One of an architect's most important tasks is to remove architecture by finding ways to eliminate irreversibility in software designs."[12] What was true when Fowler wrote this in 2003 is just as accurate today.

As we said previously, Bezos refers to reversible decisions as "two-way doors." As he says, "If you walk through and don't like what you see on the other side, you can't get back to before. We can call these Type 1 decisions. But most decisions aren't like that—they are changeable, reversible—they're two-way doors." Aim for two-way doors whenever possible.

Given the pace of change—and the decoupling/modularization of technologies across your data architecture—always strive to pick the best-of-breed solutions that work for today. Also, be prepared to upgrade or adopt better practices as the landscape evolves.

---

12 Fowler, "Who Needs an Architect?"

Principle 8: Prioritize Security

Every data engineer must assume responsibility for the security of the systems they build and maintain. We focus now on two main ideas: zero-trust security and the shared responsibility security model. These align closely to a cloud-native architecture.

Hardened-perimeter and zero-trust security models

To define *zero-trust security*, it's helpful to start by understanding the traditional hard-perimeter security model and its limitations, as detailed in Google Cloud's Five Principles:[13]

> Traditional architectures place a lot of faith in perimeter security, crudely a hardened network perimeter with "trusted things" inside and "untrusted things" outside. Unfortunately, this approach has always been vulnerable to insider attacks, as well as external threats such as spear phishing.

The 1996 film *Mission Impossible* presents a perfect example of the hard-perimeter security model and its limitations. In the movie, the CIA hosts highly sensitive data on a storage system inside a room with extremely tight physical security. Ethan Hunt infiltrates CIA headquarters and exploits a human target to gain physical access to the storage system. Once inside the secure room, he can exfiltrate data with relative ease.

For at least a decade, alarming media reports have made us aware of the growing menace of security breaches that exploit human targets inside hardened organizational security perimeters. Even as employees work on highly secure corporate networks, they remain connected to the outside world through email and mobile devices. External threats effectively become internal threats.

In a cloud-native environment, the notion of a hardened perimeter erodes further. All assets are connected to the outside world to some degree. While virtual private cloud (VPC) networks can be defined with no external connectivity, the API control plane that engineers use to define these networks still faces the internet.

The shared responsibility model

Amazon emphasizes the shared responsibility model (*https://oreil.ly/rEFoU*), which divides security into the security *of* the cloud and security *in* the cloud. AWS is responsible for the security of the cloud:[14]

---

13 Tom Grey, "5 Principles for Cloud-Native Architecture—What It Is and How to Master It," Google Cloud blog, June 19, 2019, *https://oreil.ly/4NkGf*.

14 Amazon Web Services, "Security in AWS WAF," AWS WAF documentation, *https://oreil.ly/rEFoU*.

AWS is responsible for protecting the infrastructure that runs AWS services in the AWS Cloud. AWS also provides you with services that you can use securely.

AWS users are responsible for security in the cloud:

Your responsibility is determined by the AWS service that you use. You are also responsible for other factors including the sensitivity of your data, your organization's requirements, and applicable laws and regulations.

In general, all cloud providers operate on some form of this shared responsibility model. They secure their services according to published specifications. Still, it is ultimately the user's responsibility to design a security model for their applications and data and leverage cloud capabilities to realize this model.

Data engineers as security engineers

In the corporate world today, a command-and-control approach to security is quite common, wherein security and networking teams manage perimeters and general security practices. The cloud pushes this responsibility out to engineers who are not explicitly in security roles. Because of this responsibility, in conjunction with more general erosion of the hard security perimeter, all data engineers should consider themselves security engineers.

Failure to assume these new implicit responsibilities can lead to dire consequences. Numerous data breaches have resulted from the simple error of configuring Amazon S3 buckets with public access.[15] Those who handle data must assume that they are ultimately responsible for securing it.

Principle 9: Embrace FinOps

Let's start by considering a couple of definitions of FinOps. First, the FinOps Foundation offers this:[16]

FinOps is an evolving cloud financial management discipline and cultural practice that enables organizations to get maximum business value by helping engineering, finance, technology, and business teams to collaborate on data-driven spending decisions.

In addition, J. R. Sorment and Mike Fuller provide the following definition in *Cloud FinOps*:[17]

The term "FinOps" typically refers to the emerging professional movement that advocates a collaborative working relationship between DevOps and Finance, resulting in

---

15 Ericka Chickowski, "Leaky Buckets: 10 Worst Amazon S3 Breaches," Bitdefender *Business Insights* blog, Jan 24, 2018, *https://oreil.ly/pFEFO*.

16 FinOps Foundation, "What Is FinOps," *https://oreil.ly/wJFVn*.

17 J. R. Storment and Mike Fuller, *Cloud FinOps* (Sebastapol, CA: O'Reilly, 2019), *https://oreil.ly/QV6vF*.

an iterative, data-driven management of infrastructure spending (i.e., lowering the unit economics of cloud) while simultaneously increasing the cost efficiency and, ultimately, the profitability of the cloud environment.

The cost structure of data has evolved dramatically during the cloud era. In an on-premises setting, data systems are generally acquired with a capital expenditure (described more in Chapter 4) for a new system every few years in an on-premises setting. Responsible parties have to balance their budget against desired compute and storage capacity. Overbuying entails wasted money, while underbuying means hampering future data projects and driving significant personnel time to control system load and data size; underbuying may require faster technology refresh cycles, with associated extra costs.

In the cloud era, most data systems are pay-as-you-go and readily scalable. Systems can run on a cost-per-query model, cost-per-processing-capacity model, or another variant of a pay-as-you-go model. This approach can be far more efficient than the capital expenditure approach. It is now possible to scale up for high performance, and then scale down to save money. However, the pay-as-you-go approach makes spending far more dynamic. The new challenge for data leaders is to manage budgets, priorities, and efficiency.

Cloud tooling necessitates a set of processes for managing spending and resources. In the past, data engineers thought in terms of performance engineering—maximizing the performance for data processes on a fixed set of resources and buying adequate resources for future needs. With FinOps, engineers need to learn to think about the cost structures of cloud systems. For example, what is the appropriate mix of AWS spot instances when running a distributed cluster? What is the most appropriate approach for running a sizable daily job in terms of cost-effectiveness and performance? When should the company switch from a pay-per-query model to reserved capacity?

FinOps evolves the operational monitoring model to monitor spending on an ongoing basis. Rather than simply monitor requests and CPU utilization for a web server, FinOps might monitor the ongoing cost of serverless functions handling traffic, as well as spikes in spending trigger alerts. Just as systems are designed to fail gracefully in excessive traffic, companies may consider adopting hard limits for spending, with graceful failure modes in response to spending spikes.

Ops teams should also think in terms of cost attacks. Just as a distributed denial-of-service (DDoS) attack can block access to a web server, many companies have discovered to their chagrin that excessive downloads from S3 buckets can drive spending through the roof and threaten a small startup with bankruptcy. When sharing data publicly, data teams can address these issues by setting requester-pays policies, or simply monitoring for excessive data access spending and quickly removing access if spending begins to rise to unacceptable levels.

As of this writing, FinOps is a recently formalized practice. The FinOps Foundation was started only in 2019.[18] However, we highly recommend you start thinking about FinOps early, before you encounter high cloud bills. Start your journey with the FinOps Foundation (*https://oreil.ly/4EOIB*) and O'Reilly's *Cloud FinOps*. We also suggest that data engineers involve themselves in the community process of creating FinOps practices for data engineering— in such a new practice area, a good deal of territory is yet to be mapped out.

Now that you have a high-level understanding of good data architecture principles, let's dive a bit deeper into the major concepts you'll need to design and build good data architecture.

Major Architecture Concepts

If you follow the current trends in data, it seems like new types of data tools and architectures are arriving on the scene every week. Amidst this flurry of activity, we must not lose sight of the main goal of all of these architectures: to take data and transform it into something useful for downstream consumption.

Domains and Services

> Domain: A sphere of knowledge, influence, or activity. The subject area to which the user applies a program is the domain of the software.
>
> —Eric Evans[19]

Before diving into the components of the architecture, let's briefly cover two terms you'll see come up very often: domain and services. A *domain* is the real-world subject area for which you're architecting. A *service* is a set of functionality whose goal is to accomplish a task. For example, you might have a sales order-processing service whose task is to process orders as they are created. The sales order-processing service's only job is to process orders; it doesn't provide other functionality, such as inventory management or updating user profiles.

A domain can contain multiple services. For example, you might have a sales domain with three services: orders, invoicing, and products. Each service has particular tasks that support the sales domain. Other domains may also share services (Figure 3-3). In this case, the accounting domain is responsible for basic accounting functions: invoicing, payroll, and accounts receivable (AR). Notice the accounting domain shares the invoice service with the sales domain since a sale generates an invoice,

---

18 "FinOps Foundation Soars to 300 Members and Introduces New Partner Tiers for Cloud Service Providers and Vendors," Business Wire, June 17, 2019, *https://oreil.ly/XcwYO*.

19 Eric Evans, *Domain-Driven Design Reference: Definitions and Pattern Summaries* (March 2015), *https://oreil.ly/pQ9oq*.

and accounting must keep track of invoices to ensure that payment is received. Sales and accounting own their respective domains.

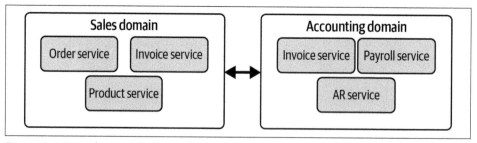

Figure 3-3. Two domains (sales and accounting) share a common service (invoices), and sales and accounting own their respective domains

When thinking about what constitutes a domain, focus on what the domain represents in the real world and work backward. In the preceding example, the sales domain should represent what happens with the sales function in your company. When architecting the sales domain, avoid cookie-cutter copying and pasting from what other companies do. Your company's sales function likely has unique aspects that require specific services to make it work the way your sales team expects.

Identify what should go in the domain. When determining what the domain should encompass and what services to include, the best advice is to simply go and talk with users and stakeholders, listen to what they're saying, and build the services that will help them do their job. Avoid the classic trap of architecting in a vacuum.

Distributed Systems, Scalability, and Designing for Failure

The discussion in this section is related to our second and third principles of data engineering architecture discussed previously: plan for failure and architect for scalability. As data engineers, we're interested in four closely related characteristics of data systems (availability and reliability were mentioned previously, but we reiterate them here for completeness):

Scalability
Allows us to increase the capacity of a system to improve performance and handle the demand. For example, we might want to scale a system to handle a high rate of queries or process a huge data set.

Elasticity
The ability of a scalable system to scale dynamically; a highly elastic system can automatically scale up and down based on the current workload. Scaling up is critical as demand increases, while scaling down saves money in a cloud environment. Modern systems sometimes scale to zero, meaning they can automatically shut down when idle.

Availability

    The percentage of time an IT service or component is in an operable state.

Reliability

    The system's probability of meeting defined standards in performing its intended function during a specified interval.

    See PagerDuty's "Why Are Availability and Reliability Crucial?" web page (*https://oreil.ly/E6il3*) for definitions and background on availability and reliability.

How are these characteristics related? If a system fails to meet performance requirements during a specified interval, it may become unresponsive. Thus low reliability can lead to low availability. On the other hand, dynamic scaling helps ensure adequate performance without manual intervention from engineers—elasticity improves reliability.

Scalability can be realized in a variety of ways. For your services and domains, does a single machine handle everything? A single machine can be scaled vertically; you can increase resources (CPU, disk, memory, I/O). But there are hard limits to possible resources on a single machine. Also, what happens if this machine dies? Given enough time, some components will eventually fail. What's your plan for backup and failover? Single machines generally can't offer high availability and reliability.

We utilize a distributed system to realize higher overall scaling capacity and increased availability and reliability. *Horizontal scaling* allows you to add more machines to satisfy load and resource requirements (Figure 3-4). Common horizontally scaled systems have a leader node that acts as the main point of contact for the instantiation, progress, and completion of workloads. When a workload is started, the leader node distributes tasks to the worker nodes within its system, completing the tasks and returning the results to the leader node. Typical modern distributed architectures also build in redundancy. Data is replicated so that if a machine dies, the other machines can pick up where the missing server left off; the cluster may add more machines to restore capacity.

Distributed systems are widespread in the various data technologies you'll use across your architecture. Almost every cloud data warehouse object storage system you use has some notion of distribution under the hood. Management details of the distributed system are typically abstracted away, allowing you to focus on high-level architecture instead of low-level plumbing. However, we highly recommend that you learn more about distributed systems because these details can be extremely helpful in understanding and improving the performance of your pipelines; Martin Kleppmann's *Designing Data-Intensive Applications* (O'Reilly) is an excellent resource.

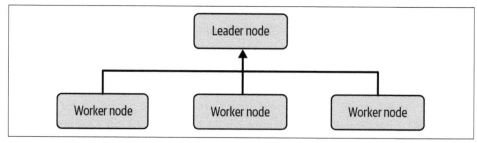

Figure 3-4. A simple horizontal distributed system utilizing a leader-follower architecture, with one leader node and three worker nodes

Tight Versus Loose Coupling: Tiers, Monoliths, and Microservices

When designing a data architecture, you choose how much interdependence you want to include within your various domains, services, and resources. On one end of the spectrum, you can choose to have extremely centralized dependencies and workflows. Every part of a domain and service is vitally dependent upon every other domain and service. This pattern is known as *tightly coupled*.

On the other end of the spectrum, you have decentralized domains and services that do not have strict dependence on each other, in a pattern known as *loose coupling*. In a loosely coupled scenario, it's easy for decentralized teams to build systems whose data may not be usable by their peers. Be sure to assign common standards, ownership, responsibility, and accountability to the teams owning their respective domains and services. Designing "good" data architecture relies on trade-offs between the tight and loose coupling of domains and services.

It's worth noting that many of the ideas in this section originate in software development. We'll try to retain the context of these big ideas' original intent and spirit—keeping them agnostic of data—while later explaining some differences you should be aware of when applying these concepts to data specifically.

Architecture tiers

As you develop your architecture, it helps to be aware of architecture tiers. Your architecture has layers—data, application, business logic, presentation, and so forth —and you need to know how to decouple these layers. Because tight coupling of modalities presents obvious vulnerabilities, keep in mind how you structure the layers of your architecture to achieve maximum reliability and flexibility. Let's look at single-tier and multitier architecture.

Single tier. In a *single-tier architecture*, your database and application are tightly coupled, residing on a single server (Figure 3-5). This server could be your laptop or a single virtual machine (VM) in the cloud. The tightly coupled nature means if the server, the database, or the application fails, the entire architecture fails. While single-tier architectures are good for prototyping and development, they are not advised for production environments because of the obvious failure risks.

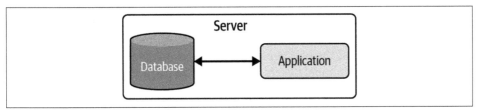

Figure 3-5. Single-tier architecture

Even when single-tier architectures build in redundancy (for example, a failover replica), they present significant limitations in other ways. For instance, it is often impractical (and not advisable) to run analytics queries against production application databases. Doing so risks overwhelming the database and causing the application to become unavailable. A single-tier architecture is fine for testing systems on a local machine but is not advised for production uses.

Multitier.   The challenges of a tightly coupled single-tier architecture are solved by decoupling the data and application. A *multitier* (also known as *n-tier*) architecture is composed of separate layers: data, application, business logic, presentation, etc. These layers are bottom-up and hierarchical, meaning the lower layer isn't necessarily dependent on the upper layers; the upper layers depend on the lower layers. The notion is to separate data from the application, and application from the presentation.

A common multitier architecture is a three-tier architecture, a widely used client-server design. A *three-tier architecture* consists of data, application logic, and presentation tiers (Figure 3-6). Each tier is isolated from the other, allowing for separation of concerns. With a three-tier architecture, you're free to use whatever technologies you prefer within each tier without the need to be monolithically focused.

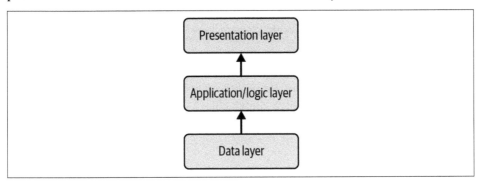

Figure 3-6. A three-tier architecture

We've seen many single-tier architectures in production. Single-tier architectures offer simplicity but also severe limitations. Eventually, an organization or application outgrows this arrangement; it works well until it doesn't. For instance, in a single-tier architecture, the data and logic layers share and compete for resources (disk, CPU, and memory) in ways that are simply avoided in a multitier architecture. Resources are spread across various tiers. Data engineers should use tiers to evaluate their layered architecture and the way dependencies are handled. Again, start simple and bake in evolution to additional tiers as your architecture becomes more complex.

In a multitier architecture, you need to consider separating your layers and the way resources are shared within layers when working with a distributed system. Distributed systems under the hood power many technologies you'll encounter across the data engineering lifecycle. First, think about whether you want resource contention with your nodes. If not, exercise a *shared-nothing architecture*: a single node handles each request, meaning other nodes do not share resources such as memory, disk, or CPU with this node or with each other. Data and resources are isolated to the node. Alternatively, various nodes can handle multiple requests and share resources but at the risk of resource contention. Another consideration is whether nodes should share the same disk and memory accessible by all nodes. This is called a *shared disk architecture* and is common when you want shared resources if a random node failure occurs.

Monoliths

The general notion of a monolith includes as much as possible under one roof; in its most extreme version, a monolith consists of a single codebase running on a single machine that provides both the application logic and user interface.

Coupling within monoliths can be viewed in two ways: technical coupling and domain coupling. *Technical coupling* refers to architectural tiers, while *domain coupling* refers to the way domains are coupled together. A monolith has varying degrees of coupling among technologies and domains. You could have an application with various layers decoupled in a multitier architecture but still share multiple domains. Or, you could have a single-tier architecture serving a single domain.

The tight coupling of a monolith implies a lack of modularity of its components. Swapping out or upgrading components in a monolith is often an exercise in trading one pain for another. Because of the tightly coupled nature, reusing components across the architecture is difficult or impossible. When evaluating how to improve a monolithic architecture, it's often a game of whack-a-mole: one component is improved, often at the expense of unknown consequences with other areas of the monolith.

Data teams will often ignore solving the growing complexity of their monolith, letting it devolve into a big ball of mud (*https://oreil.ly/2brRT*).

Chapter 4 provides a more extensive discussion comparing monoliths to distributed technologies. We also discuss the *distributed monolith*, a strange hybrid that emerges when engineers build distributed systems with excessive tight coupling.

Microservices

Compared with the attributes of a monolith—interwoven services, centralization, and tight coupling among services—microservices are the polar opposite. *Microservices architecture* comprises separate, decentralized, and loosely coupled services. Each service has a specific function and is decoupled from other services operating within its domain. If one service temporarily goes down, it won't affect the ability of other services to continue functioning.

A question that comes up often is how to convert your monolith into many microservices (Figure 3-7). This completely depends on how complex your monolith is and how much effort it will be to start extracting services out of it. It's entirely possible that your monolith cannot be broken apart, in which case, you'll want to start creating a new parallel architecture that has the services decoupled in a microservices-friendly manner. We don't suggest an entire refactor but instead break out services. The monolith didn't arrive overnight and is a technology issue as an organizational one. Be sure you get buy-in from stakeholders of the monolith if you plan to break it apart.

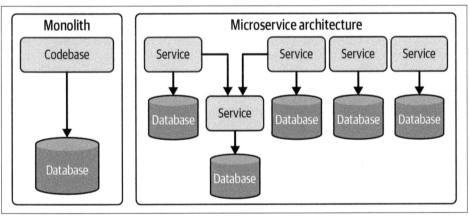

Figure 3-7. An extremely monolithic architecture runs all functionality inside a single codebase, potentially colocating a database on the same host server

If you'd like to learn more about breaking apart a monolith, we suggest reading the fantastic, pragmatic guide *Software Architecture: The Hard Parts* by Neal Ford et al. (O'Reilly).

Considerations for data architecture

As we mentioned at the start of this section, the concepts of tight versus loose coupling stem from software development, with some of these concepts dating back over 20 years. Though architectural practices in data are now adopting those from software development, it's still common to see very monolithic, tightly coupled data architectures. Some of this is due to the nature of existing data technologies and the way they integrate.

For example, data pipelines might consume data from many sources ingested into a central data warehouse. The central data warehouse is inherently monolithic. A move toward a microservices equivalent with a data warehouse is to decouple the workflow with domain-specific data pipelines connecting to corresponding domain-specific data warehouses. For example, the sales data pipeline connects to the sales-specific data warehouse, and the inventory and product domains follow a similar pattern.

Rather than dogmatically preach microservices over monoliths (among other arguments), we suggest you pragmatically use loose coupling as an ideal, while recognizing the state and limitations of the data technologies you're using within your data architecture. Incorporate reversible technology choices that allow for modularity and loose coupling whenever possible.

As you can see in Figure 3-7, you separate the components of your architecture into different layers of concern in a vertical fashion. While a multitier architecture solves the technical challenges of decoupling shared resources, it does not address the complexity of sharing domains. Along the lines of single versus multitiered architecture, you should also consider how you separate the domains of your data architecture. For example, your analyst team might rely on data from sales and inventory. The sales and inventory domains are different and should be viewed as separate.

One approach to this problem is centralization: a single team is responsible for gathering data from all domains and reconciling it for consumption across the organization. (This is a common approach in traditional data warehousing.) Another approach is the *data mesh*. With the data mesh, each software team is responsible for preparing its data for consumption across the rest of the organization. We'll say more about the data mesh later in this chapter.

Our advice: monoliths aren't necessarily bad, and it might make sense to start with one under certain conditions. Sometimes you need to move fast, and it's much simpler to start with a monolith. Just be prepared to break it into smaller pieces eventually; don't get too comfortable.

User Access: Single Versus Multitenant

As a data engineer, you have to make decisions about sharing systems across multiple teams, organizations, and customers. In some sense, all cloud services are multitenant, although this multitenancy occurs at various grains. For example, a cloud compute instance is usually on a shared server, but the VM itself provides some degree of isolation. Object storage is a multitenant system, but cloud vendors guarantee security and isolation so long as customers configure their permissions correctly.

Engineers frequently need to make decisions about multitenancy at a much smaller scale. For example, do multiple departments in a large company share the same data warehouse? Does the organization share data for multiple large customers within the same table?

We have two factors to consider in multitenancy: performance and security. With multiple large tenants within a cloud system, will the system support consistent performance for all tenants, or will there be a noisy neighbor problem? (That is, will high usage from one tenant degrade performance for other tenants?) Regarding security, data from different tenants must be properly isolated. When a company has multiple external customer tenants, these tenants should not be aware of one another, and engineers must prevent data leakage. Strategies for data isolation vary by system. For instance, it is often perfectly acceptable to use multitenant tables and isolate data through views. However, you must make certain that these views cannot leak data. Read vendor or project documentation to understand appropriate strategies and risks.

Event-Driven Architecture

Your business is rarely static. Things often happen in your business, such as getting a new customer, a new order from a customer, or an order for a product or service. These are all examples of *events* that are broadly defined as something that happened, typically a change in the *state* of something. For example, a new order might be created by a customer, or a customer might later make an update to this order.

An event-driven workflow (Figure 3-8) encompasses the ability to create, update, and asynchronously move events across various parts of the data engineering lifecycle. This workflow boils down to three main areas: event production, routing, and consumption. An event must be produced and routed to something that consumes it without tightly coupled dependencies among the producer, event router, and consumer.

Figure 3-8. In an event-driven workflow, an event is produced, routed, and then consumed

An event-driven architecture (Figure 3-9) embraces the event-driven workflow and uses this to communicate across various services. The advantage of an event-driven architecture is that it distributes the state of an event across multiple services. This is helpful if a service goes offline, a node fails in a distributed system, or you'd like multiple consumers or services to access the same events. Anytime you have loosely coupled services, this is a candidate for event-driven architecture. Many of the examples we describe later in this chapter incorporate some form of event-driven architecture.

You'll learn more about event-driven streaming and messaging systems in Chapter 5.

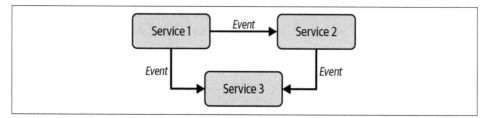

Figure 3-9. In an event-driven architecture, events are passed between loosely coupled services

Brownfield Versus Greenfield Projects

Before you design your data architecture project, you need to know whether you're starting with a clean slate or redesigning an existing architecture. Each type of project requires assessing trade-offs, albeit with different considerations and approaches. Projects roughly fall into two buckets: brownfield and greenfield.

Brownfield projects

Brownfield projects often involve refactoring and reorganizing an existing architecture and are constrained by the choices of the present and past. Because a key part of architecture is change management, you must figure out a way around these limitations and design a path forward to achieve your new business and technical objectives. Brownfield projects require a thorough understanding of the legacy architecture and the interplay of various old and new technologies. All too often, it's easy to criticize a prior team's work and decisions, but it is far better to dig deep, ask questions, and understand why decisions were made. Empathy and context go a long way in helping you diagnose problems with the existing architecture, identify opportunities, and recognize pitfalls.

You'll need to introduce your new architecture and technologies and deprecate the old stuff at some point. Let's look at a couple of popular approaches. Many teams jump headfirst into an all-at-once or big-bang overhaul of the old architecture, often figuring out deprecation as they go. Though popular, we don't advise this approach because of the associated risks and lack of a plan. This path often leads to disaster, with many irreversible and costly decisions. Your job is to make reversible, high-ROI decisions.

A popular alternative to a direct rewrite is the strangler pattern: new systems slowly and incrementally replace a legacy architecture's components.[20] Eventually, the legacy architecture is completely replaced. The attraction to the strangler pattern is its targeted and surgical approach of deprecating one piece of a system at a time. This allows for flexible and reversible decisions while assessing the impact of the deprecation on dependent systems.

It's important to note that deprecation might be "ivory tower" advice and not practical or achievable. Eradicating legacy technology or architecture might be impossible if you're at a large organization. Someone, somewhere, is using these legacy components. As someone once said, "Legacy is a condescending way to describe something that makes money."

If you can deprecate, understand there are numerous ways to deprecate your old architecture. It is critical to demonstrate value on the new platform by gradually increasing its maturity to show evidence of success and then follow an exit plan to shut down old systems.

Greenfield projects

On the opposite end of the spectrum, a *greenfield project* allows you to pioneer a fresh start, unconstrained by the history or legacy of a prior architecture. Greenfield projects tend to be easier than brownfield projects, and many data architects and engineers find them more fun! You have the opportunity to try the newest and coolest tools and architectural patterns. What could be more exciting?

You should watch out for some things before getting too carried away. We see teams get overly exuberant with shiny object syndrome. They feel compelled to reach for the latest and greatest technology fad without understanding how it will impact the value of the project. There's also a temptation to do *resume-driven development*, stacking up impressive new technologies without prioritizing the project's ultimate goals.[21] Always prioritize requirements over building something cool.

Whether you're working on a brownfield or greenfield project, always focus on the tenets of "good" data architecture. Assess trade-offs, make flexible and reversible decisions, and strive for positive ROI.

---

20 Martin Fowler, "StranglerFigApplication," June 29, 2004, *https://oreil.ly/PmqxB*.
21 Mike Loukides, "Resume Driven Development," *O'Reilly Radar*, October 13, 2004, *https://oreil.ly/BUHa8*.

Now, we'll look at examples and types of architectures—some established for decades (the data warehouse), some brand-new (the data lakehouse), and some that quickly came and went but still influence current architecture patterns (Lambda architecture).

Examples and Types of Data Architecture

Because data architecture is an abstract discipline, it helps to reason by example. In this section, we outline prominent examples and types of data architecture that are popular today. Though this set of examples is by no means exhaustive, the intention is to expose you to some of the most common data architecture patterns and to get you thinking about the requisite flexibility and trade-off analysis needed when designing a good architecture for your use case.

Data Warehouse

A *data warehouse* is a central data hub used for reporting and analysis. Data in a data warehouse is typically highly formatted and structured for analytics use cases. It's among the oldest and most well-established data architectures.

In 1989, Bill Inmon originated the notion of the data warehouse, which he described as "a subject-oriented, integrated, nonvolatile, and time-variant collection of data in support of management's decisions."[22] Though technical aspects of the data warehouse have evolved significantly, we feel this original definition still holds its weight today.

In the past, data warehouses were widely used at enterprises with significant budgets (often in the millions of dollars) to acquire data systems and pay internal teams to provide ongoing support to maintain the data warehouse. This was expensive and labor-intensive. Since then, the scalable, pay-as-you-go model has made cloud data warehouses accessible even to tiny companies. Because a third-party provider manages the data warehouse infrastructure, companies can do a lot more with fewer people, even as the complexity of their data grows.

It's worth noting two types of data warehouse architecture: organizational and technical. The *organizational data warehouse architecture* organizes data associated with certain business team structures and processes. The *technical data warehouse architecture* reflects the technical nature of the data warehouse, such as MPP. A company can have a data warehouse without an MPP system or run an MPP system that is not organized as a data warehouse. However, the technical and organizational architectures have existed in a virtuous cycle and are frequently identified with each other.

---

22 H. W. Inmon, *Building the Data Warehouse* (Hoboken: Wiley, 2005).

The organizational data warehouse architecture has two main characteristics:

Separates online analytical processing (OLAP) from production databases (online trans-action processing)
> This separation is critical as businesses grow. Moving data into a separate physical system directs load away from production systems and improves analytics performance.

Centralizes and organizes data
> Traditionally, a data warehouse pulls data from application systems by using ETL. The extract phase pulls data from source systems. The transformation phase cleans and standardizes data, organizing and imposing business logic in a highly modeled form. (Chapter 8 covers transformations and data models.) The load phase pushes data into the data warehouse target database system. Data is loaded into multiple data marts that serve the analytical needs for specific lines or business and departments. Figure 3-10 shows the general workflow. The data warehouse and ETL go hand in hand with specific business structures, including DBA and ETL developer teams that implement the direction of business leaders to ensure that data for reporting and analytics corresponds to business processes.

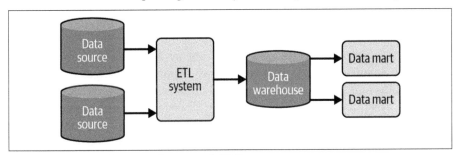

Figure 3-10. Basic data warehouse with ETL

Regarding the technical data warehouse architecture, the first MPP systems in the late 1970s became popular in the 1980s. MPPs support essentially the same SQL semantics used in relational application databases. Still, they are optimized to scan massive amounts of data in parallel and thus allow high-performance aggregation and statistical calculations. In recent years, MPP systems have increasingly shifted from a row-based to a columnar architecture to facilitate even larger data and queries, especially in cloud data warehouses. MPPs are indispensable for running performant queries for large enterprises as data and reporting needs grow.

One variation on ETL is ELT. With the ELT data warehouse architecture, data gets moved more or less directly from production systems into a staging area in the data warehouse. Staging in this setting indicates that the data is in a raw form. Rather than using an external system, transformations are handled directly in the data warehouse. The intention is to take advantage of the massive computational power of cloud data warehouses and data processing tools. Data is processed in batches, and transformed output is written into tables and views for analytics. Figure 3-11 shows the general process. ELT is also popular in a streaming arrangement, as events are streamed from a CDC process, stored in a staging area, and then subsequently transformed within the data warehouse.

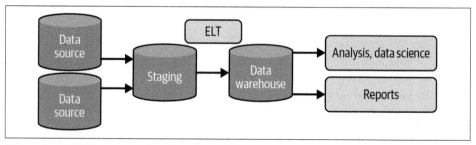

Figure 3-11. ELT—extract, load, and transform

A second version of ELT was popularized during big data growth in the Hadoop ecosystem. This is *transform-on-read ELT*, which we discuss in "Data Lake" on page 103.

The cloud data warehouse

Cloud data warehouses represent a significant evolution of the on-premises data warehouse architecture and have thus led to significant changes to the organizational architecture. Amazon Redshift kicked off the cloud data warehouse revolution. Instead of needing to appropriately size an MPP system for the next several years and sign a multimillion-dollar contract to procure the system, companies had the option of spinning up a Redshift cluster on demand, scaling it up over time as data and analytics demand grew. They could even spin up new Redshift clusters on demand to serve specific workloads and quickly delete clusters when they were no longer needed.

Google BigQuery, Snowflake, and other competitors popularized the idea of separating compute from storage. In this architecture, data is housed in object storage, allowing virtually limitless storage. This also gives users the option to spin up computing power on demand, providing ad hoc big data capabilities without the long-term cost of thousands of nodes.

Cloud data warehouses expand the capabilities of MPP systems to cover many big data use cases that required a Hadoop cluster in the very recent past. They can readily process petabytes of data in a single query. They typically support data structures that allow the storage of tens of megabytes of raw text data per row or extremely rich and complex JSON documents. As cloud data warehouses (and data lakes) mature, the line between the data warehouse and the data lake will continue to blur.

So significant is the impact of the new capabilities offered by cloud data warehouses that we might consider jettisoning the term *data warehouse* altogether. Instead, these services are evolving into a new data platform with much broader capabilities than those offered by a traditional MPP system.

Data marts

A *data mart* is a more refined subset of a warehouse designed to serve analytics and reporting, focused on a single suborganization, department, or line of business; every department has its own data mart, specific to its needs. This is in contrast to the full data warehouse that serves the broader organization or business.

Data marts exist for two reasons. First, a data mart makes data more easily accessible to analysts and report developers. Second, data marts provide an additional stage of transformation beyond that provided by the initial ETL or ELT pipelines. This can significantly improve performance if reports or analytics queries require complex joins and aggregations of data, especially when the raw data is large. Transform processes can populate the data mart with joined and aggregated data to improve performance for live queries. Figure 3-12 shows the general workflow. We discuss data marts, and modeling data for data marts, in Chapter 8.

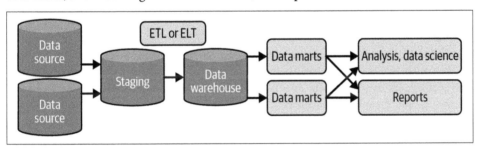

Figure 3-12. ETL or ELT plus data marts

Data Lake

Among the most popular architectures that appeared during the big data era is the *data lake*. Instead of imposing tight structural limitations on data, why not simply dump all of your data—structured and unstructured—into a central location? The data lake promised to be a democratizing force, liberating the business to drink from a fountain of limitless data. The first-generation data lake, "data lake 1.0," made solid contributions but generally failed to deliver on its promise.

Data lake 1.0 started with HDFS. As the cloud grew in popularity, these data lakes moved to cloud-based object storage, with extremely cheap storage costs and virtually limitless storage capacity. Instead of relying on a monolithic data warehouse where storage and compute are tightly coupled, the data lake allows an immense amount of data of any size and type to be stored. When this data needs to be queried or transformed, you have access to nearly unlimited computing power by spinning up a cluster on demand, and you can pick your favorite data-processing technology for the task at hand—MapReduce, Spark, Ray, Presto, Hive, etc.

Despite the promise and hype, data lake 1.0 had serious shortcomings. The data lake became a dumping ground; terms such as *data swamp*, *dark data*, and *WORN* were coined as once-promising data projects failed. Data grew to unmanageable sizes, with little in the way of schema management, data cataloging, and discovery tools. In addition, the original data lake concept was essentially write-only, creating huge headaches with the arrival of regulations such as GDPR that required targeted deletion of user records.

Processing data was also challenging. Relatively banal data transformations such as joins were a huge headache to code as MapReduce jobs. Later frameworks such as Pig and Hive somewhat improved the situation for data processing but did little to address the basic problems of data management. Simple data manipulation language (DML) operations common in SQL—deleting or updating rows—were painful to implement, generally achieved by creating entirely new tables. While big data engineers radiated a particular disdain for their counterparts in data warehousing, the latter could point out that data warehouses provided basic data management capabilities out of the box, and that SQL was an efficient tool for writing complex, performant queries and transformations.

Data lake 1.0 also failed to deliver on another core promise of the big data movement. Open source software in the Apache ecosystem was touted as a means to avoid multimillion-dollar contracts for proprietary MPP systems. Cheap, off-the-shelf hardware would replace custom vendor solutions. In reality, big data costs ballooned as the complexities of managing Hadoop clusters forced companies to hire large teams of engineers at high salaries. Companies often chose to purchase licensed, customized versions of Hadoop from vendors to avoid the exposed wires and sharp edges of the raw Apache codebase and acquire a set of scaffolding tools to make Hadoop more user-friendly. Even companies that avoided managing Hadoop clusters using cloud storage had to spend big on talent to write MapReduce jobs.

We should be careful not to understate the utility and power of first-generation data lakes. Many organizations found significant value in data lakes—especially huge, heavily data-focused Silicon Valley tech companies like Netflix and Facebook. These companies had the resources to build successful data practices and create their custom Hadoop-based tools and enhancements. But for many organizations, data lakes turned into an internal superfund site of waste, disappointment, and spiraling costs.

Convergence, Next-Generation Data Lakes, and the Data Platform

In response to the limitations of first-generation data lakes, various players have sought to enhance the concept to fully realize its promise. For example, Databricks introduced the notion of a *data lakehouse*. The lakehouse incorporates the controls, data management, and data structures found in a data warehouse while still housing data in object storage and supporting a variety of query and transformation engines. In particular, the data lakehouse supports atomicity, consistency, isolation, and durability (ACID) transactions, a big departure from the original data lake, where you simply pour in data and never update or delete it. The term *data lakehouse* suggests a convergence between data lakes and data warehouses.

The technical architecture of cloud data warehouses has evolved to be very similar to a data lake architecture. Cloud data warehouses separate compute from storage, support petabyte-scale queries, store a variety of unstructured data and semistructured objects, and integrate with advanced processing technologies such as Spark or Beam.

We believe that the trend of convergence will only continue. The data lake and the data warehouse will still exist as different architectures. In practice, their capabilities will converge so that few users will notice a boundary between them in their day-to-day work. We now see several vendors offering *data platforms* that combine data lake and data warehouse capabilities. From our perspective, AWS, Azure, Google Cloud (*https://oreil.ly/ij2QV*), Snowflake (*https://oreil.ly/NoE9p*), and Databricks are class leaders, each offering a constellation of tightly integrated tools for working with data, running the gamut from relational to completely unstructured. Instead of choosing between a data lake or data warehouse architecture, future data engineers will have the option to choose a converged data platform based on a variety of factors, including vendor, ecosystem, and relative openness.

Modern Data Stack

The *modern data stack* (Figure 3-13) is currently a trendy analytics architecture that highlights the type of abstraction we expect to see more widely used over the next several years. Whereas past data stacks relied on expensive, monolithic toolsets, the main objective of the modern data stack is to use cloud-based, plug-and-play, easy-to-use, off-the-shelf components to create a modular and cost-effective data architecture. These components include data pipelines, storage, transformation, data management/governance, monitoring, visualization, and exploration. The domain is still in flux, and the specific tools are changing and evolving rapidly, but the core aim will remain the same: to reduce complexity and increase modularization. Note that the notion of a modern data stack integrates nicely with the converged data platform idea from the previous section.

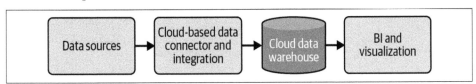

Figure 3-13. Basic components of the modern data stack

Key outcomes of the modern data stack are self-service (analytics and pipelines), agile data management, and using open source tools or simple proprietary tools with clear pricing structures. Community is a central aspect of the modern data stack as well. Unlike products of the past that had releases and roadmaps largely hidden from users, projects and companies operating in the modern data stack space typically have strong user bases and active communities that participate in the development by using the product early, suggesting features, and submitting pull requests to improve the code.

Regardless of where "modern" goes (we share our ideas in Chapter 11), we think the key concept of plug-and-play modularity with easy-to-understand pricing and implementation is the way of the future. Especially in analytics engineering, the modern data stack is and will continue to be the default choice of data architecture. Throughout the book, the architecture we reference contains pieces of the modern data stack, such as cloud-based and plug-and-play modular components.

Lambda Architecture

In the "old days" (the early to mid-2010s), the popularity of working with streaming data exploded with the emergence of Kafka as a highly scalable message queue and frameworks such as Apache Storm and Samza for streaming/real-time analytics. These technologies allowed companies to perform new types of analytics and modeling on large amounts of data, user aggregation and ranking, and product recommendations. Data engineers needed to figure out how to reconcile batch and streaming data into a single architecture. The Lambda architecture was one of the early popular responses to this problem.

In a *Lambda architecture* (Figure 3-14), you have systems operating independently of each other—batch, streaming, and serving. The source system is ideally immutable and append-only, sending data to two destinations for processing: stream and batch. In-stream processing intends to serve the data with the lowest possible latency in a "speed" layer, usually a NoSQL database. In the batch layer, data is processed and transformed in a system such as a data warehouse, creating precomputed and aggregated views of the data. The serving layer provides a combined view by aggregating query results from the two layers.

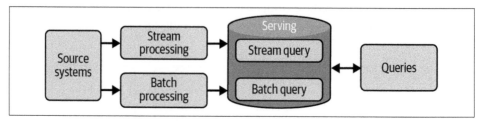

Figure 3-14. Lambda architecture

Lambda architecture has its share of challenges and criticisms. Managing multiple systems with different codebases is as difficult as it sounds, creating error-prone systems with code and data that are extremely difficult to reconcile.

We mention Lambda architecture because it still gets attention and is popular in search-engine results for data architecture. Lambda isn't our first recommendation if you're trying to combine streaming and batch data for analytics. Technology and practices have moved on.

Next, let's look at a reaction to Lambda architecture, the Kappa architecture.

Kappa Architecture

As a response to the shortcomings of Lambda architecture, Jay Kreps proposed an alternative called *Kappa architecture* (Figure 3-15).[23] The central thesis is this: why not just use a stream-processing platform as the backbone for all data handling—ingestion, storage, and serving? This facilitates a true event-based architecture. Real-time and batch processing can be applied seamlessly to the same data by reading the live event stream directly and replaying large chunks of data for batch processing.

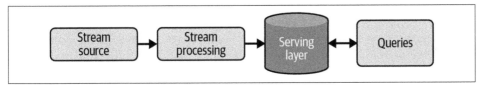

Figure 3-15. Kappa architecture

Though the original Kappa architecture article came out in 2014, we haven't seen it widely adopted. There may be a couple of reasons for this. First, streaming itself is still a bit of a mystery for many companies; it's easy to talk about, but harder than expected to execute. Second, Kappa architecture turns out to be complicated and expensive in practice. While some streaming systems can scale to huge data volumes, they are complex and expensive; batch storage and processing remain much more efficient and cost-effective for enormous historical datasets.

The Dataflow Model and Unified Batch and Streaming

Both Lambda and Kappa sought to address limitations of the Hadoop ecosystem of the 2010s by trying to duct-tape together complicated tools that were likely not natural fits in the first place. The central challenge of unifying batch and streaming data remained, and Lambda and Kappa both provided inspiration and groundwork for continued progress in this pursuit.

---

23 Jay Kreps, "Questioning the Lambda Architecture," *O'Reilly Radar*, July 2, 2014, *https://oreil.ly/wWR3n*.

One of the central problems of managing batch and stream processing is unifying multiple code paths. While the Kappa architecture relies on a unified queuing and storage layer, one still has to confront using different tools for collecting real-time statistics or running batch aggregation jobs. Today, engineers seek to solve this in several ways. Google made its mark by developing the Dataflow model (*https://oreil.ly/qrxY4*) and the Apache Beam (*https://beam.apache.org*) framework that implements this model.

The core idea in the Dataflow model is to view all data as events, as the aggregation is performed over various types of windows. Ongoing real-time event streams are *unbounded data*. Data batches are simply bounded event streams, and the boundaries provide a natural window. Engineers can choose from various windows for real-time aggregation, such as sliding or tumbling. Real-time and batch processing happens in the same system using nearly identical code.

The philosophy of "batch as a special case of streaming" is now more pervasive. Various frameworks such as Flink and Spark have adopted a similar approach.

Architecture for IoT

The *Internet of Things* (IoT) is the distributed collection of devices, aka *things*—computers, sensors, mobile devices, smart home devices, and anything else with an internet connection. Rather than generating data from direct human input (think data entry from a keyboard), IoT data is generated from devices that collect data periodically or continuously from the surrounding environment and transmit it to a destination. IoT devices are often low-powered and operate in low-resource/low bandwidth environments.

While the concept of IoT devices dates back at least a few decades, the smartphone revolution created a massive IoT swarm virtually overnight. Since then, numerous new IoT categories have emerged, such as smart thermostats, car entertainment systems, smart TVs, and smart speakers. The IoT has evolved from a futurist fantasy to a massive data engineering domain. We expect IoT to become one of the dominant ways data is generated and consumed, and this section goes a bit deeper than the others you've read.

Having a cursory understanding of IoT architecture will help you understand broader data architecture trends. Let's briefly look at some IoT architecture concepts.

Devices

Devices (also known as *things*) are the physical hardware connected to the internet, sensing the environment around them and collecting and transmitting data to a downstream destination. These devices might be used in consumer applications like a doorbell camera, smartwatch, or thermostat. The device might be an AI-powered camera that monitors an assembly line for defective components, a GPS tracker to record vehicle locations, or a Raspberry Pi programmed to download the latest tweets and brew your coffee. Any device capable of collecting data from its environment is an IoT device.

Devices should be minimally capable of collecting and transmitting data. However, the device might also crunch data or run ML on the data it collects before sending it downstream—edge computing and edge machine learning, respectively.

A data engineer doesn't necessarily need to know the inner details of IoT devices but should know what the device does, the data it collects, any edge computations or ML it runs before transmitting the data, and how often it sends data. It also helps to know the consequences of a device or internet outage, environmental or other external factors affecting data collection, and how these may impact the downstream collection of data from the device.

Interfacing with devices

A device isn't beneficial unless you can get its data. This section covers some of the key components necessary to interface with IoT devices in the wild.

IoT gateway. An *IoT gateway* is a hub for connecting devices and securely routing devices to the appropriate destinations on the internet. While you can connect a device directly to the internet without an IoT gateway, the gateway allows devices to connect using extremely little power. It acts as a way station for data retention and manages an internet connection to the final data destination.

New low-power WiFi standards are designed to make IoT gateways less critical in the future, but these are just rolling out now. Typically, a swarm of devices will utilize many IoT gateways, one at each physical location where devices are present (Figure 3-16).

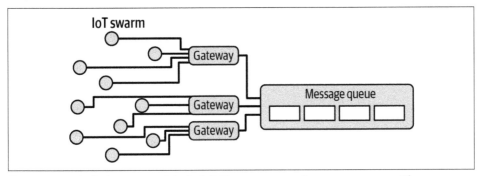

Figure 3-16. A device swarm (circles), IoT gateways, and message queue with messages (rectangles within the queue)

Ingestion. *Ingestion* begins with an IoT gateway, as discussed previously. From there, events and measurements can flow into an event ingestion architecture.

Of course, other patterns are possible. For instance, the gateway may accumulate data and upload it in batches for later analytics processing. In remote physical environments, gateways may not have connectivity to a network much of the time. They may upload all data only when they are brought into the range of a cellular or WiFi network. The point is that the diversity of IoT systems and environments presents complications—e.g., late-arriving data, data structure and schema disparities, data corruption, and connection disruption—that engineers must account for in their architectures and downstream analytics.

Storage. Storage requirements will depend a great deal on the latency requirement for the IoT devices in the system. For example, for remote sensors collecting scientific data for analysis at a later time, batch object storage may be perfectly acceptable. However, near real-time responses may be expected from a system backend that constantly analyzes data in a home monitoring and automation solution. In this case, a message queue or time-series database is more appropriate. We discuss storage systems in more detail in Chapter 6.

Serving. Serving patterns are incredibly diverse. In a batch scientific application, data might be analyzed using a cloud data warehouse and then served in a report. Data will be presented and served in numerous ways in a home-monitoring application. Data will be analyzed in the near time using a stream-processing engine or queries in a time-series database to look for critical events such as a fire, electrical outage, or break-in. Detection of an anomaly will trigger alerts to the homeowner, the fire department, or other entity. A batch analytics component also exists—for example, a monthly report on the state of the home.

One significant serving pattern for IoT looks like reverse ETL (Figure 3-17), although we tend not to use this term in the IoT context. Think of this scenario: data from sensors on manufacturing devices is collected and analyzed. The results of these measurements are processed to look for optimizations that will allow equipment to operate more efficiently. Data is sent back to reconfigure the devices and optimize them.

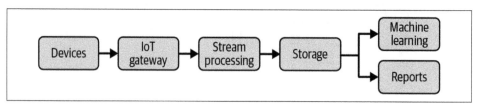

Figure 3-17. IoT serving pattern for downstream use cases

Scratching the surface of the IoT

IoT scenarios are incredibly complex, and IoT architecture and systems are also less familiar to data engineers who may have spent their careers working with business data. We hope that this introduction will encourage interested data engineers to learn more about this fascinating and rapidly evolving specialization.

Data Mesh

The *data mesh* is a recent response to sprawling monolithic data platforms, such as centralized data lakes and data warehouses, and "the great divide of data," wherein the landscape is divided between operational data and analytical data.[24] The data mesh attempts to invert the challenges of centralized data architecture, taking the concepts of domain-driven design (commonly used in software architectures) and applying them to data architecture. Because the data mesh has captured much recent attention, you should be aware of it.

A big part of the data mesh is decentralization, as Zhamak Dehghani noted in her groundbreaking article on the topic:[25]

> In order to decentralize the monolithic data platform, we need to reverse how we think about data, its locality, and ownership. Instead of flowing the data from domains into a centrally owned data lake or platform, domains need to host and serve their domain datasets in an easily consumable way.

Dehghani later identified four key components of the data mesh:[26]

- Domain-oriented decentralized data ownership and architecture
- Data as a product
- Self-serve data infrastructure as a platform
- Federated computational governance

Figure 3-18 shows a simplified version of a data mesh architecture. You can learn more about data mesh in Dehghani's book *Data Mesh* (O'Reilly).

---

24 Zhamak Dehghani, "Data Mesh Principles and Logical Architecture," MartinFowler.com, December 3, 2020, *https://oreil.ly/ezWE7*.

25 Zhamak Dehghani, "How to Move Beyond a Monolithic Data Lake to a Distributed Data Mesh," Martin-Fowler.com, May 20, 2019, *https://oreil.ly/SqMe8*.

26 Zhamak Dehghani, "Data Mesh Principles and Logical Architecture."

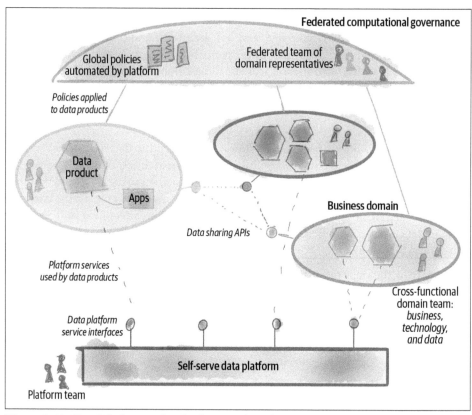

Figure 3-18. Simplified example of a data mesh architecture. Source: From Data Mesh, *by Zhamak Dehghani. Copyright © 2022 Zhamak Dehghani. Published by O'Reilly Media, Inc. Used with permission.*

Other Data Architecture Examples

Data architectures have countless other variations, such as data fabric, data hub, scaled architecture (*https://oreil.ly/MB1Ap*), metadata-first architecture (*https://oreil.ly/YkA9e*), event-driven architecture, live data stack (Chapter 11), and many more. And new architectures will continue to emerge as practices consolidate and mature, and tooling simplifies and improves. We've focused on a handful of the most critical data architecture patterns that are extremely well established, evolving rapidly, or both.

As a data engineer, pay attention to how new architectures may help your organization. Stay abreast of new developments by cultivating a high-level awareness of the data engineering ecosystem developments. Be open-minded and don't get emotionally attached to one approach. Once you've identified potential value, deepen your learning and make concrete decisions. When done right, minor tweaks—or major overhauls—in your data architecture can positively impact the business.

Who's Involved with Designing a Data Architecture?

Data architecture isn't designed in a vacuum. Bigger companies may still employ data architects, but those architects will need to be heavily in tune and current with the state of technology and data. Gone are the days of ivory tower data architecture. In the past, architecture was largely orthogonal to engineering. We expect this distinction will disappear as data engineering, and engineering in general, quickly evolves, becoming more agile, with less separation between engineering and architecture.

Ideally, a data engineer will work alongside a dedicated data architect. However, if a company is small or low in its level of data maturity, a data engineer might work double duty as an architect. Because data architecture is an undercurrent of the data engineering lifecycle, a data engineer should understand "good" architecture and the various types of data architecture.

When designing architecture, you'll work alongside business stakeholders to evaluate trade-offs. What are the trade-offs inherent in adopting a cloud data warehouse versus a data lake? What are the trade-offs of various cloud platforms? When might a unified batch/streaming framework (Beam, Flink) be an appropriate choice? Studying these choices in the abstract will prepare you to make concrete, valuable decisions.

Conclusion

You've learned how data architecture fits into the data engineering lifecycle and what makes for "good" data architecture, and you've seen several examples of data architectures. Because architecture is such a key foundation for success, we encourage you to invest the time to study it deeply and understand the trade-offs inherent in any architecture. You will be prepared to map out architecture that corresponds to your organization's unique requirements.

Next up, let's look at some approaches to choosing the right technologies to be used in data architecture and across the data engineering lifecycle.

Additional Resources

- "AnemicDomainModel" (*https://oreil.ly/Bx8fF*) by Martin Fowler
- "Big Data Architectures" (*https://oreil.ly/z7ZQY*) Azure documentation
- "BoundedContext" (*https://oreil.ly/Hx3dv*) by Martin Fowler
- "A Brief Introduction to Two Data Processing Architectures—Lambda and Kappa for Big Data" (*https://oreil.ly/CcmZi*) by Iman Samizadeh

- "The Building Blocks of a Modern Data Platform" (*https://oreil.ly/ECuIW*) by Prukalpa
- "Choosing Open Wisely" (*https://oreil.ly/79pNh*) by Benoit Dageville et al.
- "Choosing the Right Architecture for Global Data Distribution" (*https://oreil.ly/mGkrg*) Google Cloud Architecture web page
- "Column-Oriented DBMS" Wikipedia page (*https://oreil.ly/pG4DJ*)
- "A Comparison of Data Processing Frameworks" (*https://oreil.ly/XSM7H*) by Ludovik Santos
- "The Cost of Cloud, a Trillion Dollar Paradox" (*https://oreil.ly/8wBqr*) by Sarah Wang and Martin Casado
- "The Curse of the Data Lake Monster" (*https://oreil.ly/UdFHa*) by Kiran Prakash and Lucy Chambers
- *Data Architecture: A Primer for the Data Scientist* by W. H. Inmon et al. (Academic Press)
- "Data Architecture: Complex vs. Complicated" (*https://oreil.ly/akjNd*) by Dave Wells
- "Data as a Product vs. Data as a Service" (*https://oreil.ly/6svBK*) by Justin Gage
- "The Data Dichotomy: Rethinking the Way We Treat Data and Services" (*https://oreil.ly/Bk4dV*) by Ben Stopford
- "Data Fabric Architecture Is Key to Modernizing Data Management and Integration" (*https://oreil.ly/qQf3z*) by Ashutosh Gupta
- "Data Fabric Defined" (*https://oreil.ly/ECpAG*) by James Serra
- "Data Team Platform" (*https://oreil.ly/SkDj0*) by GitLab Data
- "Data Warehouse Architecture: Overview" (*https://oreil.ly/pzGKb*) by Roelant Vos
- "Data Warehouse Architecture" tutorial at Javatpoint (*https://oreil.ly/XgwiO*)
- "Defining Architecture" ISO/IEC/IEEE 42010 web page (*https://oreil.ly/CJxom*)
- "The Design and Implementation of Modern Column-Oriented Database Systems" (*https://oreil.ly/Y93uf*) by Daniel Abadi et al.
- "Disasters I've Seen in a Microservices World" (*https://oreil.ly/b1TWh*) by Joao Alves
- "DomainDrivenDesign" (*https://oreil.ly/nyMrw*) by Martin Fowler
- "Down with Pipeline Debt: Introducing Great Expectations" (*https://oreil.ly/EgVav*) by the Great Expectations project
- *EABOK* draft (*https://oreil.ly/28yWO*), edited by Paula Hagan

- EABOK website (*https://eabok.org*)
- "EagerReadDerivation" (*https://oreil.ly/ABD9d*) by Martin Fowler
- "End-to-End Serverless ETL Orchestration in AWS: A Guide" (*https://oreil.ly/xpmrY*) by Rittika Jindal
- "Enterprise Architecture" Gartner Glossary definition (*https://oreil.ly/mtam7*)
- "Enterprise Architecture's Role in Building a Data-Driven Organization" (*https://oreil.ly/n73yP*) by Ashutosh Gupta
- "Event Sourcing" (*https://oreil.ly/xrfaP*) by Martin Fowler
- "Falling Back in Love with Data Pipelines" (*https://oreil.ly/ASz07*) by Sean Knapp
- "Five Principles for Cloud-Native Architecture: What It Is and How to Master It" (*https://oreil.ly/WCYSj*) by Tom Grey
- "Focusing on Events" (*https://oreil.ly/NsFaL*) by Martin Fowler
- "Functional Data Engineering: A Modern Paradigm for Batch Data Processing" (*https://oreil.ly/ZKmuo*) by Maxime Beauchemin
- "Google Cloud Architecture Framework" Google Cloud Architecture web page (*https://oreil.ly/Cgknz*)
- "How to Beat the Cap Theorem" (*https://oreil.ly/NXLn6*) by Nathan Marz
- "How to Build a Data Architecture to Drive Innovation—Today and Tomorrow" (*https://oreil.ly/dyCpU*) by Antonio Castro et al.
- "How TOGAF Defines Enterprise Architecture (EA)" (*https://oreil.ly/b0kaG*) by Avancier Limited
- The Information Management Body of Knowledge website (*https://www.imbok.info*)
- "Introducing Dagster: An Open Source Python Library for Building Data Applications" (*https://oreil.ly/hHNqx*) by Nick Schrock
- "The Log: What Every Software Engineer Should Know About Real-Time Data's Unifying Abstraction" (*https://oreil.ly/meDK7*) by Jay Kreps
- "Microsoft Azure IoT Reference Architecture" documentation (*https://oreil.ly/UUSMY*)
- Microsoft's "Azure Architecture Center" (*https://oreil.ly/cq8PN*)
- "Modern CI Is Too Complex and Misdirected" (*https://oreil.ly/Q4RdW*) by Gregory Szorc
- "The Modern Data Stack: Past, Present, and Future" (*https://oreil.ly/lt0t4*) by Tristan Handy
- "Moving Beyond Batch vs. Streaming" (*https://oreil.ly/sHMjv*) by David Yaffe

- "A Personal Implementation of Modern Data Architecture: Getting Strava Data into Google Cloud Platform" (*https://oreil.ly/o04q2*) by Matthew Reeve
- "Polyglot Persistence" (*https://oreil.ly/aIQcv*) by Martin Fowler
- "Potemkin Data Science" (*https://oreil.ly/MFvAe*) by Michael Correll
- "Principled Data Engineering, Part I: Architectural Overview" (*https://oreil.ly/74rlm*) by Hussein Danish
- "Questioning the Lambda Architecture" (*https://oreil.ly/mc4Nx*) by Jay Kreps
- "Reliable Microservices Data Exchange with the Outbox Pattern" (*https://oreil.ly/vvyWw*) by Gunnar Morling
- "ReportingDatabase" (*https://oreil.ly/ss3HP*) by Martin Fowler
- "The Rise of the Metadata Lake" (*https://oreil.ly/fijil*) by Prukalpa
- "Run Your Data Team Like a Product Team" (*https://oreil.ly/0MjbR*) by Emilie Schario and Taylor A. Murphy
- "Separating Utility from Value Add" (*https://oreil.ly/MAy9j*) by Ross Pettit
- "The Six Principles of Modern Data Architecture" (*https://oreil.ly/wcyDV*) by Joshua Klahr
- Snowflake's "What Is Data Warehouse Architecture" web page (*https://oreil.ly/KEG4l*)
- "Software Infrastructure 2.0: A Wishlist" (*https://oreil.ly/wXMts*) by Erik Bernhardsson
- "Staying Ahead of Data Debt" (*https://oreil.ly/9JdJ1*) by Etai Mizrahi
- "Tactics vs. Strategy: SOA and the Tarpit of Irrelevancy" (*https://oreil.ly/NUbb0*) by Neal Ford
- "Test Data Quality at Scale with Deequ" (*https://oreil.ly/WG9nN*) by Dustin Lange et al.
- "Three-Tier Architecture" (*https://oreil.ly/POjK6*) by IBM Education
- TOGAF framework website (*https://oreil.ly/7yTZ5*)
- "The Top 5 Data Trends for CDOs to Watch Out for in 2021" (*https://oreil.ly/IFXFp*) by Prukalpa
- "240 Tables and No Documentation?" (*https://oreil.ly/dCReG*) by Alexey Makhotkin
- "The Ultimate Data Observability Checklist" (*https://oreil.ly/HaTwV*) by Molly Vorwerck
- "Unified Analytics: Where Batch and Streaming Come Together; SQL and Beyond" Apache Flink Roadmap (*https://oreil.ly/tCYPh*)

- "UtilityVsStrategicDichotomy" (*https://oreil.ly/YozUm*) by Martin Fowler
- "What Is a Data Lakehouse?" (*https://oreil.ly/L12pz*) by Ben Lorica et al.
- "What Is Data Architecture? A Framework for Managing Data" (*https://oreil.ly/AJgMw*) by Thor Olavsrud
- "What Is the Open Data Ecosystem and Why It's Here to Stay" (*https://oreil.ly/PoeOA*) by Casber Wang
- "What's Wrong with MLOps?" (*https://oreil.ly/c1O9I*) by Laszlo Sragner
- "What the Heck Is Data Mesh" (*https://oreil.ly/Hjnlu*) by Chris Riccomini
- "Who Needs an Architect" (*https://oreil.ly/0BNPj*) by Martin Fowler
- "Zachman Framework" Wikipedia page (*https://oreil.ly/iszvs*)

Choosing Technologies Across the Data Engineering Lifecycle

Data engineering nowadays suffers from an embarrassment of riches. We have no shortage of technologies to solve various types of data problems. Data technologies are available as turnkey offerings consumable in almost every way—open source, managed open source, proprietary software, proprietary service, and more. However, it's easy to get caught up in chasing bleeding-edge technology while losing sight of the core purpose of data engineering: designing robust and reliable systems to carry data through the full lifecycle and serve it according to the needs of end users. Just as structural engineers carefully choose technologies and materials to realize an architect's vision for a building, data engineers are tasked with making appropriate technology choices to shepherd data through the lifecycle to serve data applications and users.

Chapter 3 discussed "good" data architecture and why it matters. We now explain how to choose the right technologies to serve this architecture. Data engineers must choose good technologies to make the best possible data product. We feel the criteria to choose a good data technology is simple: does it add value to a data product and the broader business?

A lot of people confuse architecture and tools. Architecture is *strategic*; tools are *tactical*. We sometimes hear, "Our data architecture are tools X, Y, and Z." This is the wrong way to think about architecture. Architecture is the high-level design, roadmap, and blueprint of data systems that satisfy the strategic aims for the business. Architecture is the *what*, *why*, and *when*. Tools are used to make the architecture a reality; tools are the *how*.

We often see teams going "off the rails" and choosing technologies before mapping out an architecture. The reasons vary: shiny object syndrome, resume-driven development, and a lack of expertise in architecture. In practice, this prioritization of technology often means they cobble together a kind of Dr. Seuss fantasy machine rather than a true data architecture. We strongly advise against choosing technology before getting your architecture right. Architecture first, technology second.

This chapter discusses our tactical plan for making technology choices once we have a strategic architecture blueprint. The following are some considerations for choosing data technologies across the data engineering lifecycle:

- Team size and capabilities
- Speed to market
- Interoperability
- Cost optimization and business value
- Today versus the future: immutable versus transitory technologies
- Location (cloud, on prem, hybrid cloud, multicloud)
- Build versus buy
- Monolith versus modular
- Serverless versus servers
- Optimization, performance, and the benchmark wars
- The undercurrents of the data engineering lifecycle

Team Size and Capabilities

The first thing you need to assess is your team's size and its capabilities with technology. Are you on a small team (perhaps a team of one) of people who are expected to wear many hats, or is the team large enough that people work in specialized roles? Will a handful of people be responsible for multiple stages of the data engineering lifecycle, or do people cover particular niches? Your team's size will influence the types of technologies you adopt.

There is a continuum of simple to complex technologies, and a team's size roughly determines the amount of bandwidth your team can dedicate to complex solutions. We sometimes see small data teams read blog posts about a new cutting-edge technology at a giant tech company and then try to emulate these same extremely complex technologies and practices. We call this *cargo-cult engineering*, and it's generally a big mistake that consumes a lot of valuable time and money, often with little to nothing to show in return. Especially for small teams or teams with weaker technical chops, use as many managed and SaaS tools as possible, and dedicate your limited bandwidth to solving the complex problems that directly add value to the business.

Take an inventory of your team's skills. Do people lean toward low-code tools, or do they favor code-first approaches? Are people strong in certain languages like Java, Python, or Go? Technologies are available to cater to every preference on the low-code to code-heavy spectrum. Again, we suggest sticking with technologies and workflows with which the team is familiar. We've seen data teams invest a lot of time in learning the shiny new data technology, language, or tool, only to never use it in production. Learning new technologies, languages, and tools is a considerable time investment, so make these investments wisely.

Speed to Market

In technology, speed to market wins. This means choosing the right technologies that help you deliver features and data faster while maintaining high-quality standards and security. It also means working in a tight feedback loop of launching, learning, iterating, and making improvements.

Perfect is the enemy of good. Some data teams will deliberate on technology choices for months or years without reaching any decisions. Slow decisions and output are the kiss of death to data teams. We've seen more than a few data teams dissolve for moving too slow and failing to deliver the value they were hired to produce.

Deliver value early and often. As we've mentioned, use what works. Your team members will likely get better leverage with tools they already know. Avoid undifferentiated heavy lifting that engages your team in unnecessarily complex work that adds little to no value. Choose tools that help you move quickly, reliably, safely, and securely.

Interoperability

Rarely will you use only one technology or system. When choosing a technology or system, you'll need to ensure that it interacts and operates with other technologies. *Interoperability* describes how various technologies or systems connect, exchange information, and interact.

Let's say you're evaluating two technologies, A and B. How easily does technology A integrate with technology B when thinking about interoperability? This is often a spectrum of difficulty, ranging from seamless to time-intensive. Is seamless integration already baked into each product, making setup a breeze? Or do you need to do a lot of manual configuration to integrate these technologies?

Often, vendors and open source projects will target specific platforms and systems to interoperate. Most data ingestion and visualization tools have built-in integrations with popular data warehouses and data lakes. Furthermore, popular data-ingestion tools will integrate with common APIs and services, such as CRMs, accounting software, and more.

Sometimes standards are in place for interoperability. Almost all databases allow connections via Java Database Connectivity (JDBC) or Open Database Connectivity (ODBC), meaning that you can easily connect to a database by using these standards. In other cases, interoperability occurs in the absence of standards. Representational state transfer (REST) is not truly a standard for APIs; every REST API has its quirks. In these cases, it's up to the vendor or open source software (OSS) project to ensure smooth integration with other technologies and systems.

Always be aware of how simple it will be to connect your various technologies across the data engineering lifecycle. As mentioned in other chapters, we suggest designing for modularity and giving yourself the ability to easily swap out technologies as new practices and alternatives become available.

Cost Optimization and Business Value

In a perfect world, you'd get to experiment with all the latest, coolest technologies without considering cost, time investment, or value added to the business. In reality, budgets and time are finite, and the cost is a major constraint for choosing the right data architectures and technologies. Your organization expects a positive ROI from your data projects, so you must understand the basic costs you can control. Technology is a major cost driver, so your technology choices and management strategies will significantly impact your budget. We look at costs through three main lenses: total cost of ownership, opportunity cost, and FinOps.

Total Cost of Ownership

Total cost of ownership (TCO) is the total estimated cost of an initiative, including the direct and indirect costs of products and services utilized. *Direct costs* can be directly attributed to an initiative. Examples are the salaries of a team working on the initiative or the AWS bill for all services consumed. *Indirect costs*, also known as *overhead*, are independent of the initiative and must be paid regardless of where they're attributed.

Apart from direct and indirect costs, *how something is purchased* impacts the way costs are accounted for. Expenses fall into two big groups: capital expenses and operational expenses.

Capital expenses, also known as *capex*, require an up-front investment. Payment is required *today*. Before the cloud existed, companies would typically purchase hardware and software up front through large acquisition contracts. In addition, significant investments were required to host hardware in server rooms, data centers, and colocation facilities. These up-front investments—commonly hundreds of thousands to millions of dollars or more—would be treated as assets and slowly depreciate over time. From a budget perspective, capital was required to fund the entire purchase. This is capex, a significant capital outlay with a long-term plan to achieve a positive ROI on the effort and expense put forth.

Operational expenses, also known as *opex*, are the opposite of capex in certain respects. Opex is gradual and spread out over time. Whereas capex is long-term focused, opex is short-term. Opex can be pay-as-you-go or similar and allows a lot of flexibility. Opex is closer to a direct cost, making it easier to attribute to a data project.

Until recently, opex wasn't an option for large data projects. Data systems often required multimillion-dollar contracts. This has changed with the advent of the cloud, as data platform services allow engineers to pay on a consumption-based model. In general, opex allows for a far greater ability for engineering teams to choose their software and hardware. Cloud-based services let data engineers iterate quickly with various software and technology configurations, often inexpensively.

Data engineers need to be pragmatic about flexibility. The data landscape is changing too quickly to invest in long-term hardware that inevitably goes stale, can't easily scale, and potentially hampers a data engineer's flexibility to try new things. Given the upside for flexibility and low initial costs, we urge data engineers to take an opex-first approach centered on the cloud and flexible, pay-as-you-go technologies.

Total Opportunity Cost of Ownership

Any choice inherently excludes other possibilities. *Total opportunity cost of ownership* (TOCO) is the cost of lost opportunities that we incur in choosing a technology, an architecture, or a process.[1] Note that ownership in this setting doesn't require long-term purchases of hardware or licenses. Even in a cloud environment, we effectively own a technology, a stack, or a pipeline once it becomes a core part of our production data processes and is difficult to move away from. Data engineers often fail to evaluate TOCO when undertaking a new project; in our opinion, this is a massive blind spot.

If you choose data stack A, you've chosen the benefits of data stack A over all other options, effectively excluding data stacks B, C, and D. You're committed to data stack A and everything it entails—the team to support it, training, setup, and maintenance. What happens if data stack A was a poor choice? What happens when data stack A becomes obsolete? Can you still move to other data stacks?

How quickly and cheaply can you move to something newer and better? This is a critical question in the data space, where new technologies and products seem to

---

1 For more details, see "Total Opportunity Cost of Ownership" by Joseph Reis in *97 Things Every Data Engineer Should Know* (O'Reilly).

appear at an ever-faster rate. Does the expertise you've built up on data stack A translate to the next wave? Or are you able to swap out components of data stack A and buy yourself some time and options?

The first step to minimizing opportunity cost is evaluating it with eyes wide open. We've seen countless data teams get stuck with technologies that seemed good at the time and are either not flexible for future growth or simply obsolete. Inflexible data technologies are a lot like bear traps. They're easy to get into and extremely painful to escape.

FinOps

We already touched on FinOps in "Principle 9: Embrace FinOps" on page 87. As we've discussed, typical cloud spending is inherently opex: companies pay for services to run critical data processes rather than making up-front purchases and clawing back value over time. The goal of FinOps is to fully operationalize financial account-ability and business value by applying the DevOps-like practices of monitoring and dynamically adjusting systems.

In this chapter, we want to emphasize one thing about FinOps that is well embodied in this quote:[2]

> If it seems that FinOps is about saving money, then think again. FinOps is about making money. Cloud spend can drive more revenue, signal customer base growth, enable more product and feature release velocity, or even help shut down a data center.

In our setting of data engineering, the ability to iterate quickly and scale dynamically is invaluable for creating business value. This is one of the major motivations for shifting data workloads to the cloud.

Today Versus the Future: Immutable Versus Transitory Technologies

In an exciting domain like data engineering, it's all too easy to focus on a rapidly evolving future while ignoring the concrete needs of the present. The intention to build a better future is noble but often leads to overarchitecting and overengineering. Tooling chosen for the future may be stale and out-of-date when this future arrives; the future frequently looks little like what we envisioned years before.

As many life coaches would tell you, focus on the present. You should choose the best technology for the moment and near future, but in a way that supports future unknowns and evolution. Ask yourself: where are you today, and what are your goals

---

2 J. R. Storment and Mike Fuller, *Cloud FinOps* (Sebastopol, CA: O'Reilly, 2019), 6, *https://oreil.ly/RvRvX*.

for the future? Your answers to these questions should inform your decisions about your architecture and thus the technologies used within that architecture. This is done by understanding what is likely to change and what tends to stay the same.

We have two classes of tools to consider: immutable and transitory. *Immutable technologies* might be components that underpin the cloud or languages and paradigms that have stood the test of time. In the cloud, examples of immutable technologies are object storage, networking, servers, and security. Object storage such as Amazon S3 and Azure Blob Storage will be around from today until the end of the decade, and probably much longer. Storing your data in object storage is a wise choice. Object storage continues to improve in various ways and constantly offers new options, but your data will be safe and usable in object storage regardless of the rapid evolution of technology as a whole.

For languages, SQL and bash have been around for many decades, and we don't see them disappearing anytime soon. Immutable technologies benefit from the Lindy effect: the longer a technology has been established, the longer it will be used. Think of the power grid, relational databases, the C programming language, or the x86 processor architecture. We suggest applying the Lindy effect as a litmus test to determine whether a technology is potentially immutable.

Transitory technologies are those that come and go. The typical trajectory begins with a lot of hype, followed by meteoric growth in popularity, then a slow descent into obscurity. The JavaScript frontend landscape is a classic example. How many JavaScript frontend frameworks have come and gone between 2010 and 2020? Backbone.js, Ember.js, and Knockout were popular in the early 2010s, and React and Vue.js have massive mindshare today. What's the popular frontend JavaScript framework three years from now? Who knows.

New well-funded entrants and open source projects arrive on the data front every day. Every vendor will say their product will change the industry and "make the world a better place" (*https://oreil.ly/A8Fdi*). Most of these companies and projects don't get long-term traction and fade slowly into obscurity. Top VCs are making big-money bets, knowing that most of their data-tooling investments will fail. If VCs pouring millions (or billions) into data-tooling investments can't get it right, how can you possibly know which technologies to invest in for your data architecture? It's hard. Just consider the number of technologies in Matt Turck's (in)famous depictions of the ML, AI, and data (MAD) landscape (*https://oreil.ly/TWTfM*) that we introduced in Chapter 1 (Figure 4-1).

Even relatively successful technologies often fade into obscurity quickly, after a few years of rapid adoption, a victim of their success. For instance, in the early 2010s, Hive was met with rapid uptake because it allowed both analysts and engineers to query massive datasets without coding complex MapReduce jobs by hand. Inspired by the success of Hive but wishing to improve on its shortcomings, engineers developed Presto and other technologies. Hive now appears primarily in legacy deployments. Almost every technology follows this inevitable path of decline.

Figure 4-1. Matt Turck's 2021 MAD data landscape (https://oreil.ly/TWTfM)

Our Advice

Given the rapid pace of tooling and best-practice changes, we suggest evaluating tools every two years (Figure 4-2). Whenever possible, find the immutable technologies along the data engineering lifecycle, and use those as your base. Build transitory tools around the immutables.

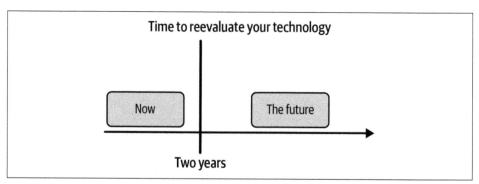

Figure 4-2. Use a two-year time horizon to reevaluate your technology choices

Given the reasonable probability of failure for many data technologies, you need to consider how easy it is to transition from a chosen technology. What are the barriers to leaving? As mentioned previously in our discussion about opportunity cost, avoid

---

"bear traps." Go into a new technology with eyes wide open, knowing the project might get abandoned, the company may not be viable, or the technology simply isn't a good fit any longer.

Location

Companies now have numerous options when deciding where to run their technology stacks. A slow shift toward the cloud culminates in a veritable stampede of companies spinning up workloads on AWS, Azure, and Google Cloud Platform (GCP). In the last decade, many CTOs have come to view their decisions around technology hosting as having existential significance for their organizations. If they move too slowly, they risk being left behind by their more agile competition; on the other hand, a poorly planned cloud migration could lead to technological failure and catastrophic costs.

Let's look at the principal places to run your technology stack: on premises, the cloud, hybrid cloud, and multicloud.

On Premises

While new startups are increasingly born in the cloud, on-premises systems are still the default for established companies. Essentially, these companies own their hardware, which may live in data centers they own or in leased colocation space. In either case, companies are operationally responsible for their hardware and the software that runs on it. If hardware fails, they have to repair or replace it. They also have to manage upgrade cycles every few years as new, updated hardware is released and older hardware ages and becomes less reliable. They must ensure that they have enough hardware to handle peaks; for an online retailer, this means hosting enough capacity to handle the load spikes of Black Friday. For data engineers in charge of on-premises systems, this means buying large-enough systems to allow good performance for peak load and large jobs without overbuying and overspending.

On the one hand, established companies have established operational practices that have served them well. Suppose a company that relies on information technology has been in business for some time. This means it has managed to juggle the cost and personnel requirements of running its hardware, managing software environments, deploying code from dev teams, and running databases and big data systems.

On the other hand, established companies see their younger, more agile competition scaling rapidly and taking advantage of cloud-managed services. They also see established competitors making forays into the cloud, allowing them to temporarily scale up enormous computing power for massive data jobs or the Black Friday shopping spike.

Companies in competitive sectors generally don't have the option to stand still. Competition is fierce, and there's always the threat of being "disrupted" by more agile competition, often backed by a large pile of venture capital dollars. Every company must keep its existing systems running efficiently while deciding what moves to make next. This could involve adopting newer DevOps practices, such as containers, Kubernetes, microservices, and continuous deployment while keeping their hardware running on premises. It could involve a complete migration to the cloud, as discussed next.

Cloud

The cloud flips the on-premises model on its head. Instead of purchasing hardware, you simply rent hardware and managed services from a cloud provider (such as AWS, Azure, or Google Cloud). These resources can often be reserved on an extremely short-term basis; VMs spin up in less than a minute, and subsequent usage is billed in per-second increments. This allows cloud users to dynamically scale resources that were inconceivable with on-premises servers.

In a cloud environment, engineers can quickly launch projects and experiment without worrying about long lead time hardware planning. They can begin running servers as soon as their code is ready to deploy. This makes the cloud model extremely appealing to startups that are tight on budget and time.

The early cloud era was dominated by infrastructure as a service (IaaS) offerings—products such as VMs and virtual disks that are essentially rented slices of hardware. Slowly, we've seen a shift toward platform as a service (PaaS), while SaaS products continue to grow at a rapid clip.

PaaS includes IaaS products but adds more sophisticated managed services to support applications. Examples are managed databases such as Amazon Relational Database Service (RDS) and Google Cloud SQL, managed streaming platforms such as Amazon Kinesis and Simple Queue Service (SQS), and managed Kubernetes such as Google Kubernetes Engine (GKE) and Azure Kubernetes Service (AKS). PaaS services allow engineers to ignore the operational details of managing individual machines and deploying frameworks across distributed systems. They provide turnkey access to complex, autoscaling systems with minimal operational overhead.

SaaS offerings move one additional step up the ladder of abstraction. SaaS typically provides a fully functioning enterprise software platform with little operational management. Examples of SaaS include Salesforce, Google Workspace, Microsoft 365, Zoom, and Fivetran. Both the major public clouds and third parties offer SaaS platforms. SaaS covers a whole spectrum of enterprise domains, including video conferencing, data management, ad tech, office applications, and CRM systems.

This chapter also discusses serverless, increasingly important in PaaS and SaaS offerings. Serverless products generally offer automated scaling from zero to extremely high usage rates. They are billed on a pay-as-you-go basis and allow engineers to operate without operational awareness of underlying servers. Many people quibble with the term *serverless*; after all, the code must run somewhere. In practice, serverless usually means *many invisible servers*.

Cloud services have become increasingly appealing to established businesses with existing data centers and IT infrastructure. Dynamic, seamless scaling is extremely valuable to businesses that deal with seasonality (e.g., retail businesses coping with Black Friday load) and web traffic load spikes. The advent of COVID-19 in 2020 was a major driver of cloud adoption, as companies recognized the value of rapidly scaling up data processes to gain insights in a highly uncertain business climate; businesses also had to cope with substantially increased load due to a spike in online shopping, web app usage, and remote work.

Before we discuss the nuances of choosing technologies in the cloud, let's first discuss why migration to the cloud requires a dramatic shift in thinking, specifically on the pricing front; this is closely related to FinOps, introduced in "FinOps" on page 124. Enterprises that migrate to the cloud often make major deployment errors by not appropriately adapting their practices to the cloud pricing model.

A Brief Detour on Cloud Economics

To understand how to use cloud services efficiently through cloud native architecture (*https://oreil.ly/uAhn8*), you need to know how clouds make money. This is an extremely complex concept and one on which cloud providers offer little transparency. Consider this sidebar a starting point for your research, discovery, and process development.

Cloud Services and Credit Default Swaps

Let's go on a little tangent about credit default swaps. Don't worry, this will make sense in a bit. Recall that credit default swaps rose to infamy after the 2007 global financial crisis. A credit default swap was a mechanism for selling different tiers of risk attached to an asset (e.g., a mortgage). It is not our intention to present this idea in any detail, but rather to offer an analogy wherein many cloud services are similar to financial derivatives; cloud providers not only slice hardware assets into small pieces through virtualization, but also sell these pieces with varying technical characteristics and risks attached. While providers are extremely tight-lipped about details of their internal systems, there are massive opportunities for optimization and scaling by understanding cloud pricing and exchanging notes with other users.

Look at the example of archival cloud storage. At the time of this writing, GCP openly admits that its archival class storage runs on the same clusters as standard cloud storage, yet the price per gigabyte per month of archival storage is roughly 1/17 that of standard storage. How is this possible?

Here's our educated guess. When purchasing cloud storage, each disk in a storage cluster has three assets that cloud providers and consumers use. First, it has a certain storage capacity—say, 10 TB. Second, it supports a certain number of input/output operations (IOPs) per second—say, 100. Third, disks support a certain maximum bandwidth, the maximum read speed for optimally organized files. A magnetic drive might be capable of reading at 200 MB/s.

Any of these limits (IOPs, storage capacity, bandwidth) is a potential bottleneck for a cloud provider. For instance, the cloud provider might have a disk storing 3 TB of data but hitting maximum IOPs. An alternative to leaving the remaining 7 TB empty is to sell the empty space without selling IOPs. Or, more specifically, sell cheap storage space and expensive IOPs to discourage reads.

Much like traders of financial derivatives, cloud vendors also deal in risk. In the case of archival storage, vendors are selling a type of insurance, but one that pays out for the insurer rather than the policy buyer in the event of a catastrophe. While data storage costs per month are extremely cheap, I risk paying a high price if I ever need to retrieve data. But this is a price that I will happily pay in a true emergency.

Similar considerations apply to nearly any cloud service. While on-premises servers are essentially sold as commodity hardware, the cost model in the cloud is more subtle. Rather than just charging for CPU cores, memory, and features, cloud vendors monetize characteristics such as durability, reliability, longevity, and predictability; a variety of compute platforms discount their offerings for workloads that are ephemeral (*https://oreil.ly/Tf8f8*) or can be arbitrarily interrupted (*https://oreil.ly/Y5jyU*) when capacity is needed elsewhere.

Cloud ≠ On Premises

This heading may seem like a silly tautology, but the belief that cloud services are just like familiar on-premises servers is a widespread cognitive error that plagues cloud migrations and leads to horrifying bills. This demonstrates a broader issue in tech that we refer to as *the curse of familiarity*. Many new technology products are intentionally designed to look like something familiar to facilitate ease of use and accelerate adoption. But, any new technology product has subtleties and wrinkles that users must learn to identify, accommodate, and optimize.

Moving on-premises servers one by one to VMs in the cloud—known as simple *lift and shift*—is a perfectly reasonable strategy for the initial phase of cloud migration, especially when a company is facing some kind of financial cliff, such as the need to sign a significant new lease or hardware contract if existing hardware is not shut down. However, companies that leave their cloud assets in this initial state are in for a rude shock. On a direct comparison basis, long-running servers in the cloud are significantly more expensive than their on-premises counterparts.

The key to finding value in the cloud is understanding and optimizing the cloud pricing model. Rather than deploying a set of long-running servers capable of handling full peak load, use autoscaling to allow workloads to scale down to minimal infrastructure when loads are light and up to massive clusters during peak times. To realize discounts through more ephemeral, less durable workloads, use reserved or spot instances, or use serverless functions in place of servers.

We often think of this optimization as leading to lower costs, but we should also strive to *increase business value* by exploiting the dynamic nature of the cloud.[3] Data engineers can create new value in the cloud by accomplishing things that were impossible in their on-premises environment. For example, it is possible to quickly spin up massive compute clusters to run complex transformations at scales that were unaffordable for on-premises hardware.

Data Gravity

In addition to basic errors such as following on-premises operational practices in the cloud, data engineers need to watch out for other aspects of cloud pricing and incentives that frequently catch users unawares.

Vendors want to lock you into their offerings. Getting data onto the platform is cheap or free on most cloud platforms, but getting data out can be extremely expensive. Be aware of data egress fees and their long-term impacts on your business before getting blindsided by a large bill. *Data gravity* is real: once data lands in a cloud, the cost to extract it and migrate processes can be very high.

Hybrid Cloud

As more established businesses migrate into the cloud, the hybrid cloud model is growing in importance. Virtually no business can migrate all of its workloads overnight. The hybrid cloud model assumes that an organization will indefinitely maintain some workloads outside the cloud.

There are many reasons to consider a hybrid cloud model. Organizations may believe that they have achieved operational excellence in certain areas, such as their application stack and associated hardware. Thus, they may migrate only to specific workloads where they see immediate benefits in the cloud environment. For example, an on-premises Spark stack is migrated to ephemeral cloud clusters, reducing the operational burden of managing software and hardware for the data engineering team and allowing rapid scaling for large data jobs.

---

3 This is a major point of emphasis in Storment and Fuller, *Cloud FinOps*.

This pattern of putting analytics in the cloud is beautiful because data flows primarily in one direction, minimizing data egress costs (Figure 4-3). That is, on-premises applications generate event data that can be pushed to the cloud essentially for free. The bulk of data remains in the cloud where it is analyzed, while smaller amounts of data are pushed back to on premises for deploying models to applications, reverse ETL, etc.

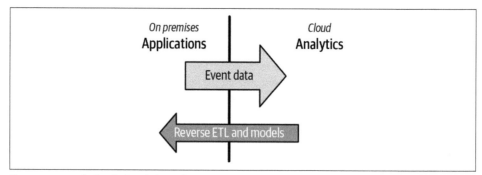

Figure 4-3. A hybrid cloud data flow model minimizing egress costs

A new generation of managed hybrid cloud service offerings also allows customers to locate cloud-managed servers in their data centers.[4] This gives users the ability to incorporate the best features in each cloud alongside on-premises infrastructure.

Multicloud

Multicloud simply refers to deploying workloads to multiple public clouds. Companies may have several motivations for multicloud deployments. SaaS platforms often wish to offer services close to existing customer cloud workloads. Snowflake and Databricks provide their SaaS offerings across multiple clouds for this reason. This is especially critical for data-intensive applications, where network latency and bandwidth limitations hamper performance, and data egress costs can be prohibitive.

Another common motivation for employing a multicloud approach is to take advantage of the best services across several clouds. For example, a company might want to handle its Google Ads and Analytics data on Google Cloud and deploy Kubernetes through GKE. And the company might also adopt Azure specifically for Microsoft workloads. Also, the company may like AWS because it has several best-in-class services (e.g., AWS Lambda) and enjoys huge mindshare, making it relatively easy to hire AWS-proficient engineers. Any mix of various cloud provider services is possible. Given the intense competition among the major cloud providers, expect them to offer more best-of-breed services, making multicloud more compelling.

---

4 Examples include Google Cloud Anthos (*https://oreil.ly/eeu0s*) and AWS Outposts (*https://oreil.ly/uaHAu*).

A multicloud methodology has several disadvantages. As we just mentioned, data egress costs and networking bottlenecks are critical. Going multicloud can introduce significant complexity. Companies must now manage a dizzying array of services across several clouds; cross-cloud integration and security present a considerable challenge; multicloud networking can be diabolically complicated.

A new generation of "cloud of clouds" services aims to facilitate multicloud with reduced complexity by offering services across clouds and seamlessly replicating data between clouds or managing workloads on several clouds through a single pane of glass. To cite one example, a Snowflake account runs in a single cloud region, but customers can readily spin up other accounts in GCP, AWS, or Azure. Snowflake provides simple scheduled data replication between these various cloud accounts. The Snowflake interface is essentially the same in all of these accounts, removing the training burden of switching between cloud-native data services.

The "cloud of clouds" space is evolving quickly; within a few years of this book's publication, many more of these services will be available. Data engineers and architects would do well to maintain awareness of this quickly changing cloud landscape.

Decentralized: Blockchain and the Edge

Though not widely used now, it's worth briefly mentioning a new trend that might become popular over the next decade: decentralized computing. Whereas today's applications mainly run on premises and in the cloud, the rise of blockchain, Web 3.0, and edge computing may invert this paradigm. For the moment, decentralized platforms have proven extremely popular but have not had a significant impact in the data space; even so, keeping an eye on these platforms is worthwhile as you assess technology decisions.

Our Advice

From our perspective, we are still at the beginning of the transition to the cloud. Thus the evidence and arguments around workload placement and migration are in flux. The cloud itself is changing, with a shift from the IaaS model built around Amazon EC2 that drove the early growth of AWS and more generally toward more managed service offerings such as AWS Glue, Google BigQuery, and Snowflake.

We've also seen the emergence of new workload placement abstractions. On-premises services are becoming more cloud-like and abstracted. Hybrid cloud services allow customers to run fully managed services within their walls while facilitating tight integration between local and remote environments. Further, the "cloud of clouds" is beginning to take shape, fueled by third-party services and public cloud vendors.

Choose technologies for the present, but look toward the future

As we mentioned in "Today Versus the Future: Immutable Versus Transitory Technologies" on page 124, you need to keep one eye on the present while planning for unknowns. Right now is a tough time to plan workload placements and migrations. Because of the fast pace of competition and change in the cloud industry, the decision space will look very different in five to ten years. It is tempting to take into account every possible future architecture permutation.

We believe that it is critical to avoid this endless trap of analysis. Instead, plan for the present. Choose the best technologies for your current needs and concrete plans for the near future. Choose your deployment platform based on real business needs while focusing on simplicity and flexibility.

In particular, don't choose a complex multicloud or hybrid-cloud strategy unless there's a compelling reason. Do you need to serve data near customers on multiple clouds? Do industry regulations require you to house certain data in your data centers? Do you have a compelling technology need for specific services on two different clouds? Choose a single-cloud deployment strategy if these scenarios don't apply to you.

On the other hand, have an escape plan. As we've emphasized before, every technology—even open source software—comes with some degree of lock-in. A single-cloud strategy has significant advantages of simplicity and integration but comes with significant lock-in attached. In this instance, we're talking about mental flexibility, the flexibility to evaluate the current state of the world and imagine alternatives. Ideally, your escape plan will remain locked behind glass, but preparing this plan will help you to make better decisions in the present and give you a way out if things go wrong in the future.

Cloud Repatriation Arguments

As we wrote this book, Sarah Wang and Martin Casado published "The Cost of Cloud, A Trillion Dollar Paradox" (*https://oreil.ly/5kc52*), an article that generated significant sound and fury in the tech space. Readers widely interpreted the article as a call for the repatriation of cloud workloads to on-premises servers. They make a somewhat more subtle argument that companies should expend significant resources to control cloud spending and should consider repatriation as a possible option.

We want to take a moment to dissect one part of their discussion. Wang and Casado cite Dropbox's repatriation of significant workloads from AWS to Dropbox-owned servers as a case study for companies considering similar repatriation moves.

You are not Dropbox, nor are you Cloudflare

We believe that this case study is frequently used without appropriate context and is a compelling example of the *false equivalence* logical fallacy. Dropbox provides particular services where ownership of hardware and data centers can offer a competitive advantage. Companies should not rely excessively on Dropbox's example when assessing cloud and on-premises deployment options.

First, it's important to understand that Dropbox stores enormous amounts of data. The company is tight-lipped about exactly how much data it hosts but says it is many exabytes and continues to grow.

Second, Dropbox handles a vast amount of network traffic. We know that its bandwidth consumption in 2017 was significant enough for the company to add "hundreds of gigabits of internet connectivity with transit providers (regional and global ISPs), and hundreds of new peering partners (where we exchange traffic directly rather than through an ISP)."[5] The data egress costs would be extremely high in a public cloud environment.

Third, Dropbox is essentially a cloud storage vendor, but one with a highly specialized storage product that combines object and block storage characteristics. Dropbox's core competence is a differential file-update system that can efficiently synchronize actively edited files among users while minimizing network and CPU usage. The product is not a good fit for object storage, block storage, or other standard cloud offerings. Dropbox has instead benefited from building a custom, highly integrated software and hardware stack.[6]

Fourth, while Dropbox moved its core product to its hardware, it continued building out other AWS workloads. This allows Dropbox to focus on building one highly tuned cloud service at an extraordinary scale rather than trying to replace multiple services. Dropbox can focus on its core competence in cloud storage and data synchronization while offloading software and hardware management in other areas, such as data analytics.[7]

Other frequently cited success stories that companies have built outside the cloud include Backblaze and Cloudflare, but these offer similar lessons. Backblaze (*https://oreil.ly/zmQ3l*) began life as a personal cloud data backup product but has since begun to offer B2 (*https://oreil.ly/y2Bh9*), an object storage service similar to Amazon S3. Backblaze currently stores over an exabyte of data. Cloudflare (*https://oreil.ly/*

---

5 Raghav Bhargava, "Evolution of Dropbox's Edge Network," Dropbox.Tech, June 19, 2017, *https://oreil.ly/RAwPf.*

6 Akhil Gupta, "Scaling to Exabytes and Beyond," Dropbox.Tech, March 14, 2016, *https://oreil.ly/5XPKv.*

7 "Dropbox Migrates 34 PB of Data to an Amazon S3 Data Lake for Analytics," AWS website, 2020, *https://oreil.ly/wpVoM.*

e3thA) claims to provide services for over 25 million internet properties, with points of presence in over 200 cities and 51 terabits per second (Tbps) of total network capacity.

Netflix offers yet another useful example. The company is famous for running its tech stack on AWS, but this is only partially true. Netflix does run video transcoding on AWS, accounting for roughly 70% of its compute needs in 2017.[8] Netflix also runs its application backend and data analytics on AWS. However, rather than using the AWS content distribution network, Netflix has built a custom CDN (*https://oreil.ly/vXuu5*) in collaboration with internet service providers, utilizing a highly specialized combination of software and hardware. For a company that consumes a substantial slice of all internet traffic,[9] building out this critical infrastructure allowed it to deliver high-quality video to a huge customer base cost-effectively.

These case studies suggest that it makes sense for companies to manage their own hardware and network connections in particular circumstances. The biggest modern success stories of companies building and maintaining hardware involve extraordinary scale (exabytes of data, terabits per second of bandwidth, etc.) and limited use cases where companies can realize a competitive advantage by engineering highly integrated hardware and software stacks. In addition, all of these companies consume massive network bandwidth, suggesting that data egress charges would be a major cost if they chose to operate fully from a public cloud.

Consider continuing to run workloads on premises or repatriating cloud workloads if you run a truly cloud-scale service. What is cloud scale? You might be at cloud scale if you are storing an exabyte of data or handling terabits per second of traffic *to and from the internet*. (Achieving a terabit per second of *internal* network traffic is fairly easy.) In addition, consider owning your servers if data egress costs are a major factor for your business. To give a concrete example of cloud scale workloads that could benefit from repatriation, Apple might gain a significant financial and performance advantage by migrating iCloud storage to its own servers.[10]

Build Versus Buy

Build versus buy is an age-old debate in technology. The argument for building is that you have end-to-end control over the solution and are not at the mercy of a vendor or open source community. The argument supporting buying comes

---

8 Todd Hoff, "The Eternal Cost Savings of Netflix's Internal Spot Market," High Scalability, December 4, 2017, *https://oreil.ly/LLoFt*.

9 Todd Spangler, "Netflix Bandwidth Consumption Eclipsed by Web Media Streaming Applications," *Variety*, September 10, 2019, *https://oreil.ly/tTm3k*.

10 Amir Efrati and Kevin McLaughlin, "Apple's Spending on Google Cloud Storage on Track to Soar 50% This Year," *The Information*, June 29, 2021, *https://oreil.ly/OlFyR*.

down to resource constraints and expertise; do you have the expertise to build a better solution than something already available? Either decision comes down to TCO, TOCO, and whether the solution provides a competitive advantage to your organization.

If you've caught on to a theme in the book so far, it's that we suggest investing in building and customizing *when doing so will provide a competitive advantage* for your business. Otherwise, stand on the shoulders of giants and *use what's already available* in the market. Given the number of open source and paid services—both of which may have communities of volunteers or highly paid teams of amazing engineers— you're foolish to build everything yourself.

As we often ask, "When you need new tires for your car, do you get the raw materials, create the tires from scratch, and install them yourself?" Like most people, you're probably buying tires and having someone install them. The same argument applies to build versus buy. We've seen teams that have built their databases from scratch. A simple open source RDBMS would have served their needs much better upon closer inspection. Imagine the amount of time and money invested in this homegrown database. Talk about low ROI for TCO and opportunity cost.

This is where the distinction between the type A and type B data engineer comes in handy. As we pointed out earlier, type A and type B roles are often embodied in the same engineer, especially in a small organization. Whenever possible, lean toward type A behavior; avoid undifferentiated heavy lifting and embrace abstraction. Use open source frameworks, or if this is too much trouble, look at buying a suitable managed or proprietary solution. Plenty of great modular services are available to choose from in either case.

The shifting reality of how companies adopt software is worth mentioning. Whereas in the past, IT used to make most of the software purchase and adoption decisions in a top-down manner, these days, the trend is for bottom-up software adoption in a company, driven by developers, data engineers, data scientists, and other technical roles. Technology adoption within companies is becoming an organic, continuous process.

Let's look at some options for open source and proprietary solutions.

Open Source Software

Open source software (OSS) is a software distribution model in which software, and the underlying codebase, is made available for general use, typically under specific licensing terms. Often OSS is created and maintained by a distributed team of collaborators. OSS is free to use, change, and distribute most of the time, but with specific caveats. For example, many licenses require that the source code of open source–derived software be included when the software is distributed.

The motivations for creating and maintaining OSS vary. Sometimes OSS is organic, springing from the mind of an individual or a small team that creates a novel solution and chooses to release it into the wild for public use. Other times, a company may make a specific tool or technology available to the public under an OSS license.

OSS has two main flavors: community managed and commercial OSS.

Community-managed OSS

OSS projects succeed with a strong community and vibrant user base. *Community-managed OSS* is a prevalent path for OSS projects. The community opens up high rates of innovations and contributions from developers worldwide with popular OSS projects.

The following are factors to consider with a community-managed OSS project:

Mindshare
> Avoid adopting OSS projects that don't have traction and popularity. Look at the number of GitHub stars, forks, and commit volume and recency. Another thing to pay attention to is community activity on related chat groups and forums. Does the project have a strong sense of community? A strong community creates a virtuous cycle of strong adoption. It also means that you'll have an easier time getting technical assistance and finding talent qualified to work with the framework.

Maturity
> How long has the project been around, how active is it today, and how usable are people finding it in production? A project's maturity indicates that people find it useful and are willing to incorporate it into their production workflows.

Troubleshooting
> How will you have to handle problems if they arise? Are you on your own to troubleshoot issues, or can the community help you solve your problem?

Project management
> Look at Git issues and the way they're addressed. Are they addressed quickly? If so, what's the process to submit an issue and get it resolved?

Team
> Is a company sponsoring the OSS project? Who are the core contributors?

Developer relations and community management
> What is the project doing to encourage uptake and adoption? Is there a vibrant chat community (e.g., in Slack) that provides encouragement and support?

Contributing

Does the project encourage and accept pull requests? What are the process and timelines for pull requests to be accepted and included in main codebase?

Roadmap

Is there a project roadmap? If so, is it clear and transparent?

Self-hosting and maintenance

Do you have the resources to host and maintain the OSS solution? If so, what's the TCO and TOCO versus buying a managed service from the OSS vendor?

Giving back to the community

If you like the project and are actively using it, consider investing in it. You can contribute to the codebase, help fix issues, and give advice in the community forums and chats. If the project allows donations, consider making one. Many OSS projects are essentially community-service projects, and the maintainers often have full-time jobs in addition to helping with the OSS project. Sadly, it's often a labor of love that doesn't afford the maintainer a living wage. If you can afford to donate, please do so.

Commercial OSS

Sometimes OSS has some drawbacks. Namely, you have to host and maintain the solution in your environment. This may be trivial or extremely complicated and cumbersome, depending on the OSS application. Commercial vendors try to solve this management headache by hosting and managing the OSS solution for you, typically as a cloud SaaS offering. Examples of such vendors include Databricks (Spark), Confluent (Kafka), DBT Labs (dbt), and there are many, many others.

This model is called *commercial OSS* (COSS). Typically, a vendor will offer the "core" of the OSS for free while charging for enhancements, curated code distributions, or fully managed services.

A vendor is often affiliated with the community OSS project. As an OSS project becomes more popular, the maintainers may create a separate business for a managed version of the OSS. This typically becomes a cloud SaaS platform built around a managed version of the open source code. This is a widespread trend: an OSS project becomes popular, an affiliated company raises truckloads of venture capital (VC) money to commercialize the OSS project, and the company scales as a fast-moving rocket ship.

At this point, the data engineer has two options. You can continue using the community-managed OSS version, which you need to continue maintaining on your own (updates, server/container maintenance, pull requests for bug fixes, etc.). Or, you can pay the vendor and let it take care of the administrative management of the COSS product.

The following are factors to consider with a commercial OSS project:

Value

Is the vendor offering a better value than if you managed the OSS technology yourself? Some vendors will add many bells and whistles to their managed offerings that aren't available in the community OSS version. Are these additions compelling to you?

Delivery model

How do you access the service? Is the product available via download, API, or web/mobile UI? Be sure you can easily access the initial version and subsequent releases.

Support

Support cannot be understated, and it's often opaque to the buyer. What is the support model for the product, and is there an extra cost for support? Frequently, vendors will sell support for an additional fee. Be sure you clearly understand the costs of obtaining support. Also, understand what is covered in support, and what is not covered. Anything that's not covered by support will be your responsibility to own and manage.

Releases and bug fixes

Is the vendor transparent about the release schedule, improvements, and bug fixes? Are these updates easily available to you?

Sales cycle and pricing

Often a vendor will offer on-demand pricing, especially for a SaaS product, and offer you a discount if you commit to an extended agreement. Be sure to understand the trade-offs of paying as you go versus paying up front. Is it worth paying a lump sum, or is your money better spent elsewhere?

Company finances

Is the company viable? If the company has raised VC funds, you can check their funding on sites like Crunchbase. How much runway does the company have, and will it still be in business in a couple of years?

Logos versus revenue

Is the company focused on growing the number of customers (logos), or is it trying to grow revenue? You may be surprised by the number of companies primarily concerned with growing their customer count, GitHub stars, or Slack channel membership without the revenue to establish sound finances.

Community support

Is the company truly supporting the community version of the OSS project? How much is the company contributing to the community OSS codebase? Controversies have arisen with certain vendors co-opting OSS projects and subsequently providing little value back to the community. How likely will the product remain viable as a community-supported open source if the company shuts down?

Note also that clouds offer their own managed open source products. If a cloud vendor sees traction with a particular product or project, expect that vendor to offer its version. This can range from simple examples (open source Linux offered on VMs) to extremely complex managed services (fully managed Kafka). The motivation for these offerings is simple: clouds make their money through consumption. More offerings in a cloud ecosystem mean a greater chance of "stickiness" and increased customer spending.

Proprietary Walled Gardens

While OSS is ubiquitous, a big market also exists for non-OSS technologies. Some of the biggest companies in the data industry sell closed source products. Let's look at two major types of *proprietary walled gardens*, independent companies and cloud-platform offerings.

Independent offerings

The data-tool landscape has seen exponential growth over the last several years. Every day, new independent offerings arise for data tools. With the ability to raise funds from VCs flush with capital, these data companies can scale and hire great engineering, sales, and marketing teams. This presents a situation where users have some great product choices in the marketplace while having to wade through endless sales and marketing clutter. At the time of this writing, the good times of freely available capital for data companies are coming to an end, but that's another long story whose consequences are still unfolding.

Often a company selling a data tool will not release it as OSS, instead offering a proprietary solution. Although you won't have the transparency of a pure OSS solution, a proprietary independent solution can work quite well, especially as a fully managed service in the cloud.

The following are things to consider with an independent offering:

Interoperability
    Make sure that the tool interoperates with other tools you've chosen (OSS, other independents, cloud offerings, etc.). Interoperability is key, so make sure you can try it before you buy.

Mindshare and market share
    Is the solution popular? Does it command a presence in the marketplace? Does it enjoy positive customer reviews?

Documentation and support

Problems and questions will inevitably arise. Is it clear how to solve your problem, either through documentation or support?

Pricing

Is the pricing understandable? Map out low-, medium-, and high-probability usage scenarios, with respective costs. Are you able to negotiate a contract, along with a discount? Is it worth it? How much flexibility do you lose if you sign a contract, both in negotiation and the ability to try new options? Are you able to obtain contractual commitments on future pricing?

Longevity

Will the company survive long enough for you to get value from its product? If the company has raised money, search around for its funding situation. Look at user reviews. Ask friends and post questions on social networks about users' experiences with the product. Make sure you know what you're getting into.

Cloud platform proprietary service offerings

Cloud vendors develop and sell their proprietary services for storage, databases, and more. Many of these solutions are internal tools used by respective sibling companies. For example, Amazon created the database DynamoDB to overcome the limitations of traditional relational databases and handle the large amounts of user and order data as Amazon.com grew into a behemoth. Amazon later offered the DynamoDB service solely on AWS; it's now a top-rated product used by companies of all sizes and maturity levels. Cloud vendors will often bundle their products to work well together. Each cloud can create stickiness with its user base by creating a strong integrated ecosystem.

The following are factors to consider with a proprietary cloud offering:

Performance versus price comparisons

Is the cloud offering substantially better than an independent or OSS version? What's the TCO of choosing a cloud's offering?

Purchase considerations

On-demand pricing can be expensive. Can you lower your cost by purchasing reserved capacity or entering into a long-term commitment agreement?

Our Advice

Build versus buy comes back to knowing your competitive advantage and where it makes sense to invest resources toward customization. In general, we favor OSS and COSS by default, which frees you to focus on improving those areas where these options are insufficient. Focus on a few areas where building something will add significant value or reduce friction substantially.

Don't treat internal operational overhead as a sunk cost. There's excellent value in upskilling your existing data team to build sophisticated systems on managed platforms rather than babysitting on-premises servers. In addition, think about how a company makes money, especially its sales and customer experience teams, which will generally indicate how you're treated during the sales cycle and when you're a paying customer.

Finally, who is responsible for the budget at your company? How does this person decide the projects and technologies that get funded? Before making the business case for COSS or managed services, does it make sense to try to use OSS first? The last thing you want is for your technology choice to be stuck in limbo while waiting for budget approval. As the old saying goes, *time kills deals.* In your case, more time spent in limbo means a higher likelihood your budget approval will die. Know beforehand who controls the budget and what will successfully get approved.

Monolith Versus Modular

Monoliths versus modular systems is another longtime debate in the software architecture space. Monolithic systems are self-contained, often performing multiple functions under a single system. The monolith camp favors the simplicity of having everything in one place. It's easier to reason about a single entity, and you can move faster because there are fewer moving parts. The *modular* camp leans toward decoupled, best-of-breed technologies performing tasks at which they are uniquely great. Especially given the rate of change in products in the data world, the argument is you should aim for interoperability among an ever-changing array of solutions.

What approach should you take in your data engineering stack? Let's explore the trade-offs.

Monolith

The *monolith* (Figure 4-4) has been a technology mainstay for decades. The old days of waterfall meant that software releases were huge, tightly coupled, and moved at a slow cadence. Large teams worked together to deliver a single working codebase. Monolithic data systems continue to this day, with older software vendors such as Informatica and open source frameworks such as Spark.

The pros of the monolith are it's easy to reason about, and it requires a lower cognitive burden and context switching since everything is self-contained. Instead of dealing with dozens of technologies, you deal with "one" technology and typically one principal programming language. Monoliths are an excellent option if you want simplicity in reasoning about your architecture and processes.

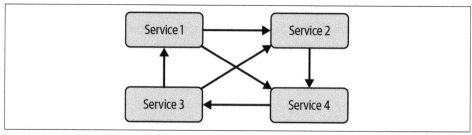

Figure 4-4. The monolith tightly couples its services

Of course, the monolith has cons. For one thing, monoliths are brittle. Because of the vast number of moving parts, updates and releases take longer and tend to bake in "the kitchen sink." If the system has a bug—hopefully, the software's been thoroughly tested before release!—it can harm the entire system.

User-induced problems also happen with monoliths. For example, we saw a monolithic ETL pipeline that took 48 hours to run. If anything broke anywhere in the pipeline, the entire process had to restart. Meanwhile, anxious business users were waiting for their reports, which were already two days late by default and usually arrived much later. Breakages were common enough that the monolithic system was eventually thrown out.

Multitenancy in a monolithic system can also be a significant problem. It can be challenging to isolate the workloads of multiple users. In an on-prem data warehouse, one user-defined function might consume enough CPU to slow the system for other users. Conflicts between dependencies and resource contention are frequent sources of headaches.

Another con of monoliths is that switching to a new system will be painful if the vendor or open source project dies. Because all of your processes are contained in the monolith, extracting yourself out of that system, and onto a new platform, will be costly in both time and money.

Modularity

Modularity (Figure 4-5) is an old concept in software engineering, but modular distributed systems truly came into vogue with the rise of microservices. Instead of relying on a massive monolith to handle your needs, why not break apart systems and processes into their self-contained areas of concern? Microservices can communicate via APIs, allowing developers to focus on their domains while making their applications accessible to other microservices. This is the trend in software engineering and is increasingly seen in modern data systems.

Figure 4-5. With modularity, each service is decoupled from another

Major tech companies have been key drivers in the microservices movement. The famous Bezos API mandate decreases coupling between applications, allowing refactoring and decomposition. Bezos also imposed the two-pizza rule (no team should be so large that two pizzas can't feed the whole group). Effectively, this means that a team will have at most five members. This cap also limits the complexity of a team's domain of responsibility—in particular, the codebase that it can manage. Whereas an extensive monolithic application might entail a group of one hundred people, dividing developers into small groups of five requires that this application be broken into small, manageable, loosely coupled pieces.

In a modular microservice environment, components are swappable, and it's possible to create a *polyglot* (multiprogramming language) application; a Java service can replace a service written in Python. Service customers need worry only about the technical specifications of the service API, not behind-the-scenes details of implementation.

Data-processing technologies have shifted toward a modular model by providing strong support for interoperability. Data is stored in object storage in a standard format such as Parquet in data lakes and lakehouses. Any processing tool that supports the format can read the data and write processed results back into the lake for processing by another tool. Cloud data warehouses support interoperation with object storage through import/export using standard formats and external tables—i.e., queries run directly on data in a data lake.

New technologies arrive on the scene at a dizzying rate in today's data ecosystem, and most get stale and outmoded quickly. Rinse and repeat. The ability to swap out tools as technology changes is invaluable. We view data modularity as a more powerful paradigm than monolithic data engineering. Modularity allows engineers to choose the best technology for each job or step along the pipeline.

The cons of modularity are that there's more to reason about. Instead of handling a single system of concern, now you potentially have countless systems to understand and operate. Interoperability is a potential headache; hopefully, these systems all play nicely together.

This very problem led us to break out orchestration as a separate undercurrent instead of placing it under data management. Orchestration is also important for monolithic data architectures; witness the success of tools like BMC Software's Control-M in the traditional data warehousing space. But orchestrating five or ten tools is dramatically more complex than orchestrating one. Orchestration becomes the glue that binds data stack modules together.

The Distributed Monolith Pattern

The *distributed monolith pattern* is a distributed architecture that still suffers from many of the limitations of monolithic architecture. The basic idea is that one runs a distributed system with different services to perform different tasks. Still, services and nodes share a common set of dependencies or a common codebase.

One standard example is a traditional Hadoop cluster. A Hadoop cluster can simultaneously host several frameworks, such as Hive, Pig, or Spark. The cluster also has many internal dependencies. In addition, the cluster runs core Hadoop components: Hadoop common libraries, HDFS, YARN, and Java. In practice, a cluster often has one version of each component installed.

A standard on-prem Hadoop system entails managing a common environment that works for all users and all jobs. Managing upgrades and installations is a significant challenge. Forcing jobs to upgrade dependencies risks breaking them; maintaining two versions of a framework entails extra complexity.

Some modern Python-based orchestration technologies—e.g., Apache Airflow—also suffer from this problem. While they utilize a highly decoupled and asynchronous architecture, every service runs the same codebase with the same dependencies. Any executor can execute any task, so a client library for a single task run in one DAG must be installed on the whole cluster. Orchestrating many tools entails installing client libraries for a host of APIs. Dependency conflicts are a constant problem.

One solution to the problems of the distributed monolith is ephemeral infrastructure in a cloud setting. Each job gets its own temporary server or cluster installed with dependencies. Each cluster remains highly monolithic, but separating jobs dramatically reduces conflicts. For example, this pattern is now quite common for Spark with services like Amazon EMR and Google Cloud Dataproc.

A second solution is to properly decompose the distributed monolith into multiple software environments using containers. We have more to say on containers in "Serverless Versus Servers" on page 147.

Our Advice

While monoliths are attractive because of ease of understanding and reduced complexity, this comes at a high cost. The cost is the potential loss of flexibility, opportunity cost, and high-friction development cycles.

Here are some things to consider when evaluating monoliths versus modular options:

Interoperability
    Architect for sharing and interoperability.

Avoiding the "bear trap"
    Something that is easy to get into might be painful or impossible to escape.

Flexibility
    Things are moving so fast in the data space right now. Committing to a monolith reduces flexibility and reversible decisions.

Serverless Versus Servers

A big trend for cloud providers is *serverless*, allowing developers and data engineers to run applications without managing servers behind the scenes. Serverless provides a quick time to value for the right use cases. For other cases, it might not be a good fit. Let's look at how to evaluate whether serverless is right for you.

Serverless

Though serverless has been around for quite some time, the serverless trend kicked off in full force with AWS Lambda in 2014. With the promise of executing small chunks of code on an as-needed basis without having to manage a server, serverless exploded in popularity. The main reasons for its popularity are cost and convenience. Instead of paying the cost of a server, why not just pay when your code is evoked?

Serverless has many flavors. Though function as a service (FaaS) is wildly popular, serverless systems predate the advent of AWS Lambda. For example, Google Cloud's BigQuery is serverless in that data engineers don't need to manage backend infrastructure, and the system scales to zero and scales up automatically to handle large queries. Just load data into the system and start querying. You pay for the amount of data your query consumes and a small cost to store your data. This payment model—paying for consumption and storage—is becoming more prevalent.

When does serverless make sense? As with many other cloud services, it depends; and data engineers would do well to understand the details of cloud pricing to predict when serverless deployments will become expensive. Looking specifically at the case of AWS Lambda, various engineers have found hacks to run batch workloads at meager costs.[11] On the other hand, serverless functions suffer from an inherent overhead inefficiency. Handling one event per function call at a high event rate can be catastrophically expensive, especially when simpler approaches like multithreading or multiprocessing are great alternatives.

---

11 Evan Sangaline, "Running FFmpeg on AWS Lambda for 1.9% the Cost of AWS Elastic Transcoder," Intoli blog, May 2, 2018, *https://oreil.ly/myzOv*.

As with other areas of ops, it's critical to monitor and model. *Monitor* to determine cost per event in a real-world environment and maximum length of serverless execution, and *model* using this cost per event to determine overall costs as event rates grow. Modeling should also include worst-case scenarios—what happens if my site gets hit by a bot swarm or DDoS attack?

Containers

In conjunction with serverless and microservices, *containers* are one of the most powerful trending operational technologies as of this writing. Containers play a role in both serverless and microservices.

Containers are often referred to as *lightweight virtual machines*. Whereas a traditional VM wraps up an entire operating system, a container packages an isolated user space (such as a filesystem and a few processes); many such containers can coexist on a single host operating system. This provides some of the principal benefits of virtualization (i.e., dependency and code isolation) without the overhead of carrying around an entire operating system kernel.

A single hardware node can host numerous containers with fine-grained resource allocations. At the time of this writing, containers continue to grow in popularity, along with Kubernetes, a container management system. Serverless environments typically run on containers behind the scenes. Indeed, Kubernetes is a kind of serverless environment because it allows developers and ops teams to deploy microservices without worrying about the details of the machines where they are deployed.

Containers provide a partial solution to problems of the distributed monolith mentioned earlier in this chapter. For example, Hadoop now supports containers, allowing each job to have its own isolated dependencies.

Container clusters do not provide the same security and isolation that full VMs offer. *Container escape*—broadly, a class of exploits whereby code in a container gains privileges outside the container at the OS level—is common enough to be considered a risk for multitenancy. While Amazon EC2 is a truly multitenant environment with VMs from many customers hosted on the same hardware, a Kubernetes cluster should host code only within an environment of mutual trust (e.g., inside the walls of a single company). In addition, code review processes and vulnerability scanning are critical to ensure that a developer doesn't introduce a security hole.

Various flavors of container platforms add additional serverless features. Containerized function platforms run containers as ephemeral units triggered by events rather than persistent services.[12] This gives users the simplicity of AWS Lambda with the full flexibility of a container environment instead of the highly restrictive Lambda runtime. And services such as AWS Fargate and Google App Engine run containers without managing a compute cluster required for Kubernetes. These services also fully isolate containers, preventing the security issues associated with multitenancy.

Abstraction will continue working its way across the data stack. Consider the impact of Kubernetes on cluster management. While you can manage your Kubernetes cluster—and many engineering teams do so—even Kubernetes is widely available as a managed service. What comes after Kubernetes? We're as excited as you to find out.

How to Evaluate Server Versus Serverless

Why would you want to run your own servers instead of using serverless? There are a few reasons. Cost is a big factor. Serverless makes less sense when the usage and cost exceed the ongoing cost of running and maintaining a server (Figure 4-6). However, at a certain scale, the economic benefits of serverless may diminish, and running servers becomes more attractive.

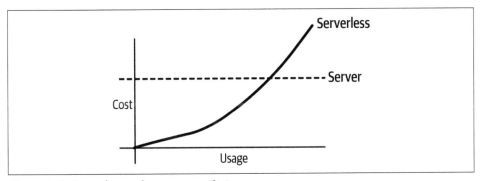

Figure 4-6. Cost of serverless versus utilizing a server

Customization, power, and control are other major reasons to favor servers over serverless. Some serverless frameworks can be underpowered or limited for certain use cases. Here are some things to consider when using servers, particularly in the cloud, where server resources are ephemeral:

Expect servers to fail.
  Server failure will happen. Avoid using a "special snowflake" server that is overly customized and brittle, as this introduces a glaring vulnerability in your architecture. Instead, treat servers as ephemeral resources that you can create as needed and then delete. If your application requires specific code to be installed on the

---

12 Examples include OpenFaaS (*http://www.openfaas.com*), Knative (*https://oreil.ly/0pT3m*), and Google Cloud Run (*https://oreil.ly/imWhI*).

server, use a boot script or build an image. Deploy code to the server through a CI/CD pipeline.

Use clusters and autoscaling.
Take advantage of the cloud's ability to grow and shrink compute resources on demand. As your application increases its usage, cluster your application servers, and use autoscaling capabilities to automatically horizontally scale your application as demand grows.

Treat your infrastructure as code.
Automation doesn't apply to just servers and should extend to your infrastructure whenever possible. Deploy your infrastructure (servers or otherwise) using deployment managers such as Terraform, AWS CloudFormation, and Google Cloud Deployment Manager.

Use containers.
For more sophisticated or heavy-duty workloads with complex installed dependencies, consider using containers on either a single server or Kubernetes.

Our Advice

Here are some key considerations to help you determine whether serverless is right for you:

Workload size and complexity
Serverless works best for simple, discrete tasks and workloads. It's not as suitable if you have many moving parts or require a lot of compute or memory horsepower. In that case, consider using containers and a container workflow orchestration framework like Kubernetes.

Execution frequency and duration
How many requests per second will your serverless application process? How long will each request take to process? Cloud serverless platforms have limits on execution frequency, concurrency, and duration. If your application can't function neatly within these limits, it is time to consider a container-oriented approach.

Requests and networking
Serverless platforms often utilize some form of simplified networking and don't support all cloud virtual networking features, such as VPCs and firewalls.

Language
What language do you typically use? If it's not one of the officially supported languages supported by the serverless platform, you should consider containers instead.

Runtime limitations

Serverless platforms don't give you complete operating system abstractions. Instead, you're limited to a specific runtime image.

Cost

Serverless functions are incredibly convenient but potentially expensive. When your serverless function processes only a few events, your costs are low; costs rise rapidly as the event count increases. This scenario is a frequent source of surprise cloud bills.

In the end, abstraction tends to win. We suggest looking at using serverless first and then servers—with containers and orchestration if possible—once you've outgrown serverless options.

Optimization, Performance, and the Benchmark Wars

Imagine that you are a billionaire shopping for new transportation. You've narrowed your choice to two options:

- 787 Business Jet
    - Range: 9,945 nautical miles (with 25 passengers)
    - Maximum speed: 0.90 Mach
    - Cruise speed: 0.85 Mach
    - Fuel capacity: 101,323 kilograms
    - Maximum takeoff weight: 227,930 kilograms
    - Maximum thrust: 128,000 pounds
- Tesla Model S Plaid
    - Range: 560 kilometers
    - Maximum speed: 322 kilometers/hour
    - 0–100 kilometers/hour: 2.1 seconds
    - Battery capacity: 100 kilowatt hours
    - Nurburgring lap time: 7 minutes, 30.9 seconds
    - Horsepower: 1020
    - Torque: 1050 lb-ft

Which of these options offers better performance? You don't have to know much about cars or aircraft to recognize that this is an idiotic comparison. One option is a wide-body private jet designed for intercontinental operation, while the other is an electric supercar.

We see such apples-to-oranges comparisons made all the time in the database space. Benchmarks either compare databases that are optimized for completely different use cases, or use test scenarios that bear no resemblance to real-world needs.

Recently, we saw a new round of benchmark wars flare up among major vendors in the data space. We applaud benchmarks and are glad to see many database vendors finally dropping DeWitt clauses from their customer contracts.[13] Even so, let the buyer beware: the data space is full of nonsensical benchmarks.[14] Here are a few common tricks used to place a thumb on the benchmark scale.

Big Data…for the 1990s

Products that claim to support "big data" at petabyte scale will often use benchmark datasets small enough to easily fit in the storage on your smartphone. For systems that rely on caching layers to deliver performance, test datasets fully reside in solid-state drive (SSD) or memory, and benchmarks can show ultra-high performance by repeatedly querying the same data. A small test dataset also minimizes RAM and SSD costs when comparing pricing.

To benchmark for real-world use cases, you must simulate anticipated real-world data and query size. Evaluate query performance and resource costs based on a detailed evaluation of your needs.

Nonsensical Cost Comparisons

Nonsensical cost comparisons are a standard trick when analyzing a price/performance or TCO. For instance, many MPP systems can't be readily created and deleted even when they reside in a cloud environment; these systems run for years on end once they've been configured. Other databases support a dynamic compute model and charge either per query or per second of use. Comparing ephemeral and non-ephemeral systems on a cost-per-second basis is nonsensical, but we see this all the time in benchmarks.

Asymmetric Optimization

The deceit of asymmetric optimization appears in many guises, but here's one example. Often a vendor will compare a row-based MPP system against a columnar database by using a benchmark that runs complex join queries on highly normalized data. The normalized data model is optimal for the row-based system, but the columnar

---

13 Justin Olsson and Reynold Xin, "Eliminating the Anti-competitive DeWitt Clause for Database Benchmarking," Databricks, November 8, 2021, *https://oreil.ly/3iFOE*.

14 For a classic of the genre, see William McKnight and Jake Dolezal, "Data Warehouse in the Cloud Benchmark," GigaOm, February 7, 2019, *https://oreil.ly/QjCmA*.

---

system would realize its full potential only with some schema changes. To make matters worse, vendors juice their systems with an extra shot of join optimization (e.g., preindexing joins) without applying comparable tuning in the competing database (e.g., putting joins in a materialized view).

Caveat Emptor

As with all things in data technology, let the buyer beware. Do your homework before blindly relying on vendor benchmarks to evaluate and choose technology.

Undercurrents and Their Impacts on Choosing Technologies

As seen in this chapter, a data engineer has a lot to consider when evaluating technologies. Whatever technology you choose, be sure to understand how it supports the undercurrents of the data engineering lifecycle. Let's briefly review them again.

Data Management

Data management is a broad area, and concerning technologies, it isn't always apparent whether a technology adopts data management as a principal concern. For example, behind the scenes, a third-party vendor may use data management best practices—regulatory compliance, security, privacy, data quality, and governance—but hide these details behind a limited UI layer. In this case, while evaluating the product, it helps to ask the company about its data management practices. Here are some sample questions you should ask:

- How are you protecting data against breaches, both from the outside and within?
- What is your product's compliance with GDPR, CCPA, and other data privacy regulations?
- Do you allow me to host my data to comply with these regulations?
- How do you ensure data quality and that I'm viewing the correct data in your solution?

There are many other questions to ask, and these are just a few of the ways to think about data management as it relates to choosing the right technologies. These same questions should also apply to the OSS solutions you're considering.

DataOps

Problems will happen. They just will. A server or database may die, a cloud's region may have an outage, you might deploy buggy code, bad data might be introduced into your data warehouse, and other unforeseen problems may occur.

When evaluating a new technology, how much control do you have over deploying new code, how will you be alerted if there's a problem, and how will you respond when there's a problem? The answer largely depends on the type of technology you're considering. If the technology is OSS, you're likely responsible for setting up monitoring, hosting, and code deployment. How will you handle issues? What's your incident response?

Much of the operations are outside your control if you're using a managed offering. Consider the vendor's SLA, the way they alert you to issues, and whether they're transparent about how they're addressing the case, including providing an ETA to a fix.

Data Architecture

As discussed in Chapter 3, good data architecture means assessing trade-offs and choosing the best tools for the job while keeping your decisions reversible. With the data landscape morphing at warp speed, the *best tool* for the job is a moving target. The main goals are to avoid unnecessary lock-in, ensure interoperability across the data stack, and produce high ROI. Choose your technologies accordingly.

Orchestration Example: Airflow

Throughout most of this chapter, we have actively avoided discussing any particular technology too extensively. We make an exception for orchestration because the space is currently dominated by one open source technology, Apache Airflow.

Maxime Beauchemin kicked off the Airflow project at Airbnb in 2014. Airflow was developed from the beginning as a noncommercial open source project. The framework quickly grew significant mindshare outside Airbnb, becoming an Apache Incubator project in 2016 and a full Apache-sponsored project in 2019.

Airflow enjoys many advantages, largely because of its dominant position in the open source marketplace. First, the Airflow open source project is extremely active, with a high rate of commits and a quick response time for bugs and security issues, and the project recently released Airflow 2, a major refactor of the codebase. Second, Airflow enjoys massive mindshare. Airflow has a vibrant, active community on many communications platforms, including Slack, Stack Overflow, and GitHub. Users can easily find answers to questions and problems. Third, Airflow is available commercially as a managed service or software distribution through many vendors, including GCP, AWS, and Astronomer.io.

Airflow also has some downsides. Airflow relies on a few core nonscalable components (the scheduler and backend database) that can become bottlenecks for performance, scale, and reliability; the scalable parts of Airflow still follow a distributed monolith pattern. (See "Monolith Versus Modular" on page 143.) Finally, Airflow

---

lacks support for many data-native constructs, such as schema management, lineage, and cataloging; and it is challenging to develop and test Airflow workflows.

We do not attempt an exhaustive discussion of Airflow alternatives here but just mention a couple of the key orchestration contenders at the time of writing. Prefect and Dagster aim to solve some of the problems discussed previously by rethinking components of the Airflow architecture. Will there be other orchestration frameworks and technologies not discussed here? Plan on it.

We highly recommend that anyone choosing an orchestration technology study the options discussed here. They should also acquaint themselves with activity in the space, as new developments will certainly occur by the time you read this.

Software Engineering

As a data engineer, you should strive for simplification and abstraction across the data stack. Buy or use prebuilt open source solutions whenever possible. Eliminating undifferentiated heavy lifting should be your big goal. Focus your resources—custom coding and tooling—on areas that give you a solid competitive advantage. For example, is hand-coding a database connection between your production database and your cloud data warehouse a competitive advantage for you? Probably not. This is very much a solved problem. Pick an off-the-shelf solution (open source or managed SaaS) instead. The world doesn't need the millionth +1 database-to-cloud data warehouse connector.

On the other hand, why do customers buy from you? Your business likely has something special about the way it does things. Maybe it's a particular algorithm that powers your fintech platform. By abstracting away a lot of the redundant workflows and processes, you can continue chipping away, refining, and customizing the things that move the needle for the business.

Conclusion

Choosing the right technologies is no easy task, especially when new technologies and patterns emerge daily. Today is possibly the most confusing time in history for evaluating and selecting technologies. Choosing technologies is a balance of use case, cost, build versus buy, and modularization. Always approach technology the same way as architecture: assess trade-offs and aim for reversible decisions.

Additional Resources

- *Cloud FinOps* by J. R. Storment and Mike Fuller (O'Reilly)
- "Cloud Infrastructure: The Definitive Guide for Beginners" (*https://oreil.ly/jyJpz*) by Matthew Smith

- "The Cost of Cloud, a Trillion Dollar Paradox" (*https://oreil.ly/WjvOT*) by Sarah Wang and Martin Casado
- FinOps Foundation's "What Is FinOps" web page (*https://oreil.ly/TO0Oz*)
- "Red Hot: The 2021 Machine Learning, AI and Data (MAD) Landscape" (*https://oreil.ly/aAy5z*) by Matt Turck
- Ternary Data's "What's Next for Analytical Databases? w/ Jordan Tigani (Mother-Duck)" video (*https://oreil.ly/8C4Gj*)
- "The Unfulfilled Promise of Serverless" (*https://oreil.ly/aF8zE*) by Corey Quinn
- "What Is the Modern Data Stack?" (*https://oreil.ly/PL3Yx*) by Charles Wang

PART II

The Data Engineering Lifecycle in Depth

CHAPTER 5

Data Generation in Source Systems

Welcome to the first stage of the data engineering lifecycle: data generation in source systems. As we described earlier, the job of a data engineer is to take data from source systems, do something with it, and make it helpful in serving downstream use cases. But before you get raw data, you must understand where the data exists, how it is generated, and its characteristics and quirks.

This chapter covers some popular operational source system patterns and the significant types of source systems. Many source systems exist for data generation, and we're not exhaustively covering them all. We'll consider the data these systems generate and things you should consider when working with source systems. We also discuss how the undercurrents of data engineering apply to this first phase of the data engineering lifecycle (Figure 5-1).

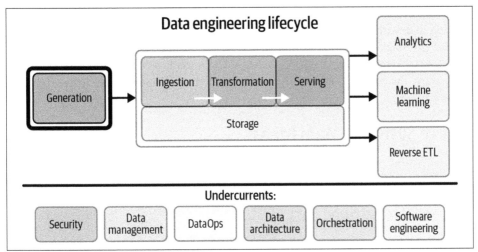

Figure 5-1. Source systems generate the data for the rest of the data engineering lifecycle

As data proliferates, especially with the rise of data sharing (discussed next), we expect that a data engineer's role will shift heavily toward understanding the interplay between data sources and destinations. The basic plumbing tasks of data engineering—moving data from A to B—will simplify dramatically. On the other hand, it will remain critical to understand the nature of data as it's created in source systems.

Sources of Data: How Is Data Created?

As you learn about the various underlying operational patterns of the systems that generate data, it's essential to understand how data is created. Data is an unorganized, context-less collection of facts and figures. It can be created in many ways, both analog and digital.

Analog data creation occurs in the real world, such as vocal speech, sign language, writing on paper, or playing an instrument. This analog data is often transient; how often have you had a verbal conversation whose contents are lost to the ether after the conversation ends?

Digital data is either created by converting analog data to digital form or is the native product of a digital system. An example of analog to digital is a mobile texting app that converts analog speech into digital text. An example of digital data creation is a credit card transaction on an ecommerce platform. A customer places an order, the transaction is charged to their credit card, and the information for the transaction is saved to various databases.

We'll utilize a few common examples in this chapter, such as data created when interacting with a website or mobile application. But in truth, data is everywhere in the world around us. We capture data from IoT devices, credit card terminals, telescope sensors, stock trades, and more.

Get familiar with your source system and how it generates data. Put in the effort to read the source system documentation and understand its patterns and quirks. If your source system is an RDBMS, learn how it operates (writes, commits, queries, etc.); learn the ins and outs of the source system that might affect your ability to ingest from it.

Source Systems: Main Ideas

Source systems produce data in various ways. This section discusses the main ideas you'll frequently encounter as you work with source systems.

Files and Unstructured Data

A *file* is a sequence of bytes, typically stored on a disk. Applications often write data to files. Files may store local parameters, events, logs, images, and audio.

In addition, files are a universal medium of data exchange. As much as data engineers wish that they could get data programmatically, much of the world still sends and receives files. For example, if you're getting data from a government agency, there's an excellent chance you'll download the data as an Excel or CSV file or receive the file in an email.

The main types of source file formats you'll run into as a data engineer—files that originate either manually or as an output from a source system process—are Excel, CSV, TXT, JSON, and XML. These files have their quirks and can be structured (Excel, CSV), semistructured (JSON, XML, CSV), or unstructured (TXT, CSV). Although you'll use certain formats heavily as a data engineer (such as Parquet, ORC, and Avro), we'll cover these later and put the spotlight here on source system files. Chapter 6 covers the technical details of files.

APIs

Application programming interfaces (APIs) are a standard way of exchanging data between systems. In theory, APIs simplify the data ingestion task for data engineers. In practice, many APIs still expose a good deal of data complexity for engineers to manage. Even with the rise of various services and frameworks, and services for automating API data ingestion, data engineers must often invest a good deal of energy into maintaining custom API connections. We discuss APIs in greater detail later in this chapter.

Application Databases (OLTP Systems)

An *application database* stores the state of an application. A standard example is a database that stores account balances for bank accounts. As customer transactions and payments happen, the application updates bank account balances.

Typically, an application database is an *online transaction processing* (OLTP) system—a database that reads and writes individual data records at a high rate. OLTP systems are often referred to as *transactional databases*, but this does not necessarily imply that the system in question supports *atomic transactions*.

More generally, OLTP databases support low latency and high concurrency. An RDBMS database can select or update a row in less than a millisecond (not accounting for network latency) and handle thousands of reads and writes per second. A document database cluster can manage even higher document commit rates at the expense of potential inconsistency. Some graph databases can also handle transactional use cases.

Fundamentally, OLTP databases work well as application backends when thousands or even millions of users might be interacting with the application simultaneously, updating and writing data concurrently. OLTP systems are less suited to use cases driven by analytics at scale, where a single query must scan a vast amount of data.

ACID

Support for atomic transactions is one of a critical set of database characteristics known together as ACID (as you may recall from Chapter 3, this stands for *atomicity, consistency, isolation, durability*). *Consistency* means that any database read will return the last written version of the retrieved item. *Isolation* entails that if two updates are in flight concurrently for the same thing, the end database state will be consistent with the sequential execution of these updates in the order they were submitted. *Durability* indicates that committed data will never be lost, even in the event of power loss.

Note that ACID characteristics are not required to support application backends, and relaxing these constraints can be a considerable boon to performance and scale. However, ACID characteristics guarantee that the database will maintain a consistent picture of the world, dramatically simplifying the app developer's task.

All engineers (data or otherwise) must understand operating with and without ACID. For instance, to improve performance, some distributed databases use relaxed consistency constraints, such as *eventual consistency*, to improve performance. Understanding the consistency model you're working with helps you prevent disasters.

Atomic transactions

An *atomic transaction* is a set of several changes that are committed as a unit. In the example in Figure 5-2, a traditional banking application running on an RDBMS executes a SQL statement that checks two account balances, one in Account A (the source) and another in Account B (the destination). Money is then moved from Account A to Account B if sufficient funds are in Account A. The entire transaction should run with updates to both account balances or fail without updating either account balance. That is, the whole operation should happen as a *transaction*.

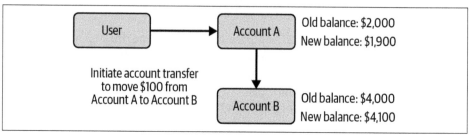

Figure 5-2. Example of an atomic transaction: a bank account transfer using OLTP

OLTP and analytics

Often, small companies run analytics directly on an OLTP. This pattern works in the short term but is ultimately not scalable. At some point, running analytical queries on OLTP runs into performance issues due to structural limitations of OLTP or resource contention with competing transactional workloads. Data engineers must understand the inner workings of OLTP and application backends to set up appropriate integrations with analytics systems without degrading production application performance.

As companies offer more analytics capabilities in SaaS applications, the need for hybrid capabilities—quick updates with combined analytics capabilities—has created new challenges for data engineers. We'll use the term *data application* to refer to applications that hybridize transactional and analytics workloads.

Online Analytical Processing System

In contrast to an OLTP system, an *online analytical processing* (OLAP) system is built to run large analytics queries and is typically inefficient at handling lookups of individual records. For example, modern column databases are optimized to scan large volumes of data, dispensing with indexes to improve scalability and scan performance. Any query typically involves scanning a minimal data block, often 100 MB or more in size. Trying to look up thousands of individual items per second in such a system will bring it to its knees unless it is combined with a caching layer designed for this use case.

Note that we're using the term *OLAP* to refer to any database system that supports high-scale interactive analytics queries; we are not limiting ourselves to systems that support OLAP cubes (multidimensional arrays of data). The *online* part of OLAP implies that the system constantly listens for incoming queries, making OLAP systems suitable for interactive analytics.

Although this chapter covers source systems, OLAPs are typically storage and query systems for analytics. Why are we talking about them in our chapter on source systems? In practical use cases, engineers often need to read data from an OLAP system. For example, a data warehouse might serve data used to train an ML model. Or, an OLAP system might serve a reverse ETL workflow, where derived data in an analytics system is sent back to a source system, such as a CRM, SaaS platform, or transactional application.

Change Data Capture

Change data capture (CDC) is a method for extracting each change event (insert, update, delete) that occurs in a database. CDC is frequently leveraged to replicate between databases in near real time or create an event stream for downstream processing.

CDC is handled differently depending on the database technology. Relational databases often generate an event log stored directly on the database server that can be processed to create a stream. (See "Database Logs" on page 165.) Many cloud NoSQL databases can send a log or event stream to a target storage location.

Logs

A *log* captures information about events that occur in systems. For example, a log may capture traffic and usage patterns on a web server. Your desktop computer's operating system (Windows, macOS, Linux) logs events as the system boots and when applications start or crash, for example.

Logs are a rich data source, potentially valuable for downstream data analysis, ML, and automation. Here are a few familiar sources of logs:

- Operating systems
- Applications
- Servers
- Containers
- Networks
- IoT devices

All logs track events and event metadata. At a minimum, a log should capture who, what, and when:

Who
> The human, system, or service account associated with the event (e.g., a web browser user agent or a user ID)

What happened
> The event and related metadata

When
> The timestamp of the event

Log encoding

Logs are encoded in a few ways:

Binary-encoded logs
> These encode data in a custom compact format for space efficiency and fast I/O. Database logs, discussed in "Database Logs" on page 165, are a standard example.

Semistructured logs

These are encoded as text in an object serialization format (JSON, more often than not). Semistructured logs are machine-readable and portable. However, they are much less efficient than binary logs. And though they are nominally machine-readable, extracting value from them often requires significant custom code.

Plain-text (unstructured) logs

These essentially store the console output from software. As such, no general-purpose standards exist. These logs can provide helpful information for data scientists and ML engineers, though extracting useful information from the raw text data might be complicated.

Log resolution

Logs are created at various resolutions and log levels. The log *resolution* refers to the amount of event data captured in a log. For example, database logs capture enough information from database events to allow reconstructing the database state at any point in time.

On the other hand, capturing all data changes in logs for a big data system often isn't practical. Instead, these logs may note only that a particular type of commit event has occurred. The *log level* refers to the conditions required to record a log entry, specifically concerning errors and debugging. Software is often configurable to log every event or to log only errors, for example.

Log latency: Batch or real time

Batch logs are often written continuously to a file. Individual log entries can be written to a messaging system such as Kafka or Pulsar for real-time applications.

Database Logs

Database logs are essential enough that they deserve more detailed coverage. Write-ahead logs—typically, binary files stored in a specific database-native format—play a crucial role in database guarantees and recoverability. The database server receives write and update requests to a database table (see Figure 5-3), storing each operation in the log before acknowledging the request. The acknowledgment comes with a log-associated guarantee: even if the server fails, it can recover its state on reboot by completing the unfinished work from the logs.

Database logs are extremely useful in data engineering, especially for CDC to generate event streams from database changes.

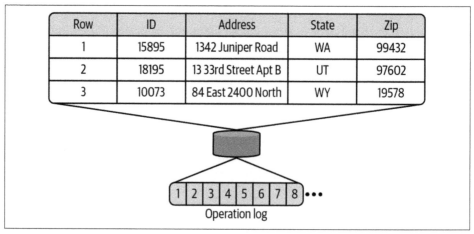

Row	ID	Address	State	Zip
1	15895	1342 Juniper Road	WA	99432
2	18195	13 33rd Street Apt B	UT	97602
3	10073	84 East 2400 North	WY	19578

```
1 2 3 4 5 6 7 8 •••
```
Operation log

Figure 5-3. Database logs record operations on a table

CRUD

CRUD, which stands for *create*, *read*, *update*, and *delete*, is a transactional pattern commonly used in programming and represents the four basic operations of persistent storage. CRUD is the most common pattern for storing application state in a database. A basic tenet of CRUD is that data must be created before being used. After the data has been created, the data can be read and updated. Finally, the data may need to be destroyed. CRUD guarantees these four operations will occur on data, regardless of its storage.

CRUD is a widely used pattern in software applications, and you'll commonly find CRUD used in APIs and databases. For example, a web application will make heavy use of CRUD for RESTful HTTP requests and storing and retrieving data from a database.

As with any database, we can use snapshot-based extraction to get data from a database where our application applies CRUD operations. On the other hand, event extraction with CDC gives us a complete history of operations and potentially allows for near real-time analytics.

Insert-Only

The *insert-only pattern* retains history directly in a table containing data. Rather than updating records, new records get inserted with a timestamp indicating when they were created (Table 5-1). For example, suppose you have a table of customer addresses. Following a CRUD pattern, you would simply update the record if the customer changed their address. With the insert-only pattern, a new address record is inserted with the same customer ID. To read the current customer address by customer ID, you would look up the latest record under that ID.

Table 5-1. An insert-only pattern produces multiple versions of a record

Record ID	Value	Timestamp
1	40	2021-09-19T00:10:23+00:00
1	51	2021-09-30T00:12:00+00:00

In a sense, the insert-only pattern maintains a database log directly in the table itself, making it especially useful if the application needs access to history. For example, the insert-only pattern would work well for a banking application designed to present customer address history.

A separate analytics insert-only pattern is often used with regular CRUD application tables. In the insert-only ETL pattern, data pipelines insert a new record in the target analytics table anytime an update occurs in the CRUD table.

Insert-only has a couple of disadvantages. First, tables can grow quite large, especially if data frequently changes, since each change is inserted into the table. Sometimes records are purged based on a record sunset date or a maximum number of record versions to keep table size reasonable. The second disadvantage is that record lookups incur extra overhead because looking up the current state involves running MAX (created_timestamp). If hundreds or thousands of records are under a single ID, this lookup operation is expensive to run.

Messages and Streams

Related to event-driven architecture, two terms that you'll often see used interchangeably are *message queue* and *streaming platform*, but a subtle but essential difference exists between the two. Defining and contrasting these terms is worthwhile since they encompass many big ideas related to source systems and practices and technologies spanning the entire data engineering lifecycle.

A *message* is raw data communicated across two or more systems (Figure 5-4). For example, we have System 1 and System 2, where System 1 sends a message to System 2. These systems could be different microservices, a server sending a message to a serverless function, etc. A message is typically sent through a *message queue* from a publisher to a consumer, and once the message is delivered, it is removed from the queue.

Figure 5-4. A message passed between two systems

Messages are discrete and singular signals in an event-driven system. For example, an IoT device might send a message with the latest temperature reading to a message queue. This message is then ingested by a service that determines whether the furnace should be turned on or off. This service sends a message to a furnace controller that takes the appropriate action. Once the message is received, and the action is taken, the message is removed from the message queue.

By contrast, a *stream* is an append-only log of event records. (Streams are ingested and stored in *event-streaming platforms*, which we discuss at greater length in "Message Queues and Event-Streaming Platforms" on page 259.) As events occur, they are accumulated in an ordered sequence (Figure 5-5); a timestamp or an ID might order events. (Note that events aren't always delivered in exact order because of the subtleties of distributed systems.)

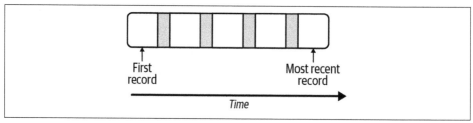

Figure 5-5. A stream, which is an ordered append-only log of records

You'll use streams when you care about what happened over many events. Because of the append-only nature of streams, records in a stream are persisted over a long retention window—often weeks or months—allowing for complex operations on records such as aggregations on multiple records or the ability to rewind to a point in time within the stream.

It's worth noting that systems that process streams can process messages, and streaming platforms are frequently used for message passing. We often accumulate messages in streams when we want to perform message analytics. In our IoT example, the temperature readings that trigger the furnace to turn on or off might also be later analyzed to determine temperature trends and statistics.

Types of Time

While time is an essential consideration for all data ingestion, it becomes that much more critical and subtle in the context of streaming, where we view data as continuous and expect to consume it shortly after it is produced. Let's look at the key types of time you'll run into when ingesting data: the time that the event is generated, when it's ingested and processed, and how long processing took (Figure 5-6).

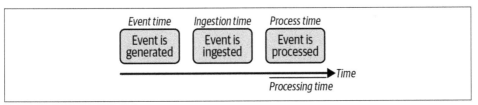

Figure 5-6. Event, ingestion, process, and processing time

Event time indicates when an event is generated in a source system, including the timestamp of the original event itself. An undetermined time lag will occur upon event creation, before the event is ingested and processed downstream. Always include timestamps for each phase through which an event travels. Log events as they occur and at each stage of time—when they're created, ingested, and processed. Use these timestamp logs to accurately track the movement of your data through your data pipelines.

After data is created, it is ingested somewhere. *Ingestion time* indicates when an event is ingested from source systems into a message queue, cache, memory, object storage, a database, or any place else that data is stored (see Chapter 6). After ingestion, data may be processed immediately; or within minutes, hours, or days; or simply persist in storage indefinitely.

Process time occurs after ingestion time, when the data is processed (typically, a transformation). *Processing time* is how long the data took to process, measured in seconds, minutes, hours, etc.

You'll want to record these various times, preferably in an automated way. Set up monitoring along your data workflows to capture when events occur, when they're ingested and processed, and how long it took to process events.

Source System Practical Details

This section discusses the practical details of interacting with modern source systems. We'll dig into the details of commonly encountered databases, APIs, and other aspects. This information will have a shorter shelf life than the main ideas discussed previously; popular API frameworks, databases, and other details will continue to change rapidly.

Nevertheless, these details are critical knowledge for working data engineers. We suggest that you study this information as baseline knowledge but read extensively to stay abreast of ongoing developments.

Databases

In this section, we'll look at common source system database technologies that you'll encounter as a data engineer and high-level considerations for working with these systems. There are as many types of databases as there are use cases for data.

Major considerations for understanding database technologies

Here, we introduce major ideas that occur across a variety of database technologies, including those that back software applications and those that support analytics use cases:

Database management system
> A database system used to store and serve data. Abbreviated as DBMS, it consists of a storage engine, query optimizer, disaster recovery, and other key components for managing the database system.

Lookups
> How does the database find and retrieve data? Indexes can help speed up lookups, but not all databases have indexes. Know whether your database uses indexes; if so, what are the best patterns for designing and maintaining them? Understand how to leverage for efficient extraction. It also helps to have a basic knowledge of the major types of indexes, including B-tree and log-structured merge-trees (LSM).

Query optimizer
> Does the database utilize an optimizer? What are its characteristics?

Scaling and distribution
> Does the database scale with demand? What scaling strategy does it deploy? Does it scale horizontally (more database nodes) or vertically (more resources on a single machine)?

Modeling patterns
> What modeling patterns work best with the database (e.g., data normalization or wide tables)? (See Chapter 8 for our discussion of data modeling.)

CRUD
> How is data queried, created, updated, and deleted in the database? Every type of database handles CRUD operations differently.

Consistency
> Is the database fully consistent, or does it support a relaxed consistency model (e.g., eventual consistency)? Does the database support optional consistency modes for reads and writes (e.g., strongly consistent reads)?

We divide databases into relational and nonrelational categories. In truth, the nonrelational category is far more diverse, but relational databases still occupy significant space in application backends.

Relational databases

A *relational database management system* (RDBMS) is one of the most common application backends. Relational databases were developed at IBM in the 1970s and popularized by Oracle in the 1980s. The growth of the internet saw the rise of the LAMP stack (Linux, Apache web server, MySQL, PHP) and an explosion of vendor and open source RDBMS options. Even with the rise of NoSQL databases (described in the following section), relational databases have remained extremely popular.

Data is stored in a table of *relations* (rows), and each relation contains multiple *fields* (columns); see Figure 5-7. Note that we use the terms *column* and *field* interchangeably throughout this book. Each relation in the table has the same *schema* (a sequence of columns with assigned static types such as string, integer, or float). Rows are typically stored as a contiguous sequence of bytes on disk.

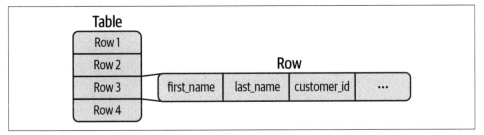

Figure 5-7. RDBMS stores and retrieves data at a row level

Tables are typically indexed by a *primary key*, a unique field for each row in the table. The indexing strategy for the primary key is closely connected with the layout of the table on disk.

Tables can also have various *foreign keys*—fields with values connected with the values of primary keys in other tables, facilitating joins, and allowing for complex schemas that spread data across multiple tables. In particular, it is possible to design a *normalized schema*. Normalization is a strategy for ensuring that data in records is not duplicated in multiple places, thus avoiding the need to update states in multiple locations at once and preventing inconsistencies (see Chapter 8).

RDBMS systems are typically ACID compliant. Combining a normalized schema, ACID compliance, and support for high transaction rates makes relational database systems ideal for storing rapidly changing application states. The challenge for data engineers is to determine how to capture state information over time.

A full discussion of the theory, history, and technology of RDBMS is beyond the scope of this book. We encourage you to study RDBMS systems, relational algebra, and strategies for normalization because they're widespread, and you'll encounter them frequently. See "Additional Resources" on page 192 for suggested books.

Nonrelational databases: NoSQL

While relational databases are terrific for many use cases, they're not a one-size-fits-all solution. We often see that people start with a relational database under the impression it's a universal appliance and shoehorn in a ton of use cases and workloads. As data and query requirements morph, the relational database collapses under its weight. At that point, you'll want to use a database that's appropriate for the specific workload under pressure. Enter nonrelational or NoSQL databases. *NoSQL*, which stands for *not only SQL*, refers to a whole class of databases that abandon the relational paradigm.

On the one hand, dropping relational constraints can improve performance, scalability, and schema flexibility. But as always in architecture, trade-offs exist. NoSQL databases also typically abandon various RDBMS characteristics, such as strong consistency, joins, or a fixed schema.

A big theme of this book is that data innovation is constant. Let's take a quick look at the history of NoSQL, as it's helpful to gain a perspective on why and how data innovations impact your work as a data engineer. In the early 2000s, tech companies such as Google and Amazon began to outgrow their relational databases and pioneered new distributed, nonrelational databases to scale their web platforms.

While the term *NoSQL* first appeared in 1998, the modern version was coined by Eric Evans in the 2000s.[1] He tells the story in a 2009 blog post (*https://oreil.ly/LOYbo*):

> I've spent the last couple of days at nosqleast (*https://oreil.ly/6xN5Y*) and one of the hot topics here is the name "nosql." Understandably, there are a lot of people who worry that the name is Bad, that it sends an inappropriate or inaccurate message. While I make no claims to the idea, I do have to accept some blame for what it is now being called. How's that? Johan Oskarsson was organizing the first meetup and asked the question "What's a good name?" on IRC; it was one of three or four suggestions that I spouted off in the span of like 45 seconds, without thinking.
>
> My regret, however, isn't about what the name says; it's about what it doesn't. When Johan originally had the idea for the first meetup, he seemed to be thinking Big Data and linearly scalable distributed systems, but the name is so vague that it opened the door to talk submissions for literally anything that stored data, and wasn't an RDBMS.

---

1 Keith D. Foote, "A Brief History of Non-Relational Databases," Dataversity, June 19, 2018, *https://oreil.ly/5Ukg2*.

NoSQL remains vague in 2022, but it's been widely adopted to describe a universe of "new school" databases, alternatives to relational databases.

There are numerous flavors of NoSQL database designed for almost any imaginable use case. Because there are far too many NoSQL databases to cover exhaustively in this section, we consider the following database types: key-value, document, wide-column, graph, search, and time series. These databases are all wildly popular and enjoy widespread adoption. A data engineer should understand these types of databases, including usage considerations, the structure of the data they store, and how to leverage each in the data engineering lifecycle.

Key-value stores. A *key-value database* is a nonrelational database that retrieves records using a key that uniquely identifies each record. This is similar to hash map or dictionary data structures presented in many programming languages but potentially more scalable. Key-value stores encompass several NoSQL database types —for example, document stores and wide column databases (discussed next).

Different types of key-value databases offer a variety of performance characteristics to serve various application needs. For example, in-memory key-value databases are popular for caching session data for web and mobile applications, where ultra-fast lookup and high concurrency are required. Storage in these systems is typically temporary; if the database shuts down, the data disappears. Such caches can reduce pressure on the main application database and serve speedy responses.

Of course, key-value stores can also serve applications requiring high-durability persistence. An ecommerce application may need to save and update massive amounts of event state changes for a user and their orders. A user logs into the ecommerce application, clicks around various screens, adds items to a shopping cart, and then checks out. Each event must be durably stored for retrieval. Key-value stores often persist data to disk and across multiple nodes to support such use cases.

Document stores. As mentioned previously, a *document store* is a specialized key-value store. In this context, a *document* is a nested object; we can usually think of each document as a JSON object for practical purposes. Documents are stored in collections and retrieved by key. A *collection* is roughly equivalent to a table in a relational database (see Table 5-2).

Table 5-2. Comparison of RDBMS and document terminology

RDBMS	Document database
Table	Collection
Row	Document, items, entity

One key difference between relational databases and document stores is that the latter does not support joins. This means that data cannot be easily *normalized*, i.e., split across multiple tables. (Applications can still join manually. Code can look up a document, extract a property, and then retrieve another document.) Ideally, all related data can be stored in the same document.

In many cases, the same data must be stored in multiple documents spread across numerous collections; software engineers must be careful to update a property everywhere it is stored. (Many document stores support a notion of transactions to facilitate this.)

Document databases generally embrace all the flexibility of JSON and don't enforce schema or types; this is a blessing and a curse. On the one hand, this allows the schema to be highly flexible and expressive. The schema can also evolve as an application grows. On the flip side, we've seen document databases become absolute nightmares to manage and query. If developers are not careful in managing schema evolution, data may become inconsistent and bloated over time. Schema evolution can also break downstream ingestion and cause headaches for data engineers if it's not communicated in a timely fashion (before deployment).

The following is an example of data that is stored in a collection called users. The collection key is the id. We also have a name (along with first and last as child elements) and an array of the user's favorite bands within each document:

```
{
  "users":[
    {
    "id":1234,
    "name":{
      "first":"Joe",
      "last":"Reis"
    },
    "favorite_bands":[
      "AC/DC",
      "Slayer",
      "WuTang Clan",
      "Action Bronson"
    ]
    },
    {
    "id":1235,
    "name":{
      "first":"Matt",
      "last":"Housley"
    },
    "favorite_bands":[
      "Dave Matthews Band",
      "Creed",
      "Nickelback"
```

```
        ]
      }
    ]
  }
}
```

To query the data in this example, you can retrieve records by key. Note that most document databases also support the creation of indexes and lookup tables to allow retrieval of documents by specific properties. This is often invaluable in application development when you need to search for documents in various ways. For example, you could set an index on name.

Another critical technical detail for data engineers is that document stores are generally not ACID compliant, unlike relational databases. Technical expertise in a particular document store is essential to understanding performance, tuning, configuration, related effects on writes, consistency, durability, etc. For example, many document stores are *eventually consistent*. Allowing data distribution across a cluster is a boon for scaling and performance but can lead to catastrophes when engineers and developers don't understand the implications.[2]

To run analytics on document stores, engineers generally must run a full scan to extract all data from a collection or employ a CDC strategy to send events to a target stream. The full scan approach can have both performance and cost implications. The scan often slows the database as it runs, and many serverless cloud offerings charge a significant fee for each full scan. In document databases, it's often helpful to create an index to help speed up queries. We discuss indexes and query patterns in Chapter 8.

Wide-column.   A *wide-column database* is optimized for storing massive amounts of data with high transaction rates and extremely low latency. These databases can scale to extremely high write rates and vast amounts of data. Specifically, wide-column databases can support petabytes of data, millions of requests per second, and sub-10ms latency. These characteristics have made wide-column databases popular in ecommerce, fintech, ad tech, IoT, and real-time personalization applications. Data engineers must be aware of the operational characteristics of the wide-column databases they work with to set up a suitable configuration, design the schema, and choose an appropriate row key to optimize performance and avoid common operational issues.

These databases support rapid scans of massive amounts of data, but they do not support complex queries. They have only a single index (the row key) for lookups. Data engineers must generally extract data and send it to a secondary analytics system to run complex queries to deal with these limitations. This can be accomplished by running large scans for the extraction or employing CDC to capture an event stream.

---

2 Nemil Dalal's excellent series on the history of MongoDB (*https://oreil.ly/pEKzk*) recounts some harrowing tales of database abuse and its consequences for fledgling startups.

Graph databases.   *Graph databases* explicitly store data with a mathematical graph structure (as a set of nodes and edges).[3] Neo4j has proven extremely popular, while Amazon, Oracle, and other vendors offer their graph database products. Roughly speaking, graph databases are a good fit when you want to analyze the connectivity between elements.

For example, you could use a document database to store one document for each user describing their properties. You could add an array element for *connections* that contains directly connected users' IDs in a social media context. It's pretty easy to determine the number of direct connections a user has, but suppose you want to know how many users can be reached by traversing two direct connections. You could answer this question by writing complex code, but each query would run slowly and consume significant resources. The document store is simply not optimized for this use case.

Graph databases are designed for precisely this type of query. Their data structures allow for queries based on the connectivity between elements; graph databases are indicated when we care about understanding complex traversals between elements. In the parlance of graphs, we store *nodes* (users in the preceding example) and *edges* (connections between users). Graph databases support rich data models for both nodes and edges. Depending on the underlying graph database engine, graph databases utilize specialized query languages such as SPARQL, Resource Description Framework (RDF), Graph Query Language (GQL), and Cypher.

As an example of a graph, consider a network of four users. User 1 follows User 2, who follows User 3 and User 4; User 3 also follows User 4 (Figure 5-8).

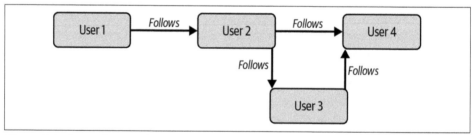

Figure 5-8. A social network graph

We anticipate that graph database applications will grow dramatically outside of tech companies; market analyses also predict rapid growth.[4] Of course, graph databases

---

3 Martin Kleppmann, *Designing Data-Intensive Applications* (Sebastopol, CA: O'Reilly, 2017), 49, *https://oreil.ly/v1NhG*.

4 Aashish Mehra, "Graph Database Market Worth $5.1 Billion by 2026: Exclusive Report by MarketsandMarkets," Cision PR Newswire, July 30, 2021, *https://oreil.ly/mGVkY*.

---

are beneficial from an operational perspective and support the kinds of complex social relationships critical to modern applications. Graph structures are also fascinating from the perspective of data science and ML, potentially revealing deep insights into human interactions and behavior.

This introduces unique challenges for data engineers who may be more accustomed to dealing with structured relations, documents, or unstructured data. Engineers must choose whether to do the following:

- Map source system graph data into one of their existing preferred paradigms
- Analyze graph data within the source system itself
- Adopt graph-specific analytics tools

Graph data can be reencoded into rows in a relational database, which may be a suitable solution depending on the analytics use case. Transactional graph databases are also designed for analytics, although large queries may overload production systems. Contemporary cloud-based graph databases support read-heavy graph analytics on massive quantities of data.

Search. A *search database* is a nonrelational database used to search your data's complex and straightforward semantic and structural characteristics. Two prominent use cases exist for a search database: text search and log analysis. Let's cover each of these separately.

Text search involves searching a body of text for keywords or phrases, matching on exact, fuzzy, or semantically similar matches. *Log analysis* is typically used for anomaly detection, real-time monitoring, security analytics, and operational analytics. Queries can be optimized and sped up with the use of indexes.

Depending on the type of company you work at, you may use search databases either regularly or not at all. Regardless, it's good to be aware they exist in case you come across them in the wild. Search databases are popular for fast search and retrieval and can be found in various applications; an ecommerce site may power its product search using a search database. As a data engineer, you might be expected to bring data from a search database (such as Elasticsearch, Apache Solr or Lucene, or Algolia) into downstream KPI reports or something similar.

Time series. A *time series* is a series of values organized by time. For example, stock prices might move as trades are executed throughout the day, or a weather sensor will take atmospheric temperatures every minute. Any events that are recorded over time—either regularly or sporadically—are time-series data. A *time-series database* is optimized for retrieving and statistical processing of time-series data.

While time-series data such as orders, shipments, logs, and so forth have been stored in relational databases for ages, these data sizes and volumes were often tiny. As data grew faster and bigger, new special-purpose databases were needed. Time-series databases address the needs of growing, high-velocity data volumes from IoT, event and application logs, ad tech, and fintech, among many other use cases. Often these workloads are write-heavy. As a result, time-series databases often utilize memory buffering to support fast writes and reads.

We should distinguish between measurement and event-based data, common in time-series databases. *Measurement data* is generated regularly, such as temperature or air-quality sensors. *Event-based data* is irregular and created every time an event occurs—for instance, when a motion sensor detects movement.

The schema for a time series typically contains a timestamp and a small set of fields. Because the data is time-dependent, the data is ordered by the timestamp. This makes time-series databases suitable for operational analytics but not great for BI use cases. Joins are not common, though some quasi time-series databases such as Apache Druid support joins. Many time-series databases are available, both as open source and paid options.

APIs

APIs are now a standard and pervasive way of exchanging data in the cloud, for SaaS platforms, and between internal company systems. Many types of API interfaces exist across the web, but we are principally interested in those built around HTTP, the most popular type on the web and in the cloud.

REST

We'll first talk about REST, currently the dominant API paradigm. As noted in Chapter 4, *REST* stands for *representational state transfer*. This set of practices and philosophies for building HTTP web APIs was laid out by Roy Fielding in 2000 in a PhD dissertation. REST is built around HTTP verbs, such as GET and PUT; in practice, modern REST uses only a handful of the verb mappings outlined in the original dissertation.

One of the principal ideas of REST is that interactions are stateless. Unlike in a Linux terminal session, there is no notion of a session with associated state variables such as a working directory; each REST call is independent. REST calls can change the system's state, but these changes are global, applying to the full system rather than a current session.

Critics point out that REST is in no way a full specification.[5] REST stipulates basic properties of interactions, but developers utilizing an API must gain a significant amount of domain knowledge to build applications or pull data effectively.

We see great variation in levels of API abstraction. In some cases, APIs are merely a thin wrapper over internals that provides the minimum functionality required to protect the system from user requests. In other examples, a REST data API is a masterpiece of engineering that prepares data for analytics applications and supports advanced reporting.

A couple of developments have simplified setting up data-ingestion pipelines from REST APIs. First, data providers frequently supply client libraries in various languages, especially in Python. Client libraries remove much of the boilerplate labor of building API interaction code. Client libraries handle critical details such as authentication and map fundamental methods into accessible classes.

Second, various services and open source libraries have emerged to interact with APIs and manage data synchronization. Many SaaS and open source vendors provide off-the-shelf connectors for common APIs. Platforms also simplify the process of building custom connectors as required.

There are numerous data APIs without client libraries or out-of-the-box connector support. As we emphasize throughout the book, engineers would do well to reduce undifferentiated heavy lifting by using off-the-shelf tools. However, low-level *plumbing* tasks still consume many resources. At virtually any large company, data engineers will need to deal with the problem of writing and maintaining custom code to pull data from APIs, which requires understanding the structure of the data as provided, developing appropriate data-extraction code, and determining a suitable data synchronization strategy.

GraphQL

GraphQL was created at Facebook as a query language for application data and an alternative to generic REST APIs. Whereas REST APIs generally restrict your queries to a specific data model, GraphQL opens up the possibility of retrieving multiple data models in a single request. This allows for more flexible and expressive queries than with REST. GraphQL is built around JSON and returns data in a shape resembling the JSON query.

There's something of a holy war between REST and GraphQL, with some engineering teams partisans of one or the other and some using both. In reality, engineers will encounter both as they interact with source systems.

---

5 For one example, see Michael S. Mikowski, "RESTful APIs: The Big Lie," August 10, 2015, *https://oreil.ly/rqja3*.

Webhooks

Webhooks are a simple event-based data-transmission pattern. The data source can be an application backend, a web page, or a mobile app. When specified events happen in the source system, this triggers a call to an HTTP endpoint hosted by the data consumer. Notice that the connection goes from the source system to the data sink, the opposite of typical APIs. For this reason, webhooks are often called *reverse APIs*.

The endpoint can do various things with the POST event data, potentially triggering a downstream process or storing the data for future use. For analytics purposes, we're interested in collecting these events. Engineers commonly use message queues to ingest data at high velocity and volume. We will talk about message queues and event streams later in this chapter.

RPC and gRPC

A *remote procedure call* (RPC) is commonly used in distributed computing. It allows you to run a procedure on a remote system.

gRPC is a remote procedure call library developed internally at Google in 2015 and later released as an open standard. Its use at Google alone would be enough to merit inclusion in our discussion. Many Google services, such as Google Ads and GCP, offer gRPC APIs. gRPC is built around the Protocol Buffers open data serialization standard, also developed by Google.

gRPC emphasizes the efficient bidirectional exchange of data over HTTP/2. *Efficiency* refers to aspects such as CPU utilization, power consumption, battery life, and bandwidth. Like GraphQL, gRPC imposes much more specific technical standards than REST, thus allowing the use of common client libraries and allowing engineers to develop a skill set that will apply to any gRPC interaction code.

Data Sharing

The core concept of cloud data sharing is that a multitenant system supports security policies for sharing data among tenants. Concretely, any public cloud object storage system with a fine-grained permission system can be a platform for data sharing. Popular cloud data-warehouse platforms also support data-sharing capabilities. Of course, data can also be shared through download or exchange over email, but a multitenant system makes the process much easier.

Many modern sharing platforms (especially cloud data warehouses) support row, column, and sensitive data filtering. Data sharing also streamlines the notion of the *data marketplace*, available on several popular clouds and data platforms. Data marketplaces provide a centralized location for data commerce, where data providers can advertise their offerings and sell them without worrying about the details of managing network access to data systems.

Data sharing can also streamline data pipelines within an organization. Data sharing allows units of an organization to manage their data and selectively share it with other units while still allowing individual units to manage their compute and query costs separately, facilitating data decentralization. This facilitates decentralized data management patterns such as data mesh.[6]

Data sharing and data mesh align closely with our philosophy of common architecture components. Choose common components (see Chapter 3) that allow the simple and efficient interchange of data and expertise rather than embracing the most exciting and sophisticated technology.

Third-Party Data Sources

The consumerization of technology means every company is essentially now a technology company. The consequence is that these companies—and increasingly government agencies—want to make their data available to their customers and users, either as part of their service or as a separate subscription. For example, the US Bureau of Labor Statistics publishes various statistics about the US labor market. The National Aeronautics and Space Administration (NASA) publishes various data from its research initiatives. Facebook shares data with businesses that advertise on its platform.

Why would companies want to make their data available? Data is sticky, and a flywheel is created by allowing users to integrate and extend their application into a user's application. Greater user adoption and usage means more data, which means users can integrate more data into their applications and data systems. The side effect is there are now almost infinite sources of third-party data.

Direct third-party data access is commonly done via APIs, through data sharing on a cloud platform, or through data download. APIs often provide deep integration capabilities, allowing customers to pull and push data. For example, many CRMs offer APIs that their users can integrate into their systems and applications. We see a common workflow to get data from a CRM, blend the CRM data through the customer scoring model, and then use reverse ETL to send that data back into CRM for salespeople to contact better-qualified leads.

Message Queues and Event-Streaming Platforms

Event-driven architectures are pervasive in software applications and are poised to grow their popularity even further. First, message queues and event-streaming platforms—critical layers in event-driven architectures—are easier to set up and manage

---

6 Martin Fowler, "How to Move Beyond a Monolithic Data Lake to a Distributed Data Mesh," Martin-Fowler.com, May 20, 2019, *https://oreil.ly/TEdJF*.

in a cloud environment. Second, the rise of data apps—applications that directly integrate real-time analytics—are growing from strength to strength. Event-driven architectures are ideal in this setting because events can both trigger work in the application and feed near real-time analytics.

Please note that streaming data (in this case, messages and streams) cuts across many data engineering lifecycle stages. Unlike an RDBMS, which is often directly attached to an application, the lines of streaming data are sometimes less clear-cut. These systems are used as source systems, but they will often cut across the data engineering lifecycle because of their transient nature. For example, you can use an event-streaming platform for message passing in an event-driven application, a source system. The same event-streaming platform can be used in the ingestion and transformation stage to process data for real-time analytics.

As source systems, message queues and event-streaming platforms are used in numerous ways, from routing messages between microservices ingesting millions of events per second of event data from web, mobile, and IoT applications. Let's look at message queues and event-streaming platforms a bit more closely.

Message queues

A *message queue* is a mechanism to asynchronously send data (usually as small individual messages, in the kilobytes) between discrete systems using a publish and subscribe model. Data is published to a message queue and is delivered to one or more subscribers (Figure 5-9). The subscriber acknowledges receipt of the message, removing it from the queue.

Figure 5-9. A simple message queue

Message queues allow applications and systems to be decoupled from each other and are widely used in microservices architectures. The message queue buffers messages to handle transient load spikes and makes messages durable through a distributed architecture with replication.

Message queues are a critical ingredient for decoupled microservices and event-driven architectures. Some things to keep in mind with message queues are frequency of delivery, message ordering, and scalability.

Message ordering and delivery. The order in which messages are created, sent, and received can significantly impact downstream subscribers. In general, order in distributed message queues is a tricky problem. Message queues often apply a fuzzy notion of order and first in, first out (FIFO). Strict FIFO means that if message A is ingested before message B, message A will always be delivered before message B. In practice, messages might be published and received out of order, especially in highly distributed message systems.

For example, Amazon SQS standard queues (*https://oreil.ly/r4lsy*) make the best effort to preserve message order. SQS also offers FIFO queues (*https://oreil.ly/8PPne*), which offer much stronger guarantees at the cost of extra overhead.

In general, don't assume that your messages will be delivered in order unless your message queue technology guarantees it. You typically need to design for out-of-order message delivery.

Delivery frequency.   Messages can be sent exactly once or at least once. If a message is sent *exactly once*, then after the subscriber acknowledges the message, the message disappears and won't be delivered again.[7] Messages sent *at least once* can be consumed by multiple subscribers or by the same subscriber more than once. This is great when duplications or redundancy don't matter.

Ideally, systems should be *idempotent*. In an idempotent system, the outcome of processing a message once is identical to the outcome of processing it multiple times. This helps to account for a variety of subtle scenarios. For example, even if our system can guarantee exactly-once delivery, a consumer might fully process a message but fail right before acknowledging processing. The message will effectively be processed twice, but an idempotent system handles this scenario gracefully.

Scalability.   The most popular message queues utilized in event-driven applications are horizontally scalable, running across multiple servers. This allows these queues to scale up and down dynamically, buffer messages when systems fall behind, and durably store messages for resilience against failure. However, this can create a variety of complications, as mentioned previously (multiple deliveries and fuzzy ordering).

Event-streaming platforms

In some ways, an *event-streaming platform* is a continuation of a message queue in that messages are passed from producers to consumers. As discussed previously in this chapter, the big difference between messages and streams is that a message queue is primarily used to route messages with certain delivery guarantees. In contrast, an event-streaming platform is used to ingest and process data in an ordered log of

---

7 Whether *exactly once* is possible is a semantical debate. Technically, exactly once delivery is impossible to guarantee, as illustrated by the Two Generals Problem (*https://oreil.ly/4VL1C*).

records. In an event-streaming platform, data is retained for a while, and it is possible to replay messages from a past point in time.

Let's describe an event related to an event-streaming platform. As mentioned in Chapter 3, an event is "something that happened, typically a change in the *state* of something." An event has the following features: a key, a value, and a timestamp. Multiple key-value timestamps might be contained in a single event. For example, an event for an ecommerce order might look like this:

```
{
    "Key":"Order # 12345",
    "Value":"SKU 123, purchase price of $100",
    "Timestamp":"2023-01-02 06:01:00"
}
```

Let's look at some of the critical characteristics of an event-streaming platform that you should be aware of as a data engineer.

Topics. In an event-streaming platform, a producer streams events to a topic, a collection of related events. A topic might contain fraud alerts, customer orders, or temperature readings from IoT devices, for example. A topic can have zero, one, or multiple producers and customers on most event-streaming platforms.

Using the preceding event example, a topic might be web orders. Also, let's send this topic to a couple of consumers, such as fulfillment and marketing. This is an excellent example of blurred lines between analytics and an event-driven system. The fulfillment subscriber will use events to trigger a fulfillment process, while marketing runs real-time analytics or trains and runs ML models to tune marketing campaigns (Figure 5-10).

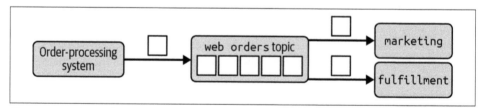

Figure 5-10. An order-processing system generates events (small squares) and publishes them to the web orders topic. Two subscribers—marketing and fulfillment—pull events from the topic.

Stream partitions. *Stream partitions* are subdivisions of a stream into multiple streams. A good analogy is a multilane freeway. Having multiple lanes allows for parallelism and higher throughput. Messages are distributed across partitions by *partition key*. Messages with the same partition key will always end up in the same partition.

In Figure 5-11, for example, each message has a numeric ID— shown inside the circle representing the message—that we use as a partition key. To determine the partition, we divide by 3 and take the remainder. Going from bottom to top, the partitions have remainder 0, 1, and 2, respectively.

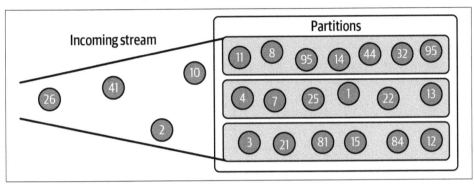

Figure 5-11. An incoming message stream broken into three partitions

Set a partition key so that messages that should be processed together have the same partition key. For example, it is common in IoT settings to want to send all messages from a particular device to the same processing server. We can achieve this by using a device ID as the partition key, and then setting up one server to consume from each partition.

A key concern with stream partitioning is ensuring that your partition key does not generate *hotspotting*—a disproportionate number of messages delivered to one partition. For example, if each IoT device were known to be located in a particular US state, we might use the state as the partition key. Given a device distribution proportional to state population, the partitions containing California, Texas, Florida, and New York might be overwhelmed, with other partitions relatively underutilized. Ensure that your partition key will distribute messages evenly across partitions.

Fault tolerance and resilience. Event-streaming platforms are typically distributed systems, with streams stored on various nodes. If a node goes down, another node replaces it, and the stream is still accessible. This means records aren't lost; you may choose to delete records, but that's another story. This fault tolerance and resilience make streaming platforms a good choice when you need a system that can reliably produce, store, and ingest event data.

Whom You'll Work With

When accessing source systems, it's essential to understand the people with whom you'll work. In our experience, good diplomacy and relationships with the stakeholders of source systems are an underrated and crucial part of successful data engineering.

Who are these stakeholders? Typically, you'll deal with two categories of stakeholders: systems and data stakeholders (Figure 5-12). A *systems stakeholder* builds and maintains the source systems; these might be software engineers, application developers, and third parties. Data stakeholders own and control access to the data you want, generally handled by IT, a data governance group, or third parties. The systems and data stakeholders are often different people or teams; sometimes, they are the same.

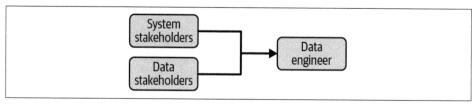

Figure 5-12. The data engineer's upstream stakeholders

You're often at the mercy of the stakeholder's ability to follow correct software engineering, database management, and development practices. Ideally, the stakeholders are doing DevOps and working in an agile manner. We suggest creating a feedback loop between data engineers and stakeholders of the source systems to create awareness of how data is consumed and used. This is among the single most overlooked areas where data engineers can get a lot of value. When something happens to the upstream source data—and something will happen, whether it's a schema or data change, a failed server or database, or other important events—you want to make sure that you're made aware of the impact these issues will have on your data engineering systems.

It might help to have a data contract in place with your upstream source system owners. What is a data contract? James Denmore offers this definition:[8]

> A data contract is a written agreement between the owner of a source system and the team ingesting data from that system for use in a data pipeline. The contract should state what data is being extracted, via what method (full, incremental), how often, as well as who (person, team) are the contacts for both the source system and the ingestion. Data contracts should be stored in a well-known and easy-to-find location such as a GitHub repo or internal documentation site. If possible, format data contracts in a standardized form so they can be integrated into the development process or queried programmatically.

---

8 James Denmore, *Data Pipelines Pocket Reference* (Sebastopol, CA: O'Reilly), *https://oreil.ly/8QdkJ*. Read the book for more information on how a data contract should be written.

In addition, consider establishing an SLA with upstream providers. An SLA provides expectations of what you can expect from the source systems you rely upon. An example of an SLA might be "data from source systems will be reliably available and of high quality." A service-level objective (SLO) measures performance against what you've agreed to in the SLA. For example, given your example SLA, an SLO might be "source systems will have 99% uptime." If a data contract or SLA/SLO seems too formal, at least verbally set expectations for source system guarantees for uptime, data quality, and anything else of importance to you. Upstream owners of source systems need to understand your requirements so they can provide you with the data you need.

Undercurrents and Their Impact on Source Systems

Unlike other parts of the data engineering lifecycle, source systems are generally outside the control of the data engineer. There's an implicit assumption (some might call it *hope*) that the stakeholders and owners of the source systems—and the data they produce—are following best practices concerning data management, DataOps (and DevOps), DODD (mentioned in Chapter 2) data architecture, orchestration, and software engineering. The data engineer should get as much upstream support as possible to ensure that the undercurrents are applied when data is generated in source systems. Doing so will make the rest of the steps in the data engineering lifecycle proceed a lot more smoothly.

How do the undercurrents impact source systems? Let's have a look.

Security

Security is critical, and the last thing you want is to accidentally create a point of vulnerability in a source system. Here are some areas to consider:

- Is the source system architected so data is secure and encrypted, both with data at rest and while data is transmitted?
- Do you have to access the source system over the public internet, or are you using a virtual private network (VPN)?
- Keep passwords, tokens, and credentials to the source system securely locked away. For example, if you're using Secure Shell (SSH) keys, use a key manager to protect your keys; the same rule applies to passwords—use a password manager or a single sign-on (SSO) provider.
- Do you trust the source system? Always be sure to trust but verify that the source system is legitimate. You don't want to be on the receiving end of data from a malicious actor.

Data Management

Data management of source systems is challenging for data engineers. In most cases, you will have only peripheral control—if any control at all—over source systems and the data they produce. To the extent possible, you should understand the way data is managed in source systems since this will directly influence how you ingest, store, and transform the data.

Here are some areas to consider:

Data governance
  Are upstream data and systems governed in a reliable, easy-to-understand fashion? Who manages the data?

Data quality
  How do you ensure data quality and integrity in upstream systems? Work with source system teams to set expectations on data and communication.

Schema
  Expect that upstream schemas will change. Where possible, collaborate with source system teams to be notified of looming schema changes.

Master data management
  Is the creation of upstream records controlled by a master data management practice or system?

Privacy and ethics
  Do you have access to raw data, or will the data be obfuscated? What are the implications of the source data? How long is it retained? Does it shift locations based on retention policies?

Regulatory
  Based upon regulations, are you supposed to access the data?

DataOps

Operational excellence—DevOps, DataOps, MLOps, XOps—should extend up and down the entire stack and support the data engineering and lifecycle. While this is ideal, it's often not fully realized.

Because you're working with stakeholders who control both the source systems and the data they produce, you need to ensure that you can observe and monitor the uptime and usage of the source systems and respond when incidents occur. For example, when the application database you depend on for CDC exceeds its I/O capacity and needs to be rescaled, how will that affect your ability to receive data from this system? Will you be able to access the data, or will it be unavailable until the database is rescaled? How will this affect reports? In another example, if the software engineering team is continuously deploying, a code change may cause unanticipated failures in the application itself. How will the failure impact your ability to access the databases powering the application? Will the data be up-to-date?

Set up a clear communication chain between data engineering and the teams supporting the source systems. Ideally, these stakeholder teams have incorporated DevOps into their workflow and culture. This will go a long way to accomplishing the goals of DataOps (a sibling of DevOps), to address and reduce errors quickly. As we mentioned earlier, data engineers need to weave themselves into the DevOps practices of stakeholders, and vice versa. Successful DataOps works when all people are on board and focus on making systems holistically work.

A few DataOps considerations are as follows:

Automation

There's the automation impacting the source system, such as code updates and new features. Then there's the DataOps automation that you've set up for your data workflows. Does an issue in the source system's automation impact your data workflow automation? If so, consider decoupling these systems so they can perform automation independently.

Observability

How will you know when there's an issue with a source system, such as an outage or a data-quality issue? Set up monitoring for source system uptime (or use the monitoring created by the team that owns the source system). Set up checks to ensure that data from the source system conforms with expectations for downstream usage. For example, is the data of good quality? Is the schema conformant? Are customer records consistent? Is data hashed as stipulated by the internal policy?

Incident response

What's your plan if something bad happens? For example, how will your data pipeline behave if a source system goes offline? What's your plan to backfill the "lost" data once the source system is back online?

Data Architecture

Similar to data management, unless you're involved in the design and maintenance of the source system architecture, you'll have little impact on the upstream source system architecture. You should also understand how the upstream architecture is designed and its strengths and weaknesses. Talk often with the teams responsible for the source systems to understand the factors discussed in this section and ensure that their systems can meet your expectations. Knowing where the architecture performs well and where it doesn't will impact how you design your data pipeline.

Here are some things to consider regarding source system architectures:

Reliability

All systems suffer from entropy at some point, and outputs will drift from what's expected. Bugs are introduced, and random glitches happen. Does the system produce predictable outputs? How often can we expect the system to fail? What's the mean time to repair to get the system back to sufficient reliability?

Durability

Everything fails. A server might die, a cloud's zone or region could go offline, or other issues may arise. You need to account for how an inevitable failure or outage will affect your managed data systems. How does the source system handle data loss from hardware failures or network outages? What's the plan for handling outages for an extended period and limiting the blast radius of an outage?

Availability

What guarantees that the source system is up, running, and available when it's supposed to be?

People

Who's in charge of the source system's design, and how will you know if breaking changes are made in the architecture? A data engineer needs to work with the teams who maintain the source systems and ensure that these systems are architected reliably. Create an SLA with the source system team to set expectations about potential system failure.

Orchestration

When orchestrating within your data engineering workflow, you'll primarily be concerned with making sure your orchestration can access the source system, which requires the correct network access, authentication, and authorization.

Here are some things to think about concerning orchestration for source systems:

Cadence and frequency

Is the data available on a fixed schedule, or can you access new data whenever you want?

Common frameworks

Do the software and data engineers use the same container manager, such as Kubernetes? Would it make sense to integrate application and data workloads into the same Kubernetes cluster? If you're using an orchestration framework like Airflow, does it make sense to integrate it with the upstream application team? There's no correct answer here, but you need to balance the benefits of integration with the risks of tight coupling.

Software Engineering

As the data landscape shifts to tools that simplify and automate access to source systems, you'll likely need to write code. Here are a few considerations when writing code to access a source system:

Networking
> Make sure your code will be able to access the network where the source system resides. Also, always think about secure networking. Are you accessing an HTTPS URL over the public internet, SSH, or a VPN?

Authentication and authorization
> Do you have the proper credentials (tokens, username/passwords) to access the source system? Where will you store these credentials so they don't appear in your code or version control? Do you have the correct IAM roles to perform the coded tasks?

Access patterns
> How are you accessing the data? Are you using an API, and how are you handling REST/GraphQL requests, response data volumes, and pagination? If you're accessing data via a database driver, is the driver compatible with the database you're accessing? For either access pattern, how are things like retries and timeouts handled?

Orchestration
> Does your code integrate with an orchestration framework, and can it be executed as an orchestrated workflow?

Parallelization
> How are you managing and scaling parallel access to source systems?

Deployment
> How are you handling the deployment of source code changes?

Conclusion

Source systems and their data are vital in the data engineering lifecycle. Data engineers tend to treat source systems as "someone else's problem"—do this at your peril! Data engineers who abuse source systems may need to look for another job when production goes down.

If there's a stick, there's also a carrot. Better collaboration with source system teams can lead to higher-quality data, more successful outcomes, and better data products. Create a bidirectional flow of communications with your counterparts on these teams; set up processes to notify of schema and application changes that affect analytics and ML. Communicate your data needs proactively to assist application teams in the data engineering process.

Be aware that the integration between data engineers and source system teams is growing. One example is reverse ETL, which has long lived in the shadows but has recently risen into prominence. We also discussed that the event-streaming platform could serve a role in event-driven architectures and analytics; a source system can also be a data engineering system. Build shared systems where it makes sense to do so.

Look for opportunities to build user-facing data products. Talk to application teams about analytics they would like to present to their users or places where ML could improve the user experience. Make application teams stakeholders in data engineering, and find ways to share your successes.

Now that you understand the types of source systems and the data they generate, we'll next look at ways to store this data.

Additional Resources

- Confluent's "Schema Evolution and Compatibility" documentation (*https://oreil.ly/6uUWM*)
- *Database Internals* by Alex Petrov (O'Reilly)
- *Database System Concepts* by Abraham (Avi) Silberschatz et al. (McGraw Hill)
- "The Log: What Every Software Engineer Should Know About Real-Time Data's Unifying Abstraction" (*https://oreil.ly/xNkWC*) by Jay Kreps
- "Modernizing Business Data Indexing" (*https://oreil.ly/4xzyq*) by Benjamin Douglas and Mohammad Mohtasham
- "NoSQL: What's in a Name" (*https://oreil.ly/z0xZH*) by Eric Evans
- "Test Data Quality at Scale with Deequ" (*https://oreil.ly/XoHFL*) by Dustin Lange et al.
- "The What, Why, and When of Single-Table Design with DynamoDB" (*https://oreil.ly/jOMTh*) by Alex DeBrie

CHAPTER 6

Storage

Storage is the cornerstone of the data engineering lifecycle (Figure 6-1) and underlies its major stages—ingestion, transformation, and serving. Data gets stored many times as it moves through the lifecycle. To paraphrase an old saying, it's storage all the way down. Whether data is needed seconds, minutes, days, months, or years later, it must persist in storage until systems are ready to consume it for further processing and transmission. Knowing the use case of the data and the way you will retrieve it in the future is the first step to choosing the proper storage solutions for your data architecture.

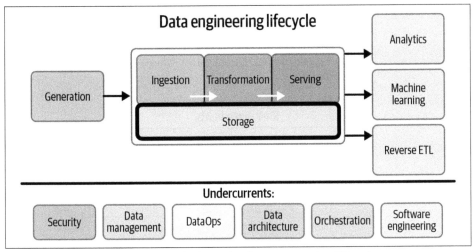

Figure 6-1. Storage plays a central role in the data engineering lifecycle

We also discussed storage in Chapter 5, but with a difference in focus and domain of control. Source systems are generally not maintained or controlled by data engineers. The storage that data engineers handle directly, which we'll focus on in this chapter, encompasses the data engineering lifecycle stages of ingesting data from source systems to serving data to deliver value with analytics, data science, etc. Many forms of storage undercut the entire data engineering lifecycle in some fashion.

To understand storage, we're going to start by studying the *raw ingredients* that compose storage systems, including hard drives, solid state drives, and system memory (see Figure 6-2). It's essential to understand the basic characteristics of physical storage technologies to assess the trade-offs inherent in any storage architecture. This section also discusses serialization and compression, key software elements of practical storage. (We defer a deeper technical discussion of serialization and compression to Appendix A.) We also discuss *caching*, which is critical in assembling storage systems.

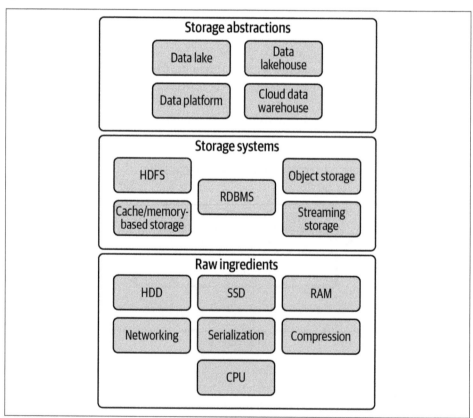

Figure 6-2. Raw ingredients, storage systems, and storage abstractions

Next, we'll look at *storage systems*. In practice, we don't directly access system memory or hard disks. These physical storage components exist inside servers and clusters that can ingest and retrieve data using various access paradigms.

Finally, we'll look at *storage abstractions*. Storage systems are assembled into a cloud data warehouse, a data lake, etc. When building data pipelines, engineers choose the appropriate abstractions for storing their data as it moves through the ingestion, transformation, and serving stages.

Raw Ingredients of Data Storage

Storage is so common that it's easy to take it for granted. We're often surprised by the number of software and data engineers who use storage every day but have little idea how it works behind the scenes or the trade-offs inherent in various storage media. As a result, we see storage used in some pretty...interesting ways. Though current managed services potentially free data engineers from the complexities of managing servers, data engineers still need to be aware of underlying components' essential characteristics, performance considerations, durability, and costs.

In most data architectures, data frequently passes through magnetic storage, SSDs, and memory as it works its way through the various processing phases of a data pipeline. Data storage and query systems generally follow complex recipes involving distributed systems, numerous services, and multiple hardware storage layers. These systems require the right raw ingredients to function correctly.

Let's look at some of the raw ingredients of data storage: disk drives, memory, networking and CPU, serialization, compression, and caching.

Magnetic Disk Drive

Magnetic disks utilize spinning platters coated with a ferromagnetic film (Figure 6-3). This film is magnetized by a read/write head during write operations to physically encode binary data. The read/write head detects the magnetic field and outputs a bitstream during read operations. Magnetic disk drives have been around for ages. They still form the backbone of bulk data storage systems because they are significantly cheaper than SSDs per gigabyte of stored data.

On the one hand, these disks have seen extraordinary improvements in performance, storage density, and cost.[1] On the other hand, SSDs dramatically outperform magnetic disks on various metrics. Currently, commercial magnetic disk drives cost roughly 3 cents per gigabyte of capacity. (Note that we'll frequently use the

---

[1] Andy Klein, "Hard Disk Drive (HDD) vs. Solid-State Drive (SSD): What's the Diff?," Backblaze blog, October 5, 2021, *https://oreil.ly/XBps8*.

abbreviations *HDD* and *SSD* to denote rotating magnetic disk and solid-state drives, respectively.)

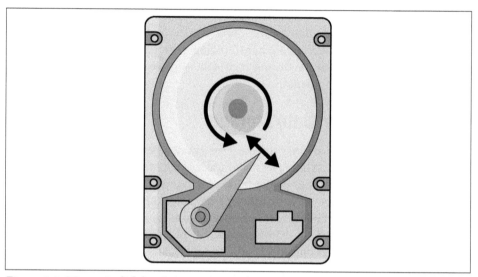

Figure 6-3. Magnetic disk head movement and rotation are essential in random access latency

IBM developed magnetic disk drive technology in the 1950s. Since then, magnetic disk capacities have grown steadily. The first commercial magnetic disk drive, the IBM 350, had a capacity of 3.75 megabytes. As of this writing, magnetic drives storing 20 TB are commercially available. In fact, magnetic disks continue to see rapid innovation, with methods such as heat-assisted magnetic recording (HAMR), shingled magnetic recording (SMR), and helium-filled disk enclosures being used to realize ever greater storage densities. In spite of the continuing improvements in drive capacity, other aspects of HDD performance are hampered by physics.

First, *disk transfer speed*, the rate at which data can be read and written, does not scale in proportion with disk capacity. Disk capacity scales with *areal density* (gigabits stored per square inch), whereas transfer speed scales with *linear density* (bits per inch). This means that if disk capacity grows by a factor of 4, transfer speed increases by only a factor of 2. Consequently, current data center drives support maximum data transfer speeds of 200–300 MB/s. To frame this another way, it takes more than 20 hours to read the entire contents of a 30 TB magnetic drive, assuming a transfer speed of 300 MB/s.

A second major limitation is seek time. To access data, the drive must physically relocate the read/write heads to the appropriate track on the disk. Third, in order to find a particular piece of data on the disk, the disk controller must wait for that data to rotate under the read/write heads. This leads to *rotational latency*. Typical commercial drives spinning at 7,200 revolutions per minute (RPM) seek time, and rotational latency, leads to over four milliseconds of overall average latency (time to access a selected piece of data). A fourth limitation is input/output operations per second (IOPS), critical for transactional databases. A magnetic drive ranges from 50 to 500 IOPS.

Various tricks can improve latency and transfer speed. Using a higher rotational speed can increase transfer rate and decrease rotational latency. Limiting the radius of the disk platter or writing data into only a narrow band on the disk reduces seek time. However, none of these techniques makes magnetic drives remotely competitive with SSDs for random access lookups. SSDs can deliver data with significantly lower latency, higher IOPS, and higher transfer speeds, partially because there is no physically rotating disk or magnetic head to wait for.

As mentioned earlier, magnetic disks are still prized in data centers for their low data-storage costs. In addition, magnetic drives can sustain extraordinarily high transfer rates through parallelism. This is the critical idea behind cloud object storage: data can be distributed across thousands of disks in clusters. Data-transfer rates go up dramatically by reading from numerous disks simultaneously, limited primarily by network performance rather than disk transfer rate. Thus, network components and CPUs are also key raw ingredients in storage systems, and we will return to these topics shortly.

Solid-State Drive

Solid-state drives (SSDs) store data as charges in flash memory cells. SSDs eliminate the mechanical components of magnetic drives; the data is read by purely electronic means. SSDs can look up random data in less than 0.1 ms (100 microseconds). In addition, SSDs can scale both data-transfer speeds and IOPS by slicing storage into partitions with numerous storage controllers running in parallel. Commercial SSDs can support transfer speeds of many gigabytes per second and tens of thousands of IOPS.

Because of these exceptional performance characteristics, SSDs have revolutionized transactional databases and are the accepted standard for commercial deployments of OLTP systems. SSDs allow relational databases such as PostgreSQL, MySQL, and SQL Server to handle thousands of transactions per second.

However, SSDs are not currently the default option for high-scale analytics data storage. Again, this comes down to cost. Commercial SSDs typically cost 20–30 cents (USD) per gigabyte of capacity, nearly 10 times the cost per capacity of a magnetic drive. Thus, object storage on magnetic disks has emerged as the leading option for large-scale data storage in data lakes and cloud data warehouses.

SSDs still play a significant role in OLAP systems. Some OLAP databases leverage SSD caching to support high-performance queries on frequently accessed data. As low-latency OLAP becomes more popular, we expect SSD usage in these systems to follow suit.

Random Access Memory

We commonly use the terms *random access memory* (RAM) and *memory* interchangeably. Strictly speaking, magnetic drives and SSDs also serve as memory that stores data for later random access retrieval, but RAM has several specific characteristics:

- It is attached to a CPU and mapped into CPU address space.
- It stores the code that CPUs execute and the data that this code directly processes.
- It is *volatile*, while magnetic drives and SSDs are *nonvolatile*. Though they may occasionally fail and corrupt or lose data, drives generally retain data when powered off. RAM loses data in less than a second when it is unpowered.
- It offers significantly higher transfer speeds and faster retrieval times than SSD storage. DDR5 memory—the latest widely used standard for RAM—offers data retrieval latency on the order of 100 ns, roughly 1,000 times faster than SSD. A typical CPU can support 100 GB/s bandwidth to attached memory and millions of IOPS. (Statistics vary dramatically depending on the number of memory channels and other configuration details.)
- It is significantly more expensive than SSD storage, at roughly $10/GB (at the time of this writing).
- It is limited in the amount of RAM attached to an individual CPU and memory controller. This adds further to complexity and cost. High-memory servers typically utilize many interconnected CPUs on one board, each with a block of attached RAM.
- It is still significantly slower than CPU cache, a type of memory located directly on the CPU die or in the same package. Cache stores frequently and recently accessed data for ultrafast retrieval during processing. CPU designs incorporate several layers of cache of varying size and performance characteristics.

When we talk about system memory, we almost always mean *dynamic RAM*, a high-density, low-cost form of memory. Dynamic RAM stores data as charges in capacitors. These capacitors leak over time, so the data must be frequently *refreshed* (read and rewritten) to prevent data loss. The hardware memory controller handles these technical details; data engineers simply need to worry about bandwidth and retrieval latency characteristics. Other forms of memory, such as *static RAM*, are used in specialized applications such as CPU caches.

Current CPUs virtually always employ the *von Neumann architecture*, with code and data stored together in the same memory space. However, CPUs typically also support the option to disable code execution in specific pages of memory for enhanced security. This feature is reminiscent of the *Harvard architecture*, which separates code and data.

RAM is used in various storage and processing systems and can be used for caching, data processing, or indexes. Several databases treat RAM as a primary storage layer, allowing ultra-fast read and write performance. In these applications, data engineers must always keep in mind the volatility of RAM. Even if data stored in memory is replicated across a cluster, a power outage that brings down several nodes could cause data loss. Architectures intended to durably store data may use battery backups and automatically dump all data to disk in the event of power loss.

Networking and CPU

Why are we mentioning networking and CPU as raw ingredients for storing data? Increasingly, storage systems are distributed to enhance performance, durability, and availability. We mentioned specifically that individual magnetic disks offer relatively low-transfer performance, but a cluster of disks parallelizes reads for significant performance scaling. While storage standards such as redundant arrays of independent disks (RAID) parallelize on a single server, cloud object storage clusters operate at a much larger scale, with disks distributed across a network and even multiple data centers and availability zones.

Availability zones are a standard cloud construct consisting of compute environments with independent power, water, and other resources. Multizonal storage enhances both the availability and durability of data.

CPUs handle the details of servicing requests, aggregating reads, and distributing writes. Storage becomes a web application with an API, backend service components, and load balancing. Network device performance and network topology are key factors in realizing high performance.

Data engineers need to understand how networking will affect the systems they build and use. Engineers constantly balance the durability and availability achieved by spreading out data geographically versus the performance and cost benefits of keeping storage in a small geographic area and close to data consumers or writers. Appendix B covers cloud networking and major relevant ideas.

Serialization

Serialization is another raw storage ingredient and a critical element of database design. The decisions around serialization will inform how well queries perform across a network, CPU overhead, query latency, and more. Designing a data lake, for example, involves choosing a base storage system (e.g., Amazon S3) and standards for serialization that balance interoperability with performance considerations.

What is serialization, exactly? Data stored in system memory by software is generally not in a format suitable for storage on disk or transmission over a network. Serialization is the process of flattening and packing data into a standard format that a reader will be able to decode. Serialization formats provide a standard of data exchange. We might encode data in a row-based manner as an XML, JSON, or CSV file and pass it to another user who can then decode it using a standard library. A serialization algorithm has logic for handling types, imposes rules on data structure, and allows exchange between programming languages and CPUs. The serialization algorithm also has rules for handling exceptions. For instance, Python objects can contain cyclic references; the serialization algorithm might throw an error or limit nesting depth on encountering a cycle.

Low-level database storage is also a form of serialization. Row-oriented relational databases organize data as rows on disk to support speedy lookups and in-place updates. Columnar databases organize data into column files to optimize for highly efficient compression and support fast scans of large data volumes. Each serialization choice comes with a set of trade-offs, and data engineers tune these choices to optimize performance to requirements.

We provide a more detailed catalog of common data serialization techniques and formats in Appendix A. We suggest that data engineers become familiar with common serialization practices and formats, especially the most popular current formats (e.g., Apache Parquet), hybrid serialization (e.g., Apache Hudi), and in-memory serialization (e.g., Apache Arrow).

Compression

Compression is another critical component of storage engineering. On a basic level, compression makes data smaller, but compression algorithms interact with other details of storage systems in complex ways.

Highly efficient compression has three main advantages in storage systems. First, the data is smaller and thus takes up less space on the disk. Second, compression increases the practical scan speed per disk. With a 10:1 compression ratio, we go from scanning 200 MB/s per magnetic disk to an effective rate of 2 GB/s per disk.

The third advantage is in network performance. Given that a network connection between an Amazon EC2 instance and S3 provides 10 gigabits per second (Gbps) of bandwidth, a 10:1 compression ratio increases effective network bandwidth to 100 Gbps.

Compression also comes with disadvantages. Compressing and decompressing data entails extra time and resource consumption to read or write data. We undertake a more detailed discussion of compression algorithms and trade-offs in Appendix A.

Caching

We've already mentioned caching in our discussion of RAM. The core idea of caching is to store frequently or recently accessed data in a fast access layer. The faster the cache, the higher the cost and the less storage space available. Less frequently accessed data is stored in cheaper, slower storage. Caches are critical for data serving, processing, and transformation.

As we analyze storage systems, it is helpful to put every type of storage we utilize inside a *cache hierarchy* (Table 6-1). Most practical data systems rely on many cache layers assembled from storage with varying performance characteristics. This starts inside CPUs; processors may deploy up to four cache tiers. We move down the hierarchy to RAM and SSDs. Cloud object storage is a lower tier that supports long-term data retention and durability while allowing for data serving and dynamic data movement in pipelines.

Table 6-1. A heuristic cache hierarchy displaying storage types with approximate pricing and performance characteristics

Storage type	Data fetch latency[a]	Bandwidth	Price
CPU cache	1 nanosecond	1 TB/s	N/A
RAM	0.1 microseconds	100 GB/s	$10/GB
SSD	0.1 milliseconds	4 GB/s	$0.20/GB
HDD	4 milliseconds	300 MB/s	$0.03/GB
Object storage	100 milliseconds	10 GB/s	$0.02/GB per month
Archival storage	12 hours	Same as object storage once data is available	$0.004/GB per month

[a] A microsecond is 1,000 nanoseconds, and a millisecond is 1,000 microseconds.

We can think of archival storage as a *reverse cache*. Archival storage provides inferior access characteristics for low costs. Archival storage is generally used for data back-ups and to meet data-retention compliance requirements. In typical scenarios, this data will be accessed only in an emergency (e.g., data in a database might be lost and need to be recovered, or a company might need to look back at historical data for legal discovery).

Data Storage Systems

This section covers the major data storage systems you'll encounter as a data engi-neer. Storage systems exist at a level of abstraction above raw ingredients. For exam-ple, magnetic disks are a raw storage ingredient, while major cloud object storage platforms and HDFS are storage systems that utilize magnetic disks. Still higher levels of storage abstraction exist, such as data lakes and lakehouses (which we cover in "Data Engineering Storage Abstractions" on page 219).

Single Machine Versus Distributed Storage

As data storage and access patterns become more complex and outgrow the usefulness of a single server, distributing data to more than one server becomes necessary. Data can be stored on multiple servers, known as *distributed storage*. This is a distributed system whose purpose is to store data in a distributed fashion (Figure 6-4).

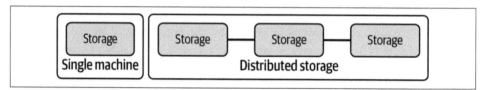

Figure 6-4. Single machine versus distributed storage on multiple servers

Distributed storage coordinates the activities of multiple servers to store, retrieve, and process data faster and at a larger scale, all while providing redundancy in case a server becomes unavailable. Distributed storage is common in architectures where you want built-in redundancy and scalability for large amounts of data. For example, object storage, Apache Spark, and cloud data warehouses rely on distributed storage architectures.

Data engineers must always be aware of the consistency paradigms of the distributed systems, which we'll explore next.

Eventual Versus Strong Consistency

A challenge with distributed systems is that your data is spread across multiple servers. How does this system keep the data consistent? Unfortunately, distributed systems pose a dilemma for storage and query accuracy. It takes time to replicate changes across the nodes of a system; often a balance exists between getting current data and getting "sorta" current data in a distributed database. Let's look at two common consistency patterns in distributed systems: eventual and strong.

We've covered ACID compliance throughout this book, starting in Chapter 5. Another acronym is *BASE*, which stands for *basically available, soft-state, eventual consistency*. Think of it as the opposite of ACID. BASE is the basis of eventual consistency. Let's briefly explore its components:

Basically available
> Consistency is not guaranteed, but database reads and writes are made on a best-effort basis, meaning consistent data is available most of the time.

Soft-state
> The state of the transaction is fuzzy, and it's uncertain whether the transaction is committed or uncommitted.

Eventual consistency
> At *some* point, reading data will return consistent values.

If reading data in an eventually consistent system is unreliable, why use it? Eventual consistency is a common trade-off in large-scale, distributed systems. If you want to scale horizontally (across multiple nodes) to process data in high volumes, then eventually, consistency is often the price you'll pay. Eventual consistency allows you to retrieve data quickly without verifying that you have the latest version across all nodes.

The opposite of eventual consistency is *strong consistency*. With strong consistency, the distributed database ensures that writes to any node are first distributed with a consensus and that any reads against the database return consistent values. You'll use strong consistency when you can tolerate higher query latency and require correct data every time you read from the database.

Generally, data engineers make decisions about consistency in three places. First, the database technology itself sets the stage for a certain level of consistency. Second, configuration parameters for the database will have an impact on consistency. Third, databases often support some consistency configuration at an individual query level. For example, DynamoDB (*https://oreil.ly/qJ6z4*) supports eventually consistent reads and strongly consistent reads. Strongly consistent reads are slower and consume more resources, so it is best to use them sparingly, but they are available when consistency is required.

You should understand how your database handles consistency. Again, data engineers are tasked with understanding technology deeply and using it to solve problems appropriately. A data engineer might need to negotiate consistency requirements with other technical and business stakeholders. Note that this is both a technology and organizational problem; ensure that you have gathered requirements from your stakeholders and choose your technologies appropriately.

File Storage

We deal with files every day, but the notion of a file is somewhat subtle. A *file* is a data entity with specific read, write, and reference characteristics used by software and operating systems. We define a file to have the following characteristics:

Finite length
> A file is a finite-length stream of bytes.

Append operations
    We can append bytes to the file up to the limits of the host storage system.

Random access
    We can read from any location in the file or write updates to any location.

Object storage behaves much like file storage but with key differences. While we set the stage for object storage by discussing file storage first, object storage is arguably much more important for the type of data engineering you'll do today. We will forward-reference the object storage discussion extensively over the next few pages.

File storage systems organize files into a directory tree. The directory reference for a file might look like this:

```
/Users/matthewhousley/output.txt
```

When this file reference is passed to the operating system, it starts at the root directory /, finds Users, matthewhousley, and finally output.txt. Working from the left, each directory is contained inside a parent directory, until we finally reach the file output.txt. This example uses Unix semantics, but Windows file reference semantics are similar. The filesystem stores each directory as metadata about the files and directories that it contains. This metadata consists of the name of each entity, relevant permission details, and a pointer to the actual entity. To find a file on disk, the operating system looks at the metadata at each hierarchy level and follows the pointer to the next subdirectory entity until finally reaching the file itself.

Note that other file-like data entities generally don't necessarily have all these properties. For example, *objects* in object storage support only the first characteristic, finite length, but are still extremely useful. We discuss this in "Object Storage" on page 209.

In cases where file storage paradigms are necessary for a pipeline, be careful with state and try to use ephemeral environments as much as possible. Even if you must process files on a server with an attached disk, use object storage for intermediate storage between processing steps. Try to reserve manual, low-level file processing for one-time ingestion steps or the exploratory stages of pipeline development.

Local disk storage

The most familiar type of file storage is an operating system–managed filesystem on a local disk partition of SSD or magnetic disk. New Technology File System (NTFS) and ext4 are popular filesystems on Windows and Linux, respectively. The operating system handles the details of storing directory entities, files, and metadata. Filesystems are designed to write data to allow for easy recovery in the event of power loss during a write, though any unwritten data will still be lost.

Local filesystems generally support full read after write consistency; reading immediately after a write will return the written data. Operating systems also employ various locking strategies to manage concurrent writing attempts to a file.

Local disk filesystems may also support advanced features such as journaling, snapshots, redundancy, the extension of the filesystem across multiple disks, full disk encryption, and compression. In "Block Storage" on page 206, we also discuss RAID.

Network-attached storage

Network-attached storage (NAS) systems provide a file storage system to clients over a network. NAS is a prevalent solution for servers; they quite often ship with built-in dedicated NAS interface hardware. While there are performance penalties to accessing the filesystem over a network, significant advantages to storage virtualization also exist, including redundancy and reliability, fine-grained control of resources, storage pooling across multiple disks for large virtual volumes, and file sharing across multiple machines. Engineers should be aware of the consistency model provided by their NAS solution, especially when multiple clients will potentially access the same data.

A popular alternative to NAS is a storage area network (SAN), but SAN systems provide block-level access without the filesystem abstraction. We cover SAN systems in "Block Storage" on page 206.

Cloud filesystem services

Cloud filesystem services provide a fully managed filesystem for use with multiple cloud VMs and applications, potentially including clients outside the cloud environment. Cloud filesystems should not be confused with standard storage attached to VMs—generally, block storage with a filesystem managed by the VM operating system. Cloud filesystems behave much like NAS solutions, but the details of networking, managing disk clusters, failures, and configuration are fully handled by the cloud vendor.

For example, Amazon Elastic File System (EFS) is an extremely popular example of a cloud filesystem service. Storage is exposed through the NFS 4 protocol (*https:// oreil.ly/GhvpT*), which is also used by NAS systems. EFS provides automatic scaling and pay-per-storage pricing with no advanced storage reservation required. The service also provides *local* read-after-write consistency (when reading from the machine that performed the write). It also offers open-after-close consistency across the full filesystem. In other words, once an application closes a file, subsequent readers will see changes saved to the closed file.

Block Storage

Fundamentally, *block storage* is the type of raw storage provided by SSDs and magnetic disks. In the cloud, virtualized block storage is the standard for VMs. These block storage abstractions allow fine control of storage size, scalability, and data durability beyond that offered by raw disks.

In our earlier discussion of SSDs and magnetic disks, we mentioned that with these random-access devices, the operating system can seek, read, and write any data on the disk. A *block* is the smallest addressable unit of data supported by a disk. This was often 512 bytes of usable data on older disks, but it has now grown to 4,096 bytes for most current disks, making writes less fine-grained but dramatically reducing the overhead of managing blocks. Blocks typically contain extra bits for error detection/correction and other metadata.

Blocks on magnetic disks are geometrically arranged on a physical platter. Two blocks on the same track can be read without moving the head, while reading two blocks on separate tracks requires a seek. Seek time can occur between blocks on an SSD, but this is infinitesimal compared to the seek time for magnetic disk tracks.

Block storage applications

Transactional database systems generally access disks at a block level to lay out data for optimal performance. For row-oriented databases, this originally meant that rows of data were written as continuous streams; the situation has grown more complicated with the arrival of SSDs and their associated seek-time performance improvements, but transactional databases still rely on the high random access performance offered by direct access to a block storage device.

Block storage also remains the default option for operating system boot disks on cloud VMs. The block device is formatted much as it would be directly on a physical disk, but the storage is usually virtualized. (See "Cloud virtualized block storage" on page 207.)

RAID

RAID stands for *redundant array of independent disks*, as noted previously. RAID simultaneously controls multiple disks to improve data durability, enhance performance, and combine capacity from multiple drives. An array can appear to the operating system as a single block device. Many encoding and parity schemes are available, depending on the desired balance between enhanced effective bandwidth and higher fault tolerance (tolerance for many disk failures).

Storage area network

Storage area network (SAN) systems provide virtualized block storage devices over a network, typically from a storage pool. SAN abstraction can allow fine-grained storage scaling and enhance performance, availability, and durability. You might encounter SAN systems if you're working with on-premises storage systems; you might also encounter a cloud version of SAN, as in the next subsection.

Cloud virtualized block storage

Cloud virtualized block storage solutions are similar to SAN but free engineers from dealing with SAN clusters and networking details. We'll look at Amazon Elastic Block Store (EBS) as a standard example; other public clouds have similar offerings. EBS is the default storage for Amazon EC2 virtual machines; other cloud providers also treat virtualized object storage as a key component of their VM offerings.

EBS offers several tiers of service with different performance characteristics. Generally, EBS performance metrics are given in IOPS and throughput (transfer speed). The higher performance tiers of EBS storage are backed by SSD disks, while magnetic disk-backed storage offers lower IOPS but costs less per gigabyte.

EBS volumes store data separate from the instance host server but in the same zone to support high performance and low latency (Figure 6-5). This allows EBS volumes to persist when an EC2 instance shuts down, when a host server fails, or even when the instance is deleted. EBS storage is suitable for applications such as databases, where data durability is a high priority. In addition, EBS replicates all data to at least two separate host machines, protecting data if a disk fails.

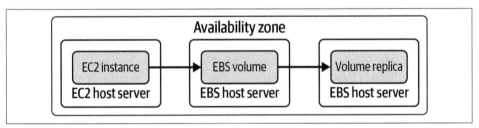

Figure 6-5. EBS volumes replicate data to multiple hosts and disks for high durability and availability, but are not resilient to the failure of an availability zone

EBS storage virtualization also supports several advanced features. For example, EBS volumes allow instantaneous point-in-time snapshots while the drive is used. Although it still takes some time for the snapshot to be replicated to S3, EBS can effectively freeze the state of data blocks when the snapshot is taken, while allowing the client machine to continue using the disk. In addition, snapshots after the initial full backup are differential; only changed blocks are written to S3 to minimize storage costs and backup time.

EBS volumes are also highly scalable. At the time of this writing, some EBS volume classes can scale up to 64 TiB, 256,000 IOPS, and 4,000 MiB/s.

Local instance volumes

Cloud providers also offer block storage volumes that are physically attached to the host server running a virtual machine. These storage volumes are generally very low cost (included with the price of the VM in the case of Amazon's EC2 instance store) and provide low latency and high IOPS.

Instance store volumes (Figure 6-6) behave essentially like a disk physically attached to a server in a data center. One key difference is that when a VM shuts down or is deleted, the contents of the locally attached disk are lost, whether or not this event was caused by intentional user action. This ensures that a new virtual machine cannot read disk contents belonging to a different customer.

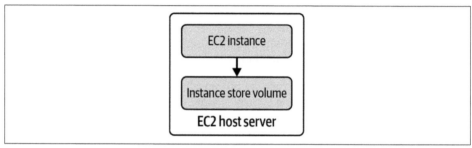

Figure 6-6. Instance store volumes offer high performance and low cost but do not protect data in the event of disk failure or VM shutdown

Locally attached disks support none of the advanced virtualization features offered by virtualized storage services like EBS. The locally attached disk is not replicated, so a physical disk failure can lose or corrupt data even if the host VM continues running. Furthermore, locally attached volumes do not support snapshots or other backup features.

Despite these limitations, locally attached disks are extremely useful. In many cases, we use disks as a local cache and hence don't need all the advanced virtualization features of a service like EBS. For example, suppose we're running AWS EMR on EC2 instances. We may be running an ephemeral job that consumes data from S3, stores it temporarily in the distributed filesystem running across the instances, processes the data, and writes the results back to S3. The EMR filesystem builds in replication and redundancy and is serving as a cache rather than permanent storage. The EC2 instance store is a perfectly suitable solution in this case and can enhance performance since data can be read and processed locally without flowing over a network (see Figure 6-7).

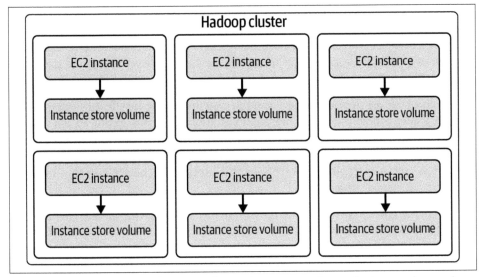

Figure 6-7. Instance store volumes can be used as a processing cache in an ephemeral Hadoop cluster

We recommend that engineers think about locally attached storage in worst-case scenarios. What are the consequences of a local disk failure? Of an accidental VM or cluster shutdown? Of a zonal or regional cloud outage? If none of these scenarios will have catastrophic consequences when data on locally attached volumes is lost, local storage may be a cost-effective and performant option. In addition, simple mitigation strategies (periodic checkpoint backups to S3) can prevent data loss.

Object Storage

Object storage contains *objects* of all shapes and sizes (Figure 6-8). The term *object storage* is somewhat confusing because *object* has several meanings in computer science. In this context, we're talking about a specialized file-like construct. It could be any type of file—TXT, CSV, JSON, images, videos, or audio.

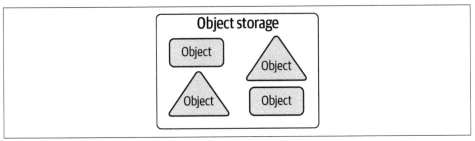

Figure 6-8. Object storage contains immutable objects of all shapes and sizes. Unlike files on a local disk, objects cannot be modified in place.

Object stores have grown in importance and popularity with the rise of big data and the cloud. Amazon S3, Azure Blob Storage, and Google Cloud Storage (GCS) are widely used object stores. In addition, many cloud data warehouses (and a growing number of databases) utilize object storage as their storage layer, and cloud data lakes generally sit on object stores.

Although many on-premises object storage systems can be installed on server clusters, we'll focus mostly on fully managed cloud object stores. From an operational perspective, one of the most attractive characteristics of cloud object storage is that it is straightforward to manage and use. Object storage was arguably one of the first "serverless" services; engineers don't need to consider the characteristics of underlying server clusters or disks.

An object store is a key-value store for immutable data objects. We lose much of the writing flexibility we expect with file storage on a local disk in an object store. Objects don't support random writes or append operations; instead, they are written once as a stream of bytes. After this initial write, objects become immutable. To change data in an object or append data to it, we must rewrite the full object. Object stores generally support random reads through range requests, but these lookups may perform much worse than random reads from data stored on an SSD.

For a software developer used to leveraging local random access file storage, the characteristics of objects might seem like constraints, but less is more; object stores don't need to support locks or change synchronization, allowing data storage across massive disk clusters. Object stores support extremely performant parallel stream writes and reads across many disks, and this parallelism is hidden from engineers, who can simply deal with the stream rather than communicating with individual disks. In a cloud environment, write speed scales with the number of streams being written up to quota limits set by the vendor. Read bandwidth can scale with the number of parallel requests, the number of virtual machines employed to read data, and the number of CPU cores. These characteristics make object storage ideal for serving high-volume web traffic or delivering data to highly parallel distributed query engines.

Typical cloud object stores save data in several availability zones, dramatically reducing the odds that storage will go fully offline or be lost in an unrecoverable way. This durability and availability are built into the cost; cloud storage vendors offer other storage classes at discounted prices in exchange for reduced durability or availability. We'll discuss this in "Storage classes and tiers" on page 214.

Cloud object storage is a key ingredient in separating compute and storage, allowing engineers to process data with ephemeral clusters and scale these clusters up and down on demand. This is a key factor in making big data available to smaller organizations that can't afford to own hardware for data jobs that they'll run only occasionally. Some major tech companies will continue to run permanent Hadoop clusters on their hardware. Still, the general trend is that most organizations will move data processing to the cloud, using an object store as essential storage and serving layer while processing data on ephemeral clusters.

In object storage, available storage space is also highly scalable, an ideal characteristic for big data systems. Storage space is constrained by the number of disks the storage provider owns, but these providers handle exabytes of data. In a cloud environment, available storage space is virtually limitless; in practice, the primary limit on storage space for public cloud customers is budget. From a practical standpoint, engineers can quickly store massive quantities of data for projects without planning months in advance for necessary servers and disks.

Object stores for data engineering applications

From the standpoint of data engineering, object stores provide excellent performance for large batch reads and batch writes. This corresponds well to the use case for massive OLAP systems. A bit of data engineering folklore says that object stores are not good for updates, but this is only partially true. Object stores are an inferior fit for transactional workloads with many small updates every second; these use cases are much better served by transactional databases or block storage systems. Object stores work well for a low rate of update operations, where each operation updates a large volume of data.

Object stores are now the gold standard of storage for data lakes. In the early days of data lakes, write once, read many (WORM) was the operational standard, but this had more to do with the complexities of managing data versions and files than the limitations of HDFS and object stores. Since then, systems such as Apache Hudi and Delta Lake have emerged to manage this complexity, and privacy regulations such as GDPR and CCPA have made deletion and update capabilities imperative. Update management for object storage is the central idea behind the data lakehouse concept, which we introduced in Chapter 3.

Object storage is an ideal repository for unstructured data in any format beyond these structured data applications. Object storage can house any binary data with no constraints on type or structure and frequently plays a role in ML pipelines for raw text, images, video, and audio.

Object lookup

As we mentioned, object stores are key-value stores. What does this mean for engineers? It's critical to understand that, unlike file stores, object stores do not utilize a directory tree to find objects. The object store uses a top-level logical container (a bucket in S3 and GCS) and references objects by key. A simple example in S3 might look like this:

```
S3://oreilly-data-engineering-book/data-example.json
```

In this case, S3://oreilly-data-engineering-book/ is the bucket name, and data-example.json is the key pointing to a particular object. S3 bucket names must be unique across all of AWS. Keys are unique within a bucket. Although cloud object stores may appear to support directory tree semantics, no true directory hierarchy exists. We might store an object with the following full path:

```
S3://oreilly-data-engineering-book/project-data/11/23/2021/data.txt
```

On the surface, this looks like subdirectories you might find in a regular file folder system: project-data, 11, 23, and 2021. Many cloud console interfaces allow users to view the objects inside a "directory," and cloud command-line tools often support Unix-style commands such as ls inside an object store directory. However, behind the scenes, the object system does not traverse a directory tree to reach the object. Instead, it simply sees a key (project-data/11/23/2021/data.txt) that happens to match directory semantics. This might seem like a minor technical detail, but engineers need to understand that certain "directory"-level operations are costly in an object store. To run aws ls S3://oreilly-data-engineering-book/project-data/11/ the object store must filter keys on the key prefix project-data/11/. If the bucket contains millions of objects, this operation might take some time, even if the "subdirectory" houses only a few objects.

Object consistency and versioning

As mentioned, object stores don't support in-place updates or appends as a general rule. We write a new object under the same key to update an object. When data engineers utilize updates in data processes, they must be aware of the consistency model for the object store they're using. Object stores may be eventually consistent or strongly consistent. For example, until recently, S3 was *eventually consistent*; after a new version of an object was written under the same key, the object store might sometimes return the old version of the object. The *eventual* part of *eventual consistency* means that after enough time has passed, the storage cluster reaches a state such that only the latest version of the object will be returned. This contrasts with the *strong consistency* model we expect of local disks attached to a server: reading after a write will return the most recently written data.

It might be desirable to impose strong consistency on an object store for various reasons, and standard methods are used to achieve this. One approach is to add a strongly consistent database (e.g., PostgreSQL) to the mix. Writing an object is now a two-step process:

1. Write the object.

2. Write the returned metadata for the object version to the strongly consistent database.

The version metadata (an object hash or an object timestamp) can uniquely identify an object version in conjunction with the object key. To read an object, a reader undertakes the following steps:

1. Fetch the latest object metadata from the strongly consistent database.

2. Query object metadata using the object key. Read the object data if it matches the metadata fetched from the consistent database.

3. If the object metadata does not match, repeat step 2 until the latest version of the object is returned.

A practical implementation has exceptions and edge cases to consider, such as when the object gets rewritten during this querying process. These steps can be managed behind an API so that an object reader sees a strongly consistent object store at the cost of higher latency for object access.

Object versioning is closely related to object consistency. When we rewrite an object under an existing key in an object store, we're essentially writing a brand-new object, setting references from the existing key to the object, and deleting the old object references. Updating all references across the cluster takes time, hence the potential for stale reads. Eventually, the storage cluster garbage collector deallocates the space dedicated to the dereferenced data, recycling disk capacity for use by new objects.

With object versioning turned on, we add additional metadata to the object that stipulates a version. While the default key reference gets updated to point to the new object, we retain other pointers to previous versions. We also maintain a version list so that clients can get a list of all object versions, and then pull a specific version. Because old versions of the object are still referenced, they aren't cleaned up by the garbage collector.

If we reference an object with a version, the consistency issue with some object storage systems disappears: the key and version metadata together form a unique reference to a particular, immutable data object. We will always get the same object back when we use this pair, provided that we haven't deleted it. The consistency issue still exists when a client requests the "default" or "latest" version of an object.

The principal overhead that engineers need to consider with object versioning is the cost of storage. Historical versions of objects generally have the same associated storage costs as current versions. Object version costs may be nearly insignificant or catastrophically expensive, depending on various factors. The data size is an issue, as is update frequency; more object versions can lead to significantly larger data size. Keep in mind that we're talking about brute-force object versioning. Object storage systems generally store full object data for each version, not differential snapshots.

Engineers also have the option of deploying storage lifecycle policies. Lifecycle policies allow automatic deletion of old object versions when certain conditions are met (e.g., when an object version reaches a certain age or many newer versions exist). Cloud vendors also offer various archival data tiers at heavily discounted prices, and the archival process can be managed using lifecycle policies.

Storage classes and tiers

Cloud vendors now offer storage classes that discount data storage pricing in exchange for reduced access or reduced durability. We use the term *reduced access* here because many of these storage tiers still make data highly available, but with high retrieval costs in exchange for reduced storage costs.

Let's look at a couple of examples in S3 since Amazon is a benchmark for cloud service standards. The S3 Standard-Infrequent Access storage class discounts monthly storage costs for increased data retrieval costs. (See "A Brief Detour on Cloud Economics" on page 129 for a theoretical discussion of the economics of cloud storage tiers.) Amazon also offers the Amazon S3 One Zone-Infrequent Access tier, replicating only to a single zone. Projected availability drops from 99.9% to 99.5% to account for the possibility of a zonal outage. Amazon still claims extremely high data durability, with the caveat that data will be lost if an availability zone is destroyed.

Further down the tiers of reduced access are the archival tiers in S3 Glacier. S3 Glacier promises a dramatic reduction in long-term storage costs for much higher access costs. Users have various retrieval speed options, from minutes to hours, with higher retrieval costs for faster access. For example, at the time of this writing, S3 Glacier Deep Archive discounts storage costs even further; Amazon advertises that storage costs start at $1 per terabyte per month. In exchange, data restoration takes 12 hours. In addition, this storage class is designed for data that will be stored 7–10 years and be accessed only one to two times per year.

Be aware of how you plan to utilize archival storage, as it's easy to get into and often costly to access data, especially if you need it more often than expected. See Chapter 4 for a more extensive discussion of archival storage economics.

Object store–backed filesystems

Object store synchronization solutions have become increasingly popular. Tools like s3fs and Amazon S3 File Gateway allow users to mount an S3 bucket as local storage. Users of these tools should be aware of the characteristics of writes to the filesystem and how these will interact with the characteristics and pricing of object storage. File Gateway, for example, handles changes to files fairly efficiently by combining portions of objects into a new object using the advanced capabilities of S3. However, high-speed transactional writing will overwhelm the update capabilities of an object store. Mounting object storage as a local filesystem works well for files that are updated infrequently.

Cache and Memory-Based Storage Systems

As discussed in "Raw Ingredients of Data Storage" on page 195, RAM offers excellent latency and transfer speeds. However, traditional RAM is extremely vulnerable to data loss because a power outage lasting even a second can erase data. RAM-based storage systems are generally focused on caching applications, presenting data for quick access and high bandwidth. Data should generally be written to a more durable medium for retention purposes.

These ultra-fast cache systems are useful when data engineers need to serve data with ultra-fast retrieval latency.

Example: Memcached and lightweight object caching

Memcached is a key-value store designed for caching database query results, API call responses, and more. Memcached uses simple data structures, supporting either string or integer types. Memcached can deliver results with very low latency while also taking the load off backend systems.

Example: Redis, memory caching with optional persistence

Like Memcached, *Redis* is a key-value store, but it supports somewhat more complex data types (such as lists or sets). Redis also builds in multiple persistence mechanisms, including snapshotting and journaling. With a typical configuration, Redis writes data roughly every two seconds. Redis is thus suitable for extremely high-performance applications but can tolerate a small amount of data loss.

The Hadoop Distributed File System

In the recent past, "Hadoop" was virtually synonymous with "big data." The Hadoop Distributed File System is based on Google File System (GFS) (*https://oreil.ly/GlIic*) and was initially engineered to process data with the MapReduce programming model (*https://oreil.ly/DscVp*). Hadoop is similar to object storage but with a key difference: Hadoop combines compute and storage on the same nodes, where object stores typically have limited support for internal processing.

Hadoop breaks large files into *blocks*, chunks of data less than a few hundred megabytes in size. The filesystem is managed by the *NameNode*, which maintains directories, file metadata, and a detailed catalog describing the location of file blocks in the cluster. In a typical configuration, each block of data is replicated to three nodes. This increases both the durability and availability of data. If a disk or node fails, the replication factor for some file blocks will fall below 3. The NameNode will instruct other nodes to replicate these file blocks so that they again reach the correct replication factor. Thus, the probability of losing data is very low, barring a *correlated failure* (e.g., an asteroid hitting the data center).

Hadoop is not simply a storage system. Hadoop combines compute resources with storage nodes to allow in-place data processing. This was originally achieved using the MapReduce programming model, which we discuss in Chapter 8.

Hadoop is dead. Long live Hadoop!

We often see claims that Hadoop is dead. This is only partially true. Hadoop is no longer a hot, bleeding-edge technology. Many Hadoop ecosystem tools such as Apache Pig are now on life support and primarily used to run legacy jobs. The pure MapReduce programming model has fallen by the wayside. HDFS remains widely used in various applications and organizations.

Hadoop still appears in many legacy installations. Many organizations that adopted Hadoop during the peak of the big data craze have no immediate plans to migrate to newer technologies. This is a good choice for companies that run massive (thousand-node) Hadoop clusters and have the resources to maintain on-premises systems effectively. Smaller companies may want to reconsider the cost overhead and scale limitations of running a small Hadoop cluster against migrating to cloud solutions.

In addition, HDFS is a key ingredient of many current big data engines, such as Amazon EMR. In fact, Apache Spark is still commonly run on HDFS clusters. We discuss this in more detail in "Separation of Compute from Storage" on page 224.

Streaming Storage

Streaming data has different storage requirements than nonstreaming data. In the case of message queues, stored data is temporal and expected to disappear after a certain duration. However, distributed, scalable streaming frameworks like Apache Kafka now allow extremely long-duration streaming data retention. Kafka supports indefinite data retention by pushing old, infrequently accessed messages down to object storage. Kafka competitors (including Amazon Kinesis, Apache Pulsar, and Google Cloud Pub/Sub) also support long data retention.

Closely related to data retention in these systems is the notion of replay. *Replay* allows a streaming system to return a range of historical stored data. Replay is the standard data-retrieval mechanism for streaming storage systems. Replay can be used to run batch queries over a time range or to reprocess data in a streaming pipeline. Chapter 7 covers replay in more depth.

Other storage engines have emerged for real-time analytics applications. In some sense, transactional databases emerged as the first real-time query engines; data becomes visible to queries as soon as it is written. However, these databases have well-known scaling and locking limitations, especially for analytics queries that run across large volumes of data. While scalable versions of row-oriented transactional databases have overcome some of these limitations, they are still not truly optimized for analytics at scale.

Indexes, Partitioning, and Clustering

Indexes provide a map of the table for particular fields and allow extremely fast lookup of individual records. Without indexes, a database would need to scan an entire table to find the records satisfying a WHERE condition.

In most RDBMSs, indexes are used for primary table keys (allowing unique identification of rows) and foreign keys (allowing joins with other tables). Indexes can also be applied to other columns to serve the needs of specific applications. Using indexes, an RDBMS can look up and update thousands of rows per second.

We do not cover transactional database records in depth in this book; numerous technical resources are available on this topic. Rather, we are interested in the evolution away from indexes in analytics-oriented storage systems and some new developments in indexes for analytics use cases.

The evolution from rows to columns

An early data warehouse was typically built on the same type of RDBMS used for transactional applications. The growing popularity of MPP systems meant a shift toward parallel processing for significant improvements in scan performance across large quantities of data for analytics purposes. However, these row-oriented MPPs still used indexes to support joins and condition checking.

In "Raw Ingredients of Data Storage" on page 195, we discuss columnar serialization. *Columnar serialization* allows a database to scan only the columns required for a particular query, sometimes dramatically reducing the amount of data read from the disk. In addition, arranging data by column packs similar values next to each other, yielding high-compression ratios with minimal compression overhead. This allows data to be scanned more quickly from disk and over a network.

Columnar databases perform poorly for transactional use cases—i.e., when we try to look up large numbers of individual rows asynchronously. However, they perform extremely well when large quantities of data must be scanned—e.g., for complex data transformations, aggregations, statistical calculations, or evaluation of complex conditions on large datasets.

In the past, columnar databases performed poorly on joins, so the advice for data engineers was to denormalize data, using wide schemas, arrays, and nested data wherever possible. Join performance for columnar databases has improved dramatically in recent years, so while there can still be performance advantages in denormalization, this is no longer a necessity. You'll learn more about normalization and denormalization in Chapter 8.

From indexes to partitions and clustering

While columnar databases allow for fast scan speeds, it's still helpful to reduce the amount of data scanned as much as possible. In addition to scanning only data in columns relevant to a query, we can partition a table into multiple subtables by splitting it on a field. It is quite common in analytics and data science use cases to scan over a time range, so date- and time-based partitioning is extremely common. Columnar databases generally support a variety of other partition schemes as well.

Clusters allow finer-grained organization of data within partitions. A clustering scheme applied within a columnar database sorts data by one or a few fields, colocating similar values. This improves performance for filtering, sorting, and joining these values.

Example: Snowflake micro-partitioning

We mention Snowflake micro-partitioning (*https://oreil.ly/nQTaP*) because it's a good example of recent developments and evolution in approaches to columnar storage. *Micro partitions* are sets of rows between 50 and 500 megabytes in uncompressed size. Snowflake uses an algorithmic approach that attempts to cluster together similar rows. This contrasts the traditional naive approach to partitioning on a single designated field, such as a date. Snowflake specifically looks for values that are repeated in a field across many rows. This allows aggressive *pruning* of queries based on predicates. For example, a WHERE clause might stipulate the following:

```
WHERE created_date='2022-01-02'
```

In such a query, Snowflake excludes any micro-partitions that don't include this date, effectively pruning this data. Snowflake also allows overlapping micro-partitions, potentially partitioning on multiple fields showing significant repeats.

Efficient pruning is facilitated by Snowflake's metadata database, which stores a description of each micro-partition, including the number of rows and value ranges for fields. At each query stage, Snowflake analyzes micro-partitions to determine which ones need to be scanned. Snowflake uses the term *hybrid columnar storage*,[2] partially referring to the fact that its tables are broken into small groups of rows, even though storage is fundamentally columnar. The metadata database plays a role similar to an index in a traditional relational database.

---

2 Benoit Dageville, "The Snowflake Elastic Data Warehouse," *SIGMOD '16: Proceedings of the 2016 International Conference on Management of Data* (June 2016): 215–226, *https://oreil.ly/Tc1su*.

Data Engineering Storage Abstractions

Data engineering storage abstractions are data organization and query patterns that sit at the heart of the data engineering lifecycle and are built atop the data storage systems discussed previously (see Figure 6-3). We introduced many of these abstractions in Chapter 3, and we will revisit them here.

The main types of abstractions we'll concern ourselves with are those that support data science, analytics, and reporting use cases. These include data warehouse, data lake, data lakehouse, data platforms, and data catalogs. We won't cover source systems, as they are discussed in Chapter 5.

The storage abstraction you require as a data engineer boils down to a few key considerations:

Purpose and use case
    You must first identify the purpose of storing the data. What is it used for?

Update patterns
    Is the abstraction optimized for bulk updates, streaming inserts, or upserts?

Cost
    What are the direct and indirect financial costs? The time to value? The opportunity costs?

Separate storage and compute
    The trend is toward separating storage and compute, but most systems hybridize separation and colocation. We cover this in "Separation of Compute from Storage" on page 224 since it affects purpose, speed, and cost.

You should know that the popularity of separating storage from compute means the lines between OLAP databases and data lakes are increasingly blurring. Major cloud data warehouses and data lakes are on a collision course. In the future, the differences between these two may be in name only since they might functionally and technically be very similar under the hood.

The Data Warehouse

Data warehouses are a standard OLAP data architecture. As discussed in Chapter 3, the term *data warehouse* refers to technology platforms (e.g., Google BigQuery and Teradata), an architecture for data centralization, and an organizational pattern within a company. In terms of storage trends, we've evolved from building data warehouses atop conventional transactional databases, row-based MPP systems (e.g., Teradata and IBM Netezza), and columnar MPP systems (e.g., Vertica and Teradata Columnar) to cloud data warehouses and data platforms. (See our data warehousing discussion in Chapter 3 for more details on MPP systems.)

In practice, cloud data warehouses are often used to organize data into a data lake, a storage area for massive amounts of unprocessed raw data, as originally conceived by James Dixon.[3] Cloud data warehouses can handle massive amounts of raw text and complex JSON documents. The limitation is that cloud data warehouses cannot handle truly unstructured data, such as images, video, or audio, unlike a true data lake. Cloud data warehouses can be coupled with object storage to provide a complete data-lake solution.

The Data Lake

The *data lake* was originally conceived as a massive store where data was retained in raw, unprocessed form. Initially, data lakes were built primarily on Hadoop systems, where cheap storage allowed for retention of massive amounts of data without the cost overhead of a proprietary MPP system.

The last five years have seen two major developments in the evolution of data lake storage. First, a major migration toward *separation of compute and storage* has occurred. In practice, this means a move away from Hadoop toward cloud object storage for long-term retention of data. Second, data engineers discovered that much of the functionality offered by MPP systems (schema management; update, merge and delete capabilities) and initially dismissed in the rush to data lakes was, in fact, extremely useful. This led to the notion of the data lakehouse.

The Data Lakehouse

The *data lakehouse* is an architecture that combines aspects of the data warehouse and the data lake. As it is generally conceived, the lakehouse stores data in object storage just like a lake. However, the lakehouse adds to this arrangement features designed to streamline data management and create an engineering experience similar to a data warehouse. This means robust table and schema support and features for managing incremental updates and deletes. Lakehouses typically also support table history and rollback; this is accomplished by retaining old versions of files and metadata.

A lakehouse system is a metadata and file-management layer deployed with data management and transformation tools. Databricks has heavily promoted the lakehouse concept with Delta Lake, an open source storage management system.

We would be remiss not to point out that the architecture of the data lakehouse is similar to the architecture used by various commercial data platforms, including BigQuery and Snowflake. These systems store data in object storage and provide

---

3 James Dixon, "Data Lakes Revisited," *James Dixon's Blog*, September 25, 2014, *https://oreil.ly/FH25v*.

automated metadata management, table history, and update/delete capabilities. The complexities of managing underlying files and storage are fully hidden from the user.

The key advantage of the data lakehouse over proprietary tools is interoperability. It's much easier to exchange data between tools when stored in an open file format. Reserializing data from a proprietary database format incurs overhead in processing, time, and cost. In a data lakehouse architecture, various tools can connect to the metadata layer and read data directly from object storage.

It is important to emphasize that much of the data in a data lakehouse may not have a table structure imposed. We can impose data warehouse features where we need them in a lakehouse, leaving other data in a raw or even unstructured format.

The data lakehouse technology is evolving rapidly. A variety of new competitors to Delta Lake have emerged, including Apache Hudi and Apache Iceberg. See Appendix A for more details.

Data Platforms

Increasingly, vendors are styling their products as *data platforms*. These vendors have created their ecosystems of interoperable tools with tight integration into the core data storage layer. In evaluating platforms, engineers must ensure that the tools offered meet their needs. Tools not directly provided in the platform can still interoperate, with extra data overhead for data interchange. Platforms also emphasize close integration with object storage for unstructured use cases, as mentioned in our discussion of cloud data warehouses.

At this point, the notion of the data platform frankly has yet to be fully fleshed out. However, the race is on to create a walled garden of data tools, both simplifying the work of data engineering and generating significant vendor lock-in.

Stream-to-Batch Storage Architecture

The stream-to-batch storage architecture has many similarities to the Lambda architecture, though some might quibble over the technical details. Essentially, data flowing through a topic in the streaming storage system is written out to multiple consumers.

Some of these consumers might be real-time processing systems that generate statistics on the stream. In addition, a batch storage consumer writes data for long-term retention and batch queries. The batch consumer could be AWS Kinesis Firehose, which can generate S3 objects based on configurable triggers (e.g., time and batch size). Systems such as BigQuery ingest streaming data into a streaming buffer. This streaming buffer is automatically reserialized into columnar object storage. The query engine supports seamless querying of both the streaming buffer and the object data to provide users a current, nearly real-time view of the table.

Big Ideas and Trends in Storage

In this section, we'll discuss some big ideas in storage—key considerations that you need to keep in mind as you build out your storage architecture. Many of these considerations are part of larger trends. For example, data catalogs fit under the trend toward "enterprisey" data engineering and data management. Separation of compute from storage is now largely an accomplished fact in cloud data systems. And data sharing is an increasingly important consideration as businesses adopt data technology.

Data Catalog

A *data catalog* is a centralized metadata store for all data across an organization. Strictly speaking, a data catalog is not a top-level data storage abstraction, but it integrates with various systems and abstractions. Data catalogs typically work across operational and analytics data sources, integrate data lineage and presentation of data relationships, and allow user editing of data descriptions.

Data catalogs are often used to provide a central place where people can view their data, queries, and data storage. As a data engineer, you'll likely be responsible for setting up and maintaining the various data integrations of data pipeline and storage systems that will integrate with the data catalog and the integrity of the data catalog itself.

Catalog application integration

Ideally, data applications are designed to integrate with catalog APIs to handle their metadata and updates directly. As catalogs are more widely used in an organization, it becomes easier to approach this ideal.

Automated scanning

In practice, cataloging systems typically need to rely on an automated scanning layer that collects metadata from various systems such as data lakes, data warehouses, and operational databases. Data catalogs can collect existing metadata and may also use scanning tools to infer metadata such as key relationships or the presence of sensitive data.

Data portal and social layer

Data catalogs also typically provide a human access layer through a web interface, where users can search for data and view data relationships. Data catalogs can be enhanced with a social layer offering Wiki functionality. This allows users to provide information on their datasets, request information from other users, and post updates as they become available.

Data catalog use cases

Data catalogs have both organizational and technical use cases. Data catalogs make metadata easily available to systems. For instance, a data catalog is a key ingredient of the data lakehouse, allowing table discoverability for queries.

Organizationally, data catalogs allow business users, analysts, data scientists, and engineers to search for data to answer questions. Data catalogs streamline cross-organizational communications and collaboration.

Data Sharing

Data sharing allows organizations and individuals to share specific data and carefully defined permissions with specific entities. Data sharing allows data scientists to share data from a sandbox with their collaborators within an organization. Across organizations, data sharing facilitates collaboration between partner businesses. For example, an ad tech company can share advertising data with its customers.

A cloud multitenant environment makes interorganizational collaboration much easier. However, it also presents new security challenges. Organizations must carefully control policies that govern who can share data with whom to prevent accidental exposure or deliberate exfiltration.

Data sharing is a core feature of many cloud data platforms. See Chapter 5 for a more extensive discussion of data sharing.

Schema

What is the expected form of the data? What is the file format? Is it structured, semistructured, or unstructured? What data types are expected? How does the data fit into a larger hierarchy? Is it connected to other data through shared keys or other relationships?

Note that schema need not be *relational*. Rather, data becomes more useful when we have as much information about its structure and organization. For images stored in a data lake, this schema information might explain the image format, resolution, and the way the images fit into a larger hierarchy.

Schema can function as a sort of Rosetta stone, instructions that tell us how to read the data. Two major schema patterns exist: schema on write and schema on read. *Schema on write* is essentially the traditional data warehouse pattern: a table has an integrated schema; any writes to the table must conform. To support schema on write, a data lake must integrate a schema metastore.

With *schema on read*, the schema is dynamically created when data is written, and a reader must determine the schema when reading the data. Ideally, schema on read is implemented using file formats that implement built-in schema information, such as Parquet or JSON. CSV files are notorious for schema inconsistency and are not recommended in this setting.

The principal advantage of schema on write is that it enforces data standards, making data easier to consume and utilize in the future. Schema on read emphasizes flexibility, allowing virtually any data to be written. This comes at the cost of greater difficulty consuming data in the future.

Separation of Compute from Storage

A key idea we revisit throughout this book is the separation of compute from storage. This has emerged as a standard data access and query pattern in today's cloud era. Data lakes, as we discussed, store data in object stores and spin up temporary compute capacity to read and process it. Most fully managed OLAP products now rely on object storage behind the scenes. To understand the motivations for separating compute and storage, we should first look at the colocation of compute and storage.

Colocation of compute and storage

Colocation of compute and storage has long been a standard method to improve database performance. For transactional databases, data colocation allows fast, low-latency disk reads and high bandwidth. Even when we virtualize storage (e.g., using Amazon EBS), data is located relatively close to the host machine.

The same basic idea applies for analytics query systems running across a cluster of machines. For example, with HDFS and MapReduce, the standard approach is to locate data blocks that need to be scanned in the cluster, and then push individual *map* jobs out to these blocks. The data scan and processing for the map step are strictly local. The *reduce* step involves shuffling data across the cluster, but keeping map steps local effectively preserves more bandwidth for shuffling, delivering better overall performance; map steps that filter heavily also dramatically reduce the amount of data to be shuffled.

Separation of compute and storage

If colocation of compute and storage delivers high performance, why the shift toward separation of compute and storage? Several motivations exist.

Ephemerality and scalability. In the cloud, we've seen a dramatic shift toward ephemerality. In general, it's cheaper to buy and host a server than to rent it from a cloud provider, *provided that you're running it 24 hours a day nonstop for years on end.* In practice, workloads vary dramatically, and significant efficiencies are realized with a pay-as-you-go model if servers can scale up and down. This is true for web servers in online retail, and it is also true for big data batch jobs that may run only periodically.

Ephemeral compute resources allow engineers to spin up massive clusters to complete jobs on time and then delete clusters when these jobs are done. The performance benefits of temporarily operating at ultra-high scale can outweigh the bandwidth limitations of object storage.

Data durability and availability. Cloud object stores significantly mitigate the risk of data loss and generally provide extremely high uptime (availability). For example, S3 stores data across multiple zones; if a natural disaster destroys a zone, data is still available from the remaining zones. Having multiple zones available also reduces the odds of a data outage. If resources in one zone go down, engineers can spin up the same resources in a different zone.

The potential for a misconfiguration that destroys data in object storage is still somewhat scary, but simple-to-deploy mitigations are available. Copying data to multiple cloud regions reduces this risk since configuration changes are generally deployed to only one region at a time. Replicating data to multiple storage providers can further reduce the risk.

Hybrid separation and colocation

The practical realities of separating compute from storage are more complicated than we've implied. In practice, we constantly hybridize colocation and separation to realize the benefits of both approaches. This hybridization is typically done in two ways: multitier caching and hybrid object storage.

With *multitier caching*, we utilize object storage for long-term data retention and access but spin up local storage to be used during queries and various stages of data pipelines. Both Google and Amazon offer versions of hybrid object storage (object storage that is tightly integrated with compute).

Let's look at examples of how some popular processing engines hybridize separation and colocation of storage and compute.

Example: AWS EMR with S3 and HDFS. Big data services like Amazon EMR spin up temporary HDFS clusters to process data. Engineers have the option of referencing both S3 and HDFS as a filesystem. A common pattern is to stand up HDFS on SSD drives, pull from S3, and save data from intermediate processing steps on local HDFS. Doing so can realize significant performance gains over processing directly from S3. Full results are written back to S3 once the cluster completes its steps, and the cluster and HDFS are deleted. Other consumers read the output data directly from S3.

Example: Apache Spark. In practice, Spark generally runs jobs on HDFS or some other ephemeral distributed filesystem to support performant storage of data between processing steps. In addition, Spark relies heavily on in-memory storage of data to improve processing. The problem with owning the infrastructure for running Spark is that dynamic RAM (DRAM) is extremely expensive; by separating compute and storage in the cloud, we can rent large quantities of memory and then release that memory when the job completes.

Example: Apache Druid. Apache Druid relies heavily on SSDs to realize high performance. Since SSDs are significantly more expensive than magnetic disks, Druid keeps only one copy of data in its cluster, reducing "live" storage costs by a factor of three.

Of course, maintaining data durability is still critical, so Druid uses an object store as its durability layer. When data is ingested, it's processed, serialized into compressed columns, and written to cluster SSDs and object storage. In the event of node failure or cluster data corruption, data can be automatically recovered to new nodes. In addition, the cluster can be shut down and then fully recovered from SSD storage.

Example: Hybrid object storage. Google's Colossus file storage system supports fine-grained control of data block location, although this functionality is not exposed directly to the public. BigQuery uses this feature to colocate customer tables in a single location, allowing ultra-high bandwidth for queries in that location.[4] We refer to this as *hybrid object storage* because it combines the clean abstractions of object storage with some advantages of colocating compute and storage. Amazon also offers some notion of hybrid object storage through S3 Select, a feature that allows users to filter S3 data directly in S3 clusters before data is returned across the network.

We speculate that public clouds will adopt hybrid object storage more widely to improve the performance of their offerings and make more efficient use of available network resources. Some may be already doing so without disclosing this publicly.

The concept of hybrid object storage underscores that there can still be advantages to having low-level access to hardware rather than relying on someone else's public cloud. Public cloud services do not expose low-level details of hardware and systems (e.g., data block locations for Colossus), but these details can be extremely useful in performance optimization and enhancement. See our discussion of cloud economics in Chapter 4.

While we're now seeing a mass migration of data to public clouds, we believe that many hyper-scale data service vendors that currently run on public clouds provided by other vendors may build their data centers in the future, albeit with deep network integration into public clouds.

---

4 Valliappa Lakshmanan and Jordan Tigani, *Google BigQuery: The Definitive Guide* (Sebastopol, CA: O'Reilly, 2019), 16–17, 188, *https://oreil.ly/5aXXu*.

Zero-copy cloning

Cloud-based systems based around object storage support *zero-copy cloning*. This typically means that a new virtual copy of an object is created (e.g., a new table) without necessarily physically copying the underlying data. Typically, new pointers are created to the raw data files, and future changes to these tables will not be recorded in the old table. For those familiar with the inner workings of object-oriented languages such as Python, this type of "shallow" copying is familiar from other contexts.

Zero-copy cloning is a compelling feature, but engineers must understand its strengths and limitations. For example, cloning an object in a data lake environment and then deleting the files in the original object might also wipe out the new object.

For fully managed object-store-based systems (e.g., Snowflake and BigQuery), engineers need to be extremely familiar with the exact limits of shallow copying. Engineers have more access to underlying object storage in data lake systems such as Databricks—a blessing and a curse. Data engineers should exercise great caution before deleting any raw files in the underlying object store. Databricks and other data lake management technologies sometimes also support a notion of *deep copying*, whereby all underlying data objects are copied. This is a more expensive process, but also more robust in the event that files are unintentionally lost or deleted.

Data Storage Lifecycle and Data Retention

Storing data isn't as simple as just saving it to object storage or disk and forgetting about it. You need to think about the data storage lifecycle and data retention. When you think about access frequency and use cases, ask, "How important is the data to downstream users, and how often do they need to access it?" This is the data storage lifecycle. Another question you should ask is, "How long should I keep this data?" Do you need to retain data indefinitely, or are you fine discarding it past a certain time frame? This is data retention. Let's dive into each of these.

Hot, warm, and cold data

Did you know that data has a temperature? Depending on how frequently data is accessed, we can roughly bucket the way it is stored into three categories of persistence: hot, warm, and cold. Query access patterns differ for each dataset (Figure 6-9). Typically, newer data is queried more often than older data. Let's look at hot, cold, and warm data in that order.

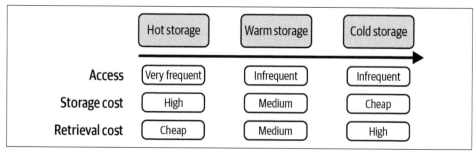

	Hot storage	Warm storage	Cold storage
Access	Very frequent	Infrequent	Infrequent
Storage cost	High	Medium	Cheap
Retrieval cost	Cheap	Medium	High

Figure 6-9. Hot, warm, and cold data costs associated with access frequency

Hot data.   *Hot data* has instant or frequent access requirements. The underlying storage for hot data is suited for fast access and reads, such as SSD or memory. Because of the type of hardware involved with hot data, storing hot data is often the most expensive form of storage. Example use cases for hot data include retrieving product recommendations and product page results. The cost of storing hot data is the highest of these three storage tiers, but retrieval is often inexpensive.

Query results cache is another example of hot data. When a query is run, some query engines will persist the query results in the cache. For a limited time, when the same query is run, instead of rerunning the same query against storage, the query results cache serves the cached results. This allows for much faster query response times versus redundantly issuing the same query repeatedly. In upcoming chapters, we cover query results caches in more detail.

Warm data.   *Warm data* is accessed semi-regularly, say, once per month. No hard and fast rules indicate how often warm data is accessed, but it's less than hot data and more than cold data. The major cloud providers offer object storage tiers that accommodate warm data. For example, S3 offers an Infrequently Accessed Tier, and Google Cloud has a similar storage tier called Nearline. Vendors give their models of recommended access frequency, and engineers can also do their cost modeling and monitoring. Storage of warm data is cheaper than hot data, with slightly more expensive retrieval costs.

Cold data.   On the other extreme, *cold data* is infrequently accessed data. The hardware used to archive cold data is typically cheap and durable, such as HDD, tape storage, and cloud-based archival systems. Cold data is mainly meant for long-term archival, when there's little to no intention to access the data. Though storing cold data is cheap, retrieving cold data is often expensive.

Storage tier considerations.   When considering the storage tier for your data, consider the costs of each tier. If you store all of your data in hot storage, all of the data can be accessed quickly. But this comes at a tremendous price! Conversely, if you store all data in cold storage to save on costs, you'll certainly lower your storage costs, but at the expense of prolonged retrieval times and high retrieval costs if you need to access data. The storage price goes down from faster/higher performing storage to lower storage.

Cold storage is popular for archiving data. Historically, cold storage involved physical backups and often mailing this data to a third party that would archive it in a literal vault. Cold storage is increasingly popular in the cloud. Every cloud vendor offers a cold data solution, and you should weigh the cost of pushing data into cold storage versus the cost and time to retrieve the data.

Data engineers need to account for spillover from hot to warm/cold storage. Memory is expensive and finite. For example, if hot data is stored in memory, it can be spilled to disk when there's too much new data to store and not enough memory. Some databases may move infrequently accessed data to warm or cold tiers, offloading the data to either HDD or object storage. The latter is increasingly more common because of the cost-effectiveness of object storage. If you're in the cloud and using managed services, disk spillover will happen automatically.

If you're using cloud-based object storage, create automated lifecycle policies for your data. This will drastically reduce your storage costs. For example, if your data needs to be accessed only once a month, move the data to an infrequent access storage tier. If your data is 180 days old and not accessed for current queries, move it to an archival storage tier. In both cases, you can automate the migration of data away from regular object storage, and you'll save money. That said, consider the retrieval costs—both in time and money—using infrequent or archival style storage tiers. Access and retrieval times and costs may vary depending on the cloud provider. Some cloud providers make it simple and cheap to migrate data into archive storage, but it is costly and slow to retrieve your data.

Data retention

Back in the early days of "big data," there was a tendency to err on the side of accumulating every piece of data possible, regardless of its usefulness. The expectation was, "we might need this data in the future." This data hoarding inevitably became unwieldy and dirty, giving rise to data swamps and regulatory crackdowns on data retention, among other consequences and nightmares. Nowadays, data engineers need to consider data retention: what data do you *need* to keep, and how *long* should you keep it? Here are some things to think about with data retention.

Value. Data is an asset, so you should know the value of the data you're storing. Of course, value is subjective and depends on what it's worth to your immediate use case and your broader organization. Is this data impossible to re-create, or can it easily be re-created by querying upstream systems? What's the impact to downstream users if this data is available versus if it is not?

Time. The value to downstream users also depends upon the age of the data. New data is typically more valuable and frequently accessed than older data. Technical limitations may determine how long you can store data in certain storage tiers. For example, if you store hot data in cache or memory, you'll likely need to set a time to live (TTL), so you can expire data after a certain point or persist it to warm or cold storage. Otherwise, your hot storage will become full, and queries against the hot data will suffer from performance lags.

Compliance. Certain regulations (e.g., HIPAA and Payment Card Industry, or PCI) might require you to keep data for a certain time. In these situations, the data simply needs to be accessible upon request, even if the likelihood of an access request is low. Other regulations might require you to hold data for only a limited period of time, and you'll need to have the ability to delete specific information on time and within compliance guidelines. You'll need a storage and archival data process—along with the ability to search the data—that fits the retention requirements of the particular regulation with which you need to comply. Of course, you'll want to balance compliance against cost.

Cost. Data is an asset that (hopefully) has an ROI. On the cost side of ROI, an obvious storage expense is associated with data. Consider the timeline in which you need to retain data. Given our discussion about hot, warm, and cold data, implement automatic data lifecycle management practices and move the data to cold storage if you don't need the data past the required retention date. Or delete data if it's truly not needed.

Single-Tenant Versus Multitenant Storage

In Chapter 3, we covered the trade-offs between single-tenant and multitenant architecture. To recap, with *single-tenant* architecture, each group of tenants (e.g., individual users, groups of users, accounts, or customers) gets its own dedicated set of resources such as networking, compute, and storage. A *multitenant* architecture inverts this and shares these resources among groups of users. Both architectures are widely used. This section looks at the implications of single-tenant and multitenant storage.

Adopting single-tenant storage means that every tenant gets their dedicated storage. In the example in Figure 6-10, each tenant gets a database. No data is shared among these databases, and storage is totally isolated. An example of using single-tenant storage is that each customer's data must be stored in isolation and cannot be blended with any other customer's data. In this case, each customer gets their own database.

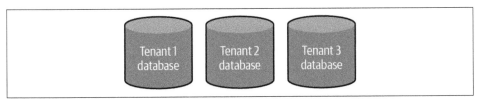

Figure 6-10. In single-tenant storage, each tenant gets their own database

Separate data storage implies separate and independent schemas, bucket structures, and everything related to storage. This means you have the liberty of designing each tenant's storage environment to be uniform or let them evolve however they may. Schema variation across customers can be an advantage and a complication; as always, consider the trade-offs. If each tenant's schema isn't uniform across all tenants, this has major consequences if you need to query multiple tenants' tables to create a unified view of all tenant data.

Multitenant storage allows for the storage of multiple tenants within a single database. For example, instead of the single-tenant scenario where customers get their own database, multiple customers may reside in the same database schemas or tables in a multitenant database. Storing multitenant data means each tenant's data is stored in the same place (Figure 6-11).

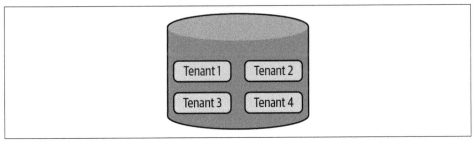

Figure 6-11. In this multitenant storage, four tenants occupy the same database

You need to be aware of querying both single and multitenant storage, which we cover in more detail in Chapter 8.

Whom You'll Work With

Storage is at the heart of data engineering infrastructure. You'll interact with the people who own your IT infrastructure—typically, DevOps, security, and cloud architects. Defining domains of responsibility between data engineering and other teams is critical. Do data engineers have the authority to deploy their infrastructure in an AWS account, or must another team handle these changes? Work with other teams to define streamlined processes so that teams can work together efficiently and quickly.

The division of responsibilities for data storage will depend significantly on the maturity of the organization involved. The data engineer will likely manage the storage systems and workflow if the company is early in its data maturity. If the company is later in its data maturity, the data engineer will probably manage a section of the storage system. This data engineer will also likely interact with engineers on either side of storage—ingestion and transformation.

The data engineer needs to ensure that the storage systems used by downstream users are securely available, contain high-quality data, have ample storage capacity, and perform when queries and transformations are run.

Undercurrents

The undercurrents for storage are significant because storage is a critical hub for all stages of the data engineering lifecycle. Unlike other undercurrents for which data might be in motion (ingestion) or queried and transformed, the undercurrents for storage differ because storage is so ubiquitous.

Security

While engineers often view security as an impediment to their work, they should embrace the idea that security is a key enabler. Robust security at rest and in motion with fine-grained data access control allows data to be shared and consumed more widely within a business. The value of data goes up significantly when this is possible.

As always, exercise the principle of least privilege. Don't give full database access to anyone unless required. This means most data engineers don't need full database access in practice. Also, pay attention to the column, row, and cell-level access controls in your database. Give users only the information they need and no more.

Data Management

Data management is critical as we read and write data with storage systems.

Data catalogs and metadata management

Data is enhanced by robust metadata. Cataloging enables data scientists, analysts, and ML engineers by enabling data discovery. Data lineage accelerates the time to track down data problems and allows consumers to locate upstream raw sources. As you build out your storage systems, invest in your metadata. Integration of a data dictionary with these other tools allows users to share and record institutional knowledge robustly.

Metadata management also significantly enhances data governance. Beyond simply enabling passive data cataloging and lineage, consider implementing analytics over these systems to get a clear, active picture of what's happening with your data.

Data versioning in object storage

Major cloud object storage systems enable data versioning. Data versioning can help with error recovery when processes fail, and data becomes corrupted. Versioning is also beneficial for tracking the history of datasets used to build models. Just as code version control allows developers to track down commits that cause bugs, data version control can aid ML engineers in tracking changes that lead to model performance degradation.

Privacy

GDPR and other privacy regulations have significantly impacted storage system design. Any data with privacy implications has a lifecycle that data engineers must manage. Data engineers must be prepared to respond to data deletion requests and selectively remove data as required. In addition, engineers can accommodate privacy and security through anonymization and masking.

DataOps

DataOps is not orthogonal to data management, and a significant area of overlap exists. DataOps concerns itself with traditional operational monitoring of storage systems and monitoring the data itself, inseparable from metadata and quality.

Systems monitoring

Data engineers must monitor storage in a variety of ways. This includes monitoring infrastructure storage components, where they exist, but also monitoring object storage and other "serverless" systems. Data engineers should take the lead on FinOps (cost management), security monitoring, and access monitoring.

Observing and monitoring data

While metadata systems as we've described are critical, good engineering must consider the entropic nature of data by actively seeking to understand its characteristics and watching for major changes. Engineers can monitor data statistics, apply anomaly detection methods or simple rules, and actively test and validate for logical inconsistencies.

Data Architecture

Chapter 3 covers the basics of data architecture, as storage is the critical underbelly of the data engineering lifecycle.

Consider the following data architecture tips. Design for required reliability and durability. Understand the upstream source systems and how that data, once ingested, will be stored and accessed. Understand the types of data models and queries that will occur downstream.

If data is expected to grow, can you negotiate storage with your cloud provider? Take an active approach to FinOps, and treat it as a central part of architecture conversations. Don't prematurely optimize, but prepare for scale if business opportunities exist in operating on large data volumes.

Lean toward fully managed systems, and understand provider SLAs. Fully managed systems are generally far more robust and scalable than systems you have to babysit.

Orchestration

Orchestration is highly entangled with storage. Storage allows data to flow through pipelines, and orchestration is the pump. Orchestration also helps engineers cope with the complexity of data systems, potentially combining many storage systems and query engines.

Software Engineering

We can think about software engineering in the context of storage in two ways. First, the code you write should perform well with your storage system. Make sure the code you write stores the data correctly and doesn't accidentally cause data, memory leaks, or performance issues. Second, define your storage infrastructure as code and use ephemeral compute resources when it's time to process your data. Because storage is increasingly distinct from compute, you can automatically spin resources up and down while keeping your data in object storage. This keeps your infrastructure clean and avoids coupling your storage and query layers.

Conclusion

Storage is everywhere and underlays many stages of the data engineering lifecycle. In this chapter, you learned about the raw ingredients, types, abstractions, and big ideas around storage systems. Gain deep knowledge of the inner workings and limitations of the storage systems you'll use. Know the types of data, activities, and workloads appropriate for your storage.

Additional Resources

- "Column-Oriented DBMS" Wikipedia page (*https://oreil.ly/FBZH0*)
- "The Design and Implementation of Modern Column-Oriented Database Systems" (*https://oreil.ly/Q570W*) by Daniel Abadi et al.
- *Designing Data-Intensive Applications* by Martin Kleppmann (O'Reilly)
- "Diving Into Delta Lake: Schema Enforcement and Evolution" (*https://oreil.ly/XSxuN*) by Burak Yavuz et al.
- "Hot Data vs. Cold Data: Why It Matters" (*https://oreil.ly/h6mbt*) by Afzaal Ahmad Zeeshan
- IDC's "Data Creation and Replication Will Grow at a Faster Rate than Installed Storage Capacity, According to the IDC Global DataSphere and StorageSphere Forecasts" press release (*https://oreil.ly/Kt784*)
- "Rowise vs. Columnar Database? Theory and in Practice" (*https://oreil.ly/SB63g*) by Mangat Rai Modi
- "Snowflake Solution Anti-Patterns: The Probable Data Scientist" (*https://oreil.ly/is1uz*) by John Aven
- "What Is a Vector Database?" (*https://oreil.ly/ktw0O*) by Bryan Turriff
- "What Is Object Storage? A Definition and Overview" (*https://oreil.ly/ZyCrz*) by Alex Chan
- "The What, When, Why, and How of Incremental Loads" (*https://oreil.ly/HcfX8*) by Tim Mitchell

CHAPTER 7

Ingestion

You've learned about the various source systems you'll likely encounter as a data engineer and about ways to store data. Let's now turn our attention to the patterns and choices that apply to ingesting data from various source systems. In this chapter, we discuss data ingestion (see Figure 7-1), the key engineering considerations for the ingestion phase, the major patterns for batch and streaming ingestion, technologies you'll encounter, whom you'll work with as you develop your data ingestion pipeline, and how the undercurrents feature in the ingestion phase.

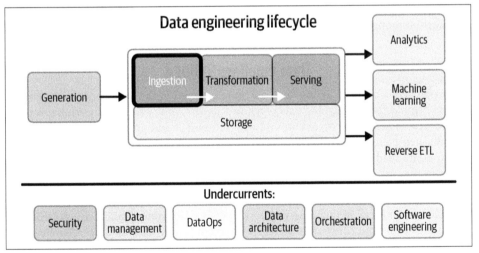

Figure 7-1. To begin processing data, we must ingest it

What Is Data Ingestion?

Data ingestion is the process of moving data from one place to another. Data ingestion implies data movement from source systems into storage in the data engineering lifecycle, with ingestion as an intermediate step (Figure 7-2).

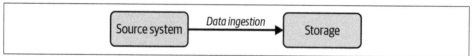

Figure 7-2. Data from system 1 is ingested into system 2

It's worth quickly contrasting data ingestion with data integration. Whereas *data ingestion* is data movement from point A to B, *data integration* combines data from disparate sources into a new dataset. For example, you can use data integration to combine data from a CRM system, advertising analytics data, and web analytics to create a user profile, which is saved to your data warehouse. Furthermore, using reverse ETL, you can send this newly created user profile *back* to your CRM so salespeople can use the data for prioritizing leads. We describe data integration more fully in Chapter 8, where we discuss data transformations; reverse ETL is covered in Chapter 9.

We also point out that data ingestion is different from *internal ingestion* within a system. Data stored in a database is copied from one table to another, or data in a stream is temporarily cached. We consider this another part of the general data transformation process covered in Chapter 8.

Data Pipelines Defined

Data pipelines begin in source systems, but ingestion is the stage where data engineers begin actively designing data pipeline activities. In the data engineering space, a good deal of ceremony occurs around data movement and processing patterns, with established patterns such as ETL, newer patterns such as ELT, and new names for long-established practices (reverse ETL) and data sharing.

All of these concepts are encompassed in the idea of a *data pipeline*. It is essential to understand the details of these various patterns and know that a modern data pipeline includes all of them. As the world moves away from a traditional monolithic approach with rigid constraints on data movement, and toward an open ecosystem of cloud services that are assembled like LEGO bricks to realize products, data engineers prioritize using the right tools to accomplish the desired outcome over adhering to a narrow philosophy of data movement.

In general, here's our definition of a data pipeline:

> A data pipeline is the combination of architecture, systems, and processes that move data through the stages of the data engineering lifecycle.
>
> Our definition is deliberately fluid—and intentionally vague—to allow data engineers to plug in whatever they need to accomplish the task at hand. A data pipeline could be a traditional ETL system, where data is ingested from an on-premises transactional system, passed through a monolithic processor, and written into a data warehouse. Or it could be a cloud-based data pipeline that pulls data from 100 sources, combines it into 20 wide tables, trains five other ML models, deploys them into production, and monitors ongoing performance. A data pipeline should be flexible enough to fit any needs along the data engineering lifecycle.
>
> Let's keep this notion of data pipelines in mind as we proceed through this chapter.

Key Engineering Considerations for the Ingestion Phase

When preparing to architect or build an ingestion system, here are some primary considerations and questions to ask yourself related to data ingestion:

- What's the use case for the data I'm ingesting?
- Can I reuse this data and avoid ingesting multiple versions of the same dataset?
- Where is the data going? What's the destination?
- How often should the data be updated from the source?
- What is the expected data volume?
- What format is the data in? Can downstream storage and transformation accept this format?
- Is the source data in good shape for immediate downstream use? That is, is the data of good quality? What post-processing is required to serve it? What are data-quality risks (e.g., could bot traffic to a website contaminate the data)?
- Does the data require in-flight processing for downstream ingestion if the data is from a streaming source?

These questions undercut batch and streaming ingestion and apply to the underlying architecture you'll create, build, and maintain. Regardless of how often the data is ingested, you'll want to consider these factors when designing your ingestion architecture:

- Bounded versus unbounded
- Frequency
- Synchronous versus asynchronous

- Serialization and deserialization
- Throughput and scalability
- Reliability and durability
- Payload
- Push versus pull versus poll patterns

Let's look at each of these.

Bounded Versus Unbounded Data

As you might recall from Chapter 3, data comes in two forms: bounded and unbounded (Figure 7-3). *Unbounded data* is data as it exists in reality, as events happen, either sporadically or continuously, ongoing and flowing. *Bounded data* is a convenient way of bucketing data across some sort of boundary, such as time.

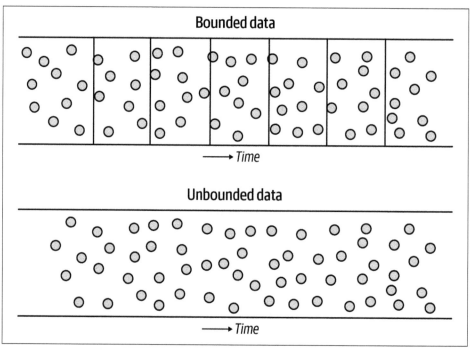

Figure 7-3. Bounded versus unbounded data

Let us adopt this mantra: *All data is unbounded until it's bounded.* Like many mantras, this one is not precisely accurate 100% of the time. The grocery list that I scribbled this afternoon is bounded data. I wrote it as a stream of consciousness (unbounded data) onto a piece of scrap paper, where the thoughts now exist as a list of things (bounded data) I need to buy at the grocery store. However, the idea is correct for practical purposes for the vast majority of data you'll handle in a business context. For example, an online retailer will process customer transactions 24 hours a day until the business fails, the economy grinds to a halt, or the sun explodes.

Business processes have long imposed artificial bounds on data by cutting discrete batches. Keep in mind the true unboundedness of your data; streaming ingestion systems are simply a tool for preserving the unbounded nature of data so that subsequent steps in the lifecycle can also process it continuously.

Frequency

One of the critical decisions that data engineers must make in designing data-ingestion processes is the data-ingestion frequency. Ingestion processes can be batch, micro-batch, or real-time.

Ingestion frequencies vary dramatically from slow to fast (Figure 7-4). On the slow end, a business might ship its tax data to an accounting firm once a year. On the faster side, a CDC system could retrieve new log updates from a source database once a minute. Even faster, a system might continuously ingest events from IoT sensors and process these within seconds. Data-ingestion frequencies are often mixed in a company, depending on the use case and technologies.

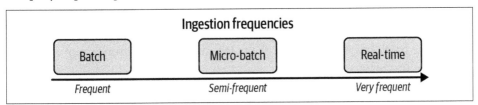

Figure 7-4. The spectrum batch to real-time ingestion frequencies

We note that "real-time" ingestion patterns are becoming increasingly common. We put "real-time" in quotation marks because no ingestion system is genuinely real-time. Any database, queue or pipeline has inherent latency in delivering data to a target system. It is more accurate to speak of *near real-time*, but we often use *real-time* for brevity. The near real-time pattern generally does away with an explicit update frequency; events are processed in the pipeline either one by one as they arrive or in micro-batches (i.e., batches over concise time intervals). For this book, we will use *real-time* and *streaming* interchangeably.

Even with a streaming data-ingestion process, batch processing downstream is relatively standard. At the time of this writing, ML models are typically trained on a batch basis, although continuous online training is becoming more prevalent. Rarely do data engineers have the option to build a purely near real-time pipeline with no batch components. Instead, they choose where batch boundaries will occur—i.e., the data engineering lifecycle data will be broken into batches. Once data reaches a batch process, the batch frequency becomes a bottleneck for all downstream processing.

In addition, streaming systems are the best fit for many data source types. In IoT applications, the typical pattern is for each sensor to write events or measurements to streaming systems as they happen. While this data can be written directly into a database, a streaming ingestion platform such as Amazon Kinesis or Apache Kafka is a better fit for the application. Software applications can adopt similar patterns by writing events to a message queue as they happen rather than waiting for an extraction process to pull events and state information from a backend database. This pattern works exceptionally well for event-driven architectures already exchanging messages through queues. And again, streaming architectures generally coexist with batch processing.

Synchronous Versus Asynchronous Ingestion

With *synchronous ingestion*, the source, ingestion, and destination have complex dependencies and are tightly coupled. As you can see in Figure 7-5, each stage of the data engineering lifecycle has processes A, B, and C directly dependent upon one another. If process A fails, processes B and C cannot start; if process B fails, process C doesn't start. This type of synchronous workflow is common in older ETL systems, where data extracted from a source system must then be transformed before being loaded into a data warehouse. Processes downstream of ingestion can't start until all data in the batch has been ingested. If the ingestion or transformation process fails, the entire process must be rerun.

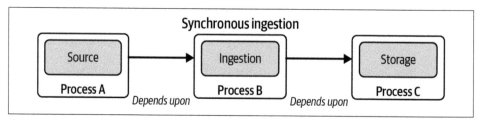

Figure 7-5. A synchronous ingestion process runs as discrete batch steps

Here's a mini case study of how *not* to design your data pipelines. At one company, the transformation process itself was a series of dozens of tightly coupled synchronous workflows, with the entire process taking over 24 hours to finish. If any step of that transformation pipeline failed, the whole transformation process had to be restarted from the beginning! In this instance, we saw process after process fail, and because of nonexistent or cryptic error messages, fixing the pipeline was a game of whack-a-mole that took over a week to diagnose and cure. Meanwhile, the business didn't have updated reports during that time. People weren't happy.

With *asynchronous ingestion*, dependencies can now operate at the level of individual events, much as they would in a software backend built from microservices (Figure 7-6). Individual events become available in storage as soon as they are ingested individually. Take the example of a web application on AWS that emits events into Amazon Kinesis Data Streams (here acting as a buffer). The stream is read by Apache Beam, which parses and enriches events, and then forwards them to a second Kinesis stream; Kinesis Data Firehose rolls up events and writes objects to Amazon S3.

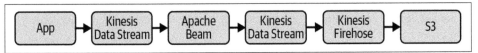

Figure 7-6. Asynchronous processing of an event stream in AWS

The big idea is that rather than relying on asynchronous processing, where a batch process runs for each stage as the input batch closes and certain time conditions are met, each stage of the asynchronous pipeline can process data items as they become available in parallel across the Beam cluster. The processing rate depends on available resources. The Kinesis Data Stream acts as the shock absorber, moderating the load so that event rate spikes will not overwhelm downstream processing. Events will move through the pipeline quickly when the event rate is low, and any backlog has cleared. Note that we could modify the scenario and use a Kinesis Data Stream for storage, eventually extracting events to S3 before they expire out of the stream.

Serialization and Deserialization

Moving data from source to destination involves serialization and deserialization. As a reminder, *serialization* means encoding the data from a source and preparing data structures for transmission and intermediate storage stages.

When ingesting data, ensure that your destination can deserialize the data it receives. We've seen data ingested from a source but then sitting inert and unusable in the destination because the data cannot be properly deserialized. See the more extensive discussion of serialization in Appendix A.

Throughput and Scalability

In theory, your ingestion should never be a bottleneck. In practice, ingestion bottlenecks are pretty standard. Data throughput and system scalability become critical as your data volumes grow and requirements change. Design your systems to scale and shrink to flexibly match the desired data throughput.

Where you're ingesting data from matters a lot. If you're receiving data as it's generated, will the upstream system have any issues that might impact your downstream ingestion pipelines? For example, suppose a source database goes down. When it comes back online and attempts to backfill the lapsed data loads, will your ingestion be able to keep up with this sudden influx of backlogged data?

Another thing to consider is your ability to handle bursty data ingestion. Data generation rarely happens at a constant rate and often ebbs and flows. Built-in buffering is required to collect events during rate spikes to prevent data from getting lost. Buffering bridges the time while the system scales and allows storage systems to accommodate bursts even in a dynamically scalable system.

Whenever possible, use managed services that handle the throughput scaling for you. While you can manually accomplish these tasks by adding more servers, shards, or workers, often this isn't value-added work, and there's a good chance you'll miss something. Much of this heavy lifting is now automated. Don't reinvent the data ingestion wheel if you don't have to.

Reliability and Durability

Reliability and durability are vital in the ingestion stages of data pipelines. *Reliability* entails high uptime and proper failover for ingestion systems. *Durability* entails making sure that data isn't lost or corrupted.

Some data sources (e.g., IoT devices and caches) may not retain data if it is not correctly ingested. Once lost, it is gone for good. In this sense, the *reliability* of ingestion systems leads directly to the *durability* of generated data. If data is ingested, downstream processes can theoretically run late if they break temporarily.

Our advice is to evaluate the risks and build an appropriate level of redundancy and self-healing based on the impact and cost of losing data. Reliability and durability have both direct and indirect costs. For example, will your ingestion process continue if an AWS zone goes down? How about a whole region? How about the power grid or the internet? Of course, nothing is free. How much will this cost you? You might be able to build a highly redundant system and have a team on call 24 hours a day to handle outages. This also means your cloud and labor costs become prohibitive (direct costs), and the ongoing work takes a significant toll on your team (indirect costs). There's no single correct answer, and you need to evaluate the costs and benefits of your reliability and durability decisions.

Don't assume that you can build a system that will reliably and durably ingest data in every possible scenario. Even the nearly infinite budget of the US federal government can't guarantee this. In many extreme scenarios, ingesting data actually won't matter. There will be little to ingest if the internet goes down, even if you build multiple air-gapped data centers in underground bunkers with independent power. Continually evaluate the trade-offs and costs of reliability and durability.

Payload

A *payload* is the dataset you're ingesting and has characteristics such as kind, shape, size, schema and data types, and metadata. Let's look at some of these characteristics to understand why this matters.

Kind

The *kind* of data you handle directly impacts how it's dealt with downstream in the data engineering lifecycle. Kind consists of type and format. Data has a type—tabular, image, video, text, etc. The type directly influences the data format or the way it is expressed in bytes, names, and file extensions. For example, a tabular kind of data may be in formats such as CSV or Parquet, with each of these formats having different byte patterns for serialization and deserialization. Another kind of data is an image, which has a format of JPG or PNG and is inherently unstructured.

Shape

Every payload has a *shape* that describes its dimensions. Data shape is critical across the data engineering lifecycle. For instance, an image's pixel and red, green, blue (RGB) dimensions are necessary for training deep learning models. As another example, if you're trying to import a CSV file into a database table, and your CSV has more columns than the database table, you'll likely get an error during the import process. Here are some examples of the shapes of various kinds of data:

Tabular
    The number of rows and columns in the dataset, commonly expressed as M rows and N columns

Semistructured JSON
    The key-value pairs and nesting depth occur with subelements

Unstructured text
    Number of words, characters, or bytes in the text body

Images
    The width, height, and RGB color depth (e.g., 8 bits per pixel)

Uncompressed audio
    Number of channels (e.g., two for stereo), sample depth (e.g., 16 bits per sample), sample rate (e.g., 48 kHz), and length (e.g., 10,003 seconds)

Size

The *size* of the data describes the number of bytes of a payload. A payload may range in size from single bytes to terabytes and larger. To reduce the size of a payload, it may be compressed into various formats such as ZIP and TAR (see the discussion of compression in Appendix A).

A massive payload can also be split into chunks, which effectively reduces the size of the payload into smaller subsections. When loading a huge file into a cloud object storage or data warehouse, this is a common practice as the small individual files are easier to transmit over a network (especially if they're compressed). The smaller chunked files are sent to their destination and then reassembled after all data has arrived.

Schema and data types

Many data payloads have a schema, such as tabular and semistructured data. As mentioned earlier in this book, a schema describes the fields and types of data within those fields. Other data, such as unstructured text, images, and audio, will not have an explicit schema or data types. However, they might come with technical file descriptions on shape, data and file format, encoding, size, etc.

Although you can connect to databases in various ways (such as file export, CDC, JDBC/ODBC), the connection is easy. The great engineering challenge is understanding the underlying schema. Applications organize data in various ways, and engineers need to be intimately familiar with the organization of the data and relevant update patterns to make sense of it. The problem has been somewhat exacerbated by the popularity of object-relational mapping (ORM), which automatically generates schemas based on object structure in languages such as Java or Python. Natural structures in an object-oriented language often map to something messy in an operational database. Data engineers may need to familiarize themselves with the class structure of application code.

Schema is not only for databases. As we've discussed, APIs present their schema complications. Many vendor APIs have friendly reporting methods that prepare data for analytics. In other cases, engineers are not so lucky. The API is a thin wrapper around underlying systems, requiring engineers to understand application internals to use the data.

Much of the work associated with ingesting from source schemas happens in the data engineering lifecycle transformation stage, which we discuss in Chapter 8. We've placed this discussion here because data engineers need to begin studying source schemas as soon they plan to ingest data from a new source.

Communication is critical for understanding source data, and engineers also have the opportunity to reverse the flow of communication and help software engineers improve data where it is produced. Later in this chapter, we'll return to this topic in "Whom You'll Work With" on page 266.

Detecting and handling upstream and downstream schema changes.   Changes in schema frequently occur in source systems and are often well out of data engineers' control. Examples of schema changes include the following:

- Adding a new column
- Changing a column type
- Creating a new table
- Renaming a column

It's becoming increasingly common for ingestion tools to automate the detection of schema changes and even auto-update target tables. Ultimately, this is something of a mixed blessing. Schema changes can still break pipelines downstream of staging and ingestion.

Engineers must still implement strategies to respond to changes automatically and alert on changes that cannot be accommodated automatically. Automation is excellent, but the analysts and data scientists who rely on this data should be informed of the schema changes that violate existing assumptions. Even if automation can accommodate a change, the new schema may adversely affect the performance of reports and models. Communication between those making schema changes and those impacted by these changes is as important as reliable automation that checks for schema changes.

Schema registries.   In streaming data, every message has a schema, and these schemas may evolve between producers and consumers. A *schema registry* is a metadata repository used to maintain schema and data type integrity in the face of constantly changing schemas. Schema registries can also track schema versions and history. It describes the data model for messages, allowing consistent serialization and deserialization between producers and consumers. Schema registries are used in most major data tools and clouds.

Metadata

In addition to the apparent characteristics we've just covered, a payload often contains metadata, which we first discussed in Chapter 2. Metadata is data about data. Metadata can be as critical as the data itself. One of the significant limitations of the early approach to the data lake—or data swamp, which could become a data superfund site—was a complete lack of attention to metadata. Without a detailed description of the data, it may be of little value. We've already discussed some types of metadata (e.g., schema) and will address them many times throughout this chapter.

Push Versus Pull Versus Poll Patterns

We mentioned push versus pull when we introduced the data engineering lifecycle in Chapter 2. A *push* strategy (Figure 7-7) involves a source system sending data to a target, while a *pull* strategy (Figure 7-8) entails a target reading data directly from a source. As we mentioned in that discussion, the lines between these strategies are blurry.

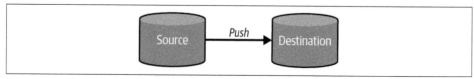

Figure 7-7. Pushing data from source to destination

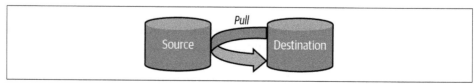

Figure 7-8. A destination pulling data from a source

Another pattern related to pulling is *polling* for data (Figure 7-9). Polling involves periodically checking a data source for any changes. When changes are detected, the destination pulls the data as it would in a regular pull situation.

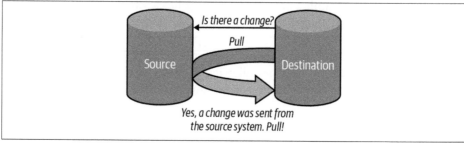

Figure 7-9. Polling for changes in a source system

Batch Ingestion Considerations

Batch ingestion, which involves processing data in bulk, is often a convenient way to ingest data. This means that data is ingested by taking a subset of data from a source system, based either on a time interval or the size of accumulated data (Figure 7-10).

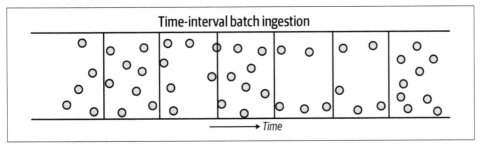

Figure 7-10. Time-interval batch ingestion

Time-interval batch ingestion is widespread in traditional business ETL for data warehousing. This pattern is often used to process data once a day, overnight during off-hours, to provide daily reporting, but other frequencies can also be used.

Size-based batch ingestion (Figure 7-11) is quite common when data is moved from a streaming-based system into object storage; ultimately, you must cut the data into discrete blocks for future processing in a data lake. Some size-based ingestion systems can break data into objects based on various criteria, such as the size in bytes of the total number of events.

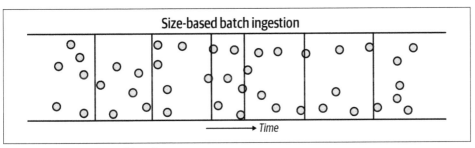

Figure 7-11. Size-based batch ingestion

Some commonly used batch ingestion patterns, which we discuss in this section, include the following:

- Snapshot or differential extraction
- File-based export and ingestion
- ETL versus ELT
- Inserts, updates, and batch size
- Data migration

Snapshot or Differential Extraction

Data engineers must choose whether to capture full snapshots of a source system or differential (sometimes called *incremental*) updates. With *full snapshots*, engineers grab the entire current state of the source system on each update read. With the *differential update* pattern, engineers can pull only the updates and changes since the last read from the source system. While differential updates are ideal for minimizing network traffic and target storage usage, full snapshot reads remain extremely common because of their simplicity.

File-Based Export and Ingestion

Data is quite often moved between databases and systems using files. Data is serialized into files in an exchangeable format, and these files are provided to an ingestion system. We consider file-based export to be a *push-based* ingestion pattern. This is because data export and preparation work is done on the source system side.

File-based ingestion has several potential advantages over a direct database connection approach. It is often undesirable to allow direct access to backend systems for security reasons. With file-based ingestion, export processes are run on the data-source side, giving source system engineers complete control over what data gets exported and how the data is preprocessed. Once files are done, they can be provided to the target system in various ways. Common file-exchange methods are object storage, secure file transfer protocol (SFTP), electronic data interchange (EDI), or secure copy (SCP).

ETL Versus ELT

Chapter 3 introduced ETL and ELT, both extremely common ingestion, storage, and transformation patterns you'll encounter in batch workloads. The following are brief definitions of the extract and load parts of ETL and ELT:

Extract

This means getting data from a source system. While *extract* seems to imply *pulling* data, it can also be push based. Extraction may also require reading metadata and schema changes.

Load

Once data is extracted, it can either be transformed (ETL) before loading it into a storage destination or simply loaded into storage for future transformation. When loading data, you should be mindful of the type of system you're loading, the schema of the data, and the performance impact of loading.

We cover ETL and ELT in greater detail in Chapter 8.

Inserts, Updates, and Batch Size

Batch-oriented systems often perform poorly when users attempt to perform many small-batch operations rather than a smaller number of large operations. For example, while it is common to insert one row at a time in a transactional database, this is a bad pattern for many columnar databases, as it forces the creation of many small, suboptimal files and forces the system to run a high number of *create object* operations. Running many small in-place update operations is an even bigger problem because it causes the database to scan each existing column file to run the update.

Understand the appropriate update patterns for the database or data store you're working with. Also, understand that certain technologies are purpose-built for high insert rates. For example, Apache Druid and Apache Pinot can handle high insert rates. SingleStore can manage hybrid workloads that combine OLAP and OLTP characteristics. BigQuery performs poorly on a high rate of vanilla SQL single-row inserts but extremely well if data is fed in through its stream buffer. Know the limits and characteristics of your tools.

Data Migration

Migrating data to a new database or environment is not usually trivial, and data needs to be moved in bulk. Sometimes this means moving data sizes that are hundreds of terabytes or much larger, often involving the migration of specific tables and moving entire databases and systems.

Data migrations probably aren't a regular occurrence as a data engineer, but you should be familiar with them. As is often the case for data ingestion, schema management is a crucial consideration. Suppose you're migrating data from one database system to a different one (say, SQL Server to Snowflake). No matter how closely the two databases resemble each other, subtle differences almost always exist in the way they handle schema. Fortunately, it is generally easy to test ingestion of a sample of data and find schema issues before undertaking a complete table migration.

Most data systems perform best when data is moved in bulk rather than as individual rows or events. File or object storage is often an excellent intermediate stage for transferring data. Also, one of the biggest challenges of database migration is not the movement of the data itself but the movement of data pipeline connections from the old system to the new one.

Be aware that many tools are available to automate various types of data migrations. Especially for large and complex migrations, we suggest looking at these options before doing this manually or writing your own migration solution.

Message and Stream Ingestion Considerations

Ingesting event data is common. This section covers issues you should consider when ingesting events, drawing on topics covered in Chapters 5 and 6.

Schema Evolution

Schema evolution is common when handling event data; fields may be added or removed, or value types might change (say, a string to an integer). Schema evolution can have unintended impacts on your data pipelines and destinations. For example, an IoT device gets a firmware update that adds a new field to the event it transmits, or a third-party API introduces changes to its event payload or countless other scenarios. All of these potentially impact your downstream capabilities.

To alleviate issues related to schema evolution, here are a few suggestions. First, if your event-processing framework has a schema registry (discussed earlier in this chapter), use it to version your schema changes. Next, a dead-letter queue (described in "Error Handling and Dead-Letter Queues" on page 253) can help you investigate issues with events that are not properly handled. Finally, the low-fidelity route (and the most effective) is regularly communicating with upstream stakeholders about potential schema changes and proactively addressing schema changes with the teams introducing these changes instead of reacting to the receiving end of breaking changes.

Late-Arriving Data

Though you probably prefer all event data to arrive on time, event data might arrive late. A group of events might occur around the same time frame (similar event times), but some might arrive later than others (late ingestion times) because of various circumstances.

For example, an IoT device might be late sending a message because of internet latency issues. This is common when ingesting data. You should be aware of late-arriving data and the impact on downstream systems and uses. Suppose you assume that ingestion or process time is the same as the event time. You may get some strange results if your reports or analysis depend on an accurate portrayal of when events occur. To handle late-arriving data, you need to set a cutoff time for when late-arriving data will no longer be processed.

Ordering and Multiple Delivery

Streaming platforms are generally built out of distributed systems, which can cause some complications. Specifically, messages may be delivered out of order and more than once (at-least-once delivery). See the event-streaming platforms discussion in Chapter 5 for more details.

Replay

Replay allows readers to request a range of messages from the history, allowing you to rewind your event history to a particular point in time. Replay is a key capability in many streaming ingestion platforms and is particularly useful when you need to reingest and reprocess data for a specific time range. For example, RabbitMQ typically deletes messages after all subscribers consume them. Kafka, Kinesis, and Pub/Sub all support event retention and replay.

Time to Live

How long will you preserve your event record? A key parameter is *maximum message retention time*, also known as the *time to live* (TTL). TTL is usually a configuration you'll set for how long you want events to live before they are acknowledged and ingested. Any unacknowledged event that's not ingested after its TTL expires automatically disappears. This is helpful to reduce backpressure and unnecessary event volume in your event-ingestion pipeline.

Find the right balance of TTL impact on our data pipeline. An extremely short TTL (milliseconds or seconds) might cause most messages to disappear before processing. A very long TTL (several weeks or months) will create a backlog of many unprocessed messages, resulting in long wait times.

Let's look at how some popular platforms handle TTL at the time of this writing. Google Cloud Pub/Sub supports retention periods of up to 7 days. Amazon Kinesis Data Streams retention can be turned up to 365 days. Kafka can be configured for indefinite retention, limited by available disk space. (Kafka also supports the option to write older messages to cloud object storage, unlocking virtually unlimited storage space and retention.)

Message Size

Message size is an easily overlooked issue: you must ensure that the streaming framework in question can handle the maximum expected message size. Amazon Kinesis supports a maximum message size of 1 MB. Kafka defaults to this maximum size but can be configured for a maximum of 20 MB or more. (Configurability may vary on managed service platforms.)

Error Handling and Dead-Letter Queues

Sometimes events aren't successfully ingested. Perhaps an event is sent to a nonexistent topic or message queue, the message size may be too large, or the event has expired past its TTL. Events that cannot be ingested need to be rerouted and stored in a separate location called a *dead-letter queue*.

A dead-letter queue segregates problematic events from events that can be accepted by the consumer (Figure 7-12). If events are not rerouted to a dead-letter queue, these erroneous events risk blocking other messages from being ingested. Data engineers can use a dead-letter queue to diagnose why event ingestions errors occur and solve data pipeline problems, and might be able to reprocess some messages in the queue after fixing the underlying cause of errors.

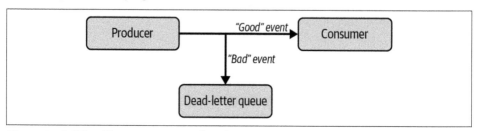

Figure 7-12. "Good" events are passed to the consumer, whereas "bad" events are stored in a dead-letter queue

Consumer Pull and Push

A consumer subscribing to a topic can get events in two ways: push and pull. Let's look at the ways some streaming technologies pull and push data. Kafka and Kinesis support only pull subscriptions. Subscribers read messages from a topic and confirm when they have been processed. In addition to pull subscriptions, Pub/Sub and RabbitMQ support push subscriptions, allowing these services to write messages to a listener.

Pull subscriptions are the default choice for most data engineering applications, but you may want to consider push capabilities for specialized applications. Note that pull-only message ingestion systems can still push if you add an extra layer to handle this.

Location

It is often desirable to integrate streaming across several locations for enhanced redundancy and to consume data close to where it is generated. As a general rule, the closer your ingestion is to where data originates, the better your bandwidth and latency. However, you need to balance this against the costs of moving data between regions to run analytics on a combined dataset. As always, data egress costs can spiral quickly. Do a careful evaluation of the trade-offs as you build out your architecture.

Ways to Ingest Data

Now that we've described some of the significant patterns underlying batch and streaming ingestion, let's focus on ways you can ingest data. Although we will cite some common ways, keep in mind that the universe of data ingestion practices and technologies is vast and growing daily.

Direct Database Connection

Data can be pulled from databases for ingestion by querying and reading over a network connection. Most commonly, this connection is made using ODBC or JDBC.

ODBC uses a driver hosted by a client accessing the database to translate commands issued to the standard ODBC API into commands issued to the database. The database returns query results over the wire, where the driver receives them and translates them back into a standard form to be read by the client. For ingestion, the application utilizing the ODBC driver is an ingestion tool. The ingestion tool may pull data through many small queries or a single large query.

JDBC is conceptually remarkably similar to ODBC. A Java driver connects to a remote database and serves as a translation layer between the standard JDBC API and the native network interface of the target database. It might seem strange to have a database API dedicated to a single programming language, but there are strong motivations for this. The Java Virtual Machine (JVM) is standard, portable across hardware architectures and operating systems, and provides the performance of compiled code through a just-in-time (JIT) compiler. The JVM is an extremely popular compiling VM for running code in a portable manner.

JDBC provides extraordinary database driver portability. ODBC drivers are shipped as OS and architecture native binaries; database vendors must maintain versions for each architecture/OS version that they wish to support. On the other hand, vendors can ship a single JDBC driver that is compatible with any JVM language (e.g., Java, Scala, Clojure, or Kotlin) and JVM data framework (i.e., Spark.) JDBC has become so popular that it is also used as an interface for non-JVM languages such as Python; the Python ecosystem provides translation tools that allow Python code to talk to a JDBC driver running on a local JVM.

JDBC and ODBC are used extensively for data ingestion from relational databases, returning to the general concept of direct database connections. Various enhancements are used to accelerate data ingestion. Many data frameworks can parallelize several simultaneous connections and partition queries to pull data in parallel. On the other hand, nothing is free; using parallel connections also increases the load on the source database.

JDBC and ODBC were long the gold standards for data ingestion from databases, but these connection standards are beginning to show their age for many data engineering applications. These connection standards struggle with nested data, and they send data as rows. This means that native nested data must be reencoded as string data to be sent over the wire, and columns from columnar databases must be reserialized as rows.

As discussed in "File-Based Export and Ingestion" on page 250, many databases now support native file export that bypasses JDBC/ODBC and exports data directly in formats such as Parquet, ORC, and Avro. Alternatively, many cloud data warehouses provide direct REST APIs.

JDBC connections should generally be integrated with other ingestion technologies. For example, we commonly use a reader process to connect to a database with JDBC, write the extracted data into multiple objects, and then orchestrate ingestion into a downstream system (see Figure 7-13). The reader process can run in a wholly ephemeral cloud instance or in an orchestration system.

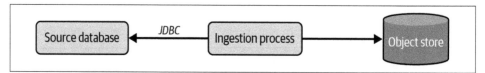

Figure 7-13. An ingestion process reads from a source database using JDBC, and then writes objects into object storage. A target database (not shown) can be triggered to ingest the data with an API call from an orchestration system.

Change Data Capture

Change data capture (CDC), introduced in Chapter 2, is the process of ingesting changes from a source database system. For example, we might have a source Post-greSQL system that supports an application and periodically or continuously ingests table changes for analytics.

Note that our discussion here is by no means exhaustive. We introduce you to common patterns but suggest that you read the documentation on a particular database to handle the details of CDC strategies.

Batch-oriented CDC

If the database table in question has an `updated_at` field containing the last time a record was written or updated, we can query the table to find all updated rows since a specified time. We set the filter timestamp based on when we last captured changed rows from the tables. This process allows us to pull changes and differentially update a target table.

This form of batch-oriented CDC has a key limitation: while we can easily determine which rows have changed since a point in time, we don't necessarily obtain all changes that were applied to these rows. Consider the example of running batch CDC on a bank account table every 24 hours. This operational table shows the current account balance for each account. When money is moved in and out of accounts, the banking application runs a transaction to update the balance.

When we run a query to return all rows in the account table that changed in the last 24 hours, we'll see records for each account that recorded a transaction. Suppose that a certain customer withdrew money five times using a debit card in the last 24 hours. Our query will return only the last account balance recorded in the 24 hour period; other records over the period won't appear. This issue can be mitigated by utilizing an insert-only schema, where each account transaction is recorded as a new record in the table (see "Insert-Only" on page 166).

Continuous CDC

Continuous CDC captures all table history and can support near real-time data ingestion, either for real-time database replication or to feed real-time streaming analytics. Rather than running periodic queries to get a batch of table changes, continuous CDC treats each write to the database as an event.

We can capture an event stream for continuous CDC in a couple of ways. One of the most common approaches with a transactional database such as PostgreSQL is *log-based CDC*. The database binary log records every change to the database sequentially (see "Database Logs" on page 165). A CDC tool can read this log and send the events to a target, such as the Apache Kafka Debezium streaming platform.

Some databases support a simplified, managed CDC paradigm. For instance, many cloud-hosted databases can be configured to directly trigger a serverless function or write to an event stream every time a change happens in the database. This completely frees engineers from worrying about the details of how events are captured in the database and forwarded.

CDC and database replication

CDC can be used to replicate between databases: events are buffered into a stream and *asynchronously* written into a second database. However, many databases natively support a tightly coupled version of replication (synchronous replication) that keeps the replica fully in sync with the primary database. Synchronous replication typically requires that the primary database and the replica are of the same type (e.g., PostgreSQL to PostgreSQL). The advantage of synchronous replication is that the secondary database can offload work from the primary database by acting as a read replica; read queries can be redirected to the replica. The query will return the same results that would be returned from the primary database.

Read replicas are often used in batch data ingestion patterns to allow large scans to run without overloading the primary production database. In addition, an application can be configured to fail over to the replica if the primary database becomes unavailable. No data will be lost in the failover because the replica is entirely in sync with the primary database.

The advantage of asynchronous CDC replication is a loosely coupled architecture pattern. While the replica might be slightly delayed from the primary database, this is often not a problem for analytics applications, and events can now be directed to a variety of targets; we might run CDC replication while simultaneously directing events to object storage and a streaming analytics processor.

CDC considerations

Like anything in technology, CDC is not free. CDC consumes various database resources, such as memory, disk bandwidth, storage, CPU time, and network bandwidth. Engineers should work with production teams and run tests before turning on CDC on production systems to avoid operational problems. Similar considerations apply to synchronous replication.

For batch CDC, be aware that running any large batch query against a transactional production system can cause excessive load. Either run such queries only at off-hours or use a read replica to avoid burdening the primary database.

APIs

> The bulk of software engineering is just plumbing.
>
> —Karl Hughes[1]

As we mentioned in Chapter 5, APIs are a data source that continues to grow in importance and popularity. A typical organization may have hundreds of external data sources such as SaaS platforms or partner companies. The hard reality is that no proper standard exists for data exchange over APIs. Data engineers can spend a significant amount of time reading documentation, communicating with external data owners, and writing and maintaining API connection code.

Three trends are slowly changing this situation. First, many vendors provide API client libraries for various programming languages that remove much of the complexity of API access.

Second, numerous data connector platforms are available now as SaaS, open source, or managed open source. These platforms provide turnkey data connectivity to many data sources; they offer frameworks for writing custom connectors for unsupported data sources. See "Managed Data Connectors" on page 260.

---

1 Karl Hughes, "The Bulk of Software Engineering Is Just Plumbing," Karl Hughes website, July 8, 2018, *https://oreil.ly/uIuqJ*.

The third trend is the emergence of data sharing (discussed in Chapter 5)—i.e., the ability to exchange data through a standard platform such as BigQuery, Snowflake, Redshift, or S3. Once data lands on one of these platforms, it is straightforward to store it, process it, or move it somewhere else. Data sharing has had a large and rapid impact in the data engineering space.

Don't reinvent the wheel when data sharing is not an option and direct API access is necessary. While a managed service might look like an expensive option, consider the value of your time and the opportunity cost of building API connectors when you could be spending your time on higher-value work.

In addition, many managed services now support building custom API connectors. This may provide API technical specifications in a standard format or writing connector code that runs in a serverless function framework (e.g., AWS Lambda) while letting the managed service handle the details of scheduling and synchronization. Again, these services can be a huge time-saver for engineers, both for development and ongoing maintenance.

Reserve your custom connection work for APIs that aren't well supported by existing frameworks; you will find that there are still plenty of these to work on. Handling custom API connections has two main aspects: software development and ops. Follow software development best practices; you should use version control, continuous delivery, and automated testing. In addition to following DevOps best practices, consider an orchestration framework, which can dramatically streamline the operational burden of data ingestion.

Message Queues and Event-Streaming Platforms

Message queues and event-streaming platforms are widespread ways to ingest real-time data from web and mobile applications, IoT sensors, and smart devices. As real-time data becomes more ubiquitous, you'll often find yourself either introducing or retrofitting ways to handle real-time data in your ingestion workflows. As such, it's essential to know how to ingest real-time data. Popular real-time data ingestion includes message queues or event-streaming platforms, which we covered in Chapter 5. Though these are both source systems, they also act as ways to ingest data. In both cases, you consume events from the publisher you subscribe to.

Recall the differences between messages and streams. A *message* is handled at the individual event level and is meant to be transient. Once a message is consumed, it is acknowledged and removed from the queue. On the other hand, a *stream* ingests events into an ordered log. The log persists for as long as you wish, allowing events to be queried over various ranges, aggregated, and combined with other streams to create new transformations published to downstream consumers. In Figure 7-14, we have two producers (producers 1 and 2) sending events to two consumers

(consumers 1 and 2). These events are combined into a new dataset and sent to a producer for downstream consumption.

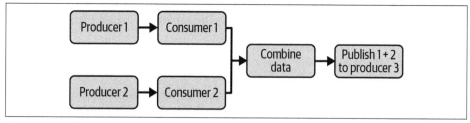

Figure 7-14. Two datasets are produced and consumed (producers 1 and 2) and then combined, with the combined data published to a new producer (producer 3)

The last point is an essential difference between batch and streaming ingestion. Whereas batch usually involves static workflows (ingest data, store it, transform it, and serve it), messages and streams are fluid. Ingestion can be nonlinear, with data being published, consumed, republished, and reconsumed. When designing your real-time ingestion workflows, keep in mind how data will flow.

Another consideration is the throughput of your real-time data pipelines. Messages and events should flow with as little latency as possible, meaning you should provision adequate partition (or shard) bandwidth and throughput. Provide sufficient memory, disk, and CPU resources for event processing, and if you're managing your real-time pipelines, incorporate autoscaling to handle spikes and save money as load decreases. For these reasons, managing your streaming platform can entail significant overhead. Consider managed services for your real-time ingestion pipelines, and focus your attention on ways to get value from your real-time data.

Managed Data Connectors

These days, if you're considering writing a data ingestion connector to a database or API, ask yourself: has this already been created? Furthermore, is there a service that will manage the nitty-gritty details of this connection for me? "APIs" on page 258 mentions the popularity of managed data connector platforms and frameworks. These tools aim to provide a standard set of connectors available out of the box to spare data engineers building complicated plumbing to connect to a particular source. Instead of creating and managing a data connector, you outsource this service to a third party.

Generally, options in the space allow users to set a target and source, ingest in various ways (e.g., CDC, replication, truncate and reload), set permissions and credentials, configure an update frequency, and begin syncing data. The vendor or cloud behind the scenes fully manages and monitors data syncs. If data synchronization fails, you'll receive an alert with logged information on the cause of the error.

We suggest using managed connector platforms instead of creating and managing your connectors. Vendors and OSS projects each typically have hundreds of prebuilt connector options and can easily create custom connectors. The creation and management of data connectors is largely undifferentiated heavy lifting these days and should be outsourced whenever possible.

Moving Data with Object Storage

Object storage is a multitenant system in public clouds, and it supports storing massive amounts of data. This makes object storage ideal for moving data in and out of data lakes, between teams, and transferring data between organizations. You can even provide short-term access to an object with a signed URL, giving a user temporary permission.

In our view, object storage is the most optimal and secure way to handle file exchange. Public cloud storage implements the latest security standards, has a robust track record of scalability and reliability, accepts files of arbitrary types and sizes, and provides high-performance data movement. We discussed object storage much more extensively in Chapter 6.

EDI

Another practical reality for data engineers is *electronic data interchange* (EDI). The term is vague enough to refer to any data movement method. It usually refers to somewhat archaic means of file exchange, such as by email or flash drive. Data engineers will find that some data sources do not support more modern means of data transport, often because of archaic IT systems or human process limitations.

Engineers can at least enhance EDI through automation. For example, they can set up a cloud-based email server that saves files onto company object storage as soon as they are received. This can trigger orchestration processes to ingest and process data. This is much more robust than an employee downloading the attached file and manually uploading it to an internal system, which we still frequently see.

Databases and File Export

Engineers should be aware of how the source database systems handle file export. Export involves large data scans that significantly load the database for many transactional systems. Source system engineers must assess when these scans can be run without affecting application performance and might opt for a strategy to mitigate the load. Export queries can be broken into smaller exports by querying over key ranges or one partition at a time. Alternatively, a read replica can reduce load. Read replicas are especially appropriate if exports happen many times a day and coincide with a high source system load.

Major cloud data warehouses are highly optimized for direct file export. For example, Snowflake, BigQuery, Redshift, and others support direct export to object storage in various formats.

Practical Issues with Common File Formats

Engineers should also be aware of the file formats to export. CSV is still ubiquitous and highly error prone at the time of this writing. Namely, CSV's default delimiter is also one of the most familiar characters in the English language—the comma! But it gets worse.

CSV is by no means a uniform format. Engineers must stipulate the delimiter, quote characters, and escaping to appropriately handle the export of string data. CSV also doesn't natively encode schema information or directly support nested structures. CSV file encoding and schema information must be configured in the target system to ensure appropriate ingestion. Autodetection is a convenience feature provided in many cloud environments but is inappropriate for production ingestion. As a best practice, engineers should record CSV encoding and schema details in file metadata.

More robust and expressive export formats include Parquet (*https://oreil.ly/D6mB5*), Avro (*https://oreil.ly/X6lOx*), Arrow (*https://oreil.ly/CUMZf*), and ORC (*https://oreil.ly/9PvA7*) or JSON (*https://oreil.ly/dDWrx*). These formats natively encode schema information and handle arbitrary string data with no particular intervention. Many of them also handle nested data structures natively so that JSON fields are stored using internal nested structures rather than simple strings. For columnar databases, columnar formats (Parquet, Arrow, ORC) allow more efficient data export because columns can be directly transcoded between formats. These formats are also generally more optimized for query engines. The Arrow file format is designed to map data directly into processing engine memory, providing high performance in data lake environments.

The disadvantage of these newer formats is that many of them are not natively supported by source systems. Data engineers are often forced to work with CSV data and then build robust exception handling and error detection to ensure data quality on ingestion. See Appendix A for a more extensive discussion of file formats.

Shell

The *shell* is an interface by which you may execute commands to ingest data. The shell can be used to script workflows for virtually any software tool, and shell scripting is still used extensively in ingestion processes. A shell script might read data from a database, reserialize it into a different file format, upload it to object storage, and trigger an ingestion process in a target database. While storing data on a single instance or server is not highly scalable, many of our data sources are not particularly large, and such approaches work just fine.

In addition, cloud vendors generally provide robust CLI-based tools. It is possible to run complex ingestion processes simply by issuing commands to the AWS CLI (*https://oreil.ly/S6Buc*). As ingestion processes grow more complicated and the SLA grows more stringent, engineers should consider moving to a proper orchestration system.

SSH

SSH is not an ingestion strategy but a protocol used with other ingestion strategies. We use SSH in a few ways. First, SSH can be used for file transfer with SCP, as mentioned earlier. Second, SSH tunnels are used to allow secure, isolated connections to databases.

Application databases should never be directly exposed on the internet. Instead, engineers can set up a bastion host—i.e., an intermediate host instance that can connect to the database in question. This host machine is exposed on the internet, although locked down for minimal access from only specified IP addresses to specified ports. To connect to the database, a remote machine first opens an SSH tunnel connection to the bastion host and then connects from the host machine to the database.

SFTP and SCP

Accessing and sending data both from secure FTP (SFTP) and secure copy (SCP) are techniques you should be familiar with, even if data engineers do not typically use these regularly (IT or security/secOps will handle this).

Engineers rightfully cringe at the mention of SFTP (occasionally, we even hear instances of FTP being used in production). Regardless, SFTP is still a practical reality for many businesses. They work with partner businesses that consume or provide data using SFTP and are unwilling to rely on other standards. To avoid data leaks, security analysis is critical in these situations.

SCP is a file-exchange protocol that runs over an SSH connection. SCP can be a secure file-transfer option if it is configured correctly. Again, adding additional network access control (defense in depth) to enhance SCP security is highly recommended.

Webhooks

Webhooks, as we discussed in Chapter 5, are often referred to as *reverse APIs*. For a typical REST data API, the data provider gives engineers API specifications that they use to write their data ingestion code. The code makes requests and receives data in responses.

With a webhook (Figure 7-15), the data provider defines an API request specification, but the data provider *makes API calls* rather than receiving them; it's the data consumer's responsibility to provide an API endpoint for the provider to call. The consumer is responsible for ingesting each request and handling data aggregation, storage, and processing.

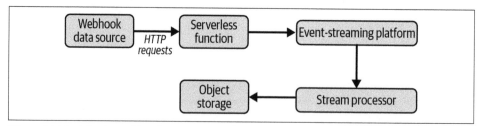

Figure 7-15. A basic webhook ingestion architecture built from cloud services

Webhook-based data ingestion architectures can be brittle, difficult to maintain, and inefficient. Using appropriate off-the-shelf tools, data engineers can build more robust webhook architectures with lower maintenance and infrastructure costs. For example, a webhook pattern in AWS might use a serverless function framework (Lambda) to receive incoming events, a managed event-streaming platform to store and buffer messages (Kinesis), a stream-processing framework to handle real-time analytics (Flink), and an object store for long-term storage (S3).

You'll notice that this architecture does much more than simply ingest the data. This underscores ingestion's entanglement with the other stages of the data engineering lifecycle; it is often impossible to define your ingestion architecture without making decisions about storage and processing.

Web Interface

Web interfaces for data access remain a practical reality for data engineers. We frequently run into situations where not all data and functionality in a SaaS platform is exposed through automated interfaces such as APIs and file drops. Instead, someone must manually access a web interface, generate a report, and download a file to a local machine. This has obvious drawbacks, such as people forgetting to run the report or having their laptop die. Where possible, choose tools and workflows that allow for automated access to data.

Web Scraping

Web scraping automatically extracts data from web pages, often by combing the web page's various HTML elements. You might scrape ecommerce sites to extract product pricing information or scrape multiple news sites for your news aggregator. Web scraping is widespread, and you may encounter it as a data engineer. It's also a murky area where ethical and legal lines are blurry.

Here is some top-level advice to be aware of before undertaking any web-scraping project. First, ask yourself if you should be web scraping or if data is available from a third party. If your decision is to web scrape, be a good citizen. Don't inadvertently create a denial-of-service (DoS) attack, and don't get your IP address blocked. Understand how much traffic you generate and pace your web-crawling activities appropriately. Just because you can spin up thousands of simultaneous Lambda functions to scrape doesn't mean you should; excessive web scraping could lead to the disabling of your AWS account.

Second, be aware of the legal implications of your activities. Again, generating DoS attacks can entail legal consequences. Actions that violate terms of service may cause headaches for your employer or you personally.

Third, web pages constantly change their HTML element structure, making it tricky to keep your web scraper updated. Ask yourself, is the headache of maintaining these systems worth the effort?

Web scraping has interesting implications for the data engineering lifecycle processing stage; engineers should think about various factors at the beginning of a web-scraping project. What do you intend to do with the data? Are you just pulling required fields from the scraped HTML by using Python code and then writing these values to a database? Do you intend to maintain the complete HTML code of the scraped websites and process this data using a framework like Spark? These decisions may lead to very different architectures downstream of ingestion.

Transfer Appliances for Data Migration

For massive quantities of data (100 TB or more), transferring data directly over the internet may be a slow and costly process. At this scale, the fastest, most efficient way to move data is not over the wire but by truck. Cloud vendors offer the ability to send your data via a physical "box of hard drives." Simply order a storage device, called a *transfer appliance*, load your data from your servers, and then send it back to the cloud vendor, which will upload your data.

The suggestion is to consider using a transfer appliance if your data size hovers around 100 TB. On the extreme end, AWS even offers Snowmobile (*https://oreil.ly/ r9vLY*), a transfer appliance sent to you in a semitrailer! Snowmobile is intended to lift and shift an entire data center, in which data sizes are in the petabytes or greater.

Transfer appliances are handy for creating hybrid-cloud or multicloud setups. For example, Amazon's data transfer appliance (AWS Snowball) supports import and export. To migrate into a second cloud, users can export their data into a Snowball device and then import it into a second transfer appliance to move data into GCP or Azure. This might sound awkward, but even when it's feasible to push data over the internet between clouds, data egress fees make this a costly proposition. Physical transfer appliances are a cheaper alternative when the data volumes are significant.

Remember that transfer appliances and data migration services are one-time data ingestion events and are not suggested for ongoing workloads. Suppose you have workloads requiring constant data movement in either a hybrid or multicloud scenario. In that case, your data sizes are presumably batching or streaming much smaller data sizes on an ongoing basis.

Data Sharing

Data sharing is growing as a popular option for consuming data (see Chapters 5 and 6). Data providers will offer datasets to third-party subscribers, either for free or at a cost. These datasets are often shared in a read-only fashion, meaning you can integrate these datasets with your own data (and other third-party datasets), but you do not own the shared dataset. In the strict sense, this isn't ingestion, where you get physical possession of the dataset. If the data provider decides to remove your access to a dataset, you'll no longer have access to it.

Many cloud platforms offer data sharing, allowing you to share your data and consume data from various providers. Some of these platforms also provide data marketplaces where companies and organizations can offer their data for sale.

Whom You'll Work With

Data ingestion sits at several organizational boundaries. In developing and managing data ingestion pipelines, data engineers will work with both people and systems sitting upstream (data producers) and downstream (data consumers).

Upstream Stakeholders

A significant disconnect often exists between those responsible for *generating data* —typically, software engineers—and the data engineers who will prepare this data for analytics and data science. Software engineers and data engineers usually sit in separate organizational silos; if they think about data engineers, they typically see them simply as downstream consumers of the data exhaust from their application, not as stakeholders.

We see this current state of affairs as a problem and a significant opportunity. Data engineers can improve the quality of their data by inviting software engineers to be stakeholders in data engineering outcomes. The vast majority of software engineers are well aware of the value of analytics and data science but don't necessarily have aligned incentives to contribute to data engineering efforts directly.

Simply improving communication is a significant first step. Often software engineers have already identified potentially valuable data for downstream consumption. Opening a communication channel encourages software engineers to get data into shape for consumers and communicate about data changes to prevent pipeline regressions.

Beyond communication, data engineers can highlight the contributions of software engineers to team members, executives, and especially product managers. Involving product managers in the outcome and treating downstream data processed as part of a product encourages them to allocate scarce software development to collaboration with data engineers. Ideally, software engineers can work partially as extensions of the data engineering team; this allows them to collaborate on various projects, such as creating an event-driven architecture to enable real-time analytics.

Downstream Stakeholders

Who is the ultimate customer for data ingestion? Data engineers focus on data practitioners and technology leaders such as data scientists, analysts, and chief technical officers. They would do well also to remember their broader circle of business stakeholders such as marketing directors, vice presidents over the supply chain, and CEOs.

Too often, we see data engineers pursuing sophisticated projects (e.g., real-time streaming buses or complex data systems) while digital marketing managers next door are left downloading Google Ads reports manually. View data engineering as a business, and recognize who your customers are. Often basic automation of ingestion processes has significant value, especially for departments like marketing that control massive budgets and sit at the heart of revenue for the business. Basic ingestion work may seem tedious, but delivering value to these core parts of the company will open up more budget and more exciting long-term data engineering opportunities.

Data engineers can also invite more executive participation in this collaborative process. For a good reason, data-driven culture is quite fashionable in business leadership circles. Still, it is up to data engineers and other data practitioners to provide executives with guidance on the best structure for a data-driven business. This means communicating the value of lowering barriers between data producers and data engineers while supporting executives in breaking down silos and setting up incentives to lead to a more unified data-driven culture.

Once again, *communication* is the watchword. Honest communication early and often with stakeholders will go a long way to ensure that your data ingestion adds value.

Undercurrents

Virtually all the undercurrents touch the ingestion phase, but we'll emphasize the most salient ones here.

Security

Moving data introduces security vulnerabilities because you have to transfer data between locations. The last thing you want is to capture or compromise the data while moving.

Consider where the data lives and where it is going. Data that needs to move within your VPC should use secure endpoints and never leave the confines of the VPC. Use a VPN or a dedicated private connection if you need to send data between the cloud and an on-premises network. This might cost money, but the security is a good investment. If your data traverses the public internet, ensure that the transmission is encrypted. It is always a good practice to encrypt data over the wire.

Data Management

Naturally, data management begins at data ingestion. This is the starting point for lineage and data cataloging; from this point on, data engineers need to think about schema changes, ethics, privacy, and compliance.

Schema changes

Schema changes (such as adding, changing, or removing columns in a database table) remain, from our perspective, an unsettled issue in data management. The traditional approach is a careful command-and-control review process. Working with clients at large enterprises, we have been quoted lead times of six months for the addition of a single field. This is an unacceptable impediment to agility.

On the opposite end of the spectrum, any schema change in the source triggers target tables to be re-created with the new schema. This solves schema problems at the ingestion stage but can still break downstream pipelines and destination storage systems.

One possible solution, which we, the authors, have meditated on for a while, is an approach pioneered by Git version control. When Linus Torvalds was developing Git, many of his choices were inspired by the limitations of Concurrent Versions System (CVS). CVS is completely centralized; it supports only one current official version of the code, stored on a central project server. To make Git a truly distributed system, Torvalds used the notion of a tree; each developer could maintain their processed branch of the code and then merge to or from other branches.

A few years ago, such an approach to data was unthinkable. On-premises MPP systems are typically operated at close to maximum storage capacity. However, storage is cheap in big data and cloud data warehouse environments. One may quite easily maintain multiple versions of a table with different schemas and even different upstream transformations. Teams can support various "development" versions of a table by using orchestration tools such as Airflow; schema changes, upstream transformation, and code changes can appear in development tables before official changes to the *main* table.

Data ethics, privacy, and compliance

Clients often ask for our advice on encrypting sensitive data in databases, which generally leads us to ask a fundamental question: do you need the sensitive data you're trying to encrypt? As it turns out, this question often gets overlooked when creating requirements and solving problems.

Data engineers should always train themselves to ask this question when setting up ingestion pipelines. They will inevitably encounter sensitive data; the natural tendency is to ingest it and forward it to the next step in the pipeline. But if this data is not needed, why collect it at all? Why not simply drop sensitive fields before data is stored? Data cannot leak if it is never collected.

Where it is truly necessary to keep track of sensitive identities, it is common practice to apply tokenization to anonymize identities in model training and analytics. But engineers should look at where this tokenization is used. If possible, hash data at ingestion time.

Data engineers cannot avoid working with highly sensitive data in some cases. Some analytics systems must present identifiable, sensitive information. Engineers must act under the highest ethical standards whenever they handle sensitive data. In addition, they can put in place a variety of practices to reduce the direct handling of sensitive data. Aim as much as possible for *touchless production* where sensitive data is involved. This means that engineers develop and test code on simulated or cleansed data in development and staging environments but automated code deployments to production.

Touchless production is an ideal that engineers should strive for, but situations inevitably arise that cannot be fully solved in development and staging environments. Some bugs may not be reproducible without looking at the live data that is triggering a regression. For these cases, put a broken-glass process in place: require at least two people to approve access to sensitive data in the production environment. This access should be tightly scoped to a particular issue and come with an expiration date.

Our last bit of advice on sensitive data: be wary of naive technological solutions to human problems. Both encryption and tokenization are often treated like privacy magic bullets. Most cloud-based storage systems and nearly all databases encrypt data at rest and in motion by default. Generally, we don't see encryption problems but data access problems. Is the solution to apply an extra layer of encryption to a single field or to control access to that field? After all, one must still tightly manage access to the encryption key. Legitimate use cases exist for single-field encryption, but watch out for ritualistic encryption.

On the tokenization front, use common sense and assess data access scenarios. If someone had the email of one of your customers, could they easily hash the email and find the customer in your data? Thoughtlessly hashing data without salting and other strategies may not protect privacy as well as you think.

DataOps

Reliable data pipelines are the cornerstone of the data engineering lifecycle. When they fail, all downstream dependencies come to a screeching halt. Data warehouses and data lakes aren't replenished with fresh data, and data scientists and analysts can't effectively do their jobs; the business is forced to fly blind.

Ensuring that your data pipelines are properly monitored is a crucial step toward reliability and effective incident response. If there's one stage in the data engineering lifecycle where monitoring is critical, it's in the ingestion stage. Weak or nonexistent monitoring means the pipelines may or may not be working. Referring back to our earlier discussion on time, be sure to track the various aspects of time—event creation, ingestion, process, and processing times. Your data pipelines should predictably process data in batches or streams. We've seen countless examples of reports and ML models generated from stale data. In one extreme case, an ingestion pipeline failure wasn't detected for six months. (One might question the concrete utility of the data in this instance, but that's another matter.) This was very much avoidable through proper monitoring.

What should you monitor? Uptime, latency, and data volumes processed are good places to start. If an ingestion job fails, how will you respond? In general, build monitoring into your pipelines from the beginning rather than waiting for deployment.

Monitoring is key, as is knowledge of the behavior of the upstream systems you depend on and how they generate data. You should be aware of the number of events generated per time interval you're concerned with (events/minute, events/second, and so on) and the average size of each event. Your data pipeline should handle both the frequency and size of the events you're ingesting.

This also applies to third-party services. In the case of these services, what you've gained in terms of lean operational efficiencies (reduced headcount) is replaced by systems you depend on being outside of your control. If you're using a third-party service (cloud, data integration service, etc.), how will you be alerted if there's an outage? What's your response plan if a service you depend on suddenly goes offline?

Sadly, no universal response plan exists for third-party failures. If you can fail over to other servers, preferably in another zone or region, definitely set this up.

If your data ingestion processes are built internally, do you have the proper testing and deployment automation to ensure that the code functions in production? And if the code is buggy or fails, can you roll it back to a working version?

Data-quality tests

We often refer to data as a silent killer. If quality, valid data is the foundation of success in today's businesses, using bad data to make decisions is much worse than having no data. Bad data has caused untold damage to businesses; these data disasters are sometimes called *datastrophes*.[2]

Data is entropic; it often changes in unexpected ways without warning. One of the inherent differences between DevOps and DataOps is that we expect software regressions only when we deploy changes, while data often presents regressions independently because of events outside our control.

DevOps engineers are typically able to detect problems by using binary conditions. Has the request failure rate breached a certain threshold? How about response latency? In the data space, regressions often manifest as subtle statistical distortions. Is a change in search-term statistics a result of customer behavior? Of a spike in bot traffic that has escaped the net? Of a site test tool deployed in some other part of the company?

Like system failures in DevOps, some data regressions are immediately visible. For example, in the early 2000s, Google provided search terms to websites when users arrived from search. In 2011, Google began withholding this information in some cases to protect user privacy better. Analysts quickly saw "not provided" bubbling to the tops of their reports.[3]

The truly dangerous data regressions are silent and can come from inside or outside a business. Application developers may change the meaning of database fields without adequately communicating with data teams. Changes to data from third-party sources may go unnoticed. In the best-case scenario, reports break in obvious ways. Often business metrics are distorted unbeknownst to decision makers.

Whenever possible, work with software engineers to fix data-quality issues at the source. It's surprising how many data-quality issues can be handled by respecting basic best practices in software engineering, such as logs to capture the history of data changes, checks (nulls, etc.), and exception handling (try, catch, etc.).

Traditional data testing tools are generally built on simple binary logic. Are nulls appearing in a non-nullable field? Are new, unexpected items showing up in a categorical column? Statistical data testing is a new realm, but one that is likely to grow dramatically in the next five years.

---

2 Andy Petrella, "Datastrophes," *Medium*, March 1, 2021, *https://oreil.ly/h6FRW*.

3 Danny Sullivan, "Dark Google: One Year Since Search Terms Went 'Not Provided,'" *MarTech*, October 19, 2012, *https://oreil.ly/Fp8ta (https://oreil.ly/Fp8ta)*.

Orchestration

Ingestion generally sits at the beginning of a large and complex data graph; since ingestion is the first stage of the data engineering lifecycle, ingested data will flow into many more data processing steps, and data from many sources will commingle in complex ways. As we've emphasized throughout this book, orchestration is a crucial process for coordinating these steps.

Organizations in an early stage of data maturity may choose to deploy ingestion processes as simple scheduled cron jobs. However, it is crucial to recognize that this approach is brittle and can slow the velocity of data engineering deployment and development.

As data pipeline complexity grows, true orchestration is necessary. By true orchestration, we mean a system capable of scheduling complete task graphs rather than individual tasks. An orchestration can start each ingestion task at the appropriate scheduled time. Downstream processing and transform steps begin as ingestion tasks are completed. Further downstream, processing steps lead to additional processing steps.

Software Engineering

The ingestion stage of the data engineering lifecycle is engineering intensive. This stage sits at the edge of the data engineering domain and often interfaces with external systems, where software and data engineers have to build a variety of custom plumbing.

Behind the scenes, ingestion is incredibly complicated, often with teams operating open source frameworks like Kafka or Pulsar, or some of the biggest tech companies running their own forked or homegrown ingestion solutions. As discussed in this chapter, managed data connectors have simplified the ingestion process, such as Fivetran, Matillion, and Airbyte. Data engineers should take advantage of the best available tools—primarily, managed tools and services that do a lot of the heavy lifting for you—and develop high software development competency in areas where it matters. It pays to use proper version control and code review processes and implement appropriate tests even for any ingestion-related code.

When writing software, your code needs to be decoupled. Avoid writing monolithic systems with tight dependencies on the source or destination systems.

Conclusion

In your work as a data engineer, ingestion will likely consume a significant part of your energy and effort. At the heart, ingestion is plumbing, connecting pipes to other pipes, ensuring that data flows consistently and securely to its destination. At times, the minutiae of ingestion may feel tedious, but the exciting data applications (e.g., analytics and ML) cannot happen without it.

As we've emphasized, we're also in the midst of a sea change, moving from batch toward streaming data pipelines. This is an opportunity for data engineers to discover interesting applications for streaming data, communicate these to the business, and deploy exciting new technologies.

Additional Resources

- Airbyte's "Connections and Sync Modes" web page (*https://oreil.ly/mCOvd*)
- Chapter 6, "Batch Is a Special Case of Streaming," in *Introduction to Apache Flink* by Ellen Friedman and Kostas Tzoumas (O'Reilly)
- "The Dataflow Model: A Practical Approach to Balancing Correctness, Latency, and Cost in Massive-Scale, Unbounded, Out-of-Order Data Processing" (*https://oreil.ly/ktS3p*) by Tyler Akidau et al.
- Google Cloud's "Streaming Pipelines" web page (*https://oreil.ly/BC1Np*)
- Microsoft's "Snapshot Window (Azure Stream Analytics)" documentation (*https://oreil.ly/O7S7L*)

CHAPTER 8

Queries, Modeling, and Transformation

Up to this point, the stages of the data engineering lifecycle have primarily been about passing data from one place to another or storing it. In this chapter, you'll learn how to make data useful. By understanding queries, modeling, and transformations (see Figure 8-1), you'll have the tools to turn raw data ingredients into something consumable by downstream stakeholders.

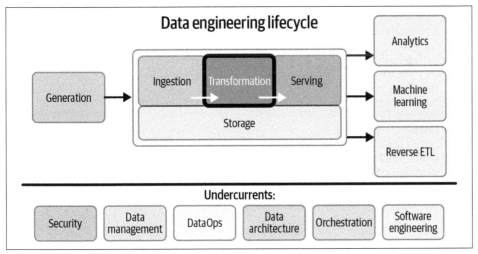

Figure 8-1. Transformations allow us to create value from data

We'll first discuss queries and the significant patterns underlying them. Second, we will look at the major data modeling patterns you can use to introduce business logic into your data. Then, we'll cover transformations, which take the logic of your data models and the results of queries and make them useful for more straightforward downstream consumption. Finally, we'll cover whom you'll work with and the undercurrents as they relate to this chapter.

A variety of techniques can be used to query, model, and transform data in SQL and NoSQL databases. This section focuses on queries made to an OLAP system, such as a data warehouse or data lake. Although many languages exist for querying, for the sake of convenience and familiarity, throughout most of this chapter, we'll focus heavily on SQL, the most popular and universal query language. Most of the concepts for OLAP databases and SQL will translate to other types of databases and query languages. This chapter assumes you have an understanding of the SQL language and related concepts like primary and foreign keys. If these ideas are unfamiliar to you, countless resources are available to help you get started.

A note on the terms used in this chapter. For convenience, we'll use the term *database* as a shorthand for a query engine and the storage it's querying; this could be a cloud data warehouse or Apache Spark querying data stored in S3. We assume the database has a storage engine that organizes the data under the hood. This extends to file-based queries (loading a CSV file into a Python notebook) and queries against file formats such as Parquet.

Also, note that this chapter focuses mainly on the query, modeling patterns, and transformations related to structured and semistructured data, which data engineers use often. Many of the practices discussed can also be applied to working with unstructured data such as images, video, and raw text.

Before we get into modeling and transforming data, let's look at queries—what they are, how they work, considerations for improving query performance, and queries on streaming data.

Queries

Queries are a fundamental part of data engineering, data science, and analysis. Before you learn about the underlying patterns and technologies for transformations, you need to understand what queries are, how they work on various data, and techniques for improving query performance.

This section primarily concerns itself with queries on tabular and semistructured data. As a data engineer, you'll most frequently query and transform these data types. Before we get into more complicated topics about queries, data modeling, and transformations, let's start by answering a pretty simple question: what is a query?

What Is a Query?

We often run into people who know how to write SQL but are unfamiliar with how a query works under the hood. Some of this introductory material on queries will be familiar to experienced data engineers; feel free to skip ahead if this applies to you.

A *query* allows you to retrieve and act on data. Recall our conversation in Chapter 5 about CRUD. When a query retrieves data, it is issuing a request to read a pattern of records. This is the *R* (read) in CRUD. You might issue a query that gets all records from a table foo, such as SELECT * FROM foo. Or, you might apply a predicate (logical condition) to filter your data by retrieving only records where the id is 1, using the SQL query SELECT * FROM foo WHERE id=1.

Many databases allow you to create, update, and delete data. These are the *CUD* in CRUD; your query will either create, mutate, or destroy existing records. Let's review some other common acronyms you'll run into when working with query languages.

Data definition language

At a high level, you first need to create the database objects before adding data. You'll use *data definition language* (DDL) commands to perform operations on database objects, such as the database itself, schemas, tables, or users; DDL defines the state of objects in your database.

Data engineers use common SQL DDL expressions: CREATE, DROP, and UPDATE. For example, you can create a database by using the DDL expression CREATE DATABASE bar. After that, you can also create new tables (CREATE table bar_table) or delete a table (DROP table bar_table).

Data manipulation language

After using DDL to define database objects, you need to add and alter data within these objects, which is the primary purpose of *data manipulation language* (DML). Some common DML commands you'll use as a data engineer are as follows:

```
SELECT
INSERT
UPDATE
DELETE
COPY
MERGE
```

For example, you can INSERT new records into a database table, UPDATE existing ones, and SELECT specific records.

Data control language

You most likely want to limit access to database objects and finely control *who* has access to *what*. *Data control language* (DCL) allows you to control access to the database objects or the data by using SQL commands such as GRANT, DENY, and REVOKE.

Let's walk through a brief example using DCL commands. A new data scientist named Sarah joins your company, and she needs read-only access to a database called *data_science_db*. You give Sarah access to this database by using the following DCL command:

```
GRANT SELECT ON data_science_db TO user_name Sarah;
```

It's a hot job market, and Sarah has worked at the company for only a few months before getting poached by a big tech company. So long, Sarah! Being a security-minded data engineer, you remove Sarah's ability to read from the database:

```
REVOKE SELECT ON data_science_db TO user_name Sarah;
```

Access-control requests and issues are common, and understanding DCL will help you resolve problems if you or a team member can't access the data they need, as well as prevent access to data they don't need.

Transaction control language

As its name suggests, *transaction control language* (TCL) supports commands that control the details of transactions. With TCL, we can define commit checkpoints, conditions when actions will be rolled back, and more. Two common TCL commands include COMMIT and ROLLBACK.

The Life of a Query

How does a query work, and what happens when a query is executed? Let's cover the high-level basics of query execution (Figure 8-2), using an example of a typical SQL query executing in a database.

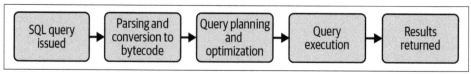

Figure 8-2. The life of a SQL query in a database

While running a query might seem simple—write code, run it, and get results—a lot is going on under the hood. When you execute a SQL query, here's a summary of what happens:

1. The database engine compiles the SQL, parsing the code to check for proper semantics and ensuring that the database objects referenced exist and that the current user has the appropriate access to these objects.

2. The SQL code is converted into bytecode. This bytecode expresses the steps that must be executed on the database engine in an efficient, machine-readable format.

3. The database's query optimizer analyzes the bytecode to determine how to execute the query, reordering and refactoring steps to use available resources as efficiently as possible.

4. The query is executed, and results are produced.

The Query Optimizer

Queries can have wildly different execution times, depending on how they're executed. A query optimizer's job is to optimize query performance and minimize costs by breaking the query into appropriate steps in an efficient order. The optimizer will assess joins, indexes, data scan size, and other factors. The query optimizer attempts to execute the query in the least expensive manner.

Query optimizers are fundamental to how your query will perform. Every database is different and executes queries in ways that are obviously and subtly different from each other. You won't directly work with a query optimizer, but understanding some of its functionality will help you write more performant queries. You'll need to know how to analyze a query's performance, using things like an explain plan or query analysis, described in the following section.

Improving Query Performance

In data engineering, you'll inevitably encounter poorly performing queries. Knowing how to identify and fix these queries is invaluable. Don't fight your database. Learn to work with its strengths and augment its weaknesses. This section shows various ways to improve your query performance.

Optimize your join strategy and schema

A single dataset (such as a table or file) is rarely useful on its own; we create value by combining it with other datasets. *Joins* are one of the most common means of combining datasets and creating new ones. We assume that you're familiar with the significant types of joins (e.g., inner, outer, left, cross) and the types of join relationships (e.g., one to one, one to many, many to one, and many to many).

Joins are critical in data engineering and are well supported and performant in many databases. Even columnar databases, which in the past had a reputation for slow join performance, now generally offer excellent performance.

A common technique for improving query performance is to *prejoin* data. If you find that analytics queries are joining the same data repeatedly, it often makes sense to join the data in advance and have queries read from the prejoined version of the data so that you're not repeating computationally intensive work. This may mean changing the schema and relaxing normalization conditions to widen tables and utilize newer data structures (such as arrays or structs) for replacing frequently joined entity relationships. Another strategy is maintaining a more normalized schema but prejoining tables for the most common analytics and data science use cases. We can simply create prejoined tables and train users to utilize these or join inside materialized views (see "Materialized Views, Federation, and Query Virtualization" on page 327).

Next, consider the details and complexity of your join conditions. Complex join logic may consume significant computational resources. We can improve performance for complex joins in a few ways.

Many row-oriented databases allow you to index a result computed from a row. For instance, PostgreSQL allows you to create an index on a string field converted to lowercase; when the optimizer encounters a query where the lower() function appears inside a predicate, it can apply the index. You can also create a new derived column for joining, though you will need to train users to join on this column.

Row Explosion

An obscure but frustrating problem is row explosion (*https://oreil.ly/kUsO9*). This occurs when we have a large number of many-to-many matches, either because of repetition in join keys or as a consequence of join logic. Suppose the join key in table A has the value this repeated five times, and the join key in table B contains this same value repeated 10 times. This leads to a cross-join of these rows: every this row from table A paired with every this row from table B. This creates 5 × 10 = 50 rows in the output. Now suppose that many other repeats are in the join key. Row explosion often generates enough rows to consume a massive quantity of database resources or even cause a query to fail.

It is also essential to know how your query optimizer handles joins. Some databases can reorder joins and predicates, while others cannot. A row explosion in an early query stage may cause the query to fail, even though a later predicate should correctly remove many of the repeats in the output. Predicate reordering can significantly reduce the computational resources required by a query.

Finally, use common table expressions (CTEs) instead of nested subqueries or temporary tables. CTEs allow users to compose complex queries together in a readable fashion, helping you understand the flow of your query. The importance of readability for complex queries cannot be understated.

In many cases, CTEs will also deliver better performance than a script that creates intermediate tables; if you have to create intermediate tables, consider creating temporary tables. If you'd like to learn more about CTEs, a quick web search will yield plenty of helpful information.

Use the explain plan and understand your query's performance

As you learned in the preceding section, the database's query optimizer influences the execution of a query. The query optimizer's explain plan will show you how the query optimizer determined its optimum lowest-cost query, the database objects used (tables, indexes, cache, etc.), and various resource consumption and performance statistics in each query stage. Some databases provide a visual representation of query stages. In contrast, others make the explain plan available via SQL with the EXPLAIN command, which displays the sequence of steps the database will take to execute the query.

In addition to using EXPLAIN to understand *how* your query will run, you should monitor your query's performance, viewing metrics on database resource consumption. The following are some areas to monitor:

- Usage of key resources such as disk, memory, and network.
- Data loading time versus processing time.
- Query execution time, number of records, the size of the data scanned, and the quantity of data shuffled.
- Competing queries that might cause resource contention in your database.
- Number of concurrent connections used versus connections available. Oversubscribed concurrent connections can have negative effects on your users who may not be able to connect to the database.

Avoid full table scans

All queries scan data, but not all scans are created equal. As a rule of thumb, you should query only the data you need. When you run SELECT * with no predicates, you're scanning the entire table and retrieving every row and column. This is very inefficient performance-wise and expensive, especially if you're using a pay-as-you-go database that charges you either for bytes scanned or compute resources utilized while a query is running.

Whenever possible, use *pruning* to reduce the quantity of data scanned in a query. Columnar and row-oriented databases require different pruning strategies. In a column-oriented database, you should select only the columns you need. Most column-oriented OLAP databases also provide additional tools for optimizing your tables for better query performance. For instance, if you have a very large table (several terabytes in size or greater), Snowflake and BigQuery give you the option to define a cluster key on a table, which orders the table's data in a way that allows queries to more efficiently access portions of very large datasets. BigQuery also allows you to partition a table into smaller segments, allowing you to query only specific partitions instead of the entire table. (Be aware that inappropriate clustering and key distribution strategies can degrade performance.)

In row-oriented databases, pruning usually centers around table indexes, which you learned in Chapter 6. The general strategy is to create table indexes that will improve performance for your most performance-sensitive queries while not overloading the table with so many indexes such that you degrade performance.

Know how your database handles commits

A database *commit* is a change within a database, such as creating, updating, or deleting a record, table, or other database objects. Many databases support *transactions*—i.e., a notion of committing several operations simultaneously in a way that maintains a consistent state. Please note that the term *transaction* is somewhat overloaded; see Chapter 5. The purpose of a transaction is to keep a consistent state of a database both while it's active and in the event of a failure. Transactions also handle isolation when multiple concurrent events might be reading, writing, and deleting from the same database objects. Without transactions, users would get potentially conflicting information when querying a database.

You should be intimately familiar with how your database handles commits and transactions, and determine the expected consistency of query results. Does your database handle writes and updates in an ACID-compliant manner? Without ACID compliance, your query might return unexpected results. This could result from a dirty read, which happens when a row is read and an uncommitted transaction has altered the row. Are dirty reads an expected behavior of your database? If so, how do you handle this? Also, be aware that during update and delete transactions, some databases create new files to represent the new state of the database and retain the old files for failure checkpoint references. In these databases, running a large number of small commits can lead to clutter and consume significant storage space that might need to be vacuumed periodically.

Let's briefly consider three databases to understand the impact of commits (note these examples are current as of the time of this writing). First, suppose we're looking at a PostgreSQL RDBMS and applying ACID transactions. Each transaction consists of a package of operations that will either fail or succeed as a group. We can also run analytics queries across many rows; these queries will present a consistent picture of the database at a point in time.

The disadvantage of the PostgreSQL approach is that it requires *row locking* (blocking reads and writes to certain rows), which can degrade performance in various ways. PostgreSQL is not optimized for large scans or the massive amounts of data appropriate for large-scale analytics applications.

Next, consider Google BigQuery. It utilizes a point-in-time full table commit model. When a read query is issued, BigQuery will read from the latest committed snapshot of the table. Whether the query runs for one second or two hours, it will read only from that snapshot and will not see any subsequent changes. BigQuery does not lock the table while I read from it. Instead, subsequent write operations will create new commits and new snapshots while the query continues to run on the snapshot where it started.

To prevent the inconsistent state, BigQuery allows only one write operation at a time. In this sense, BigQuery provides no write concurrency whatsoever. (In the sense that it can write massive amounts of data in parallel *inside a single write query*, it is highly concurrent.) If more than one client attempts to write simultaneously, write queries are queued in order of arrival. BigQuery's commit model is similar to the commit models used by Snowflake, Spark, and others.

Last, let's consider MongoDB. We refer to MongoDB as a *variable-consistency database*. Engineers have various configurable consistency options, both for the database and at the level of individual queries. MongoDB is celebrated for its extraordinary scalability and write concurrency but is somewhat notorious for issues that arise when engineers abuse it.[1]

For instance, in certain modes, MongoDB supports ultra-high write performance. However, this comes at a cost: the database will unceremoniously and silently discard writes if it gets overwhelmed with traffic. This is perfectly suitable for applications that can stand to lose some data—for example, IoT applications where we simply want many measurements but don't care about capturing all measurements. It is not a great fit for applications that need to capture exact data and statistics.

None of this is to say these are bad databases. They're all fantastic databases when they are chosen for appropriate applications and configured correctly. The same goes for virtually any database technology.

---

1 See, for example, Emin Gün Sirer, "NoSQL Meets Bitcoin and Brings Down Two Exchanges: The Story of Flexcoin and Poloniex," *Hacking, Distributed*, April 6, 2014, *https://oreil.ly/RM3QX*.

Companies don't hire engineers simply to hack on code in isolation. To be worthy of their title, engineers should develop a deep understanding of the problems they're tasked with solving and the technology tools. This applies to commit and consistency models and every other aspect of technology performance. Appropriate technology choices and configuration can ultimately differentiate extraordinary success and massive failure. Refer to Chapter 6 for a deeper discussion of consistency.

Vacuum dead records

As we just discussed, transactions incur the overhead of creating new records during certain operations, such as updates, deletes, and index operations, while retaining the old records as pointers to the last state of the database. As these old records accumulate in the database filesystem, they eventually no longer need to be referenced. You should remove these dead records in a process called *vacuuming*.

You can vacuum a single table, multiple tables, or all tables in a database. No matter how you choose to vacuum, deleting dead database records is important for a few reasons. First, it frees up space for new records, leading to less table bloat and faster queries. Second, new and relevant records mean query plans are more accurate; outdated records can lead the query optimizer to generate suboptimal and inaccurate plans. Finally, vacuuming cleans up poor indexes, allowing for better index performance.

Vacuum operations are handled differently depending on the type of database. For example, in databases backed by object storage (BigQuery, Snowflake, Databricks), the only downside of old data retention is that it uses storage space, potentially costing money depending on the storage pricing model for the database. In Snowflake, users cannot directly vacuum. Instead, they control a "time-travel" interval that determines how long table snapshots are retained before they are auto vacuumed. BigQuery utilizes a fixed seven-day history window. Databricks generally retains data indefinitely until it is manually vacuumed; vacuuming is important to control direct S3 storage costs.

Amazon Redshift handles its cluster disks in many configurations,[2] and vacuuming can impact performance and available storage. VACUUM runs automatically behind the scenes, but users may sometimes want to run it manually for tuning purposes.

Vacuuming becomes even more critical for relational databases such as PostgreSQL and MySQL. Large numbers of transactional operations can cause a rapid accumulation of dead records, and engineers working in these systems need to familiarize themselves with the details and impact of vacuuming.

---

2 Some Redshift configurations (*https://oreil.ly/WgLcV*) rely on object storage instead.

Leverage cached query results

Let's say you have an intensive query that you often run on a database that charges you for the amount of data you query. Each time a query is run, this costs you money. Instead of rerunning the same query on the database repeatedly and incurring massive charges, wouldn't it be nice if the results of the query were stored and available for instant retrieval? Thankfully, many cloud OLAP databases cache query results.

When a query is initially run, it will retrieve data from various sources, filter and join it, and output a result. This initial query—a cold query—is similar to the notion of cold data we explored in Chapter 6. For argument's sake, let's say this query took 40 seconds to run. Assuming your database caches query results, rerunning the same query might return results in 1 second or less. The results were cached, and the query didn't need to run cold. Whenever possible, leverage query cache results to reduce pressure on your database and provide a better user experience for frequently run queries. Note also that *materialized views* provide another form of query caching (see "Materialized Views, Federation, and Query Virtualization" on page 327).

Queries on Streaming Data

Streaming data is constantly in flight. As you might imagine, querying streaming data is different from batch data. To fully take advantage of a data stream, we must adapt query patterns that reflect its real-time nature. For example, systems such as Kafka and Pulsar make it easier to query streaming data sources. Let's look at some common ways to do this.

Basic query patterns on streams

Recall continuous CDC, discussed in Chapter 7. CDC, in this form, essentially sets up an analytics database as a fast follower to a production database. One of the longest-standing streaming query patterns simply entails querying the analytics database, retrieving statistical results and aggregations with a slight lag behind the production database.

The fast-follower approach.   How is this a streaming query pattern? Couldn't we accomplish the same thing simply by running our queries on the production database? In principle, yes; in practice, no. Production databases generally aren't equipped to handle production workloads and simultaneously run large analytics scans across significant quantities of data. Running such queries can slow the production application or even cause it to crash.[3] The basic CDC query pattern allows us to serve real-time analytics with a minimal impact on the production system.

---

3 The authors are aware of an incident involving a new analyst at a large grocery store chain running SELECT *
  on a production database and bringing down a critical inventory database for three days.

The fast-follower pattern can utilize a conventional transactional database as the follower, but there are significant advantages to using a proper OLAP-oriented system (Figure 8-3). Both Druid and BigQuery combine a streaming buffer with long-term columnar storage in a setup somewhat similar to the Lambda architecture (see Chapter 3). This works extremely well for computing trailing statistics on vast historical data with near real-time updates.

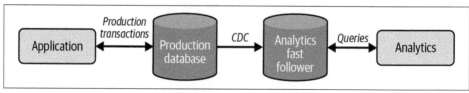

Figure 8-3. CDC with a fast-follower analytics database

The fast-follower CDC approach has critical limitations. It doesn't fundamentally rethink batch query patterns. You're still running SELECT queries against the current table state, and missing the opportunity to dynamically trigger events off changes in the stream.

The Kappa architecture.   Next, recall the Kappa architecture we discussed in Chapter 3. The principal idea of this architecture is to handle all data like events and store these events as a stream rather than a table (Figure 8-4). When production application databases are the source, Kappa architecture stores events from CDC. Event streams can also flow directly from an application backend, from a swarm of IoT devices, or any system that generates events and can push them over a network. Instead of simply treating a streaming storage system as a buffer, Kappa architecture retains events in storage during a more extended retention period, and data can be directly queried from this storage. The retention period can be pretty long (months or years). Note that this is much longer than the retention period used in purely real-time oriented systems, usually a week at most.

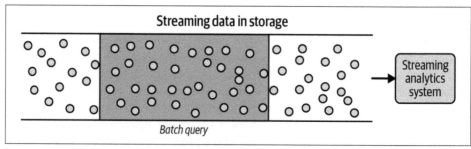

Figure 8-4. The Kappa architecture is built around streaming storage and ingest systems

The "big idea" in Kappa architecture is to treat streaming storage as a real-time transport layer and a database for retrieving and querying historical data. This happens either through the direct query capabilities of the streaming storage system or with the help of external tools. For example, Kafka KSQL supports aggregation, statistical calculations, and even sessionization. If query requirements are more complex or data needs to be combined with other data sources, an external tool such as Spark reads a time range of data from Kafka and computes the query results. The streaming storage system can also feed other applications or a stream processor such as Flink or Beam.

Windows, triggers, emitted statistics, and late-arriving data

One fundamental limitation of traditional batch queries is that this paradigm generally treats the query engine as an external observer. An actor external to the data causes the query to run—perhaps an hourly cron job or a product manager opening a dashboard.

Most widely used streaming systems, on the other hand, support the notion of computations triggered directly from the data itself. They might emit mean and median statistics every time a certain number of records are collected in the buffer or output a summary when a user session closes.

Windows are an essential feature in streaming queries and processing. Windows are small batches that are processed based on dynamic triggers. Windows are generated dynamically over time in some ways. Let's look at some common types of windows: session, fixed-time, and sliding. We'll also look at watermarks.

Session window. A *session window* groups events that occur close together, and filters out periods of inactivity when no events occur. We might say that a user session is any time interval with no inactivity gap of five minutes or more. Our batch system collects data by a user ID key, orders events, determines the gaps and session boundaries, and calculates statistics for each session. Data engineers often sessionize data retrospectively by applying time conditions to user activity on web and desktop apps.

In a streaming session, this process can happen dynamically. Note that session windows are per key; in the preceding example, each user gets their own set of windows. The system accumulates data per user. If a five-minute gap with no activity occurs, the system closes the window, sends its calculations, and flushes the data. If new events arrive for the user, the system starts a new session window.

Session windows may also make a provision for late-arriving data. Allowing data to arrive up to five minutes late to account for network conditions and system latency, the system will open the window if a late-arriving event indicates activity less than five minutes after the last event. We will have more to say about late-arriving data throughout this chapter. Figure 8-5 shows three session windows, each separated by five minutes of inactivity.

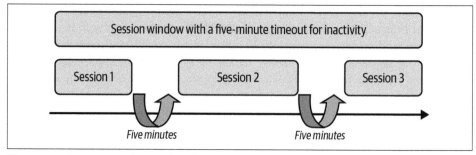

Figure 8-5. Session window with a five-minute timeout for inactivity

Making sessionization dynamic and near real-time fundamentally changes its utility. With retrospective sessionization, we could automate specific actions a day or an hour after a user session closed (e.g., a follow-up email with a coupon for a product viewed by the user). With dynamic sessionization, the user could get an alert in a mobile app that is immediately useful based on their activity in the last 15 minutes.

Fixed-time windows. A *fixed-time* (aka *tumbling*) window features fixed time periods that run on a fixed schedule and processes all data since the previous window is closed. For example, we might close a window every 20 seconds and process all data arriving from the previous window to give a mean and median statistic (Figure 8-6). Statistics would be emitted as soon as they could be calculated after the window closed.

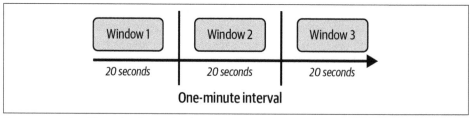

Figure 8-6. Tumbling/fixed window

This is similar to traditional batch ETL processing, where we might run a data update job every day or every hour. The streaming system allows us to generate windows more frequently and deliver results with lower latency. As we'll repeatedly emphasize, batch is a special case of streaming.

Sliding windows. Events in a sliding window are bucketed into windows of fixed time length, where separate windows might overlap. For example, we could generate a new 60-second window every 30 seconds (Figure 8-7). Just as we did before, we can emit mean and median statistics.

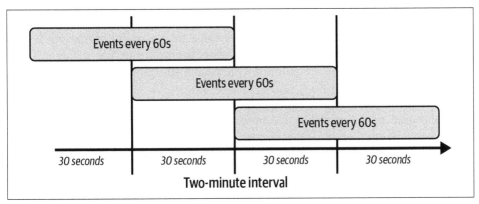

Figure 8-7. Sliding windows

The sliding can vary. For example, we might think of the window as truly sliding continuously but emitting statistics only when certain conditions (triggers) are met. Suppose we used a 30-second continuously sliding window but calculated a statistic only when a user clicked a particular banner. This would lead to an extremely high rate of output when many users click the banner, and no calculations during a lull.

Watermarks. We've covered various types of windows and their uses. As discussed in Chapter 7, data is sometimes ingested out of the order from which it originated. A *watermark* (Figure 8-8) is a threshold used by a window to determine whether data in a window is within the established time interval or whether it's considered late. If data arrives that is new to the window but older than the timestamp of the watermark, it is considered to be late-arriving data.

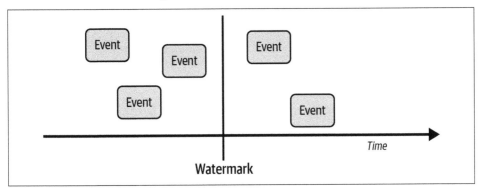

Figure 8-8. Watermark acting as a threshold for late-arriving data

Combining streams with other data

As we've mentioned before, we often derive value from data by combining it with other data. Streaming data is no different. For instance, multiple streams can be combined, or a stream can be combined with batch historical data.

Conventional table joins. Some tables may be fed by streams (Figure 8-9). The most basic approach to this problem is simply joining these two tables in a database. A stream can feed one or both of these tables.

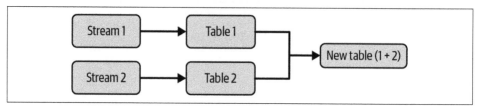

Figure 8-9. Joining two tables fed by streams

Enrichment. *Enrichment* means that we join a stream to other data (Figure 8-10). Typically, this is done to provide enhanced data into another stream. For example, suppose that an online retailer receives an event stream from a partner business containing product and user IDs. The retailer wishes to enhance these events with product details and demographic information on the users. The retailer feeds these events to a serverless function that looks up the product and user in an in-memory database (say, a cache), adds the required information to the event, and outputs the enhanced events to another stream.

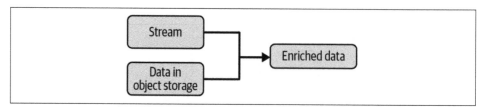

Figure 8-10. In this example, a stream is enriched with data residing in object storage, resulting in a new enriched dataset

In practice, the enrichment source could originate almost anywhere—a table in a cloud data warehouse or RDBMS, or a file in object storage. It's simply a question of reading from the source and storing the requisite enrichment data in an appropriate place for retrieval by the stream.

Stream-to-stream joining. Increasingly, streaming systems support direct stream-to-stream joining. Suppose that an online retailer wishes to join its web event data with streaming data from an ad platform. The company can feed both streams into Spark, but a variety of complications arise. For instance, the streams may have significantly different latencies for arrival at the point where the join is handled in the streaming system. The ad platform may provide its data with a five-minute delay. In addition, certain events may be significantly delayed—for example, a session close event for a user, or an event that happens on the phone offline and shows up in the stream only after the user is back in mobile network range.

As such, typical streaming join architectures rely on streaming buffers. The buffer retention interval is configurable; a longer retention interval requires more storage and other resources. Events get joined with data in the buffer and are eventually evicted after the retention interval has passed (Figure 8-11).[4]

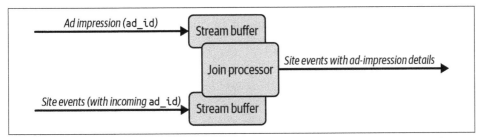

Figure 8-11. An architecture to join streams buffers each stream and joins events if related events are found during the buffer retention interval

Now that we've covered how queries work for batch and streaming data, let's discuss making your data useful by modeling it.

Data Modeling

Data modeling is something that we see overlooked disturbingly often. We often see data teams jump into building data systems without a game plan to organize their data in a way that's useful for the business. This is a mistake. Well-constructed data architectures must reflect the goals and business logic of the organization that relies on this data. Data modeling involves deliberately choosing a coherent structure for data and is a critical step to make data useful for the business.

Data modeling has been a practice for decades in one form or another. For example, various types of normalization techniques (discussed in "Normalization" on page 294) have been used to model data since the early days of RDBMSs; data warehousing modeling techniques have been around since at least the early 1990s and arguably longer. As pendulums in technology often go, data modeling became somewhat

---

4 Figure 8-11 and the example it depicts are significantly based on "Introducing Stream—Stream Joins in Apache Spark 2.3" (*https://oreil.ly/LG4EK*) by Tathagata Das and Joseph Torres (Databricks *Engineering Blog,* March 13, 2018).

unfashionable in the early to mid-2010s. The rise of data lake 1.0, NoSQL, and big data systems allowed engineers to bypass traditional data modeling, sometimes for legitimate performance gains. Other times, the lack of rigorous data modeling created data swamps, along with lots of redundant, mismatched, or simply wrong data.

Nowadays, the pendulum seems to be swinging back toward data modeling. The growing popularity of data management (in particular, data governance and data quality) is pushing the need for coherent business logic. The meteoric rise of data's prominence in companies creates a growing recognition that modeling is critical for realizing value at the higher levels of the Data Science Hierarchy of Needs pyramid. That said, we believe that new paradigms are required to truly embrace the needs of streaming data and ML. In this section, we survey current mainstream data modeling techniques and briefly muse on the future of data modeling.

What Is a Data Model?

A *data model* represents the way data relates to the real world. It reflects how the data must be structured and standardized to best reflect your organization's processes, definitions, workflows, and logic. A good data model captures how communication and work naturally flow within your organization. In contrast, a poor data model (or nonexistent one) is haphazard, confusing, and incoherent.

Some data professionals view data modeling as tedious and reserved for "big enterprises." Like most good hygiene practices—such as flossing your teeth and getting a good night's sleep—data modeling is acknowledged as a good thing to do but is often ignored in practice. Ideally, every organization should model its data if only to ensure that business logic and rules are translated at the data layer.

When modeling data, it's critical to focus on translating the model to business outcomes. A good data model should correlate with impactful business decisions. For example, a *customer* might mean different things to different departments in a company. Is someone who's bought from you over the last 30 days a customer? What if they haven't bought from you in the previous six months or a year? Carefully defining and modeling this customer data can have a massive impact on downstream reports on customer behavior or the creation of customer churn models whereby the time since the last purchase is a critical variable.

 A good data model contains consistent definitions. In practice, definitions are often messy throughout a company. Can you think of concepts or terms in your company that might mean different things to different people?

Our discussion focuses mainly on batch data modeling since that's where most data modeling techniques arose. We will also look at some approaches to modeling streaming data and general considerations for modeling.

Conceptual, Logical, and Physical Data Models

When modeling data, the idea is to move from abstract modeling concepts to concrete implementation. Along this continuum (Figure 8-12), three main data models are conceptual, logical, and physical. These models form the basis for the various modeling techniques we describe in this chapter:

Conceptual
> Contains business logic and rules and describes the system's data, such as schemas, tables, and fields (names and types). When creating a conceptual model, it's often helpful to visualize it in an entity-relationship (ER) diagram, which is a standard tool for visualizing the relationships among various entities in your data (orders, customers, products, etc.). For example, an ER diagram might encode the connections among customer ID, customer name, customer address, and customer orders. Visualizing entity relationships is highly recommended for designing a coherent conceptual data model.

Logical
> Details how the conceptual model will be implemented in practice by adding significantly more detail. For example, we would add information on the types of customer ID, customer names, and custom addresses. In addition, we would map out primary and foreign keys.

Physical
> Defines how the logical model will be implemented in a database system. We would add specific databases, schemas, and tables to our logical model, including configuration details.

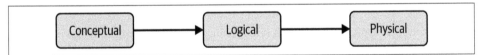

Figure 8-12. The continuum of data models: conceptual, logical, and physical

Successful data modeling involves business stakeholders at the inception of the process. Engineers need to obtain definitions and business goals for the data. Modeling data should be a full-contact sport whose goal is to provide the business with quality data for actionable insights and intelligent automation. This is a practice that everyone must continuously participate in.

Another important consideration for data modeling is the *grain* of the data, which is the resolution at which data is stored and queried. The grain is typically at the level of a primary key in a table, such as customer ID, order ID, and product ID; it's often accompanied by a date or timestamp for increased fidelity.

For example, suppose that a company has just begun to deploy BI reporting. The company is small enough that the same person is filling the role of data engineer and analyst. A request comes in for a report that summarizes daily customer orders. Specifically, the report should list all customers who ordered, the number of orders they placed that day, and the total amount they spent.

This report is inherently coarse-grained. It contains no details on spending per order or the items in each order. It is tempting for the data engineer/analyst to ingest data from the production orders database and boil it down to a reporting table with only the basic aggregated data required for the report. However, this would entail starting over when a request comes in for a report with finer-grained data aggregation.

Since the data engineer is actually quite experienced, they elect to create tables with detailed data on customer orders, including each order, item, item cost, item IDs, etc. Essentially, their tables contain all details on customer orders. The data's grain is at the customer-order level. This customer-order data can be analyzed as is, or aggregated for summary statistics on customer order activity.

In general, you should strive to model your data at the lowest level of grain possible. From here, it's easy to aggregate this highly granular dataset. The reverse isn't true, and it's generally impossible to restore details that have been aggregated away.

Normalization

Normalization is a database data modeling practice that enforces strict control over the relationships of tables and columns within a database. The goal of normalization is to remove the redundancy of data within a database and ensure referential integrity. Basically, it's *don't repeat yourself* (DRY) applied to data in a database.[5]

Normalization is typically applied to relational databases containing tables with rows and columns (we use the terms *column* and *field* interchangeably in this section). It was first introduced by relational database pioneer Edgar Codd in the early 1970s.

---

5 For more details on the DRY principle, see *The Pragmatic Programmer* by David Thomas and Andrew Hunt (Addison-Wesley Professional, 2019).

Codd outlined four main objectives of normalization:[6]

- To free the collection of relations from undesirable insertion, update, and deletion dependencies
- To reduce the need for restructuring the collection of relations, as new types of data are introduced, and thus increase the lifespan of application programs
- To make the relational model more informative to users
- To make the collection of relations neutral to the query statistics, where these statistics are liable to change as time goes by

Codd introduced the idea of *normal forms*. The normal forms are sequential, with each form incorporating the conditions of prior forms. We describe Codd's first three normal forms here:

Denormalized
No normalization. Nested and redundant data is allowed.

First normal form (1NF)
Each column is unique and has a single value. The table has a unique primary key.

Second normal form (2NF)
The requirements of 1NF, plus partial dependencies are removed.

Third normal form (3NF)
The requirements of 2NF, plus each table contains only relevant fields related to its primary key and has no transitive dependencies.

It's worth spending a moment to unpack a couple of terms we just threw at you. A *unique primary key* is a single field or set of multiple fields that uniquely determines rows in the table. Each key value occurs at most once; otherwise, a value would map to multiple rows in the table. Thus, every other value in a row is dependent on (can be determined from) the key. A *partial dependency* occurs when a subset of fields in a composite key can be used to determine a nonkey column of the table. A *transitive dependency* occurs when a nonkey field depends on another nonkey field.

Let's look at stages of normalization—from denormalized to 3NF—using an ecommerce example of customer orders (Table 8-1). We'll provide concrete explanations of each of the concepts introduced in the previous paragraph.

---

6 E. F. Codd, "Further Normalization of the Data Base Relational Model," IBM Research Laboratory (1971), *https://oreil.ly/Muajm*.

Table 8-1. OrderDetail

OrderID	OrderItems	CustomerID	CustomerName	OrderDate

100	`[{`
	`  "sku": 1,`
	`  "price": 50,`
	`  "quantity": 1,`
	`  "name:": "Thingamajig"`
	`}, {`
	`  "sku": 2,`
	`  "price": 25,`
	`  "quantity": 2,`
	`  "name:": "Whatchamacallit"`
	`}]`
		5	Joe Reis	2022-03-01

First, this denormalized OrderDetail table contains five fields. The primary key is OrderID. Notice that the OrderItems field contains a nested object with two SKUs along with their price, quantity, and name.

To convert this data to 1NF, let's move OrderItems into four fields (Table 8-2). Now we have an OrderDetail table in which fields do not contain repeats or nested data.

Table 8-2. OrderDetail without repeats or nested data

OrderID	Sku	Price	Quantity	ProductName	CustomerID	CustomerName	OrderDate
100	1	50	1	Thingamajig	5	Joe Reis	2022-03-01
100	2	25	2	Whatchamacallit	5	Joe Reis	2022-03-01

The problem is that now we don't have a unique primary key. That is, 100 occurs in the OrderID column in two different rows. To get a better grasp of the situation, let's look at a larger sample from our table (Table 8-3).

Table 8-3. OrderDetail with a larger sample

OrderID	Sku	Price	Quantity	ProductName	CustomerID	CustomerName	OrderDate
100	1	50	1	Thingamajig	5	Joe Reis	2022-03-01
100	2	25	2	Whatchamacallit	5	Joe Reis	2022-03-01
101	3	75	1	Whozeewhatzit	7	Matt Housley	2022-03-01
102	1	50	1	Thingamajig	7	Matt Housley	2022-03-01

To create a unique primary (composite) key, let's number the lines in each order by adding a column called LineItemNumber (Table 8-4).

Table 8-4. OrderDetail with LineItemNumber column

Order ID	LineItem Number	Sku	Price	Quantity	Product Name	Customer ID	Customer Name	OrderDate
100	1	1	50	1	Thingama jig	5	Joe Reis	2022-03-01
100	2	2	25	2	Whatchama callit	5	Joe Reis	2022-03-01
101	1	3	75	1	Whozee whatzit	7	Matt Housley	2022-03-01
102	1	1	50	1	Thingama jig	7	Matt Housley	2022-03-01

The composite key (OrderID, LineItemNumber) is now a unique primary key.

To reach 2NF, we need to ensure that no partial dependencies exist. A *partial dependency* is a nonkey column that is fully determined by a subset of the columns in the unique primary (composite) key; partial dependencies can occur only when the primary key is composite. In our case, the last three columns are determined by order number. To fix this problem, let's split OrderDetail into two tables: Orders and OrderLineItem (Tables 8-5 and 8-6).

Table 8-5. Orders

OrderID	CustomerID	CustomerName	OrderDate
100	5	Joe Reis	2022-03-01
101	7	Matt Housley	2022-03-01
102	7	Matt Housley	2022-03-01

Table 8-6. OrderLineItem

OrderID	LineItemNumber	Sku	Price	Quantity	ProductName
100	1	1	50	1	Thingamajig
100	2	2	25	2	Whatchamacallit
101	1	3	75	1	Whozeewhatzit
102	1	1	50	1	Thingamajig

The composite key (OrderID, LineItemNumber) is a unique primary key for Order LineItem, while OrderID is a primary key for Orders.

Notice that Sku determines ProductName in OrderLineItem. That is, Sku depends on the composite key, and ProductName depends on Sku. This is a transitive dependency. Let's break OrderLineItem into OrderLineItem and Skus (Tables 8-7 and 8-8).

Table 8-7. OrderLineItem

OrderID	LineItemNumber	Sku	Price	Quantity
100	1	1	50	1
100	2	2	25	2
101	1	3	75	1
102	1	1	50	1

Table 8-8. Skus

Sku	ProductName
1	Thingamajig
2	Whatchamacallit
3	Whozeewhatzit

Now, both OrderLineItem and Skus are in 3NF. Notice that Orders does not satisfy 3NF. What transitive dependencies are present? How would you fix this?

Additional normal forms exist (up to 6NF in the Boyce-Codd system), but these are much less common than the first three. A database is usually considered normalized if it's in third normal form, and that's the convention we use in this book.

The degree of normalization that you should apply to your data depends on your use case. No one-size-fits-all solution exists, especially in databases where some denormalization presents performance advantages. Although denormalization may seem like an antipattern, it's common in many OLAP systems that store semistructured data. Study normalization conventions and database best practices to choose an appropriate strategy.

Techniques for Modeling Batch Analytical Data

When describing data modeling for data lakes or data warehouses, you should assume that the raw data takes many forms (e.g., structured and semistructured), but the output is a structured data model of rows and columns. However, several approaches to data modeling can be used in these environments. The big approaches you'll likely encounter are Kimball, Inmon, and Data Vault.

In practice, some of these techniques can be combined. For example, we see some data teams start with Data Vault and then add a Kimball star schema alongside it. We'll also look at wide and denormalized data models and other batch data-modeling techniques you should have in your arsenal. As we discuss each of these techniques, we will use the example of modeling transactions occurring in an ecommerce order system.

Our coverage of the first three approaches—Inmon, Kimball, and Data Vault—is cursory and hardly does justice to their respective complexity and nuance. At the end of each section, we list the canonical books from their creators. For a data engineer, these books are must-reads, and we highly encourage you to read them, if only to understand how and why data modeling is central to batch analytical data.

Inmon

The father of the data warehouse, Bill Inmon, created his approach to data modeling in 1989. Before the data warehouse, the analysis would often occur directly on the source system itself, with the obvious consequence of bogging down production transactional databases with long-running queries. The goal of the data warehouse was to separate the source system from the analytical system.

Inmon defines a data warehouse the following way:[7]

> A data warehouse is a subject-oriented, integrated, nonvolatile, and time-variant collection of data in support of management's decisions. The data warehouse contains granular corporate data. Data in the data warehouse is able to be used for many different purposes, including sitting and waiting for future requirements which are unknown today.

The four critical parts of a data warehouse can be described as follows:

Subject-oriented
    The data warehouse focuses on a specific subject area, such as sales or marketing.

Integrated
    Data from disparate sources is consolidated and normalized.

Nonvolatile
    Data remains unchanged after data is stored in a data warehouse.

Time-variant
    Varying time ranges can be queried.

Let's look at each of these parts to understand its influence on an Inmon data model. First, the logical model must focus on a specific area. For instance, if the *subject orientation* is "sales," then the logical model contains all details related to sales —business keys, relationships, attributes, etc. Next, these details are *integrated* into a consolidated and highly normalized data model. Finally, the data is stored unchanged in a *nonvolatile* and *time-variant* way, meaning you can (theoretically) query the original data for as long as storage history allows. The Inmon data warehouse must

---

7 H. W. Inmon, *Building the Data Warehouse* (Hoboken: Wiley, 2005).

strictly adhere to all four of these critical parts *in support of management's decisions.* This is a subtle point, but it positions the data warehouse for analytics, not OLTP.

Here is another key characteristic of Inmon's data warehouse:[8]

> The second salient characteristic of the data warehouse is that it is integrated. Of all the aspects of a data warehouse, integration is the most important. Data is fed from multiple, disparate sources into the data warehouse. As the data is fed, it is converted, reformatted, resequenced, summarized, etc. The result is that data—once it resides in the data warehouse—has a single physical corporate image.

With Inmon's data warehouse, data is integrated from across the organization in a granular, highly normalized ER model, with a relentless emphasis on ETL. Because of the subject-oriented nature of the data warehouse, the Inmon data warehouse consists of key source databases and information systems used in an organization. Data from key business source systems is ingested and integrated into a highly normalized (3NF) data warehouse that often closely resembles the normalization structure of the source system itself; data is brought in incrementally, starting with the highest-priority business areas. The strict normalization requirement ensures as little data duplication as possible, which leads to fewer downstream analytical errors because data won't diverge or suffer from redundancies. The data warehouse represents a "single source of truth," which supports the overall business's information requirements. The data is presented for downstream reports and analysis via business and department-specific data marts, which may also be denormalized.

Let's look at how an Inmon data warehouse is used for ecommerce (Figure 8-13). The business source systems are orders, inventory, and marketing. The data from these source systems are ETLed to the data warehouse and stored in 3NF. Ideally, the data warehouse holistically encompasses the business's information. To serve data for department-specific information requests, ETL processes take data from the data warehouse, transform the data, and place it in downstream data marts to be viewed in reports.

A popular option for modeling data in a data mart is a star schema (discussed in the following section on Kimball), though any data model that provides easily accessible information is also suitable. In the preceding example, sales, marketing, and purchasing have their own star schema, fed upstream from the granular data in the data warehouse. This allows each department to have its own data structure that's unique and optimized to its specific needs.

Inmon continues to innovate in the data warehouse space, currently focusing on textual ETL in the data warehouse. He's also a prolific writer and thinker, writing over

---

8 Inmon, *Building the Data Warehouse.*

60 books and countless articles. For further reading about Inmon's data warehouse, please refer to his books listed in "Additional Resources" on page 339.

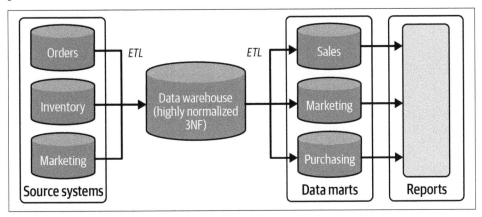

Figure 8-13. An ecommerce data warehouse

Kimball

If there are spectrums to data modeling, Kimball is very much on the opposite end of Inmon. Created by Ralph Kimball in the early 1990s, this approach to data modeling focuses less on normalization, and in some cases accepting denormalization. As Inmon says about the difference between the data warehouse and data mart, "A data mart is never a substitute for a data warehouse."[9]

Whereas Inmon integrates data from across the business in the data warehouse, and serves department-specific analytics via data marts, the Kimball model is bottom-up, encouraging you to model and serve department or business analytics in the data warehouse itself (Inmon argues this approach skews the definition of a data warehouse). The Kimball approach effectively makes the data mart the data warehouse itself. This may enable faster iteration and modeling than Inmon, with the trade-off of potential looser data integration, data redundancy, and duplication.

In Kimball's approach, data is modeled with two general types of tables: facts and dimensions. You can think of a *fact table* as a table of numbers, and *dimension tables* as qualitative data referencing a fact. Dimension tables surround a single fact table in a relationship called a *star schema* (Figure 8-14).[10] Let's look at facts, dimensions, and star schemas.

---

9 Inmon, *Building the Data Warehouse.*

10 Although dimensions and facts are often associated with Kimball, they were first used at General Mills and Dartmouth University in the 1960s and had early adoption at Nielsen and IRI, among other companies.

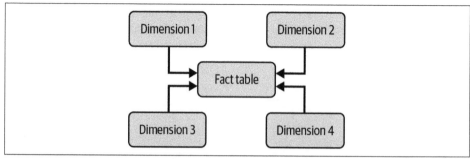

Figure 8-14. A Kimball star schema, with facts and dimensions

Fact tables.   The first type of table in a star schema is the fact table, which contains *factual*, quantitative, and event-related data. The data in a fact table is immutable because facts relate to events. Therefore, fact tables don't change and are append-only. Fact tables are typically narrow and long, meaning they have not a lot of columns but a lot of rows that represent events. Fact tables should be at the lowest grain possible.

Queries against a star schema start with the fact table. Each row of a fact table should represent the grain of the data. Avoid aggregating or deriving data within a fact table. If you need to perform aggregations or derivations, do so in a downstream query, data mart table, or view. Finally, fact tables don't reference other fact tables; they reference only dimensions.

Let's look at an example of an elementary fact table (Table 8-9). A common question in your company might be, "Show me gross sales, by each customer order, by date." Again, facts should be at the lowest grain possible—in this case, the orderID of the sale, customer, date, and gross sale amount. Notice that the data types in the fact table are all numbers (integers and floats); there are no strings. Also, in this example, CustomerKey 7 has two orders on the same day, reflecting the grain of the table. Instead, the fact table has keys that reference dimension tables containing their respective attributes, such as the customer and date information. The gross sales amount represents the total sale for the sales *event*.

Table 8-9. A fact table

OrderID	CustomerKey	DateKey	GrossSalesAmt
100	5	20220301	100.00
101	7	20220301	75.00
102	7	20220301	50.00

Dimension tables.   The second primary type of table in a Kimball data model is called a *dimension*. Dimension tables provide the reference data, attributes, and relational context for the events stored in fact tables. Dimension tables are smaller than fact tables and take an opposite shape, typically wide and short. When joined to a fact table, dimensions can describe the events' what, where, and when. Dimensions are denormalized, with the possibility of duplicate data. This is OK in the Kimball data model. Let's look at the two dimensions referenced in the earlier fact table example.

In a Kimball data model, dates are typically stored in a date dimension, allowing you to reference the date key (DateKey) between the fact and date dimension table. With the date dimension table, you can easily answer questions like, "What are my total sales in the first quarter of 2022?" or "How many more customers shop on Tuesday than Wednesday?" Notice we have five fields in addition to the date key (Table 8-10). The beauty of a date dimension is that you can add as many new fields as makes sense to analyze your data.

Table 8-10. A date dimension table

DateKey	Date-ISO	Year	Quarter	Month	Day-of-week
20220301	2022-03-01	2022	1	3	Tuesday
20220302	2022-03-02	2022	1	3	Wednesday
20220303	2022-03-03	2022	1	3	Thursday

Table 8-11 also references another dimension—the customer dimension—by the CustomerKey field. The customer dimension contains several fields that describe the customer: first and last name, zip code, and a couple of peculiar-looking date fields. Let's look at these date fields, as they illustrate another concept in the Kimball data model: a Type 2 slowly changing dimension, which we'll describe in greater detail next.

Table 8-11. A Type 2 customer dimension table

CustomerKey	FirstName	LastName	ZipCode	EFF_StartDate	EFF_EndDate
5	Joe	Reis	84108	2019-01-04	9999-01-01
7	Matt	Housley	84101	2020-05-04	2021-09-19
7	Matt	Housley	84123	2021-09-19	9999-01-01
11	Lana	Belle	90210	2022-02-04	9999-01-01

For example, take a look at CustomerKey 5, with the EFF_StartDate (EFF_StartDate means *effective start date*) of 2019-01-04 and an EFF_EndDate of 9999-01-01. This means Joe Reis's customer record was created in the customer dimension table on 2019-01-04 and has an end date of 9999-01-01. Interesting. What does this end date mean? It means the customer record is active and isn't changed.

Now let's look at Matt Housley's customer record (CustomerKey = 7). Notice the two entries for Housley's start date: 2020-05-04 and 2021-09-19. It looks like Housley changed his zip code on 2021-09-19, resulting in a change to his customer record.

When the data is queried for the most recent customer records, you will query where the end date is equal to 9999-01-01.

A slowly changing dimension (SCD) is necessary to track changes in dimensions. The preceding example is a Type 2 SCD: a new record is inserted when an existing record changes. Though SCDs can go up to seven levels, let's look at the three most common ones:

Type 1
> Overwrite existing dimension records. This is super simple and means you have no access to the deleted historical dimension records.

Type 2
> Keep a full history of dimension records. When a record changes, that specific record is flagged as changed, and a new dimension record is created that reflects the current status of the attributes. In our example, Housley moved to a new zip code, which triggered his initial record to reflect an effective end date, and a new record was created to show his new zip code.

Type 3
> A Type 3 SCD is similar to a Type 2 SCD, but instead of creating a new row, a change in a Type 3 SCD creates a new field. Using the preceding example, let's see what this looks like as a Type 3 SCD in the following tables.

In Table 8-12, Housley lives in the 84101 zip code. When Housley moves to a new zip code, the Type 3 SCD creates two new fields, one for his new zip code and the date of the change (Table 8-13). The original zip code field is also renamed to reflect that this is the older record.

Table 8-12. Type 3 slowly changing dimension

CustomerKey	FirstName	LastName	ZipCode
7	Matt	Housley	84101

Table 8-13. Type 3 customer dimension table

CustomerKey	FirstName	LastName	Original ZipCode	Current ZipCode	CurrentDate
7	Matt	Housley	84101	84123	2021-09-19

Of the types of SCDs described, Type 1 is the default behavior of most data warehouses, and Type 2 is the one we most commonly see used in practice. There's a lot to know about dimensions, and we suggest using this section as a starting point to get familiar with how dimensions work and how they're used.

Star schema.   Now that you have a basic understanding of facts and dimensions, it's time to integrate them into a star schema. The *star schema* represents the data model of the business. Unlike highly normalized approaches to data modeling, the star schema is a fact table surrounded by the necessary dimensions. This results in fewer joins than other data models, which speeds up query performance. Another advantage of a star schema is it's arguably easier for business users to understand and use.

Note that the star schema shouldn't reflect a particular report, though you can model a report in a downstream data mart or directly in your BI tool. The star schema should capture the facts and attributes of your *business logic* and be flexible enough to answer the respective critical questions.

Because a star schema has one fact table, sometimes you'll have multiple star schemas that address different facts of the business. You should strive to reduce the number of dimensions whenever possible since this reference data can potentially be reused among different fact tables. A dimension that is reused across multiple star schemas, thus sharing the same fields, is called a *conformed dimension*. A conformed dimension allows you to combine multiple fact tables across multiple star schemas. Remember, redundant data is OK with the Kimball method, but avoid replicating the same dimension tables to avoid drifting business definitions and data integrity.

The Kimball data model and star schema have a lot of nuance. You should be aware that this mode is appropriate only for batch data and not for streaming data. Because the Kimball data model is popular, there's a good chance you'll run into it.

Data Vault

Whereas Kimball and Inmon focus on the structure of business logic in the data warehouse, the *Data Vault* offers a different approach to data modeling.[11] Created in the 1990s by Dan Linstedt, the Data Vault methodology separates the structural aspects of a source system's data from its attributes. Instead of representing business logic in facts, dimensions, or highly normalized tables, a Data Vault simply loads data from source systems directly into a handful of purpose-built tables in an insert-only manner. Unlike the other data modeling approaches you've learned about, there's no notion of good, bad, or conformed data in a Data Vault.

Data moves fast these days, and data models need to be agile, flexible, and scalable; the Data Vault methodology aims to meet this need. The goal of this methodology is to keep the data as closely aligned to the business as possible, even while the business's data evolves.

---

11 The Data Vault has two versions, 1.0 and 2.0. This section focuses on Data Vault 2.0, but we'll call it *Data Vault* for the sake of brevity.

A Data Vault model consists of three main types of tables: hubs, links, and satellites (Figure 8-15). In short, a *hub* stores business keys, a *link* maintains relationships among business keys, and a *satellite* represents a business key's attributes and context. A user will query a hub, which will link to a satellite table containing the query's relevant attributes. Let's explore hubs, links, and satellites in more detail.

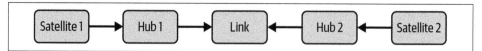

Figure 8-15. Data Vault tables: hubs, links, and satellites connected together

Hubs. Queries often involve searching by a business key, such as a customer ID or an order ID from our ecommerce example. A hub is the central entity of a Data Vault that retains a record of all unique business keys loaded into the Data Vault.

A hub always contains the following standard fields:

Hash key
> The primary key used to join data between systems. This is a calculated hash field (MD5 or similar).

Load date
> The date the data was loaded into the hub.

Record source
> The source from which the unique record was obtained.

Business key(s)
> The key used to identify a unique record.

It's important to note that a hub is insert-only, and data is not altered in a hub. Once data is loaded into a hub, it's permanent.

When designing a hub, identifying the business key is critical. Ask yourself: What is the *identifiable business element*?[12] Put another way, how do users commonly look for data? Ideally, this is discovered as you build the conceptual data model of your organization and before you start building your Data Vault.

Using our ecommerce scenario, let's look at an example of a hub for products. First, let's look at the physical design of a product hub (Table 8-14).

---

12 Kent Graziano, "Data Vault 2.0 Modeling Basics," Vertabelo, October 20, 2015, *https://oreil.ly/iuW1U*.

Table 8-14. A physical design for a product hub

HubProduct
ProductHashKey
LoadDate
RecordSource
ProductID

In practice, the product hub looks like this when populated with data (Table 8-15). In this example, three different products are loaded into a hub from an ERP system on two separate dates.

Table 8-15. A product hub populated with data

ProductHashKey	LoadDate	RecordSource	ProductID
4041fd80ab...	2020-01-02	ERP	1
de8435530d...	2021-03-09	ERP	2
cf27369bd8...	2021-03-09	ERP	3

While we're at it, let's create another hub for orders (Table 8-16) using the same schema as HubProduct, and populate it with some sample order data.

Table 8-16. An order hub populated with data

OrderHashKey	LoadDate	RecordSource	OrderID
f899139df5...	2022-03-01	Website	100
38b3eff8ba...	2022-03-01	Website	101
ec8956637a...	2022-03-01	Website	102

Links. A *link table* tracks the relationships of business keys between hubs. Link tables connect hubs, ideally at the lowest possible grain. Because link tables connect data from various hubs, they are many to many. The Data Vault model's relationships are straightforward and handled through changes to the links. This provides excellent flexibility in the inevitable event that the underlying data changes. You simply create a new link that ties business concepts (or hubs) to represent the new relationship. That's it! Now let's look at ways to view data contextually using satellites.

Back to our ecommerce example, we'd like to associate orders with products. Let's see what a link table might look like for orders and products (Table 8-17).

Table 8-17. A link table for products and orders

LinkOrderProduct
OrderProductHashKey
LoadDate

LinkOrderProduct
RecordSource
ProductHashKey
OrderHashKey

When the LinkOrderProduct table is populated, here's what it looks like (Table 8-18). Note that we're using the order's record source in this example.

Table 8-18. A link table connecting orders and products

OrderProductHashKey	LoadDate	RecordSource	ProductHashKey	OrderHashKey
ff64ec193d...	2022-03-01	Website	4041fd80ab...	f899139df5...
ff64ec193d...	2022-03-01	Website	de8435530d...	f899139df5...
e232628c25...	2022-03-01	Website	cf27369bd8...	38b3eff8ba...
26166a5871...	2022-03-01	Website	4041fd80ab...	ec8956637a...

Satellites. We've described relationships between hubs and links that involve keys, load dates, and record sources. How do you get a sense of what these relationships mean? *Satellites* are descriptive attributes that give meaning and context to hubs. Satellites can connect to either hubs or links. The only required fields in a satellite are a primary key consisting of the business key of the parent hub and a load date. Beyond that, a satellite can contain however many attributes that make sense.

Let's look at an example of a satellite for the Product hub (Table 8-19). In this example, the SatelliteProduct table contains additional information about the product, such as product name and price.

Table 8-19. SatelliteProduct

SatelliteProduct
ProductHashKey
LoadDate
RecordSource
ProductName
Price

And here's the SatelliteProduct table with some sample data (Table 8-20).

Table 8-20. A product satellite table with sample data

ProductHashKey	LoadDate	RecordSource	ProductName	Price
4041fd80ab...	2020-01-02	ERP	Thingamajig	50
de8435530d...	2021-03-09	ERP	Whatchamacallit	25
cf27369bd8...	2021-03-09	ERP	Whozeewhatzit	75

Let's tie this all together and join the hub, product, and link tables into a Data Vault (Figure 8-16).

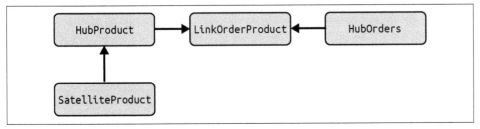

Figure 8-16. The Data Vault for orders and products

Other types of Data Vault tables exist, including point-in-time (PIT) and bridge tables. We don't cover these here, but mention them because the Data Vault is quite comprehensive. Our goal is to simply give you an overview of the Data Vault's power.

Unlike other data modeling techniques we've discussed, in a Data Vault, the business logic is created and interpreted when the data from these tables is queried. Please be aware that the Data Vault model can be used with other data modeling techniques. It's not unusual for a Data Vault to be the landing zone for analytical data, after which it's separately modeled in a data warehouse, commonly using a star schema. The Data Vault model also can be adapted for NoSQL and streaming data sources. The Data Vault is a huge topic, and this section is simply meant to make you aware of its existence.

Wide denormalized tables

The strict modeling approaches we've described, especially Kimball and Inmon, were developed when data warehouses were expensive, on premises, and heavily resource-constrained with tightly coupled compute and storage. While batch data modeling has traditionally been associated with these strict approaches, more relaxed approaches are becoming more common.

There are reasons for this. First, the popularity of the cloud means that storage is dirt cheap. It's cheaper to store data than agonize over the optimum way to represent the data in storage. Second, the popularity of nested data (JSON and similar) means schemas are flexible in source and analytical systems.

You have the option to rigidly model your data as we've described, or you can choose to throw all of your data into a single wide table. A *wide table* is just what it sounds like: a highly denormalized and very wide collection of many fields, typically created in a columnar database. A field may be a single value or contain nested data. The data is organized along with one or multiple keys; these keys are closely tied to the *grain* of the data.

A wide table can potentially have thousands of columns, whereas fewer than 100 are typical in relational databases. Wide tables are usually sparse; the vast majority of entries in a given field may be null. This is extremely expensive in a traditional relational database because the database allocates a fixed amount of space for each field entry; nulls take up virtually no space in a columnar database. A wide schema in a relational database dramatically slows reading because each row must allocate all the space specified by the wide schema, and the database must read the contents of each row in its entirety. On the other hand, a columnar database reads only columns selected in a query, and reading nulls is essentially free.

Wide tables generally arise through schema evolution; engineers gradually add fields over time. Schema evolution in a relational database is a slow and resource-heavy process. In a columnar database, adding a field is initially just a change to metadata. As data is written into the new field, new files are added to the column.

Analytics queries on wide tables often run faster than equivalent queries on highly normalized data requiring many joins. Removing joins can have a huge impact on scan performance. The wide table simply contains all of the data you would have joined in a more rigorous modeling approach. Facts and dimensions are represented in the same table. The lack of data model rigor also means not a lot of thought is involved. Load your data into a wide table and start querying it. Especially with schemas in source systems becoming more adaptive and flexible, this data usually results from high-volume transactions, meaning there's a lot of data. Storing this as nested data in your analytical storage has a lot of benefits.

Throwing all of your data into a single table might seem like heresy for a hardcore data modeler, and we've seen plenty of criticism. What are some of these criticisms? The biggest criticism is as you blend your data, you lose the business logic in your analytics. Another downside is the performance of updates to things like an element in an array, which can be very painful.

Let's look at an example of a wide table (Table 8-21), using the original denormalized table from our earlier normalization example. This table can have many more columns—hundreds or more!—and we include only a handful of columns for brevity and ease of understanding. As you can see, this table combines various data types, represented along a grain of orders for a customer on a date.

We suggest using a wide table when you don't care about data modeling, or when you have a lot of data that needs more flexibility than traditional data-modeling rigor provides. Wide tables also lend themselves to streaming data, which we'll discuss next. As data moves toward fast-moving schemas and streaming-first, we expect to see a new wave of data modeling, perhaps something along the lines of "relaxed normalization."

Table 8-21. An example of denormalized data

OrderID	OrderItems	CustomerID	Customer Name	OrderDate	Site	Site Region

100	`[{`
	  `"sku": 1,`
	  `"price": 50,`
	  `"quantity": 1,`
	  `"name:":`
	    `"Thingamajig"`
	`}, {`
	  `"sku": 2,`
	  `"price": 25,`
	  `"quantity": 2,`
	  `"name:":`
	    `"Whatchamacallit"`
	`}]`
		5	Joe Reis	2022-03-01	abc.com	US

What If You Don't Model Your Data?

You also have the option of *not* modeling your data. In this case, just query data sources directly. This pattern is often used, especially when companies are just getting started and want to get quick insights or share analytics with their users. While it allows you to get answers to various questions, you should consider the following:

- If I don't model my data, how do I know the results of my queries are consistent?

- Do I have proper definitions of business logic in the source system, and will my query produce truthful answers?

- What query load am I putting on my source systems, and how does this impact users of these systems?

At some point, you'll probably gravitate toward a stricter batch data model paradigm and a dedicated data architecture that doesn't rely on the source systems for the heavy lifting.

Modeling Streaming Data

Whereas many data-modeling techniques are well established for batch, this is not the case for streaming data. Because of the unbounded and continuous nature of streaming data, translating batch techniques like Kimball to a streaming paradigm is tricky, if not impossible. For example, given a stream of data, how would you continuously update a Type-2 slowly changing dimension without bringing your data warehouse to its knees?

The world is evolving from batch to streaming and from on premises to the cloud. The constraints of the older batch methods no longer apply. That said, big questions remain about how to model data to balance the need for business logic against fluid schema changes, fast-moving data, and self-service. What is the streaming equivalent of the preceding batch data model approaches? There isn't (yet) a consensus approach on streaming data modeling. We spoke with many experts in streaming data systems, many of whom told us that traditional batch-oriented data modeling doesn't apply to streaming. A few suggested the Data Vault as an option for streaming data modeling.

As you may recall, two main types of streams exist: event streams and CDC. Most of the time, the shape of the data in these streams is semistructured, such as JSON. The challenge with modeling streaming data is that the payload's schema might change on a whim. For example, suppose you have an IoT device that recently upgraded its firmware and introduced a new field. In that case, it's possible that your downstream destination data warehouse or processing pipeline isn't aware of this change and breaks. That's not great. As another example, a CDC system might recast a field as a different type—say, a string instead of an International Organization for Standardization (ISO) datetime format. Again, how does the destination handle this seemingly random change?

The streaming data experts we've talked with overwhelmingly suggest you anticipate changes in the source data and keep a flexible schema. This means there's no rigid data model in the analytical database. Instead, assume the source systems are providing the correct data with the right business definition and logic, as it exists today. And because storage is cheap, store the recent streaming and saved historical data in a way they can be queried together. Optimize for comprehensive analytics against a dataset with a flexible schema. Furthermore, instead of reacting to reports, why not create automation that responds to anomalies and changes in the streaming data instead?

The world of data modeling is changing, and we believe a sea change will soon occur in data model paradigms. These new approaches will likely incorporate metrics and semantic layers, data pipelines, and traditional analytics workflows in a streaming layer that sits directly on top of the source system. Since data is being generated in real time, the notion of artificially separating source and analytics systems into two distinct buckets may not make as much sense as when data moved more slowly and predictably. Time will tell…

We have more to say on the future of streaming data in Chapter 11.

Transformations

> The net result of transforming data is the ability to unify and integrate data. Once data is transformed, the data can be viewed as a single entity. But without transforming data, you cannot have a unified view of data across the organization.
>
> —Bill Inmon[13]

Now that we've covered queries and data modeling, you might be wondering, if I can model data, query it, and get results, why do I need to think about transformations? Transformations manipulate, enhance, and save data for downstream use, increasing its value in a scalable, reliable, and cost-effective manner.

Imagine running a query every time you want to view results from a particular dataset. You'd run the same query dozens or hundreds of times a day. Imagine that this query involves parsing, cleansing, joining, unioning, and aggregating across 20 datasets. To further exacerbate the pain, the query takes 30 minutes to run, consumes significant resources, and incurs substantial cloud charges over several repetitions. You and your stakeholders would probably go insane. Thankfully, you can *save the results of your query* instead, or at least run the most compute-intensive portions only once, so subsequent queries are simplified.

A transformation differs from a query. A *query* retrieves the data from various sources based on filtering and join logic. A *transformation* persists the results for consumption by additional transformations or queries. These results may be stored ephemerally or permanently.

Besides persistence, a second aspect that differentiates transformations from queries is complexity. You'll likely build complex pipelines that combine data from multiple sources and reuse intermediate results for multiple final outputs. These complex pipelines might normalize, model, aggregate, or featurize data. While you can build complex dataflows in single queries using common table expressions, scripts, or DAGs, this quickly becomes unwieldy, inconsistent, and intractable. Enter transformations.

Transformations critically rely on one of the major undercurrents in this book: orchestration. Orchestration combines many discrete operations, such as intermediate transformations, that store data temporarily or permanently for consumption by downstream transformations or serving. Increasingly, transformation pipelines span not only multiple tables and datasets but also multiple systems.

---

13 Bill Inmon, "Avoiding the Horrible Task of Integrating Data," LinkedIn Pulse, March 24, 2022, *https://oreil.ly/yLb71*.

Batch Transformations

Batch transformations run on discrete chunks of data, in contrast to streaming transformations, where data is processed continuously as it arrives. Batch transformations can run on a fixed schedule (e.g., daily, hourly, or every 15 minutes) to support ongoing reporting, analytics, and ML models. In this section, you'll learn various batch transformation patterns and technologies.

Distributed joins

The basic idea behind distributed joins is that we need to break a *logical join* (the join defined by the query logic) into much smaller *node joins* that run on individual servers in the cluster. The basic distributed join patterns apply whether one is in MapReduce (discussed in "MapReduce" on page 326), BigQuery, Snowflake, or Spark, though the details of intermediate storage between processing steps vary (on disk or in memory). In the best-case scenario, the data on one side of the join is small enough to fit on a single node (*broadcast join*). Often, a more resource-intensive *shuffle hash join* is required.

Broadcast join. A *broadcast join* is generally asymmetric, with one large table distributed across nodes and one small table that can easily fit on a single node (Figure 8-17). The query engine "broadcasts" the small table (table A) out to all nodes, where it gets joined to the parts of the large table (table B). Broadcast joins are far less compute intensive than shuffle hash joins.

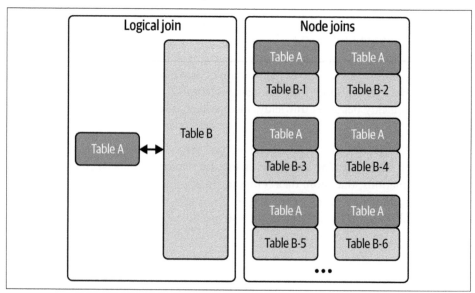

Figure 8-17. In a broadcast join, the query engine sends table A out to all nodes in the cluster to be joined with the various parts of table B

In practice, table A is often a down-filtered larger table that the query engine collects and broadcasts. One of the top priorities in query optimizers is join reordering. With the early application of filters, and movement of small tables to the left (for left joins), it is often possible to dramatically reduce the amount of data that is processed in each join. Prefiltering data to create broadcast joins where possible can dramatically improve performance and reduce resource consumption.

Shuffle hash join. If neither table is small enough to fit on a single node, the query engine will use a *shuffle hash join*. In Figure 8-18, the same nodes are represented above and below the dotted line. The area above the dotted line represents the initial partitioning of tables A and B across the nodes. In general, this partitioning will have no relation to the join key. A hashing scheme is used to repartition data by join key.

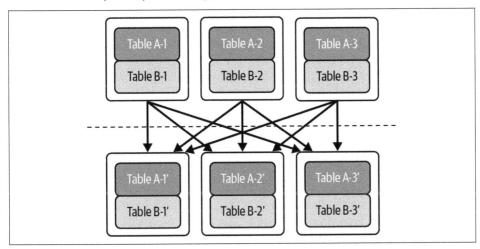

Figure 8-18. Shuffle hash join

In this example, the hashing scheme will partition the join key into three parts, with each part assigned to a node. The data is then reshuffled to the appropriate node, and the new partitions for tables A and B on each node are joined. Shuffle hash joins are generally more resource intensive than broadcast joins.

ETL, ELT, and data pipelines

As we discussed in Chapter 3, a widespread transformation pattern dating to the early days of relational databases is a batch ETL. Traditional ETL relies on an external transformation system to pull, transform, and clean data while preparing it for a target schema, such as a data mart or a Kimball star schema. The transformed data would then be loaded into a target system, such as a data warehouse, where business analytics could be performed.

The ETL pattern itself was driven by the limitations of both source and target systems. The extract phase tended to be a major bottleneck, with the constraints of the source RDBMS limiting the rate at which data could be pulled. And, the transformation was handled in a dedicated system because the target system was extremely resource-constrained in both storage and CPU capacity.

A now-popular evolution of ETL is ELT. As data warehouse systems have grown in performance and storage capacity, it has become common to simply extract raw data from a source system, import it into a data warehouse with minimal transformation, and then clean and transform it directly in the warehouse system. (See our discussion of data warehouses in Chapter 3 for a more detailed discussion of the difference between ETL and ELT.)

A second, slightly different notion of ELT was popularized with the emergence of data lakes. In this version, the data is not transformed at the time it's loaded. Indeed, massive quantities of data may be loaded with no preparation and no plan whatsoever. The assumption is that the transformation step will happen at some undetermined future time. Ingesting data without a plan is a great recipe for a data swamp. As Inmon says:[14]

> I've always been a fan of ETL because of the fact that ETL forces you to transform data before you put it into a form where you can work with it. But some organizations want to simply take the data, put it into a database, then do the transformation.... I've seen too many cases where the organization says, oh we'll just put the data in and transform it later. And guess what? Six months later, that data [has] never been touched.

We have also seen that the line between ETL and ELT can become somewhat blurry in a data lakehouse environment. With object storage as a base layer, it's no longer clear what's in the database and out of the database. The ambiguity is further exacerbated with the emergence of data federation, virtualization, and live tables. (We discuss these topics later in this section.)

Increasingly, we feel that the terms *ETL* and *ELT* should be applied only at the micro level (within individual transformation pipelines) rather than at the macro level (to describe a transformation pattern for a whole organization). Organizations no longer need to standardize on ETL or ELT but can instead focus on applying the proper technique on a case-by-case basis as they build data pipelines.

SQL and code-based transformation tools

At this juncture, the distinction between SQL-based and non-SQL-based transformation systems feels somewhat synthetic. Since the introduction of Hive on the Hadoop

---

14 Alex Woodie, "Lakehouses Prevent Data Swamps, Bill Inmon Says," Datanami, June 1, 2021, *https://oreil.ly/XMwWc*.

platform, SQL has become a first-class citizen in the big data ecosystem. For example, Spark SQL was an early feature of Apache Spark. Streaming-first frameworks such as Kafka, Flink, and Beam also support SQL, with varying features and functionality.

It is more appropriate to think about SQL-only tools versus those that support more powerful, general-purpose programming paradigms. SQL-only transformation tools span a wide variety of proprietary and open source options.

SQL is declarative…but it can still build complex data workflows. We often hear SQL dismissed because it is "not procedural." This is technically correct. SQL is a declarative language: instead of coding a data processing procedure, SQL writers stipulate the characteristics of their final data in set-theoretic language; the SQL compiler and optimizer determine the steps required to put data in this state.

People sometimes imply that because SQL is not procedural, it cannot build out complex pipelines. This is false. SQL can effectively be used to build complex DAGs using common table expressions, SQL scripts, or an orchestration tool.

To be clear, SQL has limits, but we often see engineers doing things in Python and Spark that could be more easily and efficiently done in SQL. For a better idea of the trade-offs we're talking about, let's look at a couple of examples of Spark and SQL.

Example: When to avoid SQL for batch transformations in Spark. When you're determining whether to use native Spark or PySpark code instead of Spark SQL or another SQL engine, ask yourself the following questions:

1. How difficult is it to code the transformation in SQL?
2. How readable and maintainable will the resulting SQL code be?
3. Should some of the transformation code be pushed into a custom library for future reuse across the organization?

Regarding question 1, many transformations coded in Spark could be realized in fairly simple SQL statements. On the other hand, if the transformation is not realizable in SQL, or if it would be extremely awkward to implement, native Spark is a better option. For example, we might be able to implement word stemming in SQL by placing word suffixes in a table, joining with that table, using a parsing function to find suffixes in words, and then reducing the word to its stem by using a substring function. However, this sounds like an extremely complex process with numerous edge cases to consider. A more powerful procedural programming language is a better fit here.

Question 2 is closely related. The word-stemming query will be neither readable nor maintainable.

Regarding question 3, one of the major limitations of SQL is that it doesn't include a natural notion of libraries or reusable code. One exception is that some SQL engines allow you to maintain user-defined functions (UDFs) as objects inside a database.[15] However, these aren't committed to a Git repository without an external CI/CD system to manage deployment. Furthermore, SQL doesn't have a good notion of reusability for more complex query components. Of course, reusable libraries are easy to create in Spark and PySpark.

We will add that it is possible to recycle SQL in two ways. First, we can easily reuse the *results* of a SQL query by committing to a table or creating a view. This process is often best handled in an orchestration tool such as Airflow so that downstream queries can start once the source query has finished. Second, Data Build Tool (dbt) facilitates the reuse of SQL statements and offers a templating language that makes customization easier.

Example: Optimizing Spark and other processing frameworks. Spark acolytes often complain that SQL doesn't give them control over data processing. The SQL engine takes your statements, optimizes them, and compiles them into its processing steps. (In practice, optimization may happen before or after compilation, or both.)

This is a fair complaint, but a corollary exists. With Spark and other code-heavy processing frameworks, the code writer becomes responsible for much of the optimization that is handled automatically in a SQL-based engine. The Spark API is powerful and complex, meaning it is not so easy to identify candidates for reordering, combination, or decomposition. When embracing Spark, data engineering teams need to actively engage with the problems of Spark optimization, especially for expensive, long-running jobs. This means building optimization expertise on the team and teaching individual engineers how to optimize.

A few top-level things to keep in mind when coding in native Spark:

1. Filter early and often.
2. Rely heavily on the core Spark API, and learn to understand the Spark native way of doing things. Try to rely on well-maintained public libraries if the native Spark API doesn't support your use case. Good Spark code is substantially declarative.
3. Be careful with UDFs.
4. Consider intermixing SQL.

Recommendation 1 applies to SQL optimization as well, with the difference being that Spark may not be able to reorder something that SQL would handle for you

---

15 We remind you to use UDFs responsibly. SQL UDFs often perform reasonably well. We've seen JavaScript UDFs increase query time from a few minutes to several hours.

automatically. Spark is a big data processing framework, but the less data you have to process, the less resource-heavy and more performant your code will be.

If you find yourself writing extremely complex custom code, pause and determine whether there's a more native way of doing whatever you're trying to accomplish. Learn to understand idiomatic Spark by reading public examples and working through tutorials. Is there something in the Spark API that can accomplish what you're trying to do? Is there a well-maintained and optimized public library that can help?

The third recommendation is crucial for PySpark. In general, PySpark is an API wrapper for Scala Spark. Your code pushes work into native Scala code running in the JVM by calling the API. Running Python UDFs forces data to be passed to Python, where processing is less efficient. If you find yourself using Python UDFs, look for a more Spark-native way to accomplish what you're doing. Go back to the recommendation: is there a way to accomplish your task by using the core API or a well-maintained library? If you must use UDFs, consider rewriting them in Scala or Java to improve performance.

As for recommendation 4, using SQL allows us to take advantage of the Spark Catalyst optimizer, which may be able to squeeze out more performance than we can with native Spark code. SQL is often easier to write and maintain for simple operations. Combining native Spark and SQL lets us realize the best of both worlds—powerful, general-purpose functionality combined with simplicity where applicable.

Much of the optimization advice in this section is fairly generic and would apply just as well to Apache Beam, for example. The main point is that programmable data processing APIs require a bit more optimization finesse than SQL, which is perhaps less powerful and easier to use.

Update patterns

Since transformations persist data, we will often update persisted data in place. Updating data is a major pain point for data engineering teams, especially as they transition between data engineering technologies. We're discussing DML in SQL, which we introduced earlier in the chapter.

We've mentioned several times throughout the book that the original data lake concept didn't really account for updating data. This now seems nonsensical for several reasons. Updating data has long been a key part of handling data transformation results, even though the big data community dismissed it. It is silly to rerun significant amounts of work because we have no update capabilities. Thus, the data lakehouse concept now builds in updates. Also, GDPR and other data deletion standards now *require* organizations to delete data in a targeted fashion, even in raw datasets.

Let's consider several basic update patterns.

Truncate and reload.   *Truncate* is an update pattern that doesn't update anything. It simply wipes the old data. In a truncate-and-reload update pattern, a table is cleared of data, and transformations are rerun and loaded into this table, effectively generating a new table version.

Insert only.   *Insert only* inserts new records without changing or deleting old records. Insert-only patterns can be used to maintain a current view of data—for example, if new versions of records are inserted without deleting old records. A query or view can present the current data state by finding the newest record by primary key. Note that columnar databases don't typically enforce primary keys. The primary key would be a construct used by engineers to maintain a notion of the current state of the table. The downside to this approach is that it can be extremely computationally expensive to find the latest record at query time. Alternatively, we can use a materialized view (covered later in the chapter), an insert-only table that maintains all records, and a truncate-and-reload target table that holds the current state for serving data.

 When inserting data into a column-oriented OLAP database, the common problem is that engineers transitioning from row-oriented systems attempt to use single-row inserts. This antipattern puts a massive load on the system. It also causes data to be written in many separate files; this is extremely inefficient for subsequent reads, and the data must be reclustered later. Instead, we recommend loading data in a periodic micro-batch or batch fashion.

We'll mention an exception to the advice not to insert frequently: the enhanced Lambda architecture used by BigQuery and Apache Druid, which hybridizes a streaming buffer with columnar storage. Deletes and in-place updates can still be expensive, as we'll discuss next.

Delete.   Deletion is critical when a source system deletes data and satisfies recent regulatory changes. In columnar systems and data lakes, deletes are more expensive than inserts.

When deleting data, consider whether you need to do a hard or soft delete. A *hard delete* permanently removes a record from a database, while a *soft delete* marks the record as "deleted." Hard deletes are useful when you need to remove data for performance reasons (say, a table is too big), or if there's a legal or compliance reason to do so. Soft deletes might be used when you don't want to delete a record permanently but also want to filter it out of query results.

A third approach to deletes is closely related to soft deletes: *insert deletion* inserts a new record with a `deleted` flag without modifying the previous version of the record. This allows us to follow an insert-only pattern but still account for deletions. Just note that our query to get the latest table state gets a little more complicated. We must now deduplicate, find the latest version of each record by key, and not show any record whose latest version shows deleted.

Upsert/merge. Of these update patterns, the upsert and merge patterns are the ones that consistently cause the most trouble for data engineering teams, especially for people transitioning from row-based data warehouses to column-based cloud systems.

Upserting takes a set of source records and looks for matches against a target table by using a primary key or another logical condition. (Again, it's the responsibility of the data engineering team to manage this primary key by running appropriate queries. Most columnar systems will not enforce uniqueness.) When a key match occurs, the target record gets updated (replaced by the new record). When no match exists, the database inserts the new record. The merge pattern adds to this the ability to delete records.

So, what's the problem? The upsert/merge pattern was originally designed for row-based databases. In row-based databases, updates are a natural process: the database looks up the record in question and changes it in place.

On the other hand, file-based systems don't actually support in-place file updates. All of these systems utilize copy on write (COW). If one record in a file is changed or deleted, the whole file must be rewritten with the new changes.

This is part of the reason that early adopters of big data and data lakes rejected updates: managing files and updates seemed too complicated. So they simply used an insert-only pattern and assumed that data consumers would determine the current state of the data at query time or in downstream transformations. In reality, columnar databases such as Vertica have long supported in-place updates by hiding the complexity of COW from users. They scan files, change the relevant records, write new files, and change file pointers for the table. The major columnar cloud data warehouses support updates and merges, although engineers should investigate update support if they consider adopting an exotic technology.

There are a few key things to understand here. Even though distributed columnar data systems support native update commands, merges come at a cost: the performance impact of updating or deleting a single record can be quite high. On the other hand, merges can be extremely performant for large update sets and may even outperform transactional databases.

In addition, it is important to understand that COW seldom entails rewriting the whole table. Depending on the database system in question, COW can operate at various resolutions (partition, cluster, block). To realize performant updates, focus on developing an appropriate partitioning and clustering strategy based on your needs and the innards of the database in question.

As with inserts, be careful with your update or merge frequency. We've seen many engineering teams transition between database systems and try to run near real-time merges from CDC just as they did on their old system. It simply doesn't work. No matter how good your CDC system is, this approach will bring most columnar data warehouses to their knees. We've seen systems fall weeks behind on updates, where an approach that simply merged every hour would make much more sense.

We can use various approaches to bring columnar databases closer to real time. For example, BigQuery allows us to stream insert new records into a table, and then supports specialized materialized views that present an efficient, near real-time deduplicated table view. Druid uses two-tier storage and SSDs to support ultrafast real-time queries.

Schema updates

Data has entropy and may change without your control or consent. External data sources may change their schema, or application development teams may add new fields to the schema. One advantage of columnar systems over row-based systems is that while updating the data is more difficult, updating the schema is easier. Columns can typically be added, deleted, and renamed.

In spite of these technological improvements, practical organizational schema management is more challenging. Will some schema updates be automated? (This is the approach that Fivetran uses when replicating from sources.) As convenient as this sounds, there's a risk that downstream transformations will break.

Is there a straightforward schema update request process? Suppose a data science team wants to add a column from a source that wasn't previously ingested. What will the review process look like? Will downstream processes break? (Are there queries that run SELECT * rather than using explicit column selection? This is generally bad practice in columnar databases.) How long will it take to implement the change? Is it possible to create a table fork—i.e., a new table version specific to this project?

A new interesting option has emerged for semistructured data. Borrowing an idea from document stores, many cloud data warehouses now support data types that encode arbitrary JSON data. One approach stores raw JSON in a field while storing frequently accessed data in adjacent flattened fields. This takes up additional storage space but allows for the convenience of flattened data, with the flexibility of semi-structured data for advanced users. Frequently accessed data in the JSON field can be added directly into the schema over time.

This approach works extremely well when data engineers must ingest data from an application document store with a frequently changing schema. Semistructured data available as a first-class citizen in data warehouses is extremely flexible and opens new opportunities for data analysts and data scientists since data is no longer constrained to rows and columns.

Data wrangling

Data wrangling takes messy, malformed data and turns it into useful, clean data. This is generally a batch transformation process.

Data wrangling has long been a major source of pain and job security for data engineers. For example, suppose that developers receive EDI data (see Chapter 7) from a partner business regarding transactions and invoices, potentially a mix of structured data and text. The typical process of wrangling this data involves first trying to ingest it. Often, the data is so malformed that a good deal of text preprocessing is involved. Developers may choose to ingest the data as a single text field table—an entire row ingested as a single field. Developers then begin writing queries to parse and break apart the data. Over time, they discover data anomalies and edge cases. Eventually, they will get the data into rough shape. Only then can the process of downstream transformation begin.

Data wrangling tools aim to simplify significant parts of this process. These tools often put off data engineers because they claim to be no code, which sounds unsophisticated. We prefer to think of data wrangling tools as integrated development environments (IDEs) for malformed data. In practice, data engineers spend way too much time parsing nasty data; automation tools allow data engineers to spend time on more interesting tasks. Wrangling tools may also allow engineers to hand some parsing and ingestion work off to analysts.

Graphical data-wrangling tools typically present a sample of data in a visual interface, with inferred types, statistics including distributions, anomalous data, outliers, and nulls. Users can then add processing steps to fix data issues. A step might provide instructions for dealing with mistyped data, splitting a text field into multiple parts, or joining with a lookup table.

Users can run the steps on a full dataset when the full job is ready. The job typically gets pushed to a scalable data processing system such as Spark for large datasets. After the job runs, it will return errors and unhandled exceptions. The user can further refine the recipe to deal with these outliers.

We highly recommend that both aspiring and seasoned engineers experiment with wrangling tools; major cloud providers sell their version of data-wrangling tools, and many third-party options are available. Data engineers may find that these tools significantly streamline certain parts of their jobs. Organizationally, data engineering teams may want to consider training specialists in data wrangling if they frequently ingest from new, messy data sources.

Example: Data transformation in Spark

Let's look at a practical, concrete example of data transformation. Suppose we build a pipeline that ingests data from three API sources in JSON format. This initial ingestion step is handled in Airflow. Each data source gets its prefix (filepath) in an S3 bucket.

Airflow then triggers a Spark job by calling an API. This Spark job ingests each of the three sources into a dataframe, converting the data into a relational format, with nesting in certain columns. The Spark job combines the three sources into a single table and then filters the results with a SQL statement. The results are finally written out to a Parquet-formatted Delta Lake table stored in S3.

In practice, Spark creates a DAG of steps based on the code that we write for ingesting, joining, and writing out the data. The basic ingestion of data happens in cluster memory, although one of the data sources is large enough that it must spill to disk during the ingestion process. (This data gets written to cluster storage; it will be reloaded into memory for subsequent processing steps.)

The join requires a shuffle operation. A key is used to redistribute data across the cluster; once again, a spill to disk occurs as the data is written to each node. The SQL transformation filters through the rows in memory and discards the unused rows. Finally, Spark converts the data into Parquet format, compresses it, and writes it back to S3. Airflow periodically calls back to Spark to see if the job is completed. Once it confirms that the job has finished, it marks the full Airflow DAG as completed. (Note that we have two DAG constructs here, an Airflow DAG and a DAG specific to the Spark job.)

Business logic and derived data

One of the most common use cases for transformation is to render business logic. We've placed this discussion under batch transformations because this is where this type of transformation happens most frequently, but note that it could also happen in a streaming pipeline.

Suppose that a company uses multiple specialized internal profit calculations. One version might look at profits before marketing costs, and another might look at a profit after subtracting marketing costs. Even though this appears to be a straightforward accounting exercise, each of these metrics is highly complex to render.

Profit before marketing costs might need to account for fraudulent orders; determining a reasonable profit estimate for the previous business day entails estimating what percentage of revenue and profit will ultimately be lost to orders canceled in the coming days as the fraud team investigates suspicious orders. Is there a special flag in the database that indicates an order with a high probability of fraud, or one that has been automatically canceled? Does the business assume that a certain percentage of orders will be canceled because of fraud even before the fraud-risk evaluation process has been completed for specific orders?

For profits after marketing costs, we must account for all the complexities of the previous metric, plus the marketing costs attributed to the specific order. Does the company have a naive attribution model—e.g., marketing costs attributed to items weighted by price? Marketing costs might also be attributed per department, or item category, or—in the most sophisticated organizations—per individual item based on user ad clicks.

The business logic transformation that generates this nuanced version of profit must integrate all the subtleties of attribution—i.e., a model that links orders to specific ads and advertising costs. Is attribution data stored in the guts of ETL scripts, or is it pulled from a table that is automatically generated from ad platform data?

This type of reporting data is a quintessential example of *derived data*—data computed from other data stored in a data system. Derived data critics will point out that it is challenging for the ETL to maintain consistency in the derived metrics.[16] For example, if the company updates its attribution model, this change may need to be merged into many ETL scripts for reporting. (ETL scripts are notorious for breaking the DRY principle.) Updating these ETL scripts is a manual and labor-intensive process, involving domain expertise in processing logic and previous changes. Updated scripts must also be validated for consistency and accuracy.

From our perspective, these are legitimate criticisms but not necessarily very constructive because the alternative to derived data in this instance is equally distasteful. Analysts will need to run their reporting queries if profit data is not stored in the data warehouse, including profit logic. Updating complex ETL scripts to represent changes to business logic accurately is an overwhelming, labor-intensive task, but getting analysts to update their reporting queries consistently is well-nigh impossible.

One interesting alternative is to push business logic into a *metrics layer*,[17] but still leverage the data warehouse or other tool to do the computational heavy lifting. A metrics layer encodes business logic and allows analysts and dashboard users to build complex analytics from a library of defined metrics. The metrics layer generates queries from the metrics and sends these to the database. We discuss semantic and metrics layers in more detail in Chapter 9.

---

16 Michael Blaha, "Be Careful with Derived Data," Dataversity, December 5, 2016, *https://oreil.ly/garoL*.

17 Benn Stancil, "The Missing Piece of the Modern Data Stack," *benn.substack*, April 22, 2021, *https://oreil.ly/GYf3Z*.

MapReduce

No discussion of batch transformation can be complete without touching on Map-Reduce. This isn't because MapReduce is widely used by data engineers these days. MapReduce was the defining batch data transformation pattern of the big data era, it still influences many distributed systems data engineers use today, and it's useful for data engineers to understand at a basic level. MapReduce (*https://oreil.ly/hdptb*) was introduced by Google in a follow-up to its paper on GFS. It was initially the de facto processing pattern of Hadoop, the open source analogue technology of GFS that we introduced in Chapter 6.

A simple MapReduce job consists of a collection of map tasks that read individual data blocks scattered across the nodes, followed by a shuffle that redistributes result data across the cluster and a reduce step that aggregates data on each node. For example, suppose that we wanted to run the following SQL query:

```
SELECT COUNT(*), user_id
FROM user_events
GROUP BY user_id;
```

The table data is spread across nodes in data blocks; the MapReduce job generates one map task per block. Each map task essentially runs the query on a single block —i.e., it generates a count for each user ID that appears in the block. While a block might contain hundreds of megabytes, the full table could be petabytes in size. However, the map portion of the job is a nearly perfect example of embarrassing parallelism; the data scan rate across the full cluster essentially scales linearly with the number of nodes.

We then need to aggregate (reduce) to gather results from the full cluster. We're not gathering results to a single node; rather, we redistribute results by key so that each key ends up on one and only one node. This is the shuffle step, which is often executed using a hashing algorithm on keys. Once the map results have been shuffled, we sum the results for each key. The key/count pairs can be written to the local disk on the node where they are computed. We collect the results stored across nodes to view the full query results.

Real-world MapReduce jobs can be far more complex than what we describe here. A complex query that filters with a WHERE clause joins three tables and applies a window function that would consist of many map and reduce stages.

After MapReduce

Google's original MapReduce model is extremely powerful but is now viewed as excessively rigid. It utilizes numerous short-lived ephemeral tasks that read from and write to disk. In particular, no intermediate state is preserved in memory; all data is transferred between tasks by storing it to disk or pushing it over the network. This

---

simplifies state and workflow management and minimizes memory consumption, but it can also drive high-disk bandwidth utilization and increase processing time.

The MapReduce paradigm was constructed around the idea that magnetic disk capacity and bandwidth were so cheap that it made sense to simply throw a massive amount of disk at data to realize ultra-fast queries. This worked to an extent; Map-Reduce repeatedly set data processing records during the early days of Hadoop.

However, we have lived in a post-MapReduce world for quite some time. Post-MapReduce processing does not truly discard MapReduce; it still includes the elements of map, shuffle, and reduce, but it relaxes the constraints of MapReduce to allow for in-memory caching.[18] Recall that RAM is much faster than SSD and HDDs in transfer speed and seek time. Persisting even a tiny amount of judiciously chosen data in memory can dramatically speed up specific data processing tasks and utterly crush the performance of MapReduce.

For example, Spark, BigQuery, and various other data processing frameworks were designed around in-memory processing. These frameworks treat data as a distributed set that resides in memory. If data overflows available memory, this causes a *spill to disk*. The disk is treated as a second-class data-storage layer for processing, though it is still highly valuable.

The cloud is one of the drivers for the broader adoption of memory caching; it is much more effective to lease memory during a specific processing job than to own it 24 hours a day. Advancements in leveraging memory for transformations will continue to yield gains for the foreseeable future.

Materialized Views, Federation, and Query Virtualization

In this section, we look at several techniques that virtualize query results by presenting them as table-like objects. These techniques can become part of a transformation pipeline or sit right before end-user data consumption.

Views

First, let's review views to set the stage for materialized views. A *view* is a database object that we can select from just like any other table. In practice, a view is just a query that references other tables. When we select from a view, that database creates a new query that combines the view subquery with our query. The query optimizer then optimizes and runs the full query.

---

18 "What Is the Difference Between Apache Spark and Hadoop MapReduce?," Knowledge Powerhouse YouTube video, May 20, 2017, *https://oreil.ly/WN0eX*.

Views play a variety of roles in a database. First, views can serve a security role. For example, views can select only specific columns and filter rows, thus providing restricted data access. Various views can be created for job roles depending on user data access.

Second, a view might be used to provide a current deduplicated picture of data. If we're using an insert-only pattern, a view may be used to return a deduplicated version of a table showing only the latest version of each record.

Third, views can be used to present common data access patterns. Suppose that marketing analysts must frequently run a query that joins five tables. We could create a view that joins together these five tables into a wide table. Analysts can then write queries that filter and aggregate on top of this view.

Materialized views

We mentioned materialized views in our earlier discussion of query caching. A potential disadvantage of (nonmaterialized) views is that they don't do any precomputation. In the example of a view that joins five tables, this join must run every time a marketing analyst runs a query on this view, and the join could be extremely expensive.

A materialized view does some or all of the view computation in advance. In our example, a materialized view might save the five table join results every time a change occurs in the source tables. Then, when a user references the view, they're querying from the prejoined data. A materialized view is a de facto transformation step, but the database manages execution for convenience.

Materialized views may also serve a significant query optimization role depending on the database, even for queries that don't directly reference them. Many query optimizers can identify queries that "look like" a materialized view. An analyst may run a query that uses a filter that appears in a materialized view. The optimizer will rewrite the query to select from the precomputed results.

Composable materialized views

In general, materialized views do not allow for composition—that is, a materialized view cannot select from another materialized view. However, we've recently seen the emergence of tools that support this capability. For example, Databricks has introduced the notion of *live tables*. Each table is updated as data arrives from sources. Data flows down to subsequent tables asynchronously.

Federated queries

Federated queries are a database feature that allows an OLAP database to select from an external data source, such as object storage or RDBMS. For example, let's say you need to combine data across object storage and various tables in MySQL and PostgreSQL databases. Your data warehouse can issue a federated query to these sources and return the combined results (Figure 8-19).

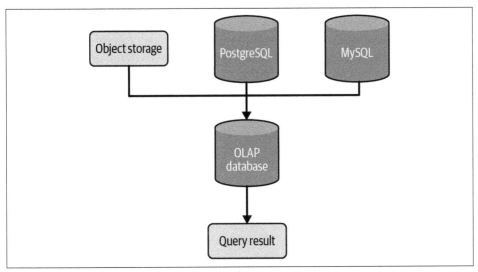

Figure 8-19. An OLAP database issues a federated query that gets data from object storage, MySQL, and PostgreSQL and returns a query result with the combined data

As another example, Snowflake supports the notion of external tables defined on S3 buckets. An external data location and a file format are defined when creating the table, but data is not yet ingested into the table. When the external table is queried, Snowflake reads from S3 and processes the data based on the parameters set at the time of the table's creation. We can even join S3 data to internal database tables. This makes Snowflake and similar databases more compatible with a data lake environment.

Some OLAP systems can convert federated queries into materialized views. This gives us much of the performance of a native table without the need to manually ingest data every time the external source changes. The materialized view gets updated whenever the external data changes.

Data virtualization

Data virtualization is closely related to federated queries, but this typically entails a data processing and query system that doesn't store data internally. Right now, Trino (e.g., Starburst) and Presto are examples par excellence. Any query/processing engine that supports external tables can serve as a data virtualization engine. The most significant considerations with data virtualization are supported external sources and performance.

A closely related concept is the notion of *query pushdown*. Suppose I wanted to query data from Snowflake, join data from a MySQL database, and filter the results. Query pushdown aims to move as much work as possible to the source databases. The engine might look for ways to push filtering predicates into the queries on the source systems. This serves two purposes: first, it offloads computation from the virtualization layer, taking advantage of the query performance of the source. Second, it potentially reduces the quantity of data that must push across the network, a critical bottleneck for virtualization performance.

Data virtualization is a good solution for organizations with data stored across various data sources. However, data virtualization should not be used haphazardly. For example, virtualizing a production MySQL database doesn't solve the core problem of analytics queries adversely impacting the production system—because Trino does not store data internally, it will pull from MySQL every time it runs a query.

Alternatively, data virtualization can be used as a component of data ingestion and processing pipelines. For instance, Trino might be used to select from MySQL once a day at midnight when the load on the production system is low. Results could be saved into S3 for consumption by downstream transformations and daily queries, protecting MySQL from direct analytics queries.

Data virtualization can be viewed as a tool that expands the data lake to many more sources by abstracting away barriers used to silo data between organizational units. An organization can store frequently accessed, transformed data in S3 and virtualize access between various parts of the company. This fits closely with the notion of a *data mesh* (discussed in Chapter 3), wherein small teams are responsible for preparing their data for analytics and sharing it with the rest of the company; virtualization can serve as a critical access layer for practical sharing.

Streaming Transformations and Processing

We've already discussed stream processing in the context of queries. The difference between streaming transformations and streaming queries is subtle and warrants more explanation.

Basics

Streaming queries run dynamically to present a current view of data, as discussed previously. *Streaming transformations* aim to prepare data for downstream consumption.

For instance, a data engineering team may have an incoming stream carrying events from an IoT source. These IoT events carry a device ID and event data. We wish to dynamically enrich these events with other device metadata, which is stored in a separate database. The stream-processing engine queries a separate database containing this metadata by device ID, generates new events with the added data, and passes it on to another stream. Live queries and triggered metrics run on this enriched stream (see Figure 8-20).

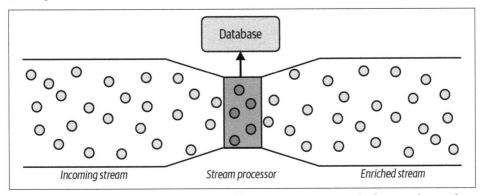

Figure 8-20. An incoming stream is carried by a streaming event platform and passed into a stream processor

Transformations and queries are a continuum

The line between transformations and queries is also blurry in batch processing, but the differences become even more subtle in the domain of streaming. For example, if we dynamically compute roll-up statistics on windows, and then send the output to a target stream, is this a transformation or a query?

Maybe we will eventually adopt new terminology for stream processing that better represents real-world use cases. For now, we will do our best with the terminology we have.

Streaming DAGs

One interesting notion closely related to stream enrichment and joins is the *streaming DAG*.[19] We first talked about this idea in our discussion of orchestration in Chapter 2. Orchestration is inherently a batch concept, but what if we wanted to enrich, merge, and split multiple streams in real time?

Let's take a simple example where streaming DAG would be useful. Suppose that we want to combine website clickstream data with IoT data. This will allow us to get a unified view of user activity by combining IoT events with clicks. Furthermore, each data stream needs to be preprocessed into a standard format (see Figure 8-21).

---

19 For a detailed application of the concept of a streaming DAG, see "Why We Moved from Apache Kafka to Apache Pulsar" by Simba Khadder, StreamNative blog, April 21, 2020, *https://oreil.ly/Rxfko*.

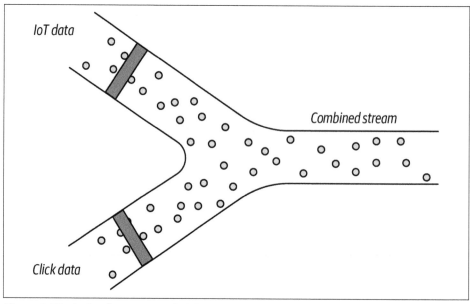

Figure 8-21. A simple streaming DAG

This has long been possible by combining a streaming store (e.g., Kafka) with a stream processor (e.g., Flink). Creating the DAG amounted to building a complex Rube Goldberg machine, with numerous topics and processing jobs connected.

Pulsar dramatically simplifies this process by treating DAGs as a core streaming abstraction. Rather than managing flows across several systems, engineers can define their streaming DAGs as code inside a single system.

Micro-batch versus true streaming

A long-running battle has been ongoing between micro-batch and true streaming approaches. Fundamentally, it's important to understand your use case, the performance requirements, and the performance capabilities of the framework in question.

Micro-batching is a way to take a batch-oriented framework and apply it in a streaming situation. A micro-batch might run anywhere from every two minutes to every second. Some micro-batch frameworks (e.g., Apache Spark Streaming) are designed for this use case and will perform well with appropriately allocated resources at a high batch frequency. (In truth, DBAs and engineers have long used micro-batching with more traditional databases; this often led to horrific performance and resource consumption.)

True streaming systems (e.g., Beam and Flink) are designed to process one event at a time. However, this comes with significant overhead. Also, it's important to note that even in these true streaming systems, many processes will still occur in batches. A basic enrichment process that adds data to individual events can deliver one event at a time with low latency. However, a triggered metric on windows may run every few seconds, every few minutes, etc.

When you're using windows and triggers (hence, batch processing), what's the window frequency? What's the acceptable latency? If you are collecting Black Friday sales metrics published every few minutes, micro-batches are probably just fine as long as you set an appropriate micro-batch frequency. On the other hand, if your ops team is computing metrics every second to detect DDoS attacks, true streaming may be in order.

When should you use one over the other? Frankly, there is no universal answer. The term *micro-batch* has often been used to dismiss competing technologies, but it may work just fine for your use case and can be superior in many respects depending on your needs. If your team already has expertise in Spark, you will be able to spin up a Spark (micro-batch) streaming solution extremely fast.

There's no substitute for domain expertise and real-world testing. Talk to experts who can present an even-handed opinion. You can also easily test the alternatives by spinning up tests on cloud infrastructure. Also, watch out for spurious benchmarks provided by vendors. Vendors are notorious for cherry-picking benchmarks and setting up artificial examples that don't match reality (recall our conversation on benchmarks in Chapter 4). Frequently, vendors will show massive advantages in their benchmark results but fail to deliver in the real world for your use case.

Whom You'll Work With

Queries, transformations, and modeling impact all stakeholders up and down the data engineering lifecycle. The data engineer is responsible for several things at this stage in the lifecycle. From a technical angle, the data engineer designs, builds, and maintains the integrity of the systems that query and transform data. The data engineer also implements data models within this system. This is the most "full-contact" stage where your focus is to add as much value as possible, both in terms of functioning systems and reliable and trustworthy data.

Upstream Stakeholders

When it comes to transformations, upstream stakeholders can be broken into two broad categories: those who control the business definitions and those who control the systems generating data.

When interfacing with upstream stakeholders about business definitions and logic, you'll need to know the data sources—what they are, how they're used, and the business logic and definitions involved. You'll work with the engineers in charge of these source systems and the business stakeholders who oversee the complementary products and apps. A data engineer might work alongside "the business" and technical stakeholders on a data model.

The data engineer needs to be involved in designing the data model and later updates because of changes in business logic or new processes. Transformations are easy enough to do; just write a query and plop the results into a table or view. Creating them so they're both performant and valuable to the business is another matter. Always keep the requirements and expectations of the business top of mind when transforming data.

The stakeholders of the upstream systems want to make sure your queries and transformations minimally impact their systems. Ensure bidirectional communication about changes to the data models (column and index changes, for example) in source systems, as these can directly impact queries, transformations, and analytical data models. Data engineers should know about schema changes, including the addition or deletion of fields, data type changes, and anything else that might materially impact the ability to query and transform data.

Downstream Stakeholders

Transformations are where data starts providing utility to downstream stakeholders. Your downstream stakeholders include many people, including data analysts, data scientists, ML engineers, and "the business." Collaborate with them to ensure the data model and transformations you provide are performant and useful. In terms of performance, queries should execute as quickly as possible in the most cost-effective way. What do we mean by *useful*? Analysts, data scientists, and ML engineers should be able to query a data source with the confidence the data is of the highest quality and completeness and can be integrated into their workflows and data products. The business should be able to trust that transformed data is accurate and actionable.

Undercurrents

The transformation stage is where your data mutates and morphs into something useful for the business. Because there are many moving parts, the undercurrents are especially critical at this stage.

Security

Queries and transformations combine disparate datasets into new datasets. Who has access to this new dataset? If someone does have access to a dataset, continue to control who has access to a dataset's column, row, and cell-level access.

Be aware of attack vectors against your database at query time. Read/write privileges to the database must be tightly monitored and controlled. Query access to the database must be controlled in the same way as you normally control access to your organization's systems and environments.

Keep credentials hidden; avoid copying and pasting passwords, access tokens, or other credentials into code or unencrypted files. It's shockingly common to see code in GitHub repositories with database usernames and passwords pasted directly in the codebase! It goes without saying, don't share passwords with other users. Finally, never allow unsecured or unencrypted data to traverse the public internet.

Data Management

Though data management is essential at the source system stage (and every other stage of the data engineering lifecycle), it's especially critical at the transformation stage. Transformation inherently creates new datasets that need to be managed. As with other stages of the data engineering lifecycle, it's critical to involve all stakeholders in data models and transformations and manage their expectations. Also, make sure everyone agrees on naming conventions that align with the respective business definitions of the data. Proper naming conventions should be reflected in easy-to-understand field names. Users can also check in a data catalog for more clarity on what the field means when it was created, who maintains the dataset, and other relevant information.

Accounting for definitional accuracy is key at the transformation stage. Does the transformation adhere to the expected business logic? Increasingly, the notion of a semantic or metrics layer that sits independent of transformations is becoming popular. Instead of enforcing business logic within the transformation at runtime, why not keep these definitions as a standalone stage before your transformation layer? While it's still early days, expect to see semantic and metrics layers becoming more popular and commonplace in data engineering and data management.

Because transformations involve mutating data, it's critical to ensure that the data you're using is free of defects and represents ground truth. If MDM is an option at your company, pursue its implementation. Conformed dimensions and other transformations rely on MDM to preserve data's original integrity and ground truth. If MDM isn't possible, work with upstream stakeholders who control the data to ensure that any data you're transforming is correct and complies with the agreed-upon business logic.

Data transformations make it potentially difficult to know how a dataset was derived along the same lines. In Chapter 6, we discussed data catalogs. As we transform data, *data lineage* tools become invaluable. Data lineage tools help both data engineers, who must understand previous transformation steps as they create new transformations, and analysts, who need to understand where data came from as they run queries and build reports.

Finally, what impact does regulatory compliance have on your data model and transformations? Are sensitive fields data masked or obfuscated if necessary? Do you have the ability to delete data in response to deletion requests? Does your data lineage tracking allow you to see data derived from deleted data and rerun transformations to remove data downstream of raw sources?

DataOps

With queries and transformations, DataOps has two areas of concern: data and systems. You need to monitor and be alerted for changes or anomalies in these areas. The field of data observability is exploding right now, with a big focus on data reliability. There's even a recent job title called *data reliability engineer*. This section emphasizes data observability and data health, which focuses on the query and transformation stage.

Let's start with the data side of DataOps. When you query data, are the inputs and outputs correct? How do you know? If this query is saved to a table, is the schema correct? How about the shape of the data and related statistics such as min/max values, null counts, and more? You should run data-quality tests on the input datasets and the transformed dataset, which will ensure that the data meets the expectations of upstream and downstream users. If there's a data-quality issue in the transformation, you should have the ability to flag this issue, roll back the changes, and investigate the root cause.

Now let's look at the Ops part of DataOps. How are the systems performing? Monitor metrics such as query queue length, query concurrency, memory usage, storage utilization, network latency, and disk I/O. Use metric data to spot bottlenecks and poor-performing queries that might be candidates for refactoring and tuning. If the query is perfectly fine, you'll have a good idea of where to tune the database itself (for instance, by clustering a table for faster lookup performance). Or, you may need to upgrade the database's compute resources. Today's cloud and SaaS databases give you a ton of flexibility for quickly upgrading (and downgrading) your system. Take a data-driven approach and use your observability metrics to pinpoint whether you have a query or a systems-related issue.

The shift toward SaaS-based analytical databases changes the cost profile of data consumption. In the days of on-premises data warehouses, the system and licenses were purchased up front, with no additional usage cost. Whereas traditional data engineers would focus on performance optimization to squeeze the maximum utility out of their expensive purchases, data engineers working with cloud data warehouses that charge on a consumption basis need to focus on cost management and cost optimization. This is the practice of *FinOps* (see Chapter 4).

Data Architecture

The general rules of good data architecture in Chapter 3 apply to the transformation stage. Build robust systems that can process and transform data without imploding. Your choices for ingestion and storage will directly impact your general architecture's ability to perform reliable queries and transformations. If the ingestion and storage are appropriate to your query and transformation patterns, you should be in a great place. On the other hand, if your queries and transformations don't work well with your upstream systems, you're in for a world of pain.

For example, we often see data teams using the wrong data pipelines and databases for the job. A data team might connect a real-time data pipeline to an RDBMS or Elasticsearch and use this as their data warehouse. These systems are not optimized for high-volume aggregated OLAP queries and will implode under this workload. This data team clearly didn't understand how their architectural choices would impact query performance. Take the time to understand the trade-offs inherent in your architecture choices; be clear about how your data model will work with ingestion and storage systems and how queries will perform.

Orchestration

Data teams often manage their transformation pipelines using simple time-based schedules—e.g., cron jobs. This works reasonably well at first but turns into a nightmare as workflows grow more complicated. Use orchestration to manage complex pipelines using a dependency-based approach. Orchestration is also the glue that allows us to assemble pipelines that span multiple systems.

Software Engineering

When writing transformation code, you can use many languages—such as SQL, Python, and JVM-based languages—platforms ranging from data warehouses to distributed computing clusters, and everything in between. Each language and platform has its strengths and quirks, so you should know the best practices of your tools. For example, you might write data transformations in Python, powered by a distributed system such as Spark or Dask. When running a data transformation, are you using a UDF when a native function might work much better? We've seen cases where poorly written, sluggish UDFs were replaced by a built-in SQL command, with instant and dramatic improvement in performance.

The rise of analytics engineering brings software engineering practices to end users, with the notion of *analytics as code*. Analytics engineering transformation tools like dbt have exploded in popularity, giving analysts and data scientists the ability to write in-database transformations using SQL, without the direct intervention of a DBA or a data engineer. In this case, the data engineer is responsible for setting up the code repository and CI/CD pipeline used by the analysts and data scientists. This is a big change in the role of a data engineer, who would historically build and manage the underlying infrastructure and create the data transformations. As data tools lower the barriers to entry and become more democratized across data teams, it will be interesting to see how the workflows of data teams change.

Using a GUI-based low-code tool, you'll get useful visualizations of the transformation workflow. You still need to understand what's going on under the hood. These GUI-based transformation tools will often generate SQL or some other language behind the scenes. While the point of a low-code tool is to alleviate the need to be involved in low-level details, understanding the code behind the scenes will help with debugging and performance optimization. Blindly assuming that the tool is generating performant code is a mistake.

We suggest that data engineers pay particular attention to software engineering best practices at the query and transformation stage. While it's tempting to simply throw more processing resources at a dataset, knowing how to write clean, performant code is a much better approach.

Conclusion

Transformations sit at the heart of data pipelines. It's critical to keep in mind the purpose of transformations. Ultimately, engineers are not hired to play with the latest technological toys but to serve their customers. Transformations are where data adds value and ROI to the business.

Our opinion is that it is possible to adopt exciting transformation technologies *and* serve stakeholders. Chapter 11 talks about the *live data stack*, essentially reconfiguring the data stack around streaming data ingestion and bringing transformation workflows closer to the source system applications themselves. Engineering teams that think about real-time data as the technology for the sake of technology will repeat the mistakes of the big data era. But in reality, the majority of organizations that we work with have a business use case that would benefit from streaming data. Identifying these use cases and focusing on the value before choosing technologies and complex systems is key.

As we head into the serving stage of the data engineering lifecycle in Chapter 9, reflect on technology as a tool for realizing organizational goals. If you're a working data engineer, think about how improvements in transformation systems could help you to serve your end customers better. If you're just embarking on a path toward data engineering, think about the kinds of business problems you're interested in solving with technology.

Additional Resources

- "Building a Real-Time Data Vault in Snowflake" (*https://oreil.ly/KiQtd*) by Dmytro Yaroshenko and Kent Graziano
- *Building a Scalable Data Warehouse with Data Vault 2.0* (Morgan Kaufmann) by Daniel Linstedt and Michael Olschimke
- *Building the Data Warehouse* (Wiley), *Corporate Information Factory*, and *The Unified Star Schema* (Technics Publications) by W. H. (Bill) Inmon
- "Caching in Snowflake Data Warehouse" Snowflake Community page (*https://oreil.ly/opMFi*)
- "Data Warehouse: The Choice of Inmon vs. Kimball" (*https://oreil.ly/pjuuz*) by Ian Abramson
- *The Data Warehouse Toolkit* by Ralph Kimball and Margy Ross (Wiley)
- "Data Vault—An Overview" (*https://oreil.ly/Vxsm6*) by John Ryan
- "Data Vault 2.0 Modeling Basics" (*https://oreil.ly/DLvaI*) by Kent Graziano
- "A Detailed Guide on SQL Query Optimization" tutorial (*https://oreil.ly/WNate*) by Megha
- "Difference Between Kimball and Inmon" (*https://oreil.ly/i8Eki*) by manmeetjuneja5
- "Eventual vs. Strong Consistency in Distributed Databases" (*https://oreil.ly/IU3H1*) by Saurabh.v
- "The Evolution of the Corporate Information Factory" (*https://oreil.ly/j0pRS*) by Bill Inmon
- Gavroshe USA's "DW 2.0" web page (*https://oreil.ly/y1lgO*)
- Google Cloud's "Using Cached Query Results" documentation (*https://oreil.ly/lGNHw*)
- Holistics' "Cannot Combine Fields Due to Fan-Out Issues?" FAQ page (*https://oreil.ly/r5fjk*)
- "How a SQL Database Engine Works," (*https://oreil.ly/V0WkU*) by Dennis Pham
- "How Should Organizations Structure Their Data?" (*https://oreil.ly/00d2b*) by Michael Berk
- "Inmon or Kimball: Which Approach Is Suitable for Your Data Warehouse?" (*https://oreil.ly/ghHPL*) by Sansu George
- "Introduction to Data Vault Modeling" document, (*https://oreil.ly/3rrU0*) compiled by Kent Graziano and Dan Linstedt

- "Introduction to Data Warehousing" (*https://oreil.ly/RpmFV*), "Introduction to Dimensional Modelling for Data Warehousing" (*https://oreil.ly/N1uUg*), and "Introduction to Data Vault for Data Warehousing" (*https://oreil.ly/aPDUx*) by Simon Kitching

- Kimball Group's "Four-Step Dimensional Design Process" (*https://oreil.ly/jj2wI*), "Conformed Dimensions" (*https://oreil.ly/A9s6x*), and "Dimensional Modeling Techniques" (*https://oreil.ly/EPzNZ*) web pages

- "Kimball vs. Inmon vs. Vault" Reddit thread (*https://oreil.ly/9Kzbq*)

- "Modeling of Real-Time Streaming Data?" Stack Exchange thread (*https://oreil.ly/wC9oD*)

- "The New 'Unified Star Schema' Paradigm in Analytics Data Modeling Review" (*https://oreil.ly/jWFHk*) by Andriy Zabavskyy

- Oracle's "Slowly Changing Dimensions" tutorial (*https://oreil.ly/liRfT*)

- ScienceDirect's "Corporate Information Factory" web page (*https://oreil.ly/u2fNq*)

- "A Simple Explanation of Symmetric Aggregates or 'Why on Earth Does My SQL Look Like That?'" (*https://oreil.ly/7CD96*) by Lloyd Tabb

- "Streaming Event Modeling" (*https://oreil.ly/KQwMQ*) by Paul Stanton

- "Types of Data Warehousing Architecture" (*https://oreil.ly/gHEJX*) by Amritha Fernando

- US patent for "Method and Apparatus for Functional Integration of Metadata" (*https://oreil.ly/C3URp*)

- Zentut's "Bill Inmon Data Warehouse" web page (*https://oreil.ly/FvZ6K*)

CHAPTER 9

Serving Data for Analytics, Machine Learning, and Reverse ETL

Congratulations! You've reached the final stage of the data engineering lifecycle—serving data for downstream use cases (see Figure 9-1). In this chapter, you'll learn about various ways to serve data for three major use cases you'll encounter as a data engineer. First, you'll serve data for analytics and BI. You'll prepare data for use in statistical analysis, reporting, and dashboards. This is the most traditional area of data serving. Arguably, it predates IT and databases, but it is as important as ever for stakeholders to have visibility into the business, organizational, and financial processes.

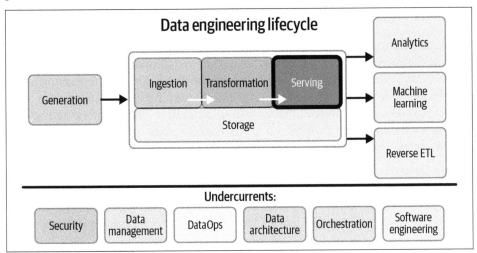

Figure 9-1. Serving delivers data for use cases

Second, you'll serve data for ML applications. ML is not possible without high-quality data, appropriately prepared. Data engineers work with data scientists and ML engineers to acquire, transform, and deliver the data necessary for model training.

Third, you'll serve data through reverse ETL. *Reverse ETL* is the process of sending data back to data sources. For example, we might acquire data from an ad tech platform, run a statistical process on this data to determine cost-per-click bids, and then feed this data back into the ad tech platform. Reverse ETL is highly entangled with BI and ML.

Before we get into these three major ways of serving data, let's look at some general considerations.

General Considerations for Serving Data

Before we get further into serving data, we have a few big considerations. First and foremost is trust. People need to trust the data you're providing. Additionally, you need to understand your use cases and users, the data products that will be produced, how you'll be serving data (self-service or not), data definitions and logic, and data mesh. The considerations we'll discuss here are general and apply to any of the three ways of serving data. Understanding these considerations will help you be much more effective in serving your data customers.

Trust

> It takes 20 years to build a reputation and five minutes to ruin it. If you think about that, you'll do things differently.
>
> —Warren Buffett[1]

Above all else, trust is the root consideration in serving data; end users need to trust the data they're receiving. The fanciest, most sophisticated data architecture and serving layer are irrelevant if end users don't believe the data is a reliable representation of their business. A loss of trust is often a silent death knell for a data project, even if the project isn't officially canceled until months or years later. The job of a data engineer is to serve the best data possible, so you'll want to make sure your data products always contain high-quality and trustworthy data.

As you learn to serve data throughout this chapter, we'll reinforce the idea of baking trust into your data and discuss pragmatic ways to accomplish this. We see too many cases in which data teams are fixated on pushing out data without asking whether stakeholders trust it in the first place. Often, stakeholders lose trust in the data. Once

---

1 Quoted in Benjamin Snyder, "7 Insights from Legendary Investor Warren Buffett," CNBC *Make It*, May 1, 2017, *https://oreil.ly/QEqF9*.

trust is gone, earning it back is insanely difficult. This inevitably leads to the business not performing to its fullest potential with data and data teams losing credibility (and possibly being dissolved).

To realize data quality and build stakeholder trust, utilize data validation and data observability processes, in conjunction with visually inspecting and confirming validity with stakeholders. *Data validation* is analyzing data to ensure that it accurately represents financial information, customer interactions, and sales. *Data observability* provides an ongoing view of data and data processes. These processes must be applied *throughout the data engineering lifecycle* to realize a good result as we reach the end. We'll discuss these further in "Undercurrents" on page 364.

In addition to building trust in data quality, it is incumbent on engineers to build trust in their SLAs and SLOs with their end users and upstream stakeholders. Once users come to depend on data to accomplish business processes, they will require that data is consistently available and up-to-date per the commitments made by data engineers. High-quality data is of little value if it's not available as expected when it's time to make a critical business decision. Note, the SLAs and SLOs may also take the form of *data contracts* (see Chapter 5), formally or informally.

We talked about SLAs in Chapter 5, but discussing them again here is worthwhile. SLAs come in a variety of forms. Regardless of its form, an SLA tells users what to expect from your data product; it is a contract between you and your stakeholders. An example of an SLA might be, "Data will be reliably available and of high quality." An SLO is a key part of an SLA and describes the ways you'll measure performance against what you've agreed to. For example, given the preceding example SLA, an SLO might be, "Our data pipelines to your dashboard or ML workflow will have 99% uptime, with 95% of data free of defects." Be sure expectations are clear and you have the ability to verify you're operating within your agreed SLA and SLO parameters.

It's not enough to simply agree on an SLA. Ongoing communication is a central feature of a good SLA. Have you communicated possible issues that might affect your SLA or SLO expectations? What's your process for remediation and improvement?

Trust is everything. It takes a long time to earn, and it's easy to lose.

What's the Use Case, and Who's the User?

The serving stage is about data in action. But what is a *productive* use of data? You need to consider two things to answer this question: what's the use case, and who's the user?

The use case for data goes well beyond viewing reports and dashboards. Data is at its best when it leads to *action*. Will an executive make a strategic decision from a report? Will a user of a mobile food delivery app receive a coupon that entices them to purchase in the next two minutes? The data is often used in more than one use case—e.g., to train an ML model that does lead scoring and populates a CRM (reverse ETL). High-quality, high-impact data will inherently attract many interesting use cases. But in seeking use cases, always ask, "What *action* will this data trigger, and *who* will be performing this action?," with the appropriate follow-up question, "Can this action be automated?"

Whenever possible, prioritize use cases with the highest possible ROI. Data engineers love to obsess over the technical implementation details of the systems they build while ignoring the basic question of purpose. Engineers want to do what they do best: engineer things. When engineers recognize the need to focus on value and use cases, they become much more valuable and effective in their roles.

When starting a new data project, working backward is helpful. While it's tempting to focus on tools, we encourage you to start with the use case and the users. Here are some questions to ask yourself as you get started:

- Who will use the data, and how will they use it?
- What do stakeholders expect?
- How can I collaborate with data stakeholders (e.g., data scientists, analysts, business users) to understand how the data I'm working with will be used?

Again, always approach data engineering from the perspective of the user and their use case. By understanding their expectations and goals, you can work backward to create amazing data products more easily. Let's take a moment to expand on our discussion of a data product.

Data Products

> A good definition of a data product is a product that facilitates an end goal through the use of data.
>
> —D. J. Patil[2]

Data products aren't created in a vacuum. Like so many other organizational processes that we've discussed, making data products is a full-contact sport, involving a mix of product and business alongside technology. It's important to involve key stakeholders in developing a data product. In most companies, a data engineer is a couple of steps removed from the end users of a data product; a good data engineer will seek to fully understand outcomes for direct users such as data analysts and data scientists or customers external to the company.

---

2 D. J. Patil, "Data Jujitsu: The Art of Turning Data into Product," *O'Reilly Radar*, July 17, 2012, *https://oreil.ly/IYS9x*.

When creating a data product, it's useful to think of the "jobs to be done."[3] A user "hires" a product for a "job to be done." This means you need to know what the user wants—i.e., their motivation for "hiring" your product. A classic engineering mistake is simply building without understanding the requirements, needs of the end user, or product/market fit. This disaster happens when you build data products nobody wants to use.

A good data product has positive feedback loops. More usage of a data product generates more useful data, which is used to improve the data product. Rinse and repeat.

When building a data product, keep these considerations in mind:

- When someone uses the data product, what do they hope to accomplish? All too often, data products are made without a clear understanding of the outcome expected by the user.

- Will the data product serve internal or external users? In Chapter 2, we discussed internal- and external-facing data engineering. When creating a data product, knowing whether your customer is internal or external facing will impact the way data is served.

- What are the outcomes and ROI of the data product you're building?

Building data products that people will use and love is critical. Nothing will ruin the adoption of a data product more than unwanted utility and loss of trust in the data outputs. Pay attention to the adoption and usage of data products, and be willing to adjust to make users happy.

Self-Service or Not?

How will users interface with your data product? Will a business director request a report from the data team, or can this director simply build the report? Self-service data products—giving the user the ability to build data products on their own—have been a common aspiration of data users for many years. What's better than just giving the end user the ability to directly create reports, analyses, and ML models?

Today, self-service BI and data science is still mostly aspirational. While we occasionally see companies successfully doing self-service with data, this is rare. Most of the time, attempts at self-service data begin with great intentions but ultimately fail; self-service data is tough to implement in practice. Thus, the analyst or data scientist

---

3 Clayton M. Christensen et al., "Know Your Customers' 'Jobs to Be Done,'" *Harvard Business Review*, September 2016, *https://oreil.ly/3uU4j*.

is left to perform the heavy lifting of providing ad hoc reports and maintaining dashboards.

Why is self-service data so hard? The answer is nuanced, but it generally involves understanding the end user. If the user is an executive who needs to understand how the business is doing, that person probably just wants a predefined dashboard of clear and actionable metrics. The executive will likely ignore any self-serve tools for creating custom data views. If reports provoke further questions, they might have analysts at their disposal to pursue a deeper investigation. On the other hand, a user who is an analyst might already be pursuing self-service analytics via more powerful tools such as SQL. Self-service analytics through a BI layer is not useful. The same considerations apply to data science. Although granting self-service ML to "citizen data scientists" has been a goal of many automated ML vendors, adoption is still nascent for the same reasons as self-service analytics. In these two extreme cases, a self-service data product is a wrong tool for the job.

Successful self-service data projects boil down to having the right audience. Identify the self-service users and the "job" they want to do. What are they trying to accomplish by using a self-service data product versus partnering with a data analyst to get the job done? A group of executives with a background in data forms an ideal audience for self-service; they likely want to slice and dice data themselves without needing to dust off their languishing SQL skills. Business leaders willing to invest the time to learn data skills through a company initiative and training program could also realize significant value from self-service.

Determine how you will provide data to this group. What are their time requirements for new data? What happens if they inevitably want more data or change the scope of what's required from self-service? More data often means more questions, which requires more data. You'll need to anticipate the growing needs of your self-service users. You also need to understand the fine balance between flexibility and guardrails that will help your audience find value and insights without incorrect results and confusion.

Data Definitions and Logic

As we've emphatically discussed, the utility of data in an organization is ultimately derived from its correctness and trustworthiness. Critically, the correctness of data goes beyond faithful reproduction of event values from source systems. Data correctness also encompasses proper data definitions and logic; these must be baked into data through all lifecycle stages, from source systems to data pipelines to BI tools and much more.

Data definition refers to the meaning of data as it is understood throughout the organization. For example, *customer* has a precise meaning within a company and across departments. When the definition of a customer varies, these must be documented and made available to everyone who uses the data.

Data logic stipulates formulas for deriving metrics from data—say, gross sales or customer lifetime value. Proper data logic must encode data definitions and details of statistical calculations. To compute customer churn metrics, we would need a definition: who is a customer? To calculate net profits, we would need a set of logical rules to determine which expenses to deduct from gross revenue.

Frequently, we see data definitions and logic taken for granted, often passed around the organization in the form of institutional knowledge. *Institutional knowledge* takes on a life of its own, often at the expense of anecdotes replacing data-driven insights, decisions, and actions. Instead, formally declaring data definitions and logic both in a data catalog and within the systems of the data engineering lifecycle goes a long way to ensuring data correctness, consistency, and trustworthiness.

Data definitions can be served in many ways, sometimes explicitly, but mostly implicitly. By *implicit*, we mean that anytime you serve data for a query, a dashboard, or an ML model, the data and derived metrics are presented consistently and correctly. When you write a SQL query, you're implicitly assuming that the inputs to this query are correct, including upstream pipeline logic and definitions. This is where data modeling (described in Chapter 8) is incredibly useful to capture data definitions and logic in a way that's understandable and usable by multiple end users.

Using a semantic layer, you consolidate business definitions and logic in a reusable fashion. Write once, use anywhere. This paradigm is an object-oriented approach to metrics, calculations, and logic. We'll have more to say in "Semantic and Metrics Layers" on page 359.

Data Mesh

Data mesh will increasingly be a consideration when serving data. Data mesh fundamentally changes the way data is served within an organization. Instead of siloed data teams serving their internal constituents, every domain team takes on two aspects of decentralized, peer-to-peer data serving.

First, teams are responsible for serving data *to other teams* by preparing it for consumption. Data must be good for use in data apps, dashboards, analytics, and BI tools across the organization. Second, each team potentially runs its dashboards and analytics for *self-service*. Teams consume data from across the organization based on the particular needs in their domain. Data consumed from other teams may also make its way into the software designed by a domain team through embedded analytics or an ML feature.

This dramatically changes the details and structure of serving. We introduced the concept of a data mesh in Chapter 3. Now that we've covered some general considerations for serving data, let's look at the first major area: analytics.

Analytics

The first data-serving use case you'll likely encounter is *analytics*, which is discovering, exploring, identifying, and making visible key insights and patterns within data. Analytics has many aspects. As a practice, analytics is carried out using statistical methods, reporting, BI tools, and more. As a data engineer, knowing the various types and techniques of analytics is key to accomplishing your work. This section aims to show how you'll serve data for analytics and presents some points to think about to help your analysts succeed.

Before you even serve data for analytics, the first thing you need to do (which should sound familiar after reading the preceding section) is identify the end use case. Is the user looking at historical trends? Should users be immediately and automatically notified of an anomaly, such as a fraud alert? Is someone consuming a real-time dashboard on a mobile application? These examples highlight the differences between business analytics (usually BI), operational analytics, and embedded analytics. Each of these analytics categories has different goals and unique serving requirements. Let's look at how you'll serve data for these types of analytics.

Business Analytics

Business analytics uses historical and current data to make strategic and actionable decisions. The types of decisions tend to factor in longer-term trends and often involve a mix of statistical and trend analysis, alongside domain expertise and human judgment. Business analysis is as much an art as it is a science.

Business analytics typically falls into a few big areas—dashboards, reports, and ad hoc analysis. A business analyst might focus on one or all of these categories. Let's quickly look at the differences between these practices and related tools. Understanding an analyst's workflow will help you, the data engineer, understand how to serve data.

A *dashboard* concisely shows decision makers how an organization is performing against a handful of core metrics, such as sales and customer retention. These core metrics are presented as visualizations (e.g., charts or heatmaps), summary statistics, or even a single number. This is similar to a car dashboard, which gives you a single readout of the critical things you need to know while driving a vehicle. An organization may have more than one dashboard, with C-level executives using an overarching dashboard and their direct reports using dashboards with their particular metrics, KPIs, or objectives and key results (OKRs). Analysts help create and maintain these dashboards. Once business stakeholders embrace and rely on a dashboard, the analyst usually responds to requests to look into a potential issue with a metric or add a new metric to the dashboard. Currently, you might use BI platforms to create dashboards, such as Tableau, Looker, Sisense, Power BI, or Apache Superset/Preset.

Analysts are often tasked by business stakeholders with creating a *report*. The goal of a report is to use data to drive insights and action. An analyst working at an online retail company is asked to investigate which factors are driving a higher-than-expected rate of returns for women's running shorts. The analyst runs some SQL queries in the data warehouse, aggregates the return codes that customers provide as the reason for their return, and discovers that the fabric in the running shorts is of inferior quality, often wearing out within a few uses. Stakeholders such as manufacturing and quality control are notified of these findings. Furthermore, the findings are summarized in a report and distributed in the same BI tool where the dashboard resides.

The analyst was asked to dig into a potential issue and come back with insights. This represents an example of *ad hoc analysis*. Reports typically start as ad hoc requests. If the results of the ad hoc analysis are impactful, they often end up in a report or dashboard. The technologies used for reports and ad hoc analysis are similar to dashboards but may include Excel, Python, R-based notebooks, SQL queries, and much more.

Good analysts constantly engage with the business and dive into the data to answer questions and uncover hidden and counterintuitive trends and insights. They also work with data engineers to provide feedback on data quality, reliability issues, and requests for new datasets. The data engineer is responsible for addressing this feedback and providing new datasets for the analyst to use.

Returning to the running shorts example, suppose that after communicating their findings, analysts learn that manufacturing can provide them with various supply-chain details regarding the materials used in the running shorts. Data engineers undertake a project to ingest this data into the data warehouse. Once the supply-chain data is present, analysts can correlate specific garment serial numbers with the supplier of the fabric used in the item. They discover that most failures are tied to one of their three suppliers, and the factory stops using fabric from this supplier.

The data for business analytics is frequently served in batch mode from a data warehouse or a data lake. This varies wildly across companies, departments, and even data teams within companies. New data might be available every second, every minute, every 30 minutes, every day, or once a week. The frequency of the batches can vary for several reasons. One key thing to note is that engineers working on analytics problems should consider various potential applications of data—current and future. It is common to have mixed data update frequencies to serve use cases appropriately but remember that the frequency of ingestion sets a ceiling on downstream frequency. If streaming applications exist for the data, it should be ingested as a stream even if some downstream processing and serving steps are handled in batches.

Of course, data engineers must address various backend technical considerations in serving business analytics. Some BI tools store data in an internal storage layer. Other tools run queries on your data lake or data warehouse. This is advantageous because you can take full advantage of your OLAP database's power. As we've discussed in earlier chapters, the downside is cost, access control, and latency.

Operational Analytics

If business analytics is about using data to discover actionable insights, then operational analytics uses data to take *immediate action*:

> Operational analytics versus business analytics =
> immediate action versus actionable insights

The big difference between operational and business analytics is *time*. Data used in business analytics takes a longer view of the question under consideration. Up-to-the-second updates are nice to know but won't materially impact the quality or outcome. Operational analytics is quite the opposite, as real-time updates can be impactful in addressing a problem when it occurs.

An example of operational analytics is real-time application monitoring. Many software engineering teams want to know how their application is performing; if issues arise, they want to be notified immediately. The engineering team might have a dashboard (see, e.g., Figure 9-2) that shows the key metrics such as requests per second, database I/O, or whatever metrics are important. Certain conditions can trigger scaling events, adding more capacity if servers are overloaded. If certain thresholds are breached, the monitoring system might also send alerts via text message, group chat, and email.

Business and Operational Analytics

The line between business and operational analytics has begun to blur. As streaming and low-latency data become more pervasive, it is only natural to apply operational approaches to business analytics problems; in addition to monitoring website performance on Black Friday, an online retailer could also analyze and present sales, revenue, and the impact of advertising campaigns in real time.

The data architectures will change to fit into a world where you can have both your red hot and warm data in one place. The central question you should always ask yourself, and your stakeholders, is this: if you have streaming data, what are you

---

going to do with it? What action should you take? Correct action creates impact and value. Real-time data without action is an unrelenting distraction.

In the long term, we predict that streaming will supplant batch. Data products over the next 10 years will likely be streaming-first, with the ability to seamlessly blend historical data. After real-time collection, data can still be consumed and processed in batches as required.

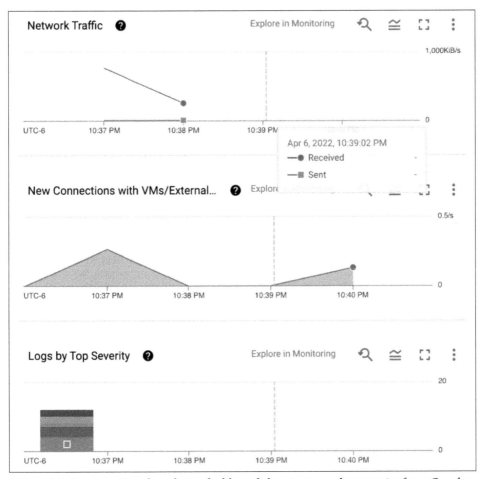

Figure 9-2. An operational analytics dashboard showing some key metrics from Google Compute Engine

Let's return once again to our running shorts example. Using analytics to discover bad fabric in the supply chain was a huge success; business leaders and data engineers want to find more opportunities to utilize data to improve product quality. The data engineers suggest deploying real-time analytics at the factory. The plant already uses a variety of machines capable of streaming real-time data. In addition, the plant has cameras recording video on the manufacturing line. Right now, technicians watch the footage in real time, look for defective items, and alert those running the line when they see a high rate of snags appearing in items.

Data engineers realize that they can use an off-the-shelf cloud machine vision tool to identify defects in real time automatically. Defect data is tied to specific item serial numbers and streamed. From here, a real-time analytics process can tie defective items to streaming events from machines further up the assembly line.

Using this approach, factory floor analysts discover that the quality of raw fabric stock varies significantly from box to box. When the monitoring system shows a high rate of snag defects, line workers can remove the defective box and charge it back to the supplier.

Seeing the success of this quality improvement project, the supplier decides to adopt similar quality-control processes. Data engineers from the retailer work with the supplier to deploy their real-time data analytics, dramatically improving the quality of their fabric stock.

Embedded Analytics

Whereas business and operational analytics are internally focused, a recent trend is external-facing or embedded analytics. With so much data powering applications, companies increasingly provide analytics to end users. These are typically referred to as *data applications*, often with analytics dashboards embedded within the application itself. Also known as *embedded analytics*, these end-user-facing dashboards give users key metrics about their relationship with the application.

A smart thermostat has a mobile application that shows the temperature in real time and up-to-date power consumption metrics, allowing the user to create a better energy-efficient heating or cooling schedule. In another example, a third-party ecommerce platform provides its sellers a real-time dashboard on sales, inventory, and returns. The seller has the option to use this information to offer deals to customers in near real time. In both cases, an application allows users to make real-time decisions (manually or automatically) based on data.

The landscape of embedded analytics is snowballing, and we expect that such data applications will become increasingly pervasive within the next few years. As a data engineer, you're probably not creating the embedded analytics frontend, as the application developers handle that. Since you're responsible for the databases serving the embedded analytics, you'll need to understand the speed and latency requirements for embedded analytics.

Performance for embedded analytics encompasses three problems. First, app users are not as tolerant of infrequent batch processing as internal company analysts; users of a recruiting SaaS platform may expect to see a change in their statistics as soon as they upload a new resume. Users want low *data latency*. Second, users of data apps expect fast *query performance*. When they adjust parameters in an analytics dashboard, they want to see refreshed results appear in seconds. Third, data apps must often support extremely high query rates across many dashboards and numerous customers. High *concurrency* is critical.

Google and other early major players in the data apps space developed exotic technologies to cope with these challenges. For new startups, the default is to use conventional transactional databases for data applications. As their customer bases expand, they outgrow their initial architecture. They have access to a new generation of databases that combine high performance—fast queries, high concurrency, and near real-time updates—with relative ease of use (e.g., SQL-based analytics).

Machine Learning

The second major area for serving data is machine learning. ML is increasingly common, so we'll assume you're at least familiar with the concept. With the rise of ML engineering (itself almost a parallel universe to data engineering), you might ask yourself where a data engineer fits into the picture.

Admittedly, the boundary between ML, data science, data engineering, and ML engineering is increasingly fuzzy, and this boundary varies dramatically between organizations. In some organizations, ML engineers take over data processing for ML applications right after data collection or may even form an entirely separate and parallel data organization that handles the entire lifecycle for all ML applications. Data engineers handle all data processing in other settings and then hand off data to ML engineers for model training. Data engineers may even handle some extremely ML-specific tasks, such as featurization of data.

Let's return to our example of quality for control of running shorts produced by an online retailer. Suppose that streaming data has been implemented in the factory that makes the raw fabric stock for the shorts. Data scientists discovered that the quality of the manufactured fabric is susceptible to characteristics of the input raw polyester, temperature, humidity, and various tunable parameters of the loom that weaves the fabric. Data scientists develop a basic model to optimize loom parameters. ML engineers automate model training and set up a process to automatically tune the loom based on input parameters. Data and ML engineers work together to design a featurization pipeline, and data engineers implement and maintain the pipeline.

What a Data Engineer Should Know About ML

Before we discuss serving data for ML, you may ask yourself how much ML you need to know as a data engineer. ML is an incredibly vast topic, and we won't attempt to teach you the field; countless books and courses are available to learn ML.

While a data engineer doesn't need to have a deep understanding of ML, it helps tremendously to know the basics of how classical ML works and the fundamentals of deep learning. Knowing the basics of ML will go a long way in helping you work alongside data scientists in building data products.

Here are some areas of ML that we think a data engineer should be familiar with:

- The difference between supervised, unsupervised, and semisupervised learning.
- The difference between classification and regression techniques.
- The various techniques for handling time-series data. This includes time-series analysis, as well as time-series forecasting.
- When to use the "classical" techniques (logistic regression, tree-based learning, support vector machines) versus deep learning. We constantly see data scientists immediately jump to deep learning when it's overkill. As a data engineer, your basic knowledge of ML can help you spot whether an ML technique is appropriate and scales the data you'll need to provide.
- When would you use automated machine learning (AutoML) versus handcrafting an ML model? What are the trade-offs with each approach regarding the data being used?
- What are data-wrangling techniques used for structured and unstructured data?
- All data that is used for ML is converted to numbers. If you're serving structured or semistructured data, ensure that the data can be properly converted during the feature-engineering process.
- How to encode categorical data and the embeddings for various types of data.
- The difference between batch and online learning. Which approach is appropriate for your use case?
- How does the data engineering lifecycle intersect with the ML lifecycle at your company? Will you be responsible for interfacing with or supporting ML technologies such as feature stores or ML observability?
- Know when it's appropriate to train locally, on a cluster, or at the edge. When would you use a GPU over a CPU? The type of hardware you use largely depends on the type of ML problem you're solving, the technique you're using, and the size of your dataset.

- Know the difference between the applications of batch and streaming data in training ML models. For example, batch data often fits well with offline model training, while streaming data works with online training.
- What are data cascades (*https://oreil.ly/FBV4g*), and how might they impact ML models?
- Are results returned in real time or in batch? For example, a batch speech transcription model might process speech samples and return text in batch after an API call. A product recommendation model might need to operate in real time as the customer interacts with an online retail site.
- The use of structured versus unstructured data. We might cluster tabular (structured) customer data or recognize images (unstructured) by using a neural net.

ML is a *vast* subject area, and this book won't teach you these topics, or even ML generalities. If you'd like to learn more about ML, we suggest reading *Hands on Machine Learning with Scikit-Learn, Keras, and TensorFlow* by Aurélien Géron (O'Reilly); countless other ML courses and books are available online. Because the books and online courses evolve so rapidly, do your research on what seems like a good fit for you.

Ways to Serve Data for Analytics and ML

As with analytics, data engineers provide data scientists and ML engineers with the data they need to do their jobs. We have placed serving for ML alongside analytics because the pipelines and processes are extremely similar. There are many ways to serve data for analytics and ML. Some common ways to serve this data include files, databases, query engines, and data sharing. Let's briefly look at each.

File Exchange

File exchange is ubiquitous in data serving. We process data and generate files to pass to data consumers.

Keep in mind that a file might be used for many purposes. A data scientist might load a text file (unstructured data) of customer messages to analyze the sentiments of customer complaints. A business unit might receive invoice data from a partner company as a collection of CSVs (structured data), and an analyst must perform some statistical analysis on these files. Or, a data vendor might provide an online retailer with images of products on a competitor's website (unstructured data) for automated classification using computer vision.

The way you serve files depends on several factors, such as these:

- Use case—business analytics, operational analytics, embedded analytics
- The data consumer's data-handling processes
- The size and number of individual files in storage
- Who is accessing this file
- Data type—structured, semistructured, or unstructured

The second bullet point is one of the main considerations. It is often necessary to serve data through files rather than data sharing because the data consumer cannot use a sharing platform.

The simplest file to serve is something along the lines of emailing a single Excel file. This is still a common workflow even in an era when files can be collaboratively shared. The problem with emailing files is each recipient gets their version of the file. If a recipient edits the file, these edits are specific to that user's file. Deviations among files inevitably result. And what happens if you no longer want the recipient to have access to the file? If the file is emailed, you have very little recourse to retrieve the file. If you need a coherent, consistent version of a file, we suggest using a collaboration platform such as Microsoft 365 or Google Docs.

Of course, serving single files is hard to scale, and your needs will eventually outgrow simple cloud file storage. You'll likely grow into an object storage bucket if you have a handful of large files, or a data lake if you have a steady supply of files. Object storage can store any type of blob file and is especially useful for semistructured or unstructured files.

We'll note that we generally consider file exchange through object storage (data lake) to land under "data sharing" rather than file exchange since the process can be significantly more scalable and streamlined than ad hoc file exchange.

Databases

Databases are a critical layer in serving data for analytics and ML. For this discussion, we'll implicitly keep our focus on serving data from OLAP databases (e.g., data warehouses and data lakes). In the previous chapter, you learned about querying databases. Serving data involves querying a database and then consuming those results for a use case. An analyst or data scientist might query a database by using a SQL editor and export those results to a CSV file for consumption by a downstream application, or analyze the results in a notebook (described in "Serving Data in Notebooks" on page 360).

Serving data from a database carries a variety of benefits. A database imposes order and structure on the data through schema; databases can offer fine-grained permission controls at the table, column, and row level, allowing database adminis-trators to craft complex access policies for various roles; and databases can offer high serving performance for large, computationally intensive queries and high query concurrency.

BI systems usually share the data processing workload with a source database, but the boundary between processing in the two systems varies. For example, a Tableau server runs an initial query to pull data from a database and stores it locally. Basic OLAP/BI slicing and dicing (interactive filtering and aggregation) runs directly on the server from the local data copy. On the other hand, Looker (and similar modern BI systems) relies on a computational model called *query pushdown*; Looker enco-des data processing logic in a specialized language (LookML), combines this with dynamic user input to generate SQL queries, runs these against the source database, and presents the output. (See "Semantic and Metrics Layers" on page 359.) Both Tableau and Looker have various configuration options for caching results to reduce the processing burden for frequently run queries.

A data scientist might connect to a database, extract data, and perform feature engineering and selection. This converted dataset is then fed into an ML model; the offline model is trained and produces predictive results.

Data engineers are quite often tasked with managing the database-serving layer. This includes management of performance and costs. In databases that separate compute and storage, this is a somewhat more subtle optimization problem than in the days of fixed on-premises infrastructure. For example, it is now possible to spin up a new Spark cluster or Snowflake warehouse for each analytical or ML workload. It is generally recommended to at least split out clusters by major use cases, such as ETL and serving for analytics and data science. Often data teams choose to slice more finely, assigning one warehouse per major area. This makes it possible for different teams to budget for their query costs under the supervision of a data engineering team.

Also, recall the three performance considerations that we discussed in "Embedded Analytics" on page 352. These are data latency, query performance, and concurrency. A system that can ingest directly from a stream can lower data latency. And many database architectures rely on SSD or memory caching to enhance query perfor-mance and concurrency to serve the challenging use cases inherent in embedded analytics.

Increasingly, data platforms like Snowflake and Databricks allow analysts and data scientists to operate under a single environment, providing SQL editors and data science notebooks under one roof. Because compute and storage are separated, the analysts and data scientists can consume the underlying data in various ways without interfering with each other. This will allow high throughput and faster delivery of data products to stakeholders.

Streaming Systems

Streaming analytics are increasingly important in the realm of serving. At a high level, understand that this type of serving may involve *emitted metrics*, which are different from traditional queries.

Also, we see operational analytics databases playing a growing role in this area (see "Operational Analytics" on page 350). These databases allow queries to run across a large range of historical data, encompassing up-to-the-second current data. Essentially, they combine aspects of OLAP databases with stream-processing systems. Increasingly, you'll work with streaming systems to serve data for analytics and ML, so get familiar with this paradigm.

You've learned about streaming systems throughout the book. For an idea of where it's going, read about the live data stack in Chapter 11.

Query Federation

As you learned in Chapter 8, query federation pulls data from multiple sources, such as data lakes, RDBMSs, and data warehouses. Federation is becoming more popular as distributed query virtualization engines gain recognition as ways to serve queries without going through the trouble of centralizing data in an OLAP system. Today, you can find OSS options like Trino and Presto and managed services such as Starburst. Some of these offerings describe themselves as ways to enable the data mesh; time will tell how that unfolds.

When serving data for federated queries, you should be aware that the end user might be querying several systems—OLTP, OLAP, APIs, filesystems, etc. (Figure 9-3). Instead of serving data from a single system, you're now serving data from multiple systems, each with its usage patterns, quirks, and nuances. This poses challenges for serving data. If federated queries touch live production source systems, you must ensure that the federated query won't consume excessive resources in the source.

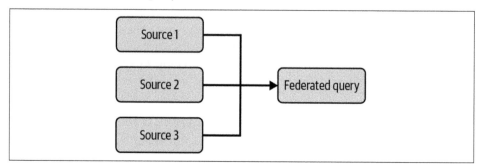

Figure 9-3. A federated query with three data sources

In our experience, federated queries are ideally suited when you want flexibility in analyzing data or the source data needs to be tightly controlled. Federation allows ad hoc queries for performing exploratory analysis, blending data from various systems without the complexity of setting up data pipelines or ETL. This will allow you to determine whether the performance of a federated query is sufficient for ongoing purposes or you need to set up ingestion on some or all data sources and centralize the data in an OLAP database or data lake.

Federated queries also provide read-only access to source systems, which is great when you don't want to serve files, database access, or data dumps. The end user reads only the version of the data they're supposed to access and nothing more. Query federation is a great option to explore for situations where access and compliance are critical.

Data Sharing

Chapter 5 includes an extensive discussion of data sharing. Any data exchange between organizations or units within a larger organization can be viewed as data sharing. Still, we mean specifically sharing through massively multitenant storage systems in a cloud environment. Data sharing generally turns data serving into a security and access control problem.

The actual queries are now handled by the data consumers (analysts and data scientists) rather than the engineers sourcing the data. Whether serving data in a data mesh within an organization, providing data to the public, or serving to partner businesses, data sharing is a compelling serving model. Data sharing is increasingly a core feature of major data platforms like Snowflake, Redshift, and BigQuery allowing companies to share data safely and securely with each other.

Semantic and Metrics Layers

When data engineers think about serving, they naturally tend to gravitate toward the data processing and storage technologies—i.e., will you use Spark or a cloud data warehouse? Is your data stored in object storage or cached in a fleet of SSDs? But powerful processing engines that deliver quick query results across vast datasets don't inherently make for quality business analytics. When fed poor-quality data or poor-quality queries, powerful query engines quickly return bad results.

Where data quality focuses on characteristics of the data itself and various techniques to filter or improve bad data, query quality is a question of building a query with appropriate logic that returns accurate answers to business questions. Writing high-quality ETL queries and reporting is time-intensive, detailed work. Various tools can help automate this process while facilitating consistency, maintenance, and continuous improvement.

Fundamentally, a *metrics layer* is a tool for maintaining and computing business logic.[4] (A *semantic layer* is extremely similar conceptually,[5] and *headless BI* is another closely related term.) This layer can live in a BI tool or in software that builds transformation queries. Two concrete examples are Looker and Data Build Tool (dbt).

For instance, Looker's LookML allows users to define virtual, complex business logic. Reports and dashboards point to specific LookML for computing metrics. Looker allows users to define standard metrics and reference them in many downstream queries; this is meant to solve the traditional problem of repetition and inconsistency in traditional ETL scripts. Looker uses LookML to generate SQL queries, which are pushed down to the database. Results can be persisted in the Looker server or in the database itself for large result sets.

dbt allows users to define complex SQL data flows encompassing many queries and standard definitions of business metrics, much like Looker. Unlike Looker, dbt runs exclusively in the transform layer, although this can include pushing queries into views that are computed at query time. Whereas Looker focuses on serving queries and reporting, dbt can serve as a robust data pipeline orchestration tool for analytics engineers.

We believe that metrics layer tools will grow more popular with wider adoption and more entrants, as well as move upstream toward the application. Metrics layer tools help solve a central question in analytics that has plagued organizations since people have analyzed data: "Are these numbers correct?" Many new entrants are in the space beside the ones we've mentioned.

Serving Data in Notebooks

Data scientists often use notebooks in their day-to-day work. Whether it's exploring data, engineering features, or training a model, the data scientist will likely use a notebook. At this writing, the most popular notebook platform is Jupyter Notebook, along with its next-generation iteration, JupyterLab. Jupyter is open source and can be hosted locally on a laptop, on a server, or through various cloud-managed services. *Jupyter* stands for *Julia, Python, and R* —the latter two are popular for data science applications, especially notebooks. Regardless of the language used, the first thing you'll need to consider is how data can be accessed from a notebook.

Data scientists will programmatically connect to a data source, such as an API, a database, a data warehouse, or a data lake (Figure 9-4). In a notebook, all connections

---

4 Benn Stancil, "The Missing Piece of the Modern Data Stack," *benn.substack*, April 22, 2021, *https://oreil.ly/wQyPb*.

5 Srini Kadamati, "Understanding the Superset Semantic Layer," Preset blog, December 21, 2021, *https://oreil.ly/6smWC*.

are created using the appropriate built-in or imported libraries to load a file from a filepath, connect to an API endpoint, or make an ODBC connection to a database. A remote connection may require the correct credentials and privileges to establish a connection. Once connected, a user may need the correct access to tables (and rows/columns) or files stored in object storage. The data engineer will often assist the data scientist in finding the right data and then ensure that they have the right permissions to access the rows and columns required.

Let's look at an incredibly common workflow for data scientists: running a local notebook and loading data into a pandas dataframe. *Pandas* is a prevalent Python library used for data manipulation and analysis and is commonly used to load data (say, a CSV file) into a Jupyter notebook. When pandas loads a dataset, it stores this dataset in memory.

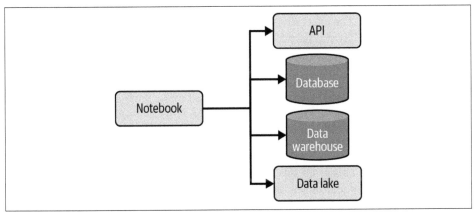

Figure 9-4. A notebook can be served data from many sources, such as object storage or a database, data warehouse, or data lake

Credential Handling

Incorrectly handled credentials in notebooks and data science code are a major security risk; we constantly see credentials mishandled in this domain. It is common to embed credentials directly in code, where they often leak into version control repos. Credentials are also frequently passed around through messages and email.

We encourage data engineers to audit data science security practices and work collaboratively on improvements. Data scientists are highly receptive to these conversations if they are given alternatives. Data engineers should set standards for handling credentials. Credentials should never be embedded in code; ideally, data scientists use credential managers or CLI tools to manage access.

What happens when the dataset size exceeds the local machine's available memory? This inevitably happens given the limited memory of laptops and workstations: it stops a data science project dead in its tracks. It's time to consider more scalable options. First, move to a cloud-based notebook where the underlying storage and memory for the notebook can be flexibly scaled. Upon outgrowing this option, look at distributed execution systems; popular Python-based options include Dask, Ray, and Spark. If a full-fledged cloud-managed offering seems appealing, consider setting up a data science workflow using Amazon SageMaker, Google Cloud Vertex AI, or Microsoft Azure Machine Learning. Finally, open source end-to-end ML workflow options such as Kubeflow and MLflow make it easy to scale ML workloads in Kubernetes and Spark, respectively. The point is to get data scientists off their laptops and take advantage of the cloud's power and scalability.

Data engineers and ML engineers play a key role in facilitating the move to scalable cloud infrastructure. The exact division of labor depends a great deal on the details of your organization. They should take the lead in setting up cloud infrastructure, overseeing the management of environments, and training data scientists on cloud-based tools.

Cloud environments require significant operational work, such as managing versions and updates, controlling access, and maintaining SLAs. As with other operational work, a significant payoff can result when "data science ops" are done well.

Notebooks may even become a part of production data science; notebooks are widely deployed at Netflix. This is an interesting approach with advantages and trade-offs. Productionized notebooks allow data scientists to get their work into production much faster, but they are also inherently a substandard form of production. The alternative is to have ML and data engineers convert notebooks for production use, placing a significant burden on these teams. A hybrid of these approaches may be ideal, with notebooks used for "light" production and a full productionization process for high-value projects.

Reverse ETL

Today, *reverse ETL* is a buzzword that describes serving data by loading it from an OLAP database back into a source system. That said, any data engineer who's worked in the field for more than a few years has probably done some variation of reverse ETL. Reverse ETL grew in popularity in the late 2010s/early 2020s and is increasingly recognized as a formal data engineering responsibility.

A data engineer might pull customers and order data from a CRM and store it in a data warehouse. This data is used to train a lead scoring model, whose results are returned to the data warehouse. Your company's sales team wants access to these scored leads to try to generate more sales. You have a few options to get the results of this lead scoring model into the hands of the sales team. You can put the results in a dashboard for them to view. Or you might email the results to them as an Excel file.

The challenge with these approaches is that they are not connected to the CRM, where a salesperson does their work. Why not just put the scored leads back into the CRM? As we mentioned, successful data products reduce friction with the end user. In this case, the end user is the sales team.

Using reverse ETL and loading the scored leads back into the CRM is the easiest and best approach for this data product. Reverse ETL takes processed data from the output side of the data engineering lifecycle and feeds it back into source systems (Figure 9-5).

Instead of reverse ETL, we, the authors, half-jokingly call it bidirectional load and transform (BLT) (*https://oreil.ly/SJmZn*). The term *reverse ETL* doesn't quite accurately describe what's happening in this process. Regardless, the term has stuck in the popular imagination and press, so we'll use it throughout the book. More broadly, whether the term *reverse ETL* sticks around is anyone's guess, but the practice of loading data from OLAP systems back into source systems will remain important.

How do you begin serving data with reverse ETL? While you can roll your reverse ETL solution, many off-the-shelf reverse ETL options are available. We suggest using open source, or a commercial managed service. That said, the reverse ETL space is changing extremely quickly. No clear winners have emerged, and many reverse ETL products will be absorbed by major clouds or other data product vendors. Choose carefully.

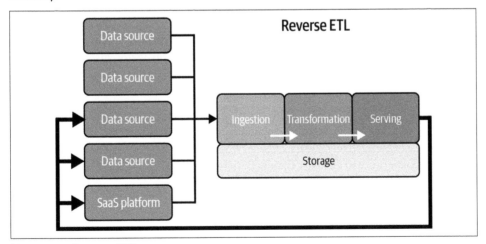

Figure 9-5. Reverse ETL

We do have a few words of warning regarding reverse ETL. Reverse ETL inherently creates feedback loops. For example, imagine that we download Google Ads data, use a model to compute new bids, load the bids back into Google Ads, and start the process again. Suppose that because of an error in your bid model, the bids trend ever higher, and your ads get more and more clicks. You can quickly waste massive amounts of money! Be careful, and build in monitoring and guardrails.

Whom You'll Work With

As we've discussed, in the serving stage, a data engineer will interface with a lot of stakeholders. These include (but aren't limited to) the following:

- Data analysts
- Data scientists
- MLOps/ML engineers
- The business—nondata or nontechnical stakeholders, managers, and executives

As a reminder, the data engineer operates in a *support* role for these stakeholders and is not necessarily responsible for the end uses of data. For example, a data engineer supplies the data for a report that analysts interpret, but the data engineer isn't responsible for these interpretations. Instead, the data engineer is responsible for producing the highest-quality data products possible.

A data engineer should be aware of feedback loops between the data engineering lifecycle and the broader use of data once it's in the hands of stakeholders. Data is rarely static, and the outside world will influence the data that is ingested and served and reingested and re-served.

A big consideration for data engineers in the serving stage of the lifecycle is the separation of duties and concerns. If you're at an early-stage company, the data engineer may also be an ML engineer or data scientist; this is not sustainable. As the company grows, you need to establish a clear division of duties with other data team members.

Adopting a data mesh dramatically reorganizes team responsibilities, and every domain team takes on aspects of serving. For a data mesh to be successful, each team must work effectively on its data-serving responsibilities, and teams must also effectively collaborate to ensure organizational success.

Undercurrents

The undercurrents come to finality with serving. Remember that the data engineering lifecycle is just that—a lifecycle. What goes around comes around. We see many instances where serving data highlights something missed earlier in the lifecycle. Always be on the lookout for how the undercurrents can help you spot ways to improve data products.

We're fond of saying, "Data is a silent killer," and the undercurrents come to a head in the serving stage. Serving is your final chance to make sure your data is in great shape before it gets into the hands of end users.

Security

The same security principles apply whether sharing data with people or systems. We often see data shared indiscriminately, with little to no access controls or thought as to what the data will be used for. This is a huge mistake that can have catastrophic results, such as a data breach and the resulting fines, bad press, and lost jobs. Take security seriously, especially in this stage of the lifecycle. Of all the lifecycle stages, serving presents the largest security surface.

As always, exercise the principle of least privilege both for people and systems, and provide only the access required for the purpose at hand and the job to be done. What data does an executive need versus an analyst or data scientist? What about an ML pipeline or reverse ETL process? These users and destinations all have different data needs, and access should be provided accordingly. Avoid giving carte blanche permissions to everyone and everything.

Serving data is often read-only unless a person or process needs to update data in the system from which it is queried. People should be given read-only access to specific databases and datasets unless their role requires something more advanced like write or update access. This can be accomplished by combining groups of users with certain IAM roles (i.e., analysts group, data scientist group) or custom IAM roles if this makes sense. For systems, provide service accounts and roles in a similar fashion. For both users and systems, narrow access to a dataset's fields, rows, columns, and cells if this is warranted. Access controls should be as fine-grained as possible and revoked when access is no longer required.

Access controls are critical when serving data in a multitenant environment. Make sure users can access only *their* data and nothing more. A good approach is to mediate access through filtered views, thus alleviating the security risks inherent in sharing access to a common table. Another suggestion is to use data sharing in your workflows, which allows for read-only granular controls between you and people consuming your data.

Check how often data products are used and whether it makes sense to stop sharing certain data products. It's extremely common for an executive to urgently request an analyst to create a report, only to have this report very quickly go unused. If data products aren't used, ask the users if they're still needed. If not, kill off the data product. This means one less security vulnerability floating around.

Finally, you should view access control and security not as impediments to serving but as key enablers. We're aware of many instances where complex, advanced data systems were built, potentially having a significant impact on a company. Because security was not implemented correctly, few people were allowed to access the data, so it languished. Fine-grained, robust access control means that more interesting data analytics and ML can be done while still protecting the business and its customers.

Data Management

You've been incorporating data management along the data engineering lifecycle, and the impact of your efforts will soon become apparent as people use your data products. At the serving stage, you're mainly concerned with ensuring that people can access high-quality and trustworthy data.

As we mentioned at the beginning of this chapter, trust is perhaps the most critical variable in data serving. If people trust their data, they will use it; untrusted data will go unused. Be sure to make data trust and data improvement an active process by providing feedback loops. As users interact with data, they can report problems and request improvements. Actively communicate back to your users as changes are made.

What data do people need to do their jobs? Especially with regulatory and compliance concerns weighing on data teams, giving people access to the raw data—even with limited fields and rows—poses a problem of tracing data back to an entity, such as a person or a group of people. Thankfully, advancements in data obfuscation allow you to serve synthetic, scrambled, or anonymized data to end users. These "fake" datasets should sufficiently allow an analyst or data scientist to get the necessary signal from the data, but in a way that makes identifying protected information difficult. Though this isn't a perfect process—with enough effort, many datasets can be de-anonymized or reverse-engineered—it at least reduces the risk of data leakage.

Also, incorporate semantic and metrics layers into your serving layer, alongside rigorous data modeling that properly expresses business logic and definitions. This provides a single source of truth, whether for analytics, ML, reverse ETL, or other serving uses.

DataOps

The steps you take in data management—data quality, governance, and security—are monitored in DataOps. Essentially, DataOps operationalizes data management. The following are some things to monitor:

- Data health and data downtime
- Latency of systems serving data—dashboards, databases, etc.
- Data quality
- Data and system security and access
- Data and model versions being served
- Uptime to achieve an SLO

A variety of new tools have sprung up to address various monitoring aspects. For example, many popular data observability tools aim to minimize *data downtime* and maximize data quality. Observability tools may cross over from data to ML, supporting monitoring of models and model performance. More conventional DevOps monitoring is also critical to DataOps—e.g., you need to monitor whether connections are stable among storage, transformation, and serving.

As in every stage of the data engineering lifecycle, version-control code and operationalize deployment. This applies to analytical code, data logic code, ML scripts, and orchestration jobs. Use multiple stages of deployment (dev, test, prod) for reports and models.

Data Architecture

Serving data should have the same architectural considerations as other data engineering lifecycle stages. At the serving stage, feedback loops must be fast and tight. Users should be able to access the data they need as quickly as possible when they need it.

Data scientists are notorious for doing most development on their local machines. As discussed earlier, encourage them to migrate these workflows to common systems in a cloud environment, where data teams can collaborate in dev, test, and production environments and create proper production architectures. Facilitate your analysts and data scientists by supporting tools for publishing data insights with little encumbrance.

Orchestration

Data serving is the last stage of the data engineering lifecycle. Because serving is downstream of so many processes, it's an area of extremely complex overlap. Orchestration is not simply a way of organizing and automating complex work but a means of coordinating data flow across teams so that data is made available to consumers at the promised time.

Ownership of orchestration is a key organizational decision. Will orchestration be centralized or decentralized? A decentralized approach allows small teams to manage their data flows, but it can increase the burden of cross-team coordination. Instead of simply managing flows within a single system, directly triggering the completion of DAGs or tasks belonging to other teams, teams must pass messages or queries between systems.

A centralized approach means that work is easier to coordinate, but significant gatekeeping must also exist to protect a single production asset. For example, a poorly written DAG can bring Airflow to a halt. The centralized approach would mean bringing down data processes and serving across the whole organization. Centralized orchestration management requires high standards, automated testing of DAGs, and gatekeeping.

If orchestration is centralized, who will own it? When a company has a DataOps team, orchestration usually lands here. Often, a team involved in serving is a natural fit because it has a fairly holistic view of all data engineering lifecycle stages. This could be the DBAs, analytics engineers, data engineers, or ML engineers. ML engineers coordinate complex model-training processes but may or may not want to add the operational complexity of managing orchestration to an already crowded docket of responsibilities.

Software Engineering

Compared to a few years ago, serving data has become simpler. The need to write code has been drastically simplified. Data has also become more code-first, with the proliferation of open source frameworks focused on simplifying the serving of data. Many ways exist to serve data to end users, and a data engineer's focus should be on knowing how these systems work and how data is delivered.

Despite the simplicity of serving data, if code is involved, a data engineer should still understand how the main serving interfaces work. For example, a data engineer may need to translate the code a data scientist is running locally on a notebook and convert it into a report or a basic ML model to operate.

Another area where data engineers will be useful is understanding the impact of how code and queries will perform against the storage systems. Analysts can generate SQL in various programmatic ways, including LookML, Jinja via dbt, various object-relational mapping (ORM) tools, and metrics layers. When these programmatic layers compile to SQL, how will this SQL perform? A data engineer can suggest optimizations where the SQL code might not perform as well as handwritten SQL.

The rise of analytics and ML IaC means the role of writing code is moving toward building the systems that support data scientists and analysts. Data engineers might be responsible for setting up the CI/CD pipelines and building processes for their data team. They would also do well to train and support their data team in using the Data/MLOps infrastructure they've built so that these data teams can be as self-sufficient as possible.

For embedded analytics, data engineers may need to work with application developers to ensure that queries are returned quickly and cost-effectively. The application developer will control the frontend code that users deal with. The data engineer is there to ensure that developers receive the correct payloads as they're requested.

Conclusion

The data engineering lifecycle has a logical ending at the serving stage. As with all lifecycles, a feedback loop occurs (Figure 9-6). You should view the serving stage as a chance to learn what's working and what can be improved. Listen to your stakeholders. If they bring up issues—and they inevitably will—try not to take offense. Instead, use this as an opportunity to improve what you've built.

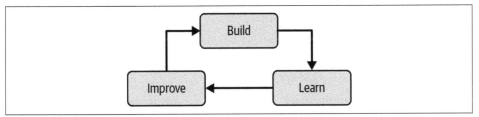

Figure 9-6. Build, learn, improve

A good data engineer is always open to new feedback and constantly finds ways to improve their craft. Now that we've taken a journey through the data engineering lifecycle, you know how to design, architect, build, maintain, and improve your data engineering systems and products. Let's turn our attention to Part III of the book, where we'll cover some aspects of data engineering we're constantly asked about and that, frankly, deserve more attention.

Additional Resources

- "Data as a Product vs. Data Products: What Are the Differences?" (*https://oreil.ly/fRAA5*) by Xavier Gumara Rigol
- "Data Jujitsu: The Art of Turning Data into Product" (*https://oreil.ly/5TH6Q*) by D. J. Patil
- *Data Mesh* by Zhamak Dehghani (O'Reilly)
- "Data Mesh Principles and Logical Architecture" (*https://oreil.ly/JqaW6*) by Zhamak Dehghani
- "Designing Data Products" (*https://oreil.ly/BKqu4*) by Seth O'Regan

- "The Evolution of Data Products" (*https://oreil.ly/DNk8x*) and "What Is Data Science" (*https://oreil.ly/xWL0w*) by Mike Loukides
- Forrester's "Self-Service Business Intelligence: Dissolving the Barriers to Creative Decision-Support Solutions" blog article (*https://oreil.ly/c3bpO*)
- "Fundamentals of Self-Service Machine Learning" (*https://oreil.ly/aALpB*) by Paramita (Guha) Ghosh
- "The Future of BI Is Headless" (*https://oreil.ly/INa17*) by ZD
- "How to Build Great Data Products" (*https://oreil.ly/9cI55*) by Emily Glassberg Sands
- "How to Structure a Data Analytics Team" (*https://oreil.ly/mGtii*) by Niall Napier
- "Know Your Customers' 'Jobs to Be Done'" (*https://oreil.ly/1W1JV*) by Clayton M. Christensen et al.
- "The Missing Piece of the Modern Data Stack" (*https://oreil.ly/NYs1A*) and "Why Is Self-Serve Still a Problem?" (*https://oreil.ly/0vYvs*) by Benn Stancil
- "Self-Service Analytics" in the Gartner Glossary (*https://oreil.ly/NG1yA*)
- Ternary Data's "What's Next for Analytical Databases? w/ Jordan Tigani (MotherDuck)" video (*https://oreil.ly/8C4Gj*)
- "Understanding the Superset Semantic Layer" (*https://oreil.ly/YqURr*) by Srini Kadamati
- "What Do Modern Self-Service BI and Data Analytics Really Mean?" (*https://oreil.ly/Q9Ux8*) by Harry Dix
- "What Is Operational Analytics (and How Is It Changing How We Work with Data)?" (*https://oreil.ly/5yU4p*) by Sylvain Giuliani
- "What Is User-Facing Analytics?" (*https://oreil.ly/HliJe*) by Chinmon Soman

PART III

Security, Privacy, and the Future of Data Engineering

CHAPTER 10

Security and Privacy

Now that you've learned about the data engineering lifecycle, we'd like to reiterate the importance of security and share some straightforward practices you can incorporate in your day-to-day workflow. Security is vital to the practice of data engineering. This should be blindingly obvious, but we're constantly amazed at how often data engineers view security as an afterthought. We believe that security is the first thing a data engineer needs to think about in every aspect of their job and every stage of the data engineering lifecycle. You deal with sensitive data, information, and access daily. Your organization, customers, and business partners expect these valuable assets to be handled with the utmost care and concern. One security breach or a data leak can leave your business dead in the water; your career and reputation are ruined if it's your fault.

Security is a key ingredient for privacy. Privacy has long been critical to trust in the corporate information technology space; engineers directly or indirectly handle data related to people's private lives. This includes financial information, data on private communications (emails, texts, phone calls), medical history, educational records, and job history. A company that leaked this information or misused it could find itself a pariah when the breach came to light.

Increasingly, privacy is a matter of significant legal importance. For example, the Family Educational Rights and Privacy Act (FERPA) went into effect in the US in the 1970s; the Health Insurance Portability and Accountability Act (HIPAA) followed in the 1990s; GDPR was passed in Europe in the mid-2010s. Several US-based privacy bills have passed or will soon. This is just a tiny sampling of privacy-related statutes (and we believe just the beginning). Still, the penalties for violation of any of these laws can be significant, even devastating, to a business. And because data systems are woven into the fabric of education, health care, and business, data engineers handle sensitive data related to each of these laws.

A data engineer's exact security and privacy responsibilities will vary significantly between organizations. At a small startup, a data engineer may do double duty as a data security engineer. A large tech company will have armies of security engineers and security researchers. Even in this situation, data engineers will often be able to identify security practices and technology vulnerabilities within their own teams and systems that they can report and mitigate in collaboration with dedicated security personnel.

Because security and privacy are critical to data engineering (security being an undercurrent), we want to spend some more time covering security and privacy. In this chapter, we lay out some things data engineers should consider around security, particularly in people, processes, and technology (in that order). This isn't a complete list, but it lays out the major things we wish would improve based on our experience.

People

The weakest link in security and privacy is *you*. Security is often compromised at the human level, so conduct yourself as if you're always a target. A bot or human actor is trying to infiltrate your sensitive credentials and information at any given time. This is our reality, and it's not going away. Take a defensive posture with everything you do online and offline. Exercise the power of negative thinking and always be paranoid.

The Power of Negative Thinking

In a world obsessed with positive thinking, negative thinking is distasteful. However, American surgeon Atul Gawande wrote a 2007 op-ed in the *New York Times* (*https:// oreil.ly/UtwPM*) on precisely this subject. His central thesis is that positive thinking can blind us to the possibility of terrorist attacks or medical emergencies and deter preparation. Negative thinking allows us to consider disastrous scenarios and act to prevent them.

Data engineers should actively think through the scenarios for data utilization and collect sensitive data only if there is an actual need downstream. The best way to protect private and sensitive data is to avoid ingesting this data in the first place.

Data engineers should think about the attack and leak scenarios with any data pipeline or storage system they utilize. When deciding on security strategies, ensure that your approach delivers proper security and not just the illusion of safety.

Always Be Paranoid

Always exercise caution when someone asks you for your credentials. When in doubt—and you should always be in extreme doubt when asked for credentials— hold off and get second opinions from your coworkers and friends. Confirm with other people that the request is indeed legitimate. A quick chat or phone call is cheaper than a ransomware attack triggered through an email click. Trust nobody at face value when asked for credentials, sensitive data, or confidential information, including from your coworkers.

You are also the first line of defense in respecting privacy and ethics. Are you uncomfortable with sensitive data you've been tasked to collect? Do you have ethical questions about the way data is being handled in a project? Raise your concerns with colleagues and leadership. Ensure that your work is both legally compliant and ethical.

Processes

When people follow regular security processes, security becomes part of the job. Make security a habit, regularly practice real security, exercise the principle of least privilege, and understand the shared responsibility model in the cloud.

Security Theater Versus Security Habit

With our corporate clients, we see a pervasive focus on compliance (with internal rules, laws, recommendations from standards bodies), but not enough attention to potentially bad scenarios. Unfortunately, this creates an illusion of security but often leaves gaping holes that would be evident with a few minutes of reflection.

Security needs to be simple and effective enough to become habitual throughout an organization. We're amazed at the number of companies with security policies in the hundreds of pages that nobody reads, the annual security policy review that people immediately forget, all in checking a box for a security audit. This is security theater, where security is done in the letter of compliance (SOC-2, ISO 27001, and related) without real *commitment*.

Instead, pursue the spirit of genuine and habitual security; bake a security mindset into your culture. Security doesn't need to be complicated. For example, at our company, we run security training and policy review at least once a month to ingrain this into our team's DNA and update each other on security practices we can improve. Security must not be an afterthought for your data team. Everyone is responsible and has a role to play. It must be the priority for you and everyone else you work with.

Active Security

Returning to the idea of negative thinking, *active security* entails thinking about and researching security threats in a dynamic and changing world. Rather than simply deploying scheduled simulated phishing attacks, you can take an active security posture by researching successful phishing attacks and thinking through your organizational security vulnerabilities. Rather than simply adopting a standard compliance checklist, you can think about internal vulnerabilities specific to your organization and incentives employees might have to leak or misuse private information.

We have more to say about active security in "Technology" on page 378.

The Principle of Least Privilege

The *principle of least privilege* means that a person or system should be given only the privileges and data they need to complete the task at hand and nothing more. Often, we see an antipattern in the cloud: a regular user is given administrative access to everything, when that person may need just a handful of IAM roles to do their work. Giving someone carte blanche administrative access is a huge mistake and should never happen under the principle of least privilege.

Instead, provide the user (or group they belong to) the IAM roles they need when they need them. When these roles are no longer needed, take them away. The same rule applies to service accounts. Treat humans and machines the same way: give them only the privileges and data they need to do their jobs, and only for the timespan when needed.

Of course, the principle of least privilege is also critical to privacy. Your users and customers expect that people will look at their sensitive data only when necessary. Make sure that this is the case. Implement column, row, and cell-level access controls around sensitive data; consider masking PII and other sensitive data and create views that contain only the information the viewer needs to access. Some data must be retained but should be accessed only in an emergency. Put this data behind a *broken glass process*: users can access it only after going through an emergency approval process to fix a problem, query critical historical information, etc. Access is revoked immediately once the work is done.

Shared Responsibility in the Cloud

Security is a shared responsibility in the cloud. The cloud vendor is responsible for ensuring the physical security of its data center and hardware. At the same time, you are responsible for the security of the applications and systems you build and maintain in the cloud. Most cloud security breaches continue to be caused by end users, not the cloud. Breaches occur because of unintended misconfigurations, mistakes, oversights, and sloppiness.

Always Back Up Your Data

Data disappears. Sometimes it's a dead hard drive or server; in other cases, someone might accidentally delete a database or an object storage bucket. A bad actor can also lock away data. Ransomware attacks are widespread these days. Some insurance companies are reducing payouts in the event of an attack, leaving you on the hook both to recover your data and pay the bad actor who's holding it hostage. You need to back up your data regularly, both for disaster recovery and continuity of business operations, if a version of your data is compromised in a ransomware attack. Additionally, test the restoration of your data backups on a regular basis.

Data backup doesn't strictly fit under security and privacy practices; it goes under the larger heading of *disaster prevention*, but it's adjacent to security, especially in the era of ransomware attacks.

An Example Security Policy

This section presents a sample security policy regarding credentials, devices, and sensitive information. Notice that we don't overcomplicate things; instead, we give people a short list of practical actions they can take immediately.

Example Security Policy

Protect Your Credentials

Protect your credentials at all costs. Here are some ground rules for credentials:

- Use a single-sign-on (SSO) for everything. Avoid passwords whenever possible, and use SSO as the default.
- Use multifactor authentication with SSO.
- Don't share passwords or credentials. This includes client passwords and credentials. If in doubt, see the person you report to. If that person is in doubt, keep digging until you find an answer.
- Beware of phishing and scam calls. Don't ever give your passwords out. (Again, prioritize SSO.)
- Disable or delete old credentials. Preferably the latter.
- Don't put your credentials in code. Handle secrets as configuration and never commit them to version control. Use a secrets manager where possible.
- Always exercise the principle of least privilege. Never give more access than is required to do the job. This applies to all credentials and privileges in the cloud and on premises.

Protect Your Devices

- Use device management for all devices used by employees. If an employee leaves the company or your device gets lost, the device can be remotely wiped.
- Use multifactor authentication for all devices.

- Sign in to your device using your company email credentials.
- All policies covering credentials and behavior apply to your device(s).
- Treat your device as an extension of yourself. Don't let your assigned device(s) out of your sight.
- When screen sharing, be aware of exactly what you're sharing to protect sensitive information and communications. Share only single documents, browser tabs, or windows, and avoid sharing your full desktop. Share only what's required to convey your point.
- Use "do not disturb" mode when on video calls; this prevents messages from appearing during calls or recordings.

Software Update Policy

- Restart your web browser when you see an update alert.
- Run minor OS updates on company and personal devices.
- The company will identify critical major OS updates and provide guidance.
- Don't use the beta version of an OS.
- Wait a week or two for new major OS version releases.

These are some basic examples of how security can be simple and effective. Based on your company's security profile, you may need to add more requirements for people to follow. And again, always remember that people are your weakest link in security.

Technology

After you've addressed security with people and processes, it's time to look at how you leverage technology to secure your systems and data assets. The following are some significant areas you should prioritize.

Patch and Update Systems

Software gets stale, and security vulnerabilities are constantly discovered. To avoid exposing a security flaw in an older version of the tools you're using, always patch and update operating systems and software as new updates become available. Thankfully, many SaaS and cloud-managed services automatically perform upgrades and other maintenance without your intervention. To update your own code and dependencies, either automate builds or set alerts on releases and vulnerabilities so you can be prompted to perform the updates manually.

Encryption

Encryption is not a magic bullet. It will do little to protect you in the event of a *human* security breach that grants access to credentials. Encryption is a baseline requirement for any organization that respects security and privacy. It will protect you from basic attacks, such as network traffic interception.

Let's look separately at encryption at rest and in transit.

Encryption at rest

Be sure your data is encrypted when it is at rest (on a storage device). Your company laptops should have full-disk encryption enabled to protect data if a device is stolen. Implement server-side encryption for all data stored in servers, filesystems, databases, and object storage in the cloud. All data backups for archival purposes should also be encrypted. Finally, incorporate application-level encryption where applicable.

Encryption over the wire

Encryption over the wire is now the default for current protocols. For instance, HTTPS is generally required for modern cloud APIs. Data engineers should always be aware of how keys are handled; bad key handling is a significant source of data leaks. In addition, HTTPS does nothing to protect data if bucket permissions are left open to the public, another cause of several data scandals over the last decade.

Engineers should also be aware of the security limitations of older protocols. For example, FTP is simply not secure on a public network. While this may not appear to be a problem when data is already public, FTP is vulnerable to man-in-the-middle attacks, whereby an attacker intercepts downloaded data and changes it before it arrives at the client. It is best to simply avoid FTP.

Make sure everything is encrypted over the wire, even with legacy protocols. When in doubt, use robust technology with encryption baked in.

Logging, Monitoring, and Alerting

Hackers and bad actors typically don't announce that they're infiltrating your systems. Most companies don't find out about security incidents until well after the fact. Part of DataOps is to observe, detect, and alert on incidents. As a data engineer, you should set up automated monitoring, logging, and alerting to be aware of peculiar events when they happen in your systems. If possible, set up automatic anomaly detection.

Here are some areas you should monitor:

Access

Who's accessing what, when, and from where? What new accesses were granted? Are there strange patterns with your current users that might indicate their account is compromised, such as trying to access systems they don't usually access or shouldn't have access to? Do you see new unrecognized users accessing your system? Be sure to regularly comb through access logs, users, and their roles to ensure that everything looks OK.

Resources

Monitor your disk, CPU, memory, and I/O for patterns that seem out of the ordinary. Did your resources suddenly change? If so, this might indicate a security breach.

Billing

Especially with SaaS and cloud-managed services, you need to oversee costs. Set up budget alerts to make sure your spending is within expectations. If an unexpected spike occurs in your billing, this might indicate someone or something is utilizing your resources for malicious purposes.

Excess permissions

Increasingly, vendors are providing tools that monitor for permissions that are *not utilized* by a user or service account over some time. These tools can often be configured to automatically alert an administrator or remove permissions after a specified elapsed time.

For example, suppose that a particular analyst hasn't accessed Redshift for six months. These permissions can be removed, closing a potential security hole. If the analyst needs to access Redshift in the future, they can put in a ticket to restore permissions.

It's best to combine these areas in your monitoring to get a cross-sectional view of your resource, access, and billing profile. We suggest setting up a dashboard for everyone on the data team to view monitoring and receive alerts when something seems out of the ordinary. Couple this with an effective incident response plan to manage security breaches when they occur, and run through the plan on a regular basis so you are prepared.

Network Access

We often see data engineers doing pretty wild things regarding network access. In several instances, we've seen publicly available Amazon S3 buckets housing lots of sensitive data. We've also witnessed Amazon EC2 instances with inbound SSH access open to the whole world for 0.0.0.0/0 (all IPs) or databases with open access to all inbound requests over the public internet. These are just a few examples of terrible network security practices.

In principle, network security should be left to security experts at your company. (In practice, you may need to assume significant responsibility for network security in a small company.) As a data engineer, you will encounter databases, object storage, and servers so often that you should at least be aware of simple measures you can take to make sure you're in line with good network access practices. Understand what IPs and ports are open, to whom, and why. Allow the incoming IP addresses of the systems and users that will access these ports (a.k.a. whitelisting IPs) and avoid broadly opening connections for any reason. When accessing the cloud or a SaaS tool, use an encrypted connection. For example, don't use an unencrypted website from a coffee shop.

Also, while this book has focused almost entirely on running workloads in the cloud, we add a brief note here about hosting on-premises servers. Recall that in Chapter 3, we discussed the difference between a hardened perimeter and zero-trust security. The cloud is generally closer to zero-trust security—every action requires authentication. We believe that the cloud is a more secure option for most organizations because it imposes zero-trust practices and allows companies to leverage the army of security engineers employed by the public clouds.

However, sometimes hardened perimeter security still makes sense; we find some solace in the knowledge that nuclear missile silos are air gapped (not connected to any networks). Air-gapped servers are the ultimate example of a hardened security perimeter. Just keep in mind that even on premises, air-gapped servers are vulnerable to human security failings.

Security for Low-Level Data Engineering

For engineers who work in the guts of data storage and processing systems, it is critical to consider the security implications of every element. Any software library, storage system, or compute node is a potential security vulnerability. A flaw in an obscure logging library might allow attackers to bypass access controls or encryption. Even CPU architectures and microcode represent potential vulnerabilities; sensitive data can be vulnerable (*https://meltdownattack.com*) when it's at rest in memory or a CPU cache. No link in the chain can be taken for granted.

Of course, this book is principally about high-level data engineering—stitching together tools to handle the entire lifecycle. Thus, we'll leave it to you to dig into the gory technical details.

Internal security research

We discussed the idea of *active security* in "Processes" on page 375. We also highly recommend adopting an *active security* approach to technology. Specifically, this means that every technology employee should think about security problems.

Why is this important? Every technology contributor develops a domain of technical expertise. Even if your company employs an army of security researchers, data engineers will become intimately familiar with specific data systems and cloud services in their purview. Experts in a particular technology are well positioned to identify security holes in this technology.

Encourage every data engineer to be actively involved in security. When they identify potential security risks in their systems, they should think through mitigations and take an active role in deploying these.

Conclusion

Security needs to be a habit of mind and action; treat data like your wallet or smartphone. Although you won't likely be in charge of security for your company, knowing basic security practices and keeping security top of mind will help reduce the risk of data security breaches at your organization.

Additional Resources

- *Building Secure and Reliable Systems* by Heather Adkins et al. (O'Reilly)
- Open Web Application Security Project (OWASP) publications (*https://owasp.org*)
- *Practical Cloud Security* by Chris Dotson (O'Reilly)

CHAPTER 11

The Future of Data Engineering

This book grew out of the authors' recognition that warp speed changes in the field have created a significant knowledge gap for existing data engineers, people interested in moving into a career in data engineering, technology managers, and executives who want to better understand how data engineering fits into their companies. When we started thinking about how to organize this book, we got quite a bit of pushback from friends who'd ask, "How dare you write about a field that is changing so quickly?!" In many ways, they're right. It certainly feels like the field of data engineering—and, really, all things data—is changing daily. Sifting through the noise and finding the signal of *what's unlikely to change* was among the most challenging parts of organizing and writing this book.

In this book, we focus on big ideas that we feel will be useful for the next several years—hence the continuum of the data engineering lifecycle and its undercurrents. The order of operations and names of best practices and technologies might change, but the primary stages of the lifecycle will likely remain intact for many years to come. We're keenly aware that technology continues to change at an exhausting pace; working in the technology sector in our present era can feel like a rollercoaster ride or perhaps a hall of mirrors.

Several years ago, data engineering didn't even exist as a field or job title. Now you're reading a book called *Fundamentals of Data Engineering*! You've learned all about the fundamentals of data engineering—its lifecycle, undercurrents, technologies, and best practices. You might be asking yourself, what's next in data engineering? While nobody can predict the future, we have a good perspective on the past, the present, and current trends. We've been fortunate to watch the genesis and evolution of data engineering from a front-row seat. This final chapter presents our thoughts on the future, including observations of ongoing developments and wild future speculation.

The Data Engineering Lifecycle Isn't Going Away

While data science has received the bulk of the attention in recent years, data engineering is rapidly maturing into a distinct and visible field. It's one of the fastest-growing careers in technology, with no signs of losing momentum. As companies realize they first need to build a data foundation before moving to "sexier" things like AI and ML, data engineering will continue growing in popularity and importance. This progress centers around the data engineering lifecycle.

Some question whether increasingly simple tools and practices will lead to the disappearance of data engineers. This thinking is shallow, lazy, and shortsighted. As organizations leverage data in new ways, new foundations, systems, and workflows will be needed to address these needs. Data engineers sit at the center of designing, architecting, building, and maintaining these systems. If tooling becomes easier to use, data engineers will move up the value chain to focus on higher-level work. The data engineering lifecycle isn't going away anytime soon.

The Decline of Complexity and the Rise of Easy-to-Use Data Tools

Simplified, easy-to-use tools continue to lower the barrier to entry for data engineering. This is a great thing, especially given the shortage of data engineers we've discussed. The trend toward simplicity will continue. Data engineering isn't dependent on a particular technology or data size. It's also not just for large companies. In the 2000s, deploying "big data" technologies required a large team and deep pockets. The ascendance of SaaS-managed services has largely removed the complexity of understanding the guts of various "big data" systems. Data engineering is now something that *all* companies can do.

Big data is a victim of its extraordinary success. For example, Google BigQuery, a descendant of GFS and MapReduce, can query petabytes of data. Once reserved for internal use at Google, this insanely powerful technology is now available to anybody with a GCP account. Users simply pay for the data they store and query rather than having to build a massive infrastructure stack. Snowflake, Amazon EMR, and many other hyper-scalable cloud data solutions compete in the space and offer similar capabilities.

The cloud is responsible for a significant shift in the usage of open source tools. Even in the early 2010s, using open source typically entailed downloading the code and configuring it yourself. Nowadays, many open source data tools are available as managed cloud services that compete directly with proprietary services. Linux is available preconfigured and installed on server instances on all major clouds. Serverless platforms like AWS Lambda and Google Cloud Functions allow you to deploy

---

event-driven applications in minutes, using mainstream languages such as Python, Java, and Go running atop Linux behind the scenes. Engineers wishing to use Apache Airflow can adopt Google's Cloud Composer or AWS's managed Airflow service. Managed Kubernetes allows us to build highly scalable microservice architectures. And so on.

This fundamentally changes the conversation around open source code. In many cases, managed open source is just as easy to use as its proprietary service competitors. Companies with highly specialized needs can also deploy managed open source, then move to self-managed open source later if they need to customize the underlying code.

Another significant trend is the growth in popularity of off-the-shelf data connectors (at the time of this writing, popular ones include Fivetran and Airbyte). Data engineers have traditionally spent a lot of time and resources building and maintaining plumbing to connect to external data sources. The new generation of managed connectors is highly compelling, even for highly technical engineers, as they begin to recognize the value of recapturing time and mental bandwidth for other projects. API connectors will be an outsourced problem so that data engineers can focus on the unique issues that drive their businesses.

The intersection of red-hot competition in the data-tooling space with a growing number of data engineers means data tools will continue decreasing in complexity while adding even more functionality and features. This simplification will only grow the practice of data engineering, as more and more companies find opportunities to discover value in data.

The Cloud-Scale Data OS and Improved Interoperability

Let's briefly review some of the inner workings of (single-device) operating systems, then tie this back to data and the cloud. Whether you're utilizing a smartphone, a laptop, an application server, or a smart thermostat, these devices rely on an operating system to provide essential services and orchestrate tasks and processes. For example, I can see roughly 300 processes running on the MacBook Pro that I'm typing on. Among other things, I see services such as WindowServer (responsible for providing windows in a graphical interface) and CoreAudio (tasked with providing low-level audio capabilities).

When I run an application on this machine, it doesn't directly access sound and graphics hardware. Instead, it sends commands to operating system services to draw windows and play sound. These commands are issued to standard APIs; a specification tells software developers how to communicate with operating system services. The operating system *orchestrates* a boot process to provide these services, starting each service in the correct order based on dependencies among them; it also maintains services by monitoring them and restarting them in the correct order in case of a failure.

Now let's return to data in the cloud. The simplified data services that we've mentioned throughout this book (e.g., Google Cloud BigQuery, Azure Blob Storage, Snowflake, and AWS Lambda) resemble operating system services, but at a much larger scale, running across many machines rather than a single server.

Now that these simplified services are available, the next frontier of evolution for this notion of a cloud data operating system will happen at a higher level of abstraction. Benn Stancil called for the emergence of standardized data APIs for building data pipelines and data applications.[1] We predict that data engineering will gradually coalesce around a handful of data interoperability standards. Object storage in the cloud will grow in importance as a batch interface layer between various data services. New generation file formats (such as Parquet and Avro) are already taking over for the purposes of cloud data interchange, significantly improving on the dreadful interoperability of CSV and the poor performance of raw JSON.

Another critical ingredient of a data API ecosystem is a metadata catalog that describes schemas and data hierarchies. Currently, this role is largely filled by the legacy Hive Metastore. We expect that new entrants will emerge to take its place. Metadata will play a crucial role in data interoperability, both across applications and systems and across clouds and networks, driving automation and simplification.

We will also see significant improvements in the scaffolding that manages cloud data services. Apache Airflow has emerged as the first truly cloud-oriented data orchestration platform, but we are on the cusp of significant enhancement. Airflow will grow in capabilities, building on its massive mindshare. New entrants such as Dagster and Prefect will compete by rebuilding orchestration architecture from the ground up.

This next generation of data orchestration platforms will feature enhanced data integration and data awareness. Orchestration platforms will integrate with data cataloging and lineage, becoming significantly more data-aware in the process. In addition, orchestration platforms will build IaC capabilities (similar to Terraform) and code deployment features (like GitHub Actions and Jenkins). This will allow engineers to code a pipeline and then pass it to the orchestration platform to automatically build, test, deploy, and monitor. Engineers will be able to write infrastructure specifications directly into their pipelines; missing infrastructure and services (e.g., Snowflake databases, Databricks clusters, and Amazon Kinesis streams) will be deployed the first time the pipeline runs.

---

1 Benn Stancil, "The Data OS," *benn.substack*, September 3, 2021, *https://oreil.ly/HetE9*.

We will also see significant enhancements in the domain of *live data*—e.g., streaming pipelines and databases capable of ingesting and querying streaming data. In the past, building a streaming DAG was an extremely complex process with a high ongoing operational burden (see Chapter 8). Tools like Apache Pulsar point the way toward a future in which streaming DAGs can be deployed with complex transformations using relatively simple code. We have already seen the emergence of managed stream processors (such as Amazon Kinesis Data Analytics and Google Cloud Dataflow), but we will see a new generation of orchestration tools for managing these services, stitching them together, and monitoring them. We discuss live data in "The Live Data Stack" on page 389.

What does this enhanced abstraction mean for data engineers? As we've already argued in this chapter, the role of the data engineer won't go away, but it will evolve significantly. By comparison, more sophisticated mobile operating systems and frameworks have not eliminated mobile app developers. Instead, mobile app developers can now focus on building better-quality, more sophisticated applications. We expect similar developments for data engineering as the cloud-scale data OS paradigm increases interoperability and simplicity across various applications and systems.

"Enterprisey" Data Engineering

The increasing simplification of data tools and the emergence and documentation of best practices means data engineering will become more "enterprisey."[2] This will make many readers violently cringe. The term *enterprise*, for some, conjures Kafkaesque nightmares of faceless committees dressed in overly starched blue shirts and khakis, endless red tape, and waterfall-managed development projects with constantly slipping schedules and ballooning budgets. In short, some of you read "enterprise" and imagine a soulless place where innovation goes to die.

Fortunately, this is not what we're talking about; we're referring to some of the *good* things that larger companies do with data—management, operations, governance, and other "boring" stuff. We're presently living through the golden age of "enterprisey" data management tools. Technologies and practices once reserved for giant organizations are trickling downstream. The once hard parts of big data and streaming data have now largely been abstracted away, with the focus shifting to ease of use, interoperability, and other refinements.

---

2 Ben Rogojan, "Three Data Engineering Experts Share Their Thoughts on Where Data Is Headed," *Better Programming*, May 27, 2021, *https://oreil.ly/IsY4W*.

This allows data engineers working on new tooling to find opportunities in the abstractions of data management, DataOps, and all the other undercurrents of data engineering. Data engineers will become "enterprisey." Speaking of which…

Titles and Responsibilities Will Morph…

While the data engineering lifecycle isn't going anywhere anytime soon, the boundaries between software engineering, data engineering, data science, and ML engineering are increasingly fuzzy. In fact, like the authors, many data scientists are transformed into data engineers through an organic process; tasked with doing "data science" but lacking the tools to do their jobs, they take on the job of designing and building systems to serve the data engineering lifecycle.

As simplicity moves up the stack, data scientists will spend a smaller slice of their time gathering and munging data. But this trend will extend beyond data scientists. Simplification also means data engineers will spend less time on low-level tasks in the data engineering lifecycle (managing servers, configuration, etc.), and "enterprisey" data engineering will become more prevalent.

As data becomes more tightly embedded in every business's processes, new roles will emerge in the realm of data and algorithms. One possibility is a role that sits between ML engineering and data engineering. As ML toolsets become easier to use and managed cloud ML services grow in capabilities, ML is shifting away from ad hoc exploration and model development to become an operational discipline.

This new ML-focused engineer who straddles this divide will know algorithms, ML techniques, model optimization, model monitoring, and data monitoring. However, their primary role will be to create or utilize the systems that automatically train models, monitor performance, and operationalize the full ML process for model types that are well understood. They will also monitor data pipelines and quality, overlapping into the current realm of data engineering. ML engineers will become more specialized to work on model types that are closer to research and less well understood.

Another area in which titles may morph is at the intersection of software engineering and data engineering. Data applications, which blend traditional software applications with analytics, will drive this trend. Software engineers will need to have a much deeper understanding of data engineering. They will develop expertise in things like streaming, data pipelines, data modeling, and data quality. We will move beyond the "throw it over the wall" approach that is now pervasive. Data engineers will be integrated into application development teams, and software developers will acquire data engineering skills. The boundaries that exist between application backend systems and data engineering tools will be lowered as well, with deep integration through streaming and event-driven architectures.

Moving Beyond the Modern Data Stack, Toward the Live Data Stack

We'll be frank: the modern data stack (MDS) isn't so modern. We applaud the MDS for bringing a great selection of powerful data tools to the masses, lowering prices, and empowering data analysts to take control of their data stack. The rise of ELT, cloud data warehouses, and the abstraction of SaaS data pipelines certainly changed the game for many companies, opening up new powers for BI, analytics, and data science.

Having said that, the MDS is basically a repackaging of old data warehouse practices using modern cloud and SaaS technologies; because the MDS is built around the cloud data warehouse paradigm, it has some serious limitations when compared to the potential of next-generation real-time data applications. From our point of view, the world is moving beyond the use of data-warehouse-based internal-facing analytics and data science, toward powering entire businesses and applications in real time with next-generation real-time databases.

What's driving this evolution? In many cases, analytics (BI and operational analytics) will be replaced by automation. Presently, most dashboards and reports answer questions concerning *what* and *when*. Ask yourself, "If I'm asking a *what* or *when* question, what action do I take next?" If the action is repetitive, it is a candidate for automation. Why look at a report to determine whether to take action when you can instead automate the action based on events as they occur?

And it goes much further than this. Why does using a product like TikTok, Uber, Google, or DoorDash feel like magic? While it seems to you like a click of a button to watch a short video, order a ride or a meal, or find a search result, a lot is happening under the hood. These products are examples of true real-time data applications, delivering the actions you need at the click of a button while performing extremely sophisticated data processing and ML behind the scenes with miniscule latency. Presently, this level of sophistication is locked away behind custom-built technologies at large technology companies, but this sophistication and power are becoming democratized, similar to the way the MDS brought cloud-scale data warehouses and pipelines to the masses. The data world will soon go "live."

The Live Data Stack

This democratization of real-time technologies will lead us to the successor to the MDS: the *live data stack* will soon be accessible and pervasive. The live data stack, depicted in Figure 11-1, will fuse real-time analytics and ML into applications by using streaming technologies, covering the full data lifecycle from application source systems to data processing to ML, and back.

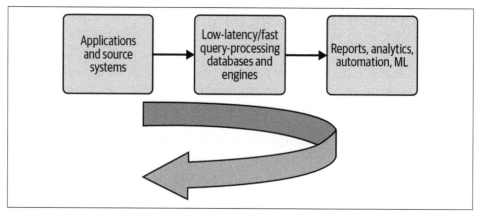

Figure 11-1. In the live data stack, data and intelligence moves in real time between the application and supporting systems

Just as the MDS took advantage of the cloud and brought on-premises data warehouse and pipeline technologies to the masses, the live data stack takes real-time data application technologies used at elite tech companies and makes them available to companies of all sizes as easy-to-use cloud-based offerings. This will open up a new world of possibilities for creating even better user experiences and business value.

Streaming Pipelines and Real-Time Analytical Databases

The MDS limits itself to batch techniques that treat data as bounded. In contrast, real-time data applications treat data as an unbounded, continuous stream. Streaming pipelines and real-time analytical databases are the two core technologies that will facilitate the move from the MDS to the live data stack. While these technologies have been around for some time, rapidly maturing managed cloud services will see them be deployed much more widely.

Streaming technologies will continue to see extreme growth for the foreseeable future. This will happen in conjunction with a clearer focus on the business utility of streaming data. Up to the present, streaming systems have frequently been treated like an expensive novelty or a dumb pipe for getting data from A to B. In the future, streaming will radically transform organizational technology and business processes; data architects and engineers will take the lead in these fundamental changes.

Real-time analytical databases enable both fast ingestion and subsecond queries on this data. This data can be enriched or combined with historical datasets. When combined with a streaming pipeline and automation, or dashboard that is capable of real-time analytics, a whole new level of possibilities opens up. No longer are you constrained by slow-running ELT processes, 15-minute updates, or other slow-moving parts. Data moves in a continuous flow. As streaming ingestion becomes more prevalent, batch ingestion will be less and less common. Why create a batch bottleneck at the head of your data pipeline? We'll eventually look at batch ingestion the same way we now look at dial-up modems.

In conjunction with the rise of streams, we expect a back-to-the-future moment for data transformations. We'll shift away from ELT—in database transformations—to something that looks more like ETL. We provisionally refer to this as *stream, transform, and load* (STL). In a streaming context, extraction is an ongoing, continuous process. Of course, batch transformations won't entirely go away. Batch will still be very useful for model training, quarterly reporting, and more. But streaming transformation will become the norm.

While the data warehouse and data lake are great for housing large amounts of data and performing ad hoc queries, they are not so well optimized for low-latency data ingestion or queries on rapidly moving data. The live data stack will be powered by OLAP databases that are purpose-built for streaming. Today, databases like Druid, ClickHouse, Rockset, and Firebolt are leading the way in powering the backend of the next generation of data applications. We expect that streaming technologies will continue to evolve rapidly and that new technologies will proliferate.

Another area we think is ripe for disruption is data modeling, where there hasn't been serious innovation since the early 2000s. The traditional batch-oriented data modeling techniques you learned about in Chapter 8 aren't suited for streaming data. New data-modeling techniques will occur not within the data warehouse but in the systems that generate the data. We expect data modeling will involve some notion of an upstream definitions layer—including semantics, metrics, lineage, and data definitions (see Chapter 9)—beginning where data is generated in the application. Modeling will also happen at every stage as data flows and evolves through the full lifecycle.

The Fusion of Data with Applications

We expect the next revolution will be the fusion of the application and data layers. Right now, applications sit in one area, and the MDS sits in another. To make matters worse, data is created with no regard for how it will be used for analytics. Consequently, lots of duct tape is needed to make systems talk with one another. This patchwork, siloed setup is awkward and ungainly.

Soon, application stacks will be data stacks, and vice versa. Applications will integrate real-time automation and decision making, powered by the streaming pipelines and ML. The data engineering lifecycle won't necessarily change, but the time between stages of the lifecycle will drastically shorten. A lot of innovation will occur in new technologies and practices that will improve the experience of engineering the live data stack. Pay attention to emerging database technologies designed to address the mix of OLTP and OLAP use cases; feature stores may also play a similar role for ML use cases.

The Tight Feedback Between Applications and ML

Another area we're excited about is the fusion of applications and ML. Today, applications and ML are disjointed systems, like applications and analytics. Software engineers do their thing over here, data scientists and ML engineers do their thing over there.

ML is well-suited for scenarios where data is generated at such a high rate and volume that humans cannot feasibly process it by hand. As data sizes and velocity grow, this applies to every scenario. High volumes of fast-moving data, coupled with sophisticated workflows and actions, are candidates for ML. As data feedback loops become shorter, we expect most applications to integrate ML. As data moves more quickly, the feedback loop between applications and ML will tighten. The applications in the live data stack are intelligent and able to adapt in real time to changes in the data. This creates a cycle of ever-smarter applications and increasing business value.

Dark Matter Data and the Rise of...Spreadsheets?!

We've talked about fast-moving data and how feedback loops will shrink as applications, data, and ML work more closely together. This section might seem odd, but we need to address something that's widely ignored in today's data world, especially by engineers.

What's the most widely used data platform? It's the humble spreadsheet. Depending on the estimates you read, the user base of spreadsheets is between 700 million and 2 billion people. Spreadsheets are the dark matter of the data world. A good deal of data analytics runs in spreadsheets and never makes its way into the sophisticated data systems that we describe in this book. In many organizations, spreadsheets handle financial reporting, supply-chain analytics, and even CRM.

At heart, what is a spreadsheet? A *spreadsheet* is an interactive data application that supports complex analytics. Unlike purely code-based tools such as pandas (Python Data Analysis Library), spreadsheets are accessible to a whole spectrum of users, ranging from those who just know how to open files and look at reports to power users who can script sophisticated procedural data processing. So far, BI tools have failed to bring comparable interactivity to databases. Users who interact with the UI are typically limited to slicing and dicing data within certain guardrails, not general-purpose programmable analytics.

We predict that a new class of tools will emerge that combines the interactive analytics capabilities of a spreadsheet with the backend power of cloud OLAP systems. Indeed, some candidates are already in the running. The ultimate winner in this product category may continue to use spreadsheet paradigms, or may define entirely new interface idioms for interacting with data.

Conclusion

Thank you for joining us on this journey through data engineering! We traversed good architecture, the stages of the data engineering lifecycle, and security best practices. We've discussed strategies for choosing technologies at a time when our field continues to change at an extraordinary pace. In this chapter, we laid out our wild speculation about the near and intermediate future.

Some aspects of our prognostication sit on a relatively secure footing. The simplification of managed tooling and the rise of "enterprisey" data engineering have proceeded day by day as we've written this book. Other predictions are much more speculative in nature; we see hints of an emerging *live data stack*, but this entails a significant paradigm shift for both individual engineers and the organizations that employ them. Perhaps the trend toward real-time data will stall once again, with most companies continuing to focus on basic batch processing. Surely, other trends exist that we have completely failed to identify. The evolution of technology involves complex interactions of technology and culture. Both are unpredictable.

Data engineering is a vast topic; while we could not go into any technical depth in individual areas, we hope that we have succeeded in creating a kind of travel guide that will help current data engineers, future data engineers, and those who work adjacent to the field to find their way in a domain that is in flux. We advise you to continue exploration on your own. As you discover interesting topics and ideas in this book, continue the conversation as part of a community. Identify domain experts who can help you to uncover the strengths and pitfalls of trendy technologies and practices. Read extensively from the latest books, blog posts, and papers. Participate in meetups and listen to talks. Ask questions and share your own expertise. Keep an eye on vendor announcements to stay abreast of the latest developments, taking all claims with a healthy grain of salt.

Through this process, you can choose technology. Next, you will need to adopt technology and develop expertise, perhaps as an individual contributor, perhaps within your team as a lead, perhaps across an entire technology organization. As you do this, don't lose sight of the larger goals of data engineering. Focus on the lifecycle, on serving your customers—internal and external—on your business, on serving and on your larger goals.

Regarding the future, many of you will play a role in determining what comes next. Technology trends are defined not only by those who create the underlying technology but also by those who adopt it and put it to good use. Successful tool *use* is as critical as tool *creation*. Find opportunities to apply real-time technology that will improve the user experience, create value, and define entirely new types of applications. It is this kind of practical application that will materialize the *live data stack* as a new industry standard; or perhaps some other new technology trend that we failed to identify will win the day.

Finally, we wish you an exciting career! We chose to work in data engineering, to consult, and to write this book not simply because it was trendy but because it was fascinating. We hope that we've managed to convey to you a bit of the joy we've found working in this field.

Serialization and Compression Technical Details

Data engineers working in the cloud are generally freed from the complexities of managing object storage systems. Still, they need to understand details of serialization and deserialization formats. As we mentioned in Chapter 6 about storage raw ingredients, serialization and compression algorithms go hand in hand.

Serialization Formats

Many serialization algorithms and formats are available to data engineers. While the abundance of options is a significant source of pain in data engineering, they are also a massive opportunity for performance improvements. We've sometimes seen job performance improve by a factor of 100 simply by switching from CSV to Parquet serialization. As data moves through a pipeline, engineers will also manage reserialization—conversion from one format to another. Sometimes data engineers have no choice but to accept data in an ancient, nasty form; they must design processes to deserialize this format and handle exceptions, and then clean up and convert data for consistent, fast downstream processing and consumption.

Row-Based Serialization

As its name suggests, *row-based serialization* organizes data by row. CSV format is an archetypal row-based format. For semistructured data (data objects that support nesting and schema variation), row-oriented serialization entails storing each object as a unit.

CSV: The nonstandard standard

We discussed CSV in Chapter 7. CSV is a serialization format that data engineers love to hate. The term *CSV* is essentially a catchall for delimited text, but there is flexibility in conventions of escaping, quote characters, delimiter, and more.

Data engineers should avoid using CSV files in pipelines because they are highly error-prone and deliver poor performance. Engineers are often required to use CSV format to exchange data with systems and business processes outside their control. CSV is a common format for data archival. If you use CSV for archival, include a complete technical description of the serialization configuration for your files so that future consumers can ingest the data.

XML

Extensible Markup Language (XML) was popular when HTML and the internet were new, but it is now viewed as legacy; it is generally slow to deserialize and serialize for data engineering applications. XML is another standard that data engineers are often forced to interact with as they exchange data with legacy systems and software. JSON has largely replaced XML for plain-text object serialization.

JSON and JSONL

JavaScript Object Notation (JSON) has emerged as the new standard for data exchange over APIs, and it has also become an extremely popular format for data storage. In the context of databases, the popularity of JSON has grown apace with the rise of MongoDB and other document stores. Databases such as Snowflake, BigQuery, and SQL Server also offer extensive native support, facilitating easy data exchange between applications, APIs, and database systems.

JSON Lines (JSONL) is a specialized version of JSON for storing bulk semistructured data in files. JSONL stores a sequence of JSON objects, with objects delimited by line breaks. From our perspective, JSONL is an extremely useful format for storing data right after it is ingested from API or applications. However, many columnar formats offer significantly better performance. Consider moving to another format for intermediate pipeline stages and serving.

Avro

Avro is a row-oriented data format designed for RPCs and data serialization. Avro encodes data into a binary format, with schema metadata specified in JSON. Avro is popular in the Hadoop ecosystem and is also supported by various cloud data tools.

Columnar Serialization

The serialization formats we've discussed so far are row-oriented. Data is encoded as complete relations (CSV) or documents (XML and JSON), and these are written into files sequentially.

With *columnar serialization*, data organization is essentially pivoted by storing each column into its own set of files. One obvious advantage to columnar storage is that it allows us to read data from only a subset of fields rather than having to read full rows at once. This is a common scenario in analytics applications and can dramatically reduce the amount of data that must be scanned to execute a query.

Storing data as columns also puts similar values next to each other, allowing us to encode columnar data efficiently. One common technique involves looking for repeated values and tokenizing these, a simple but highly efficient compression method for columns with large numbers of repeats.

Even when columns don't contain large numbers of repeated values, they may manifest high redundancy. Suppose that we organized customer support messages into a single column of data. We likely see the same themes and verbiage again and again across these messages, allowing data compression algorithms to realize a high ratio. For this reason, columnar storage is usually combined with compression, allowing us to maximize disk and network bandwidth resources.

Columnar storage and compression come with some disadvantages too. We cannot easily access individual data records; we must reconstruct records by reading data from several column files. Record updates are also challenging. To change one field in one record, we must decompress the column file, modify it, recompress it, and write it back to storage. To avoid rewriting full columns on each update, columns are broken into many files, typically using partitioning and clustering strategies that organize data according to query and update patterns for the table. Even so, the overhead for updating a single row is horrendous. Columnar databases are a terrible fit for transactional workloads, so transactional databases generally utilize some form of row- or record-oriented storage.

Parquet

Parquet stores data in a columnar format and is designed to realize excellent read and write performance in a data lake environment. Parquet solves a few problems that frequently bedevil data engineers. Parquet-encoded data builds in schema information and natively supports nested data, unlike CSV. Furthermore, Parquet is portable; while databases such as BigQuery and Snowflake serialize data in proprietary columnar formats and offer excellent query performance on data stored internally, a huge performance hit occurs when interoperating with external tools. Data must be deserialized, reserialized into an exchangeable format, and exported to use data lake tools such as Spark and Presto. Parquet files in a data lake may be a superior option to proprietary cloud data warehouses in a polyglot tool environment.

Parquet format is used with various compression algorithms; speed optimized compression algorithms such as Snappy (discussed later in this appendix) are especially popular.

ORC

Optimized Row Columnar (ORC) is a columnar storage format similar to Parquet. ORC was very popular for use with Apache Hive; while still widely used, we generally see it much less than Apache Parquet, and it enjoys somewhat less support in modern cloud ecosystem tools. For example, Snowflake and BigQuery support Parquet file import and export; while they can read from ORC files, neither tool can export to ORC.

Apache Arrow or in-memory serialization

When we introduced serialization as a storage raw ingredient at the beginning of this chapter, we mentioned that software could store data in complex objects scattered in memory and connected by pointers, or more orderly, densely packed structures such as Fortran and C arrays. Generally, densely packed in-memory data structures were limited to simple types (e.g., INT64) or fixed-width data structures (e.g., fixed-width strings). More complex structures (e.g., JSON documents) could not be densely stored in memory and required serialization for storage and transfer between systems.

The idea of Apache Arrow (*https://arrow.apache.org*) is to rethink serialization by utilizing a binary data format that is suitable for both in-memory processing and export.[1] This allows us to avoid the overhead of serialization and deserialization; we simply use the same format for in-memory processing, export over the network, and long-term storage. Arrow relies on columnar storage, where each column essentially gets its own chunks of memory. For nested data, we use a technique called *shredding*, which maps each location in the schema of JSON documents into a separate column.

This technique means that we can store a data file on disk, swap it directly into program address space by using virtual memory, and begin running a query against the data without deserialization overhead. In fact, we can swap chunks of the file into memory as we scan it, and then swap them back out to avoid running out of memory for large datasets.

---

1 Dejan Simic, "Apache Arrow: Read DataFrame with Zero Memory," *Towards Data Science*, June 25, 2020, *https://oreil.ly/TDAdY*.

One obvious headache with this approach is that different programming languages serialize data in different ways. To address this issue, the Arrow Project has created software libraries for a variety of programming languages (including C, Go, Java, JavaScript, MATLAB, Python, R, and Rust) that allow these languages to interoperate with Arrow data in memory. In some cases, these libraries use an interface between the chosen language and low-level code in another language (e.g., C) to read and write from Arrow. This allows high interoperability between languages without extra serialization overhead. For example, a Scala program can use the Java library to write arrow data and then pass it as a message to a Python program.

Arrow is seeing rapid uptake with a variety of popular frameworks such as Apache Spark. Arrow has also spanned a new data warehouse product; Dremio (*https:// www.dremio.com*) is a query engine and data warehouse built around Arrow serialization to support fast queries.

Hybrid Serialization

We use the term *hybrid serialization* to refer to technologies that combine multiple serialization techniques or integrate serialization with additional abstraction layers, such as schema management. We cite as examples Apache Hudi and Apache Iceberg.

Hudi

Hudi stands for *Hadoop Update Delete Incremental*. This table management technology combines multiple serialization techniques to allow columnar database performance for analytics queries while also supporting atomic, transactional updates. A typical Hudi application is a table that is updated from a CDC stream from a transactional application database. The stream is captured into a row-oriented serialization format, while the bulk of the table is retained in a columnar format. A query runs over both columnar and row-oriented files to return results for the current state of the table. Periodically, a repacking process runs that combines the row and columnar files into updated columnar files to maximize query efficiency.

Iceberg

Like Hudi, Iceberg is a table management technology. Iceberg can track all files that make up a table. It can also track files in each table snapshot over time, allowing table time travel in a data lake environment. Iceberg supports schema evolution and can readily manage tables at a petabyte scale.

Database Storage Engines

To round out the discussion of serialization, we briefly discuss database storage engines. All databases have an underlying storage engine; many don't expose their storage engines as a separate abstraction (for example, BigQuery, Snowflake). Some (notably, MySQL) support fully pluggable storage engines. Others (e.g., SQL Server) offer major storage engine configuration options (columnar versus row-based storage) that dramatically affect database behavior.

Typically, the storage engine is a separate software layer from the query engine. The storage engine manages all aspects of how data is stored on a disk, including serialization, the physical arrangement of data, and indexes.

Storage engines have seen significant innovation in the 2000s and 2010s. While storage engines in the past were optimized for direct access to spinning disks, modern storage engines are much better optimized to support the performance characteristics of SSDs. Storage engines also offer improved support for modern types and data structures, such as variable-length strings, arrays, and nested data.

Another major change in storage engines is a shift toward columnar storage for analytics and data warehouse applications. SQL Server, PostgreSQL, and MySQL offer robust columnar storage support.

Compression: gzip, bzip2, Snappy, Etc.

The math behind compression algorithms is complex, but the basic idea is easy to understand: compression algorithms look for redundancy and repetition in data, then reencode data to reduce redundancy. When we want to read the raw data, we *decompress* it by reversing the algorithm and putting the redundancy back in.

For example, you've noticed that certain words appear repeatedly in reading this book. Running some quick analytics on the text, you could identify the words that occur most frequently and create shortened tokens for these words. To compress, you would replace common words with their tokens; to decompress, you would replace the tokens with their respective words.

Perhaps we could use this naive technique to realize a compression ratio of 2:1 or more. Compression algorithms utilize more sophisticated mathematical techniques to identify and remove redundancy; they can often realize compression ratios of 10:1 on text data.

Note that we're talking about *lossless compression algorithms*. Decompressing data encoded with a lossless algorithm recovers a bit-for-bit exact copy of the original data. *Lossy compression algorithms* for audio, images, and video aim for sensory fidelity; decompression recovers something that sounds like or looks like the original but is not an exact copy. Data engineers might deal with lossy compression algorithms in media processing pipelines but not in serialization for analytics, where exact data fidelity is required.

Traditional compression engines such as gzip and bzip2 compress text data extremely well; they are frequently applied to JSON, JSONL, XML, CSV, and other text-based data formats. Engineers have created a new generation of compression algorithms that prioritize speed and CPU efficiency over compression ratio in recent years. Major examples are Snappy, Zstandard, LZFSE, and LZ4. These algorithms are frequently used to compress data in data lakes or columnar databases to optimize for fast query performance.

Cloud Networking

This appendix discusses some factors data engineers should consider about networking in the cloud. Data engineers frequently encounter networking in their careers and often ignore it despite its importance.

Cloud Network Topology

A *cloud network topology* describes how various components in the cloud are arranged and connected, such as cloud services, networks, locations (zones, regions), and more. Data engineers should always know how cloud network topology will affect connectivity across the data systems they build. Microsoft Azure, Google Cloud Platform (GCP), and Amazon Web Services (AWS) all use remarkably similar resource hierarchies of availability zones and regions. At the time of this writing, GCP has added one additional layer, discussed in "GCP-Specific Networking and Multiregional Redundancy" on page 405.

Data Egress Charges

Chapter 4 discusses cloud economics and how actual provider costs don't necessarily drive cloud pricing. Regarding networking, clouds allow inbound traffic for free but charge for outbound traffic to the internet. Outbound traffic is not inherently cheaper, but clouds use this method to create a moat around their services and increase the stickiness of stored data, a practice that has been widely criticized.[1] Note that data egress charges can also apply to data passing between availability zones and regions within a cloud.

---

1 Matthew Prince and Nitin Rao, "AWS's Egregious Egress," *The Cloudflare Blog*, July 23, 2021, *https://oreil.ly/NZqKa*.

Availability Zones

The *availability zone* is the smallest unit of network topology that public clouds make visible to customers (Figure B-1). While a zone can potentially consist of multiple data centers, cloud customers cannot control resource placement at this level.

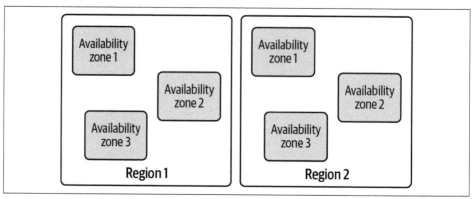

Figure B-1. Availability zones in two separate regions

Generally, clouds support their highest network bandwidth and lowest latency between systems and services within a zone. High throughput data workloads should run on clusters located in a single zone for performance and cost reasons. For example, an ephemeral Amazon EMR cluster should generally sit in a single availability zone.

In addition, network traffic sent to VMs within a zone is free, but with a significant caveat: traffic must be sent to private IP addresses. The major clouds utilize virtual networks known as *virtual private clouds* (VPCs). Virtual machines have private IP addresses within the VPC. They may also be assigned public IP addresses to communicate with the outside world and receive traffic from the internet, but communications using external IP addresses can incur data egress charges.

Regions

A *region* is a collection of two or more availability zones. Data centers require many resources to run (electrical power, water, etc.). The resources of separate availability zones are independent so that a local power outage doesn't take down multiple availability zones. Engineers can build highly resilient, separate infrastructure even within a single region by running servers in multiple zones or creating automated cross-zone failover processes.

Offering multiple regions allows engineers to put resources close to any of their users. *Close* means that users can realize good network performance in connecting to services, minimizing physical distance along the network path, and a minimal number of hops through routers. Both physical distance and network hops can increase latency and decrease performance. Major cloud providers continue to add new regions.

In general, regions support fast, low-latency networking between zones; networking performance between zones will be worse than within a single zone and incur nominal data egress charges between VMs. Network data movement between regions is even slower and may incur higher egress fees.

In general, object storage is a regional resource. Some data may pass between zones to reach a virtual machine, but this is mainly invisible to cloud customers, and there are no direct networking charges for this. (Of course, customers are still responsible for object access costs.)

Despite regions' geo-redundant design, many major cloud service failures have affected entire regions, an example of *correlated failure*. Engineers often deploy code and configuration to entire regions; the regional failures we've observed have generally resulted from code or configuration problems occurring at the regional level.

GCP-Specific Networking and Multiregional Redundancy

GCP offers a handful of unique abstractions that engineers should be aware of if they work in this cloud. The first is the *multiregion*, a layer in the resource hierarchy; a multiregion contains multiple regions. Current multiregions are US (data centers in the United States), EU (data centers in European Union member states), and ASIA.

Several GCP resources support multiregions, including Cloud Storage and BigQuery. Data is stored in multiple zones within the multiregion in a geo-redundant manner so that it should remain available in the event of a regional failure. Multiregional storage is also designed to deliver data efficiently to users within the multiregion without setting up complex replication processes between regions. In addition, there are no data egress fees for VMs in a multiregion to access Cloud Storage data in the same multiregion.

Cloud customers can set up multiregional infrastructure on AWS or Azure. In the case of databases or object storage, this involves duplicating data between regions to increase redundancy and put data closer to users.

Google also essentially owns significantly more global-scale networking resources than other cloud providers, something it offers to its customers as *premium-tier networking*. Premium-tier networking allows traffic between zones and regions to pass entirely over Google-owned networks without traversing the public internet.

Direct Network Connections to the Clouds

Each major public cloud offers enhanced connectivity options, allowing customers to integrate their networks with a cloud region or VPC directly. For example, Amazon offers AWS Direct Connect. In addition to providing higher bandwidth and lower latency, these connection options often offer dramatic discounts on data egress charges. In a typical scenario in the US, AWS egress charges drop from 9 cents per gigabyte over the public internet to 2 cents per gigabyte over direct connect.

CDNs

Content delivery networks (CDNs) can offer dramatic performance enhancements and discounts for delivering data assets to the public or customers. Cloud providers offer CDN options and many other providers, such as Cloudflare. CDNs work best when delivering the same data repeatedly, but make sure that you read the fine print. Remember that CDNs don't work everywhere, and certain countries may block internet traffic and CDN delivery.

The Future of Data Egress Fees

Data egress fees are a significant impediment to interoperability, data sharing, and data movement to the cloud. Right now, data egress fees are a moat designed to prevent public cloud customers from leaving or deploying across multiple clouds.

But interesting signals indicate that change may be on the horizon. In particular, Zoom's announcement in 2020 near the beginning of the COVID-19 pandemic that it chose Oracle as its cloud infrastructure provider caught the attention of many cloud watchers.[2] How did Oracle win this significant cloud contract for critical remote work infrastructure against the cloud heavyweights? AWS expert Corey Quinn offers a reasonably straightforward answer.[3] By his back-of-the-envelope calculation, Zoom's AWS monthly data egress fees would run over $11 million at list price; Oracle's would cost less than $2 million.

We suspect that GCP, AWS, or Azure will announce significant cuts in egress fees in the next few years, leading to a sea change in the cloud business model. It's also entirely possible that egress fees go away, similar to how limited and expensive cell-phone minutes disappeared decades ago.

---

2 Mark Haranas and Steven Burke, "Oracle Bests Cloud Rivals to Win Blockbuster Cloud Deal," CRN, April 28, 2020, *https://oreil.ly/LkqOi.*

3 Corey Quinn, "Why Zoom Chose Oracle Cloud Over AWS and Maybe You Should Too," Last Week in AWS, April 28, 2020, *https://oreil.ly/Lx5uu.*

Index

Symbols

separation of compute from storage,
224-227
cloud virtualized block storage, 207
Cloudflare, 135-136
clustering, 217
code-based transformation tools, 316
cold data, 41, 228
cold storage, 229
collaborative architecture, 83
collections, 173
colocation, 224
Colossus file storage system, 226
columnar serialization, 217, 397-399
columns, 171, 217, 294
comma-separated values (CSV) format, 396
command-and-control architecture, 83, 87
commercial open source software (COSS), 139
commits, 282
common table expressions (CTEs), 281
community-managed open source software,
138
completeness, 57
compliance, 230, 269
components, choosing, 80
composable materialized views, 328
compression algorithms, 200, 400
compute, separating from storage, 224-227
conceptual data models, 293
concurrency, 353
conformed dimension, 305
consistency, 162, 170, 175, 212
consumers (from a stream), 167, 254
container escape, 148
container platforms, 148-149
content delivery networks (CDNs), 406
continuous change data capture, 257, 285
COOs (chief operating officers), 29
copy on write (COW), 321
correlated failure, 216
COSS (commercial open source software), 139
cost
    cloud economics, 129
    cloud repatriation arguments, 134
    of cloud services, xv
    cost structure of data, 88
    data egress costs, 132, 135, 403, 406
    of data migration, 265
    data storage expenses, 230
    direct costs, 122

of distributed monolith pattern, 146
indirect costs, 122
overseeing, 380
of running servers, 149
of serverless approach, 147, 151
total cost of ownership, 122
total opportunity cost of ownership, 123
cost comparisons, 152
cost optimization and business value, 122-124
    FinOps, 124
    importance of, 122
    total cost of ownership, 122
    total opportunity cost of ownership, 123
COW (copy on write), 321
create, read, update, and delete (CRUD), 166,
170
credit default swaps, 129
CRUD (create, read, update, and delete), 166,
170
CSV (comma-separated values) format, 396
CTEs (common table expressions), 281
CTOs (chief technology officers), 29
curse of familiarity, 130

D

DAGs (directed acyclic graphs), 66, 324, 331
DAMA (Data Management Association Inter-
    national), 52
dark data, 104
dashboards, 348
data (see also generation stage; source systems)
    analog data, 160
    backing up, 376
    bounded versus unbounded, 240
    cold data, 41, 228
    combining streams with other data, 290
    cost structure of, 88
    deleting, 320
    digital data, 160
    durability and availability of, 225
    grain of, 294
    hot data, 41, 228
    internal and external, 25
    kinds of, 245
    late-arriving data, 252
    lukewarm data, 41, 228
    prejoining data, 280
    productive uses of, 343
    self-service data, 345

data engineering lifecycle (see also undercur-
    rents)
    definition of term, xiv
    future of, 383
    generation stage, 37-39
    ingestion stage, 41-44
    relationship to data lifecycle, 36
    serving data stage, 46-50
    stages of, 5, 19, 35
    storage stage, 40-41
    transformation stage, 45-46
data engineers
    background and skills of, 17
    big data engineers, 8
    business leadership and, 28-31
    business responsibilities of, 18
    cargo-cult engineering, 120
    continuum of roles for, 21
    versus data architects, 66
    data lifecycle engineers, 10
    definition of term, 4
    designing data architectures, 113
    evolution into data lifecycle engineers, 35
    new architectures and developments, 112
    other management roles and, 31
    product managers and, 30
    project managers and, 30
    as security engineers, 87
    technical responsibilities of, 19-21, 159
    within organizations, 22-28
data ethics and privacy, 61, 87, 269
data featurization, 46
data generation (see generation stage)
data gravity, 131
data ingestion (see ingestion stage)
data integration, 60, 238
data lakehouses, 105, 220
data lakes, 103, 220, 316
data latency, 353
data lifecycle, 36
data lifecycle engineers, 10
data lifecycle management, 60
data lineage, 59
data lineage tools, 335
data logic, 347
data management
    data accountability, 57
    data governance, 53
    data integration, 60

data lifecycle management, 60
data lineage, 59
data modeling and design, 59
data quality, 57
definition of term, 52
discoverability, 54
ethics and privacy, 61, 87
facets of, 53
impact on data ingestion, 268
impact on data storage, 232
impact on queries, transformations, and
    modeling, 335
impact on serving data, 366
impact on source systems, 188
impact on technology selection, 153
master data management, 58
metadata, 54-56
Data Management Association International
    (DAMA), 52
Data Management Body of Knowledge
    (DMBOK), 52, 77
Data Management Maturity (DMM), 13-17
data manipulation language (DML), 277
data marketplaces, 180
data marts, 103
data maturity, 13-17
data mesh, 96, 111, 330, 347
data migration, 251
data modeling
    alternatives to, 311
    business outcomes and, 292
    conceptual, logical, and physical models,
        293
    considerations for successful, 293
    definition of term, 291
    deriving business insights through, 59
    examples of, 291
    future of, 391
    normalization, 294
    purpose of, 292
    stakeholders of, 333
    techniques for batch analytical data,
        298-310
    combining, 298
    Data Vault, 305
    dimension tables, 302
    fact tables, 302
    hubs (Data Vault), 306
    Inmon, 299

dead database records, 284
dead-letter queues, 253
decentralized computing, 133
decision-making, eliminating irreversible decisions, 85
decompression, 400
decoupling, 85, 92
defensive posture, 374
deletion, 320
denormalization, 217, 295, 309
derived data, 324
deserialization, 243
devices, 108
DevOps engineers, 26
differential update pattern, 250
digital data, 160
dimension tables, 301-305
direct costs, 122
directed acyclic graphs (DAGs), 66, 324, 331
disaster prevention, 377
discoverability, 54
disk transfer speed, 196
distributed joins, 314
distributed monolith pattern, 146
distributed storage, 202
distributed systems, 90
DMBOK (Data Management Body of Knowledge), 52, 77
DML (data manipulation language), 277
DMM (Data Management Maturity), 13
document stores, 173
documents, 173
DODD (Data Observability Driven Development), 60, 64
domain coupling, 94
domains, 89
don't repeat yourself (DRY), 294
downstream stakeholders, 26
Dropbox, 135-136
durability, 162, 225, 244
dynamic RAM (DRAM), 198, 225

E

EA (enterprise architecture), 74-77
EABOK (Enterprise Architecture Book of Knowledge), 75, 83
EBS (Amazon Elastic Block Store), 207
edge computing, 133
edges (in a graph), 176

efficiency, 180
elastic systems, 82, 90
electronic data interchange (EDI), 261
ELT (extract, load, and transform), 101, 250, 316
embedded analytics, 47, 352
emitted metrics, 358
encryption, 379
enrichment, 290
enterprise architecture (EA), 74-77
Enterprise Architecture Book of Knowledge (EABOK), 75, 83
ephemerality, 224
error handling, 253
ethics, 61, 87, 269
ETL (see extract, transform, load process)
event time, 169
event-based data, 178, 252-254
event-driven architecture, 97
event-driven systems, 167
event-streaming platforms, 168, 181, 183-185, 259
eventual consistency, 162, 175, 202, 212
explain plan, 281
Extensible Markup Language (XML), 396
external data, 26
external-facing data engineers, 23
extract (ETL), 250
extract, load, and transform (ELT), 101, 250, 316
extract, transform, load (ETL) process
  batch data transformations, 315
  data warehouses and, 101
  versus ELT, 250
  push versus pull models of data ingestion, 44
  reverse ETL, 49, 362-364

F

fact tables, 301
failure, planning for, 81, 90
Family Educational Rights and Privacy Act (FERPA), 373
fast-follower change data capture approach, 285
fault tolerance, 185
featurization, 46
federated queries, 328, 358
FERPA (Family Educational Rights and Privacy Act), 373

W

warm data, 228
waterfall project management, 83
watermarks, 289
web interfaces, 264
web scraping, 264
webhooks, 180, 263
wide denormalized tables, 309
wide tables, 309
wide-column databases, 175

windowing methods, 69, 108, 287-289
write once, read never (WORN), 104

X

XML (Extensible Markup Language), 396

Z

zero-copy cloning, 227
zero-trust security models, 86

About the Authors

Joe Reis is a business-minded data nerd who's worked in the data industry for 20 years, with responsibilities ranging from statistical modeling, forecasting, machine learning, data engineering, data architecture, and almost everything else in between. Joe is the CEO and cofounder of Ternary Data, a data engineering and architecture consulting firm based in Salt Lake City, Utah. In addition, he volunteers with several technology groups and teaches at the University of Utah. In his spare time, Joe likes to rock climb, produce electronic music, and take his kids on crazy adventures.

Matt Housley is a data engineering consultant and cloud specialist. After some early programming experience with Logo, Basic, and 6502 assembly, he completed a PhD in mathematics at the University of Utah. Matt then began working in data science, eventually specializing in cloud-based data engineering. He cofounded Ternary Data with Joe Reis, where he leverages his teaching experience to train future data engineers and advise teams on robust data architecture. Matt and Joe also pontificate on all things data on *The Monday Morning Data Chat*.

Colophon

The animal on the cover of *Fundamentals of Data Engineering* is the white-eared puffbird (*Nystalus chacuru*).

So named for the conspicuous patch of white at their ears, as well as for their fluffy plumage, these small, rotund birds are found across a wide swath of central South America, where they inhabit forest edges and savanna.

White-eared puffbirds are sit-and-wait hunters, perching in open spaces for long periods and feeding opportunistically on insects, lizards, and even small mammals that happen to come near. They are most often found alone or in pairs and are relatively quiet birds, vocalizing only rarely.

The International Union for Conservation of Nature has listed the white-eared puffbird as being of *least concern*, due, in part, to their extensive range and stable population. Many of the animals on O'Reilly covers are endangered; all of them are important to the world.

The cover illustration is by Karen Montgomery, based on an antique line engraving from Shaw's *General Zoology*. The cover fonts are Gilroy Semibold and Guardian Sans. The text font is Adobe Minion Pro; the heading font is Adobe Myriad Condensed; and the code font is Dalton Maag's Ubuntu Mono.

O'REILLY®

Learn from experts.
Become one yourself.

Books | Live online courses
Instant answers | Virtual events
Videos | Interactive learning

Get started at oreilly.com.